ARISTOTLE

DICTIONARY

ARISTOTLE
DICTIONARY

edited by Thomas P. Kiernan

with an Introduction by Theodore E. James

PHILOSOPHICAL LIBRARY
New York

72-530

Library of Congress Catalog Card No. 61-10609

Translations by H. E. Wedeck, T. Taylor, and others.

Printed in the United States of America.

ARISTOTLE

DICTIONARY

Foreword

Aristotle was born at Stagira in Thrace, in the year 384 B.C., son of Nicomachus, a Doctor and personal physician of the King of Macedonia, Amyntas II. At the age of seventeen Aristotle was sent to Athens in continuance of his studies. The profession of medicine had been in his family for many generations, and perhaps because he was brought up in an atmosphere that was closely related to medicine and to the theories of the healing art, such a background could explain his gift, later to be manifested across broad areas of knowledge, for the concrete and the positive, for experiment and analysis.

Upon his arrival in Athens, he became a member of Plato's Academy, and for twenty years he was in the discipleship of Plato until the latter's death in 348-7 B.C. While at the Academy, Aristotle found in Plato a friend and teacher for whom he had the greatest reverence, and although Aristotle's eventual teachings were to be to a large degree grounded on disagreements with Platonic theory, he was, during his apprenticeship, a devoted student of his master.

After Plato's death, Aristotle left the Academy with Xenocrates and journeyed to Assos, where, under the sponsorship of Hermias, ruler of Atarneus, he established a Platonic community in which he put forth the beginnings of his own autonomous teachings. Three years later, after having married Pythias, the daughter of Hermias, he went to Mitylene on the island of Lesbos, where he met Theophrastus, who was to become his most ardent and celebrated disciple.

By this time he had acquired a modest reputation throughout Greece, and in 342 he was summoned to Pella by King Philip of

3

Macedonia in order to take the principal hand in the education of the King's son, Alexander, who was then thirteen years old, and who was subsequently to play so great a role on the political stage of the era as Alexander the Great. When Alexander assumed the reins of the kingdom in 336-5, Aristotle left Macedonia for Athens, by way of Stagira, his birthplace, which had been rebuilt by Alexander in compensation for Aristotle's pedagogical services.

Returning to Athens in 335-4, Aristotle founded his own school, the Lyceum. For ten years he lived and worked there, presenting the great body of his system in the form of lectures. In 323, following the death of Alexander the Great, there was in Greece a great reaction against the Macedonian suzerainty, and Aristotle found himself in peril because of his association with Alexander and because the Lyceum was established under Macedonian protection. He therefore fled to Chalcis, the birthplace of his mother, where he lived for a year before his death in 322-1.

* * *

The circumstances surrounding Aristotle's writings are lodged in a curious paradox. The writings which he designated for general publication—the esoteric works—and which were well known in antiquity, are now for the most part lost and unknown, whereas those which were written for presentation to his students and colleagues—the pedagogical works—and which were relatively obscure in antiquity, are those which have survived. These latter works are, of course, extremely complicated and axiomatic in style due to the fact that they were intended for limited and highly specialized scholarly consumption. On the other hand, those works written for public consumption were of a much more graceful literary style, fluidly oratorical and discursive, and in quite stark contrast to the prosaic severity of his scholastic writings. There remain of his public works only fragments, the most numerous of which belong to the dialogues *Protrepticus* and *Eudemus*. These fragments come out of his earliest writing period, when he was still under the direct influence of Plato. It

4

is evident that in this earliest period—it is generally agreed that his work falls into three main periods—he held without much reservation to the Platonic philosophy.

In his second period Aristotle began to separate himself from Platonic theory, becoming less the poetic philosophizer and more the empirical scientist. He criticized Plato's theory of Forms or Ideas, and took profound issue with the formerly held distinction between matter and form, negating the contention that these two terms constitute a dualism. He maintained, on the other hand, that matter and form are indissolubly united to form what is truly real being.

Aristotle's third period was that of his engagement in the Lyceum, where his genius for the organization of detailed research in the realms of nature and history awesomely manifested itself. The method and spirit of intensely incisive research into the phenomena of nature and history, which Aristotle fathered, represented something completely new in the Greek culture, and of course it still has its ramifications in the contemporary world. And yet there is no evidence from which to conclude that Aristotle, the growing empiricist, ever abandoned the more poetical flight through metaphysical speculation.

The Aristotelian system, or Aristotelianism, is not a radical contradiction of Platonism, as has often been held. Rather it is, if not a continuance of Plato's theories, at least an extension of Platonic thought. Historically speaking, Aristotelianism is the development of Platonism, through critical examination based on empirical evidence and physical fact, into a new metaphysics constructed on synthesis. Plato's metaphysics was a subjective, one-sided flower of the imagination. Aristotle's was a comprehensive and intricately landscaped garden of empirically supported logic.

T.P.K.

ARISTOTLE

Introduction

Writings

The writings attributed to Aristotle have been classified according to three historical periods:

A. While under the direct influence of the Academy (367-347 B.C.). This is evident from both content and form (the dialogue). He wrote *The Eudemus,* or On The Soul, in which he admits Plato's doctrine of reminiscence, the prior existence of the soul and his proofs of the immortality of the soul, as well as the existence of Idea-Forms. The *Protrepticus* appears to have been a letter to Themison of Cyprus or a treatise dedicated to him extolling the life of the philosopher. This may have been a model for Cicero's *Hortensius,* which created such an enthusiasm in the young Augustine for the intellectual life. It is said that the first 27 volumes in the catalogue of the works of Aristotle given by Diogenes Laertius are in dialogue form and belong to this and the succeeding period. Those which appear to be notes on Platonic dialogues are definitely in this period; others, such as the *On Philosophy* appear to be later. Some of the titles are: *On Justice, On Poets, Politicus, Gryllus* (on Rhetoric), *Statesman, Sophist, Eroticus, Symposium, On Riches, Menexenus.* It is probable that parts of the *Organon* and the *Physics* and, perhaps, Book 3 of the *De Anima* were written at this time.

B. During his stay at Assos, Mitylene and at the court of Philip of Macedon. This is considered by some to be the period of his own personal development in a direction away from Platonism. He wrote *On Philosophy* in which he shows how his idea of the meaning of this theoretical science differs from that of Plato. Here we have a basic difference concerning fundamentals. He criticizes the theory of Ideas and introduces the idea of an unmoved mover, without the multiplicity of unmoved movers found in the later Metaphysics. There is an argument for the existence of God taken from the grades of perfection found in things (the 4th way in St. Thomas Aquinas' classification). He also criticizes the doctrine of "creation" as found in the Timaeus and asserts the eternity of the world. The original draft of parts of the *Metaphysics* goes back to this period. The *Eudemean Ethics* are considered by some to belong to this period; perhaps parts of the *Politics*, (those dealing with the Ideal State), parts of the *De Generatione et Corruptione*, also.

C. At the Lyceum (335-323). This is the period of his concentration on exact scientific observation as the necessary foundation for the metaphysical structure he has erected. This viewpoint was a direct outcome of the early Ionian scientific investigations but in its Aristotelian form quite new and revolutionary in Greek philosophy. The works that we have from this period appear to be merely lecture-notes, finely and carefully prepared, but without any attempt at literary excellence. The ideas are the important thing; the style, or lack of it, is relatively unimportant. The arrangement of the works that we have is not necessarily the order of delivery or composition; the actual sequence in any one work is not necessary either. Andronicus of Rhodes, head of the Peripatetic School at Athens during Cicero's student days, is supposed to have edited and classified the Aristotelian works that are attributed to this period. In his classification the works include the following:

1. *The Organon* (the instrument of the search for truth):

a) *The Categories,* which treat of simple terms and their differentiation into ten basic predicaments or ultimate classificatory categories.

b) *On the Proposition,* the combinations of terms in which one term is affirmed or denied of another. It also includes the simple relation of immediate inference.

c) *The Prior Analytics,* on the syllogism in general from the point of view of its formal structure.

d) *The Posterior Analytics,* on the particular kind of syllogisms which is a demonstration or scientific proof based on true and primary premises, which state the cause of the conclusion.

e) *The Topics,* on dialectical reasoning, that is, argument based on generally accepted rather than scientific premises.

f) *The Sophistical Refutations,* which treat of fallacious arguments, how they are composed, the deficiencies of the matter and the form of argumentation and how we can refute and avoid fallacious reasoning.

2. *The Metaphysics,* a collection of lectures given at different times concerning reality insofar forth as it is real, the basic principles of reality and the Prime Reality, God.

3. Works on *Natural Philosophy:*

a) *The Physics,* containing 8 books about nature and motion in general; the last book deals with the Primal Mover.

b) *On the Heavens,* explains the motion of body and local motion.

c) *On Generation and Corruption,* considers the motion towards the acquisition of form, the first mobiles, the elements, and their general transmutations.

d) *On Meteorology,* considers the special transmutations of the elements and the explanations of thunder, lightning, meteors, comets, the rainbow, etc.

e) *On Minerals,* deals with inanimate, mixed mobile things.

f) *On the Soul,* treats of animated things in general and

man in particular especially in regard to the first act of his natural physical body. Man's senses, internal as well as external, his appetites and his duplex intellect are discussed.

g) *On Sense and the Sensible, On Sleep and Waking, On Memory and Recollection, On Dreams, On Divination through Dreams, On the Length and Shortness of Life, On Youth and Old Age, On Life and Death, On Respiration*, all included in what goes by the general title of *Parva Naturalia*.

h) *The History of Animals, On the Parts of Animals, On the Migration of Animals, On the Generation of Animals*.

i) *The Problemata*: encyclopedic collection of problems relating to random discussions or important issues for incorporation into a general work.

4. Moral treatises.

a) *The Nichomachean Ethics*: concerning the good life for man in all its aspects; on happiness and the means to achieve it.

b) *The Politics*: the structure of the State as involving a collection of households, the function of the individuals relative to the State; kinds of States and their relative values.

c) *Constitution of the Athenian State*.

d) *Magna Moralia*: Aristotelian in content but probably a digest-summary of the Eudemean and Nichomachean Ethics.

5. Aesthetics

a) *Poetics*: an incomplete treatise on tragedy and its relationships to comedy, epic and other poetic forms.

b) Records of dramatic performances, Winners of dramatic contests, Notes on the Homeric Problem, Notes on poetry in general.

6. *Rhetoric*: on the meaning of rhetoric, the kinds of speeches, the goal of rhetoric, the basic principles of persuasion, the emotions and their relation to persuasion, etc.

Socrates thought that the method of procedure in the acquisition of science must be changed if the errors of the Pre-Socratics were to be avoided. He sought exact definitions, especially in the field of morality, which seemed to him to deserve the main, if not the only, attention of man. The procedural activity for the acquisition of these stable, eternal essences of things was induction. According to Aristotle this was, indeed, Socrates' greatest claim to pre-eminence as a philosopher: to have seen that the important thing in science is the essence, expressible in a definition and that the only valid way of acquiring an understanding of the essences of things was by the inductive procedure of examining individual instances in variable circumstances. For Aristotle this implied the possession by man of an abstractive or separative function in the employment of which he was enabled to go from the multiple individual instances presented in experience to the universal law applicable to each.

Plato strove to perfect the Socratic method and, also to apply it to the whole of science as well as to the area of ethical conduct. But in his attempt to universalize the method he erred greatly, according to Aristotle, by separating the world of essential natures from the world of sensibly perceived realities and thus by setting up an isolated intelligible realm of Ideal-Forms. That hypothesis, which he nowhere proves, leads to absurdity and, as a matter of fact, is quite useless from the scientific point of view. Maybe Plato did not see how any other hypothesis could explain both the mutability of sense objects and the stability of science. But it is absurd to place the essence of a thing outside the thing of which it is the essence. If Ideal-Forms are required to explain the existence of the one as regards the many, why, then, are there not Ideas of all the universals, which are instances of the one among the many? Why are there not Ideas of accidents, of negations, of priva-

11

tions and of artificial products? Every predicate applicable to every thing would needs have an eternal Ideal-Pattern in the intelligible realm. And, again, how are we to conceive of that "participation" which Plato could never explain or, at least, could explain only obscurely by metaphor and myth? If the Ideas are outside things, how can they help us to know things? If there must be posited an intelligible man to explain why Callias is one of many similar men, by what reason must you reject a *third man* in order to explain how Callias and the intelligible Idea of man are the same, and so on? True, Plato seems to have been acquainted with these problems (Parmenides) and therefore sought refuge in the Pythagorean theory of Ideal-Numbers. But what kind of causality can *they* exercise? And, how can Ideas, among themselves heterogeneous, be assimilated to numbers, among themselves homogeneous, since they pertain to the genus of quantity? To Aristotle the doctrine of Platonic Ideas seemed to be but a beautiful poetic dream. He would draw up a radically different explanation.

As Socrates foresaw, exact definitions must be sought; but the means of acquiring them must be, in addition to common sense and the common discussions, the examinations of the opinions of his learned predecessors, the collection of observations and the making of experiments. These, however, are but a mere preparation for science. Science must proceed deductively, by the inferring of properties from the essence. In general, Aristotle follows this procedure:

1. He determines accurately the subject-matter of the investigation, and its problematic.

2. He describes historically the diverse solutions proposed to the problem under consideration.

3. He inserts reasons for doubting the previous solutions.

4. He indicates his own solution with appropriate evidence and reasoning.

5. He refutes the other solutions proposed. (On occa-

sion he refutes the contrary-solutions as soon as he gives them in their historical setting.)

Division of the Sciences

According to Aristotle sciences are either theoretical, practical or productive (poietic). The theoretical sciences, also called speculative by Cicero and Boethius, are so named because their end is knowledge itself for its own sake. Called theoretic from the basic root signifying 'vision,' they involve contemplation of the truth as revealed in the science in question. They are not, as such, interested in any activity in the world of material goods, whether it be human action involving moral behavior or the productive activity of human artistry.

The speculative sciences are classified in accordance with the different grades of separation from the material conditions of all objects of sense experience:

1. Physics (natural philosophy) which considers material things in so far as they are involved in movement.

2. Mathematics, which considers things of sensible experience in so far as they are involved in quantification, that is, numerable or measurable.

3. Metaphysics, which considers all things insofar forth as they are entities.

This schema of classification is based upon the power obviously present in all men of considering mentally in isolation certain aspects of sensible objects which exist in conjunction. It is quite clear that every object of sense experience is extended in three dimensions, for which reason it is discernible as a body, is numerable and measurable, that it is subject to movement either by qualitative variation, quantitative increase and decrease, generation and corruption or by change of place, and that it is an entity, a reality, a being, a something which is. When the mind considers one aspect of sensible things by itself it is performing

13

a mental activity of separation, which may be called abstraction, and which results in a formal viewpoint distinctive of a theoretical science. The subject-matter studied may be the same in all speculative disciplines, but the formal viewpoint or vision contemplated definitely leads to the theoretical distinctions proposed by Aristotle.

The practical sciences are differentiated from the speculative ones by the difference of ends or goals. Speculative sciences are concerned with knowledge for its own sake; practical sciences are concerned with knowledge for use as regards material objects. In the realm of practical sciences, they are differentiated from each other by the immediacy or finality of the goal in view. Since some material goods are means to an end, the practical science concerned with the end will be superior to the one concerned with the means, in the same ordered relationship, of course. The practical sciences are Ethics and Politics, each of which has many discernible parts. The Productive Sciences are quite clear from the name and will involve considerations about all types of making in the realm of materiality, such as fortifications, shoes, homes, clothes and even human bodies in regard to which medicine is a health-making activity. All study should begin with the *Organon*, which is not, strictly speaking, a science but an instrument of all sciences, a propaedeutic or introduction.

The Organon

The general aim of the Organon is to outline the means of proceeding correctly in the use of the mind in order to obtain scientific knowledge in the strict sense. Six treatises make up the total contents of the *Organon* and they have been designated as *The Categories, On Interpretation, The Prior Analytics, The Posterior Analytics, The Topics* and *The Sophistical Refutations*. As will be evident from what follows, there is a definite order and arrangement of themes and subject-matter in the treatises as we have them catalogued by Andronicus of Rhodes. And, though there is no evidence for such a physical arrangement in the treatises themselves, nor any statements from Aristotle to demand such an order of treatment, such a disposition of the treatises was quite probably traditional and it does have the sanction of the Lyceum and later Peripatetics. The *Categories* may not have been written by Aristotle himself, though some of the reasons presented to substantiate this surmise are not at all scientifically conclusive. But whatever the status of the categories as to their actual composer, it is quite clear that the ideas emphasized are, for the most part, in complete accord with the general philosophical teaching found elsewhere in the Aristotelian corpus. The division of the ten categories is repeated by name in *The Topics,* eight are again mentioned in the *Physics* and *Posterior Analytics* in a context where the remaining two were not a propos to the subject being discussed and seven are repeated in the *Metaphysics* under similar circumstances. All in all I would consider that the contents of the treatise entitled *The Categories* is Aristotelian and helpful as a propaedeutic to the other works of Aristotle.

The central core of the *Organon* is concerned with scientific proof. Scientific proof is a demonstration in which certain things being given something else necessarily follows; its external form is the syllogism. Scientific proof concerns necessary conclusions derived necessarily from premises which themselves involve true and necessary matter. It is quite clear, then, that science is the power or virtue of the mind which involves conclusions of this special type; it is a quality of the first grade, acquired by repeated exercise, which makes the knower proficient as regards deriving scientific conclusions. Hence the essential core of the *Organon* is duplex: the *Prior* and *Posterior Analytics,* the former concerned with the pattern and the latter with the subject-matter of scientific proof. Like the middle term in a perfect syllogism these two treatises are middle in position as well

15

as middle in universal importance and they are preceded and followed by two pairs of ancillary treatises, the *Categories* and *On Interpretation* as major extremes and the *Topics* and *Sophistical Refutations* as minor extremes.

To understand the prior and posterior resolution of scientific argumentation back to its ultimate constituents certain concepts and terms must be familiar and the proper combination of them into judgments expressed in propositions must be known. Once we grasp the overall picture of what science involves, then we are able to see the reason for a preliminary discussion of concepts-terms and judgments-propositions. One could not understand the formal pattern of correct reasoning nor the ingredients of science, in the strict sense, unless he be aware of the implications of certain simple, univocal terms predicable of a subject and indicating basic and irreducible scientific categories of classification. The distinction of the categories must be clear as regards their essence, properties and applicabilities since they are the ingredients of science. Moreover, there is a fundamental opposition between science and opinion, the subject-matter of the *Topics*, which cannot be understood if the nature and types of opposition are not known. The premises of a syllogism are prior to the conclusion in one sense and, yet, science is simultaneous with the premises, in another. What do we mean by 'prior'? What do we mean by 'simultaneous'? Science is a quality of mind acquired by an alteration which is a kind of movement. How does this type of movement differ from the other five varieties? Again, one may be said to have or to possess science. In what way does one have a habit of conclusions? Certainly, not in the way in which one is said to have a wife or a coat or a ring on his finger.

Of the fifteen chapters compiled together as *The Categories* six (4-9) take up and explain the categories proper and one each is devoted to the following: the way terms are related to things, the two forms of speech and the distinctions between to be present in and predicable of some-

16

thing, the relations of coordinate and subordinate genera, opposites of different kinds, contraries, the prior, simultaneous, six kinds of movement and six kinds of having.

At the very beginning of chapter one Aristotle takes a stand on the role and function of language which indicates clearly his epistemological realism. The *Categories,* and the whole of the *Organon* for that matter, are not concerned with a so-called pure formalism of dialectical discussion. In later treatises of the *Organon,* especially in the *Prior Analytics,* it is true that variable symbols are introduced in order to emphasize the formal structure of argumentation in contrast with its content. But in no wise does Aristotle consider that Logic or the *Organon* of correct thinking is a content-less exercise or empty pattern of thought. The *Prior Analytics* is concerned with the *form* of thought but we must not miss the fact that it is the form of *thought* and that thought involves a *content* of things. So he starts off by distinguishing homonyms from synonyms and paronyms. Words are artificial constructs created by men to be names of things. Upon examining words adapted to our current usage we find that the same term may be used to refer to things which actually are essentially different and have different definitions expressing what they are, as 'animal' is applied to man and to a sketch of an ox. In such a case the term is a homonym and the things are equivocally named. Some words fool us precisely because they can have different meanings in different contexts and we are not always sure of the context intended. Other words are clear because both the name and the definition are the same when applied to different things, as 'animal' when applied to man and ox. Paronyms are applied derivatively, that is, one word derives its root from another but the termination of the word is different, as grammarian is derived from grammar.

We see here the triangular relationship of thing, thought and term which is so basic to Aristotle's thought. We find it applied here in the preliminaries of Logic, also, in the *Physics, Metaphysics, Ethics, Poetics* and *Rhetoric.* It is a concrete indication of Aristotelian realism. We encounter material things in our everyday experience; this experience calls forth some thought in our mind, we conceive some understanding of the thing; we fabricate a term to express our understanding of the thing. Thus, the term is an artificial and instrumental sign of the thing through the mediation of the thought, which is a natural and formal sign of the thing. Synonymous terms or univocals are the important ones from the standpoint of scientific argumentation. The terms in a syllogism must be applied univocally. The ingredients of science must depend upon the univocal.

Simple forms of speech like 'man' are the terms that make up the propositions which are complex forms of expression and which serve as the premises of syllogisms. The simple terms are segregated into the categories of scientific classification when they are predicable of a subject. But whether they are also present in a subject, like knowledge itself, or not so present, as second substance, is incidental. The individual existent is neither present in a subject nor predicable of a subject precisely because the individual is the ultimate subject of all predication and predicability applies only to the universal. Hence, also, the reason why Aristotle says that there is no science of the individual as individual.

Science, of course, would demand that when one thing is predicated of another, whatever is predicable of the original predicate would also be predicable of the original subject, as, if man is predicated of John and animal predicated of man, then animal is predicable of John. We must be careful, too, of the relationship of different genera in scientific classification. If genera are different and coordinate, their differences are different; whereas, if one genus is subordinate to another, there is nothing to prevent their having the same differences.

For a thorough understanding of this relationship of genera and differences it would be helpful to have a full clarification of the meaning of genus and difference. Such is found formally expressed in the *Topics* but even here in the *Categories* the ingredients for a clear knowledge of them are evident upon a few moments of reflection. Some of the Neo-platonists, especially Porphyry and Boethius, preferred a more explicit statement of the relationships of genus and difference along with those of species, property and accident, and, as a matter of fact, thought that one could not understand, save with the greatest of difficulties, the categories of Aristotle without a prior knowledge of the five predicables. Porphyry's *Isagoge* attempted a clarification of these notions as a propaedeutic to the understanding of the categories, as well as of division, definition and demonstration. He, thus, drew up an organon to the *Organon*. Since his time a prior acquaintance with the five predicables has been considered as an essentially useful preliminary at this point in the development of Logic.

From a thorough scrutiny of the Aristotelian texts here, in the *Topics* and throughout the *Physics, Metaphysics, Ethics* and even *Poetics* it appears that the ten categories are direct universal classifications of material reality whereas the five predicables are reflex or second intention universal classifications of the relationship of the categories to the individuals of our experience. Genus is a more general classification of species because of an element possessed in common by different species. Species is a classification in terms of sameness of total essence of those individuals which differ only numerically. The specific difference distinguishes one species from another in the same genus; property is not of the essence; it is not an essential characteristic but it is necessarily connected with the essence. If you have the essence, you have it and vice versa. Accident is only incidentally related to the essence of the thing. For example, animal is the genus of man and brutes; rational is man's specific difference; rational animal is the species; artistic is the property; six feet tall is an accident.

With this as a background let us approach the main topic of this first treatise in the *Organon*. Aristotle reminds us that there are ten simple expressions of discourse which

19

signify substance (man), quantity (3 feet), quality (white & grammatical), relation (double), where (in the Lyceum), when (yesterday), position (reclining), possession or 'to have' (armor), action (to cut), passion (to be cut). No one of these terms involves an affirmation or negation and, therefore, the designation 'true' or 'false' is inapplicable to them as such. But affirmations and negations are necessarily composed of such terms.

Substance is either primary or secondary. Primary substance is the individual existent which does not exist in a subject nor is it predicable of a subject; secondary substance is the universal which does not exist in a subject, because it is a substance, but it is predicable of a subject, because it is expressive of a content common to many individuals. Primary substances are more properly substance since they underlie everything else and since everything else is either present in first substance or predicable of it. It is secondary substance which is one of the ten categories. Of the predicables, species is more truly called substance than genus is, because it is more closely related to primary substance. The definition of anything is most properly given by stating the species.

There are six characteristics of all substances. First, they are never present in a subject. Second, they are always predicated univocally (only applicable to second substance). Third, all substances signify the individual. Fourth, substance has no contrary. Fifth, substance does not admit of more or less, i.e., there are no degrees of substance since one man, e.g., is just as much man as any other man. Sixth, while remaining numerically one and the same it is capable of admitting contrary qualities alternately. This latter is the most distinctive mark of substance, its property as it were. And it is by changing accidentally that substances are capable of admitting contrary qualities. A substance cannot have contrary qualities at the same time, in the same respect.

Quantity signifies the numerable or measurable aspects of substances. Quantity is either discrete, like number since

20

its parts are separate, or continuous, like lines, time, place whose parts have a common boundary. The characteristics of quantity are: first, quantities have no contraries (there is no contrary of 3 feet); second, quantity does not admit of more or less (one 3 is no more nor less than another); third, its most distinctive characteristic, its property so to speak, is that only of it is equality and inequality predicated. Quantity *is* that in virtue of which things are said to be equal or unequal.

Relation signifies a reference of one to another. It applies to things insofar as they are said to be *of* or *referred to* something else, as knowledge of, perception of, attitude to. It is possible for relatives to have contraries, though it is not necessarily the case. Ignorance is the contrary of knowledge and vice of virtue, but double and triple have no contraries. Relatives can admit of degrees, but not always, as in the previous example. All relatives have correlatives, if properly defined. Some correlatives come into existence simultaneously e.g. double-half, master-slave. But this is not true of all, e.g. knowledge and the knowable; the knowable is prior. If someone definitely apprehends a relative he will also definitely apprehend that to which it is relative.

Quality is that in virtue of which *such* and *such* is predicated. There are four types of quality: first, habit or disposition; habit is more lasting and more firmly established, i.e. more permanent and difficult to alter, e.g. the various kinds of knowledge and virtues; disposition, which is an arrangement of parts, is a condition easily changed and quickly gives place to its opposite, as heat-cold, disease-health; second, inborn capacity or incapacity as health-sickness, hardness or softness; third, affective qualities and affections which, since they are the sensible qualities possessed by things they are capable of producing an affection in the way of perception, e.g., color; fourth, figure and shape.

The characteristics of quality are: first, one quality may be the contrary of another and qualified things, too, may be contrary in virtue of the qualities possessed; second, qualities admit of more and less and one and the same thing may exhibit a quality in a greater or lesser degree at different times; although it is a disputed point whether habits and dispositions admit of more or less, it is true that things which are so qualified may vary in the degree in which they possess them. Of course, figure and shape do not admit of variation of degree; one thing is not more triangular than another though one may be larger than another. The distinctive mark of quality is that likeness and unlikeness are predicated only with reference to quality.

Action and *passion* are easily understood; they, too, admit of contraries and degrees. *When, where* and *possession* present no special difficulties according to Aristotle but he obviously did find someone who had some difficulties with possession since he adds a short chapter at the end in which he distinguished eight types of it: as regards any quality, any quantity, apparel, something on a part of us (e.g. a ring on the hand), something possessed as a part (a hand), the content of something (a jar has wine), the acquired, as a house or field, having a wife, etc.

Three other terms merit special discussion by Aristotle before he closes the treatise on the Categories. As will be clear they are essential to an understanding and distinction of the categories and their proper application. The first deals with 'opposites' of which there are four kinds: first, opposed as correlatives; second, opposed as contraries either with or without a medium; third, opposition between privatives and positives or between privatives and habits; fourth, opposed as affirmatives and negatives. Of opposites the contraries are the more difficult to understand since they involve two positives; contradictories involve a positive and its negation; privatives are opposed to the positive habit and hence are in reference to a suitable subject. The second term which must be distinguished is 'prior' since there are five senses in which something may be said to be prior to another. There is a priority of time, priority of sequential dependence (the sequence of their being cannot be reversed), priority of order (letters are prior to syllables), priority of nature, priority of cause and effect. The simultaneous is distinguished as regards time and nature.

There are six types of movement: generation, destruction, increase, diminution, alteration, change of place. Speaking generally, rest is the contrary of movement. Change in the reverse direction is most truly the contrary of place and either rest in its quality or change in the direction of the contrary quality may be considered the contrary of the qualitative form of movement, i.e. alteration. A thorough discussion of these various types of movement occupies most of the material in the treatises in *Physics*. In general, since the categories are simple expressions of real beings and their characteristics the explanation given here in terms of the ten ways of thinking and talking about things finds realistic completion in the *Physics* and *Metaphysics* where we find them as the ten ways in which things exist. There is a real relation between thing, thought and term; things exist, we think about them and express our thoughts in appropriate terms.

Peri Hermeneias

The title of the second treatise in the *Organon* has been variously translated, though most references to the work employ the Latin *De Interpretatione*. Now an interpretation is an expression or explanation clarifying a point of view or judgment on anything. So we will consider that we are dealing here with the judgment as manifested by a proposition, which is composed of a noun and verb, at least, which is either an affirmation or denial and which is either true or false. Of the fourteen chapters one is introductory, in which he relates this work to the previous one, then follow a chapter each on nouns and verbs as the integral parts of a proposition, one on the proposition in general, and then ten chapters on the types of propositions used in expressing our judgments or interpretations of things, their characteristics, their relative oppositions and comparative truth-values.

Aristotle is clear in the very first chapter that he is mainly concerned with the mental activities and not just oral or written signs. Referring to a previous discussion of the same topic in the treatise *On The Soul* he insists that words are symbols of mental experiences of the soul, which experiences are the same in all men even though the spoken and written languages of peoples are different, the written being the symbol of the spoken. Again a reference to the thing, thought, term relationship mentioned in the *Categories*. This second work is mainly concerned with the mental activity of judging which is expressed externally in the symbolic representation of a proposition, composed of a subject of predication and an assertion or denial of something about such a subject. Thus, even though the mental activity is the subject-matter of the discussion, this is not a psychological study because the point of view is logical, i.e. it concerns the formal relationship of subject and predicate in the interpretative activity of the mind.

Thoughts, as well as their oral or written expression by terms or words, are neither true nor false in their simple state. It is only when they express the activity of mental combination and/or separation that they are susceptible of such a designation. There is a truth-value if and only if 'is' or 'is not' is employed as a means of affirming or denying something of something. This 'is' or 'is not' need not be formally expressed as such. 'The man runs' is expressive of an interpretation. Such a statement could be also framed in terms of 'is' as a third element in the sentence, 'the man is running.' In some instances the use of 'is' as a third element gives additional possible combinations: 'man is just'—'man is not just,' 'man is not not-just'—'man is not—just'; or again, 'every man is just'—'every man is not-just,' 'not every man is not-just'; 'not-man is just'—'not-man is not-just,' 'not-man is not just'—'not-man is not not-just.'

Nouns and verbs are expressive of thoughts. Both are artificial symbols signifying by convention, the former without the temporal reference. A verb, besides its basic function of signifying a meaning carries a notion of time and is always a sign of predication, i.e. of something said about a subject or something said to be in a subject. This is especially true in the case of forms of the verb 'to be.' For 'to be' and 'not to be' are not themselves, of themselves, alone, significant of a fact; nor is 'being' merely as 'being.' Forms of the verb 'to be' co-signify. That is, they signify only in conjunction with the things joined by them, since they are expressive of a relationship of predication or inherence or non-inherence. The primary function of the verb 'to be' is that of a copula, a link joining subject and predicate and indicating a positive or negative relationship.

A sentence is a form of speech that signifies by conventional agreement and it differs from a noun and verb because some of its constitutive elements are significant by themselves. 'Ouse,' as a part of 'mouse,' is not significative. 'Mouse' as a part of 'a mouse is an animal' is significative. Every sentence is not only the natural expression of a natural organ of speech but it is also expressive by convention of a meaning understood. Yet only those sentences which are declarative statements and susceptible of the true and the false are proposition. Thus a petition is a sentence but not a proposition. Propositions, not questions nor vocatives nor commands nor deprecations, are the immediate ingredients of scientific argumentation. We must understand the proposition before we can comprehend the syllogism.

Every proposition is either simple or complex, depending on whether it involves a simple affirmation or denial, or is one only by conjunction. 'Man is an animal' is simple. 'Man is an animal and man is a substance' is complex. An affirmation is a proposition positively asserting something of something; a negation is a proposition removing something from something: 'no man is a stone.' In regard to any situation it is possible to make a positive or negative proposition and thus, every affirmation has an opposite negation and vice versa. Such a pair of statements would be contradictories.

25

Propositions concern either a universal subject or an individual; the universal is such that it is predicable of many, the individual is not thus predicated. What makes the subject of a proposition universal is not the subject quantifier 'every' or 'none.' The subject term itself is either predicable of many or not; if it is, it is universal. When a universal term is used as subject, then the proposition itself may be of singular character, particular character or universal character. 'Every man is wise' is a proposition with a universal subject 'man,' because it is predicable of many, and it is of universal character or universal applicability. 'Some man is wise' is a proposition with a universal subject 'man' but it is only of particular or limited character because of the subject quantifier 'some.' 'This man is wise' is a proposition with a universal subject but the sentence is of singular or individual character because of the restrictive 'this.' 'Callias is a man' is a proposition with an individual subject with singular applicability. If anyone would express both an affirmative and negative proposition universally about the same universal these propositions would be contraries, as 'every man is rich' and 'no man is rich.' Note here a caution: though it is true that in the negative proposition the predicate is a universal or distributed term and predicated universally, the same is not the case in affirmative propositions. The proposition 'every man is every animal' is not true; a fortiori as regards 'some man is every animal.' Thus the predicate in an affirmative proposition is always undistributed, whereas the predicate in a negative proposition is always distributed.

Propositions are contradictorily opposed when with the subject remaining the same the affirmation is applied universally and the negation not, as 'every man is white' is contradictorily opposed to 'not every man is white,' which is equivalent to 'some man is not white.' The same is true as regards the opposition between the negative universally applied and the affirmative not, as "no man is white" and "some man is white." The cross-diagonals of what is called the "square of opposition" are these four propositions. When both affirmation and negation are universally applied the propositions are contraries. The contradictories of a pair of contraries are sub-contraries. The truth-value of these types of propositions can be easily established. Contradictories cannot be simultaneously true or false. Contraries cannot be simultaneously true but can be false at the same time. Contradictories of contraries can be true at the same time but not false simultaneously. The same type of contradictory opposition is evidenced in regard to the positive and negative predication about individual subjects, as "Socrates is white"—"Socrates is not white."

In this discussion of the formal opposition between all possible types of propositions we can perform an immediate inference of reason as to the truth-value of any proposition, provided we are given that the A proposition (universal affirmative, universally predicated) or the E proposition (universal negative, universally predicated) is true or provided that we are given that the particular affirmative (I) or the particular negative (O) is false. If by supposition the A is true then the E is false, the I is true and the O is false. But how can we determine as a matter of fact that A is true or that I is false? In general, a proposition will be true if it expresses that what is, is or that what is not, is not. It will be false if it states that what is, is not or that what is not, is. If a thing is white, the proposition stating such will be true and the proposition stating the opposite will be false. The method of establishing the truth of an A proposition is induction which will be discussed later. And, whether we are aware of its truth or falsity or not, every proposition concerning the present, past or future will be either true or false; as regards the future the truth or falsity is, of course, still undetermined.

The conversion of a subject and predicate in a sentence, that is, their mutual change of location, involves no change in meaning but we must be careful of the distribution of the terms. The A statement converts to the I, "every man is an animal" converts to "some animal is a man"; I converts to I; E converts to E; O never converts. "Some stone is not a man" cannot convert to "some man is not a stone" because the applicability of stone would be increased from undistributed (some) to distributed (none).

Aristotle is quite forceful in his distinction between existential and logical predication. To say that Homer is a poet is not the same as saying that Homer *is*. The verb 'is' is used incidentally of Homer, the statement asserting that Homer is a poet and not that Homer *is* in the independent sense of that word. It is possible that a proposition may be assertive of the existence of a subject but when a subject and predicate are conjoined by 'is' as a copula only then the relationship asserted is logical rather than existential even though the logical would ultimately be founded in the existential as regards its truth-value.

This treatise is brought to a close by the consideration of the modal propositions concerning possibility, impossibility, contingency and necessity, their logical sequences and the reply to the questions as to whether the contrary of an affirmation is a denial or another affirmation. The relationships of contradiction and contrariety are schematized in four groups of four each, e.g. "it may be" is contrasted with "it cannot be," "it may not be" and "it cannot not be" plus the interrelated contingent, necessary and impossibles. As a result of this analysis he concludes to the contrasting existential status of the actual and potential. Whatever exists of necessity is actual. Actuality is absolutely prior to potentiality. Some things are actualities without potentialities (the primary or separated substances), others are combinations of actuality and potentiality whose actuality is by nature prior to potentiality but posterior in time, and, the class of pure possibilities or potentialities, which were not, are not and will not be, but can be. The question about contraries is resolved in favor of the negative: the contrary of an affirmation is a negation.

28

The *Prior* and *Posterior Analytics* make up the most fundamental parts of the Aristotelian treatment of Logic. The former is concerned, for the most part, with the purely formal structure of scientific reasoning; the latter with the necessary matter involved in scientific proof. The *Prior Analytics* is composed of seventy-three chapters unevenly divided into two books: Alpha or Book I contains forty-six chapters, Beta the remainder. In contrast the *Posterior Analytics* is made up of thirty-four chapters in Book I and nineteen in Book II.

The subject-matter of the investigation in the *Prior Analytics* is scientific demonstration. In order to understand it we must be familiar with the signification of terms, premise, syllogism and the difference between a perfect and imperfect syllogism; also, the meaning of being included in or excluded from the whole of anything and what we mean when we predicate of all or none (*de omni* or *de nullo*).

A premise is a statement affirming or denying something of something. Every premise is either universal, particular or indefinite. The universal asserts that something belongs to all or none; the particular that it belongs to some or not to some or not to all; indefinite, that something belongs or does not belong without the designation of the universal or particular. The demonstrative premise as here employed differs from the dialectical, since the demonstrative is an assertion of one part of a contradiction, whereas the dialectical is an interrogation of contradiction. The demonstrative premise lays down something as a premise from which the argument proceeds, whereas the dialectical posits a question which may have diverse responses. It would be well to keep this statement of the nature of a demonstrative premise well in mind when we analyze the structure of the figures of demonstration. There it will be evident that, in spite of the formal wording of the syllogistic structure and in opposition to Lukasiewicz' formalistic interpretation, the premises of the syllogism are categorical propositions involving inferential and implicational relationships, not just implications. A premise will be demonstrative if it is not only an affirmation or denial of something of something but also if it is true and derived from the first principles. Subject and predicate are terms of the premise and with the two premises make up a syllogism, which is a discourse in which certain things being posited something else different from the posited follows from the very fact that they are laid down. A perfect syllogism needs nothing else except what is given to lead necessarily to a conclusion. Also, to round out the preliminaries, Aristotle concludes chapter one by asserting that 'to be included in' another is the same as 'to be predicated of' another. To say that one term is included in another as in a whole is the same as for it to be predicated of all. "A is included in B" is equivalent to "A is predicated of every B." One term is predicated of all of another whenever no instance of the thing can be in which the term cannot be asserted and vice versa as regards 'to be predicated of none.'

In chapters two and three Aristotle repeats the rules of conversion of propositions mentioned in the *Peri Hermeneias* and applies them to propositions whether they state that something is or must be or may be an attribute of something else. These simple categoricals, contingent or necessary propositions may be positive or negative and, also, either universal, particular or indefinite.

With these presuppositions we now enter into the construction of the three schemata of syllogistic argumentation. The perfect syllogism is made up of three terms so related that if the major extreme (i.e. the predicate of the conclusion and predicate of the first or major premise) is contained in the middle, as in a whole, and the middle is either contained in or excluded from the first, the major term will be included in or excluded from the minor term. Aristotle calls this schemata *the perfect* syllogism because the middle term is both middle in position and middle in universality and syllogistic reasoning is essentially an activity of proceeding from the greater universality to the lesser. The middle term is the one which is contained in another and contains another in itself; it is the one repeated in the premises; it is the *common third* with which the subject and predicate of the conclusion are compared. For, after all, the reasoning activity is entered into because the mind cannot see any direct and immediate connection between two terms when they are compared singly to each other. When the mind is able to compare the two terms with a *common third* and when it sees that each agrees with it (the middle) or that one agrees and the other doesn't, then the mind can conclude that the extremes are related or not. The extremes are the terms, one of which is contained in the middle and the other of which contains the middle, if you are considering the positive relationship. The negative syllogism contains a middle which excludes the major extreme and is included in the minor extreme. Hence the major extreme is excluded from the minor. The major term contains the middle, because of greater universality, and the middle contains the minor. The first figure would be schematized as

M=middle
P=predicate
S=subject

| M | P | (major premise) |
S	M	(minor premise)
S	P	(conclusion)

The only valid moods in this figure (i.e. valid combinations of propositions) would be three universal affirmatives (A-A-A, the traditional B*a*rb*a*r*a*), negative, affirmative and negative universals (E-A-E, C*e*l*a*r*e*nt), universal, particular, particular affirmative (A-I-I, D*a*r*ii*), and universal negative, particular affirmative, particular negative (E-I-O, F*e*r*io*).

31

Any other combination of propositions is not conducive to a valid syllogism in this schema called the first figure. Also, from a reflective examination of these valid moods we see that the general rules for this figure are: the major premise must be universal; the minor premise must be affirmative, otherwise no conclusion. From an analysis of other possible combinations we see that there is no conclusion from two negative premises, that the middle term must be distributed at least once, that the conclusion is negative if one premise is negative, that the conclusion is particular if one premise is particular, that a term distributed in the conclusion must be distributed in the premises and, the very obvious conclusion, that a syllogism can involve only three distinct terms.

The second figure (or middle figure as Aristotle calls it) is found whenever the same thing belongs to every individual of one kind and to none of another or is present to every one of each or to none of either. The pattern here is

$$
\begin{array}{cc}
P & M \\
S & M \\
\hline
S & P
\end{array}
$$

the middle term being predicated of both extremes. If the major premise is universal affirmative the minor will be negative, either universal or particular. Thus the major premise is always universal and one premise must be negative in order to have the middle term distributed at least once. This constitutes a valid syllogism but it cannot be perfect since the middle term is neither middle in universality nor position, since it is predicated of both extremes. All conclusions in this figure will be negative and the only legitimate moods are E-A-E (Cesare) A-E-E (Camestres), E-I-O (Festino), A-O-O (Baroco).

When one thing is present with every one of the same thing and the other with none, or when both are present with every one of the same or to none, this is the last Aristotelian figure. Schematically

$$
\begin{array}{cc}
M & P \\
M & S \\
\hline
S & P
\end{array}
$$

The middle term is the subject in both premises, the extremes are the predicates; the major extreme being the furthest from the middle and the middle being last in position. A syllogism cannot be perfect in this figure either, but it can be valid provided that the minor premise is affirmative and the conclusion particular. Thus the valid moods are A-A-I (*Darapti*), E-A-O (*Felapton*), I-A-O (*Disamis*), A-I-I (*Datisi*), O-A-O (*Baroco*), E-I-O (*Ferison*).

Although all the valid syllogisms of the middle and third figures are imperfect they can be made perfect by reducing them to the first figure. This is done either ostensively, by conversion and/or mutation of the terms, or by a reduction through contradiction. The A-O-O (*Baroco*) in the middle figure and the O-A-O (*Bocardo*) in the third are reducible *per impossibile* to A-A-A in the first figure. The mnemonic terms found in medieval Latin treatises on Logic are of assistance in the activity of reducing all moods to the moods of the perfect syllogism in the first figure. The vowels in these words stand for the quality and quantity of the proposition involved (A-E-I-O); the initial consonant identifies the terminus of the reduction, e.g. B is reduced to Barbara, C to Celarent, D to Darii, F to Ferio; of the interior consonants employed *d, l, n, r, t* are merely euphonic separators and non-significative as regards reduction; *s* means *simple conversion*, small *p* indicates *partial conversion*, *m* means *mutation* or transposition of premises and *c* indicates *contradiction*: all letters qualify the preceding propositions.

The first figure contains four valid moods: Barbara, Celarent, Darii, Ferio. In the middle figure Cesare is reduced to Celarent by a simple conversion of the major premise; Camestres becomes Celarent by a transposition of the major and minor premises and simple conversion of the minor and the conclusion. Festino becomes Ferio by a simple conversion of the major premise. As was mentioned before, Baroco becomes Barbara by demonstrating that the contradictory of the minor premise is validly concluded from the original major premise if you take as a minor premise the assumed validity of the contradictory of the original conclusion. Thus you would have the original major A, the new minor A and the new conclusion A, which is the contradictory of the original minor.

Of the moods of the third figure Darapti, Datisi and Disamis become Darii: Darapti by partial conversion of the minor premise, Datisi by simple conversion of the minor and Disamis by transposition of the premises and simple conversion of the original major and, also, the conclusion. Felapton and Ferison become Ferio by conversion of the minor, the former partially and the latter simply. Bocardo is reduced to Barbara by assuming as a major premise the contradictory of the conclusion of Bocardo. The assumed major A, with the given minor A gives a conclusion A which is the contradictory of the original major, thereby demonstrating by the first figure that the original mood was valid.

A demonstration to the impossible differs from the ostensive reduction in that it admits what it wishes to subvert leading to an acknowledged falsehood, but the ostensive commences from the assumed premises. Both assume two propositions but the ostensive assumes those from which the original syllogism is formed. The demonstration to the impossible assumes one of the original premises and the contradictory of the conclusion.

It is interesting to note here in the discussion of the reduction of the syllogisms to the first figure that only three figures are discussed and that the second figure is consistently referred to as the *middle* figure. This would be an added piece of evidence for the assertion that there are only

34

three figures set up by Aristotle, even though he is aware that arrangements of terms in a so-called fourth figure are valid and reducible to the first figure. The fourth figure would be a mutated first figure. It is, also, clear that his discussion of the valid figures of demonstration makes it evident that the variables are replaceable by any terms, that the conclusion is inferred or deduced from the premises and that the relationship between premises and conclusion is not just one of simple implication. This is evident again when Aristotle gives examples of hypothetical implication of the type of "if A, then B; but A, therefore B" and "if A, then B, but not B, therefore not A." This is quite simply the conditional or hypothetical syllogism with its two valid figures.

After discussing the figures of the syllogism Aristotle investigates modal and non-modal propositions in combination in each of the figures. In the first figure, if the major premise is necessary and the minor non-modal the conclusion will be necessary, as "if A is assumed to be necessarily present or not present with B, but B to be present with C, A will necessarily be present or not with C." In the second figure, when a necessary premise is joined with a non-modal premise the conclusion follows the negative necessary premise, but if the affirmative be necessary the conclusion will not be necessary. In the third figure, if either premise be necessary and both are universal affirmative, the conclusion will be necessary. And, if one be negative and necessary the conclusion will be necessary, otherwise not. A similar discussion is carried on concerning two contingent propositions in each figure and, also, regarding one in combination with a non-modal proposition and with a necessary proposition.

In recapitulation, every syllogism will be composed of no more than three terms included in no more than two premises. And, in working our problems of proof we must realize that the universal affirmative is proved only through the first figure and in one mood; the universal negative through the first figure in one way and through the second in two ways; the particular affirmative through the first figure in one way and through the last figure in three ways; the particular negative is proved in all figures: in the first in one mood, in the middle in two and in the last in three ways. Thus, it is most difficult to construct a syllogism in proof of the universal affirmative and most easy to subvert or destroy such an argument, since the A proposition is proved only in one figure and one mood whereas its contradictory O is proved in three figures and six moods. E is proved in two figures and three moods and its contradictory in two figures and four moods.

Facility in argumentation consists in the proficiency and speed of discovering middle terms as well as the understanding of those things which are not predicated of others (i.e. singulars), those which are predicated of others but have nothing predicated of them (the ultimate genera) and the intermediate class of those predicated of others and of which others are predicated. It, also, helps to know what to assume in your premises in order to prove the desired conclusion in the appropriate figure and mood. Above all we must recognize the difference between demonstrative and dialectical syllogistics, the latter of which is constructed of probable propositions. In the application of argumentation to the different disciplines experience is the best help, as, e.g. the experience in astronomy gives astronomical propositions, etc.

The third section of the preliminary consideration of the syllogistic forms deals with the practical construction of demonstrations. We have seen how syllogisms are constructed and the ways of discovering appropriate propositions and terms. Now we must actively analyze them in regard to the three figures. First, we must select the appropriate propositions as propositions rather than divide them according to terms. Secondly, we must determine whether the proposition is universal or particular. If universal be careful to accept what is implied about the par-

ticulars subsumed under it. Thirdly, check whether anything superfluous has been assumed and anything necessary
omitted, reducing all the propositions to but two premises.
Thus we must assume two propositions and divide the terms
so that the middle is in both. If the middle predicates and
is predicated of, or if it predicates and another is denied of
it, then there will be the first figure; but if it predicates and
is denied, there will be the middle figure; and, if other things
are predicated of it, and one thing is denied, but another
predicated, there will be the last figure. Be careful of errors
of construction arising from improper quantification of
propositions, from inaccurate exposition of terms and from
use of indefinite nouns and verbs. Remember, also, that
predication may be assumed to be possible in as many ways
as the categories are divided, that reduplicatives should be
annexed to the major term rather than the middle, that
terms should be reduced to their simplest expression, that
definite articles be added only according to the requirement
of the conclusion (e.g. pleasure is good vs. pleasure is *the*
good), that the appropriate figure is to be determined by
inspection of the conclusion, that hypothetical syllogisms
cannot be reduced to categoricals, that syllogisms are reducible from one figure to another by certain definite procedures and that oppositions of propositions must be accurately determined.

The second book of the *Prior Analytics* contains several
very important corollaries and further incidental clarifications about types of argumentations which lead to the considerations elaborated in the *Posterior Analytics, Topics* and
Sophistical Refutations. For example, Aristotle analyzes the
truth-value of syllogistic propositions and shows that the
two premises are either both true, both false or one true
and the other false, whereas the conclusion must of necessity be either true or false. From true premises, the false
cannot be inferred but from false premises the truth may be
syllogistically deduced as a matter of fact in virtue of the
formal structure but not because of the content of the

premises. This is shown to be the case in certain moods of the three figures.

Demonstration in a circle is also illustrated in each of the figures, as is the conversion of syllogisms, deduction to the impossible and the method of concluding from opposite propositions in each figure. Begging the question is illustrated as also the fallacies of false cause and false reasoning generally. We are told how to avoid a catasyllogism or the use of a syllogistic conclusion against its proposer; when there will be a possible refutation (elenchus) of a syllogism and when we are deceived by opinion though apparently knowing the opposite. This may happen when one has universal knowledge as regards a class of things, say triangles, but is not sure whether a certain thing is or is not a triangle. For just as to know is predicated in a three-fold manner: either as to the universal or the proper or actual exercise, so also in deception. So nothing prevents a man from knowing and being deceived about the same thing, but not in the same way. One may know two propositions without exercising this knowledge together and thus would have universal knowledge and particular but be uncertain about a conclusion which would follow necessarily from these premises if they were arranged as premises in an appropriate figure.

Every kind of demonstration whether scientific, dialectical, rhetorical or otherwise is produced through the three figures, for we accept everything either through the syllogism or as derived by induction. Here the discussion of induction is from the purely formal point of view of logic and in relation to the deductive procedure of the syllogism, since although what is known by induction is prior to us, what is contained in the syllogism is by nature more known. In induction the logical pattern is to show that one extreme belongs to the middle because of the other extreme, whereas in deduction one extreme is joined with the other through the middle. An example given by Aristotle is: "if B is the middle of A C and we show through C that A is with B for thus we make inductions. Thus let A be long-lived, B void of bile, C every thing long-lived as men, horse, mule." In such an inductive procedure C is taken to include all singulars of the type, "for induction is produced through all."

Somewhat different from induction is the argument from example wherein the major extreme is shown to be present with the middle through something similar to the minor extreme. If one wishes to show that it is bad to make war against the Thebans we must assume that it is bad to war against neighbors, as the war by the Thebans against the Phocians was bad. This is an argument of part to part; induction utilizes all individuals.

Abduction is a technical term that classifies an argumentative procedure perhaps midway between demonstration and the dialectical syllogism. In it the first term is known to be with the middle but it is not evident that the middle is with the last, though it is more credible than the conclusion. Or, again, if the means of establishing the minor are less than the media for the conclusion, we have an abduction, or *apagoge* in contrast with induction which is an *epagoge*.

Objection or instantia (enstasis) is a premise contrary to a premise and may be partial or total in its opposition to the original syllogistic proposition, major or minor. It may be stated universally or particularly in either the first or last figure alone. As when anyone asserts that "such or such is present with every individual," we object either that it is with none (first fig.) or not with a certain one (third fig.), and similarly against negatives.

The probable and a sign are not the same since the probable is what is generally approved or accepted as, e.g. that lovers show affection, and a sign is a demonstrative premise necessary or generally approved, as that which when it exists something else is, is a sign of something else being. An enthymeme is a syllogism composed of probabilities or signs and the sign may be assumed in as many ways as the middle in the third figure. Yet it is invalid in the middle figure. If one proposition is stated, there is only a sign; but, if another is assumed there is a syllogism. What follows from the extremes are signs. A practical application of an inference from sign would be when we infer a character from an external disposition of the body. This would be possible and valid if it is granted that body and soul are changed together by natural affections and if we grant that there is a proper sign corresponding to each affection in regard to each kind of animal. If large extremities are a sign of courage, whenever we find large extremities we would grant existence of courage.

Posterior Analytics

The treatise entitled *Posterior Analytics* is composed of two books; the first treats of the nature of demonstration and its subsidiary problems in thirty-four chapters; the second deals with the subjects of scientific investigation and their relationships with definition, division and other logical devices. It includes nineteen chapters.

Scientific knowledge is called either doctrine or intellectual discipline depending on whether it is possessed actually by the teacher (doctrine) or received in the pupil by means of the activity of learning (discipline). In either case it depends upon pre-existent knowledge which was ultimately or originally derived by induction from sense experience of individuals. In this activity certain fundamental principles are seen to be immediately self-evident (per se) and hence incapable of demonstration. All others are demonstrated by means of those that are self-evident. The most perfect example of demonstrated knowledge is found in the mathematical disciplines; in the other arts there is something analogous. Arguments through syllogisms teach only insofar as one is ready to accept the contents of the premises. The conclusion depends upon the knowledge of the premises. Induction points out the universal by means of the previous knowledge of the individuals. Rhetoricians persuade by a similar procedure, either by example, which is a form of induction related to the moral and political, or by enthymemes, which are syllogisms formed from probabilities or signs as was explained in the *Prior Analytics*. The pre-existent knowledge, then, presupposed as regards scientific knowledge is either knowledge of the fact of existence or knowledge of the subject-matter, or, in some cases, both. In regard to the subject-matter the knowledge must be either universal or proper and thus we can resolve the dilemma in the *Meno* as to whether the slave boy learns nothing or learns what he knows. He may be said to know in a general universal way what he now learns in a proper way, as one could in general know that every triangle has angles equal to two right angles but learn by induction that a certain figure in a semi-circle is a triangle and has two angles.

We have unrestricted scientific knowledge of anything when we know the cause on account of which it is, that it is the cause and that the thing could not be otherwise. The cause is necessary for the existence of the thing so that given the cause you have the thing and you cannot have the thing without the cause. Such would be the case when the middle term is the cause of the conclusion, when we know that it is the cause of the conclusion and know that the conclusion must necessarily follow from the middle term. Demonstration is, then, a scientific syllogism since, from the very fact of having it, we know. It gives knowledge of the highest type of and by itself.

The premises in a scientific syllogism must be "true, first, immediate, better known than and prior to and cause of the conclusion." They must be "true," for we cannot know what does not exist; "first" and "immediate" or otherwise we will not know them since knowledge is either by demonstration, and there is no demonstration of the principles of demonstration, or they are known immediately; "cause of," "better known than" and "prior to" the conclusion because we know scientifically when we know the cause or causes, "prior," since they are causes and every cause is "prior" to the effect, "better known than" because they are better known naturally and simply, since they contain the universal reason why. To understand this latter requirement of the principles of scientific knowing we must distinguish what is prior in nature (more removed from sense as the universal) from what is prior to us (the individual) and what is better known simply (the universal) from what is better known to us (the individual). Those things are said to be "first" which are the proper or peculiar principles from which a particular demonstration is made and these "firsts" are immediate propositions to which there is no other prior, relatively or absolutely.

Propositions are either dialectic or demonstrative; the dialectic involves the probable, the demonstrative the necessary. An immediate syllogistic principle is called a "thesis" if it cannot be demonstrated and if knowledge of it is not required as an essential step in the subsequent demonstration; what must be necessarily known in order to acquire knowledge by demonstration is called "an axiom." A "thesis" which assumes either part of a contradiction is called "an hypothesis" if it asserts existence or non-existence; it is a *definition* if it merely concerns *what* the thing is and not *that* it is.

Since a syllogism productive of science is a demonstration from necessary premises we must be sure we understand this type of proposition. Such will include universal propositions significative *of every* and *per se*. That is said to be *of every* which is true in every instance, as if animal is predicated *of every* man, if it is truly said on any occasion that a certain thing is a man, then it is true that it is an animal. That is said to be *per se* which is an essential attribute; either a) what is inherent in the definition of a thing or b) what is in a subject such that the subject is contained in the definition of the attribute (e.g. nose included in the definition of snub) or c) what is not predi-

42

cated of any other subject or d) what is necessarily connected with another. The opposite of *per se* would be *per accidens*, accidentally, incidentally, accidental, or incidental. That is *universal* which is both predicated *of every*, as true in every instance, and *per se*, so far forth as the thing is. As was clear in the discussion of the patterns of argumentation in the *Prior Analytics* at least one premise must be universal; in order to have scientific demonstration the premises must involve *essential* or *per se* attributes which are true in every instance. The universality involved in strict scientific demonstration is the primary universality, relatively or absolutely as the case may be. For example, to see that angles of a triangle are equal to two right angles not because something is a *bronze* isosceles triangle, nor because it is an *isosceles* triangle but because it is a *triangle*, i.e. a plane figure bounded by three straight lines. In a syllogism, then, when the middle term is of necessary matter the conclusion is also necessary and, therefore, science in the strict sense. Here Aristotle gives a clear statement of the inferential and deductive character of science: "let A be of necessity predicated of B and this of C, it is necessary that A belong to C."

Of common accidents there is no scientific demonstration because such accidents are not *per se, true in every instance* and *necessary*. We must remember that three elements are involved in every demonstration: 1) the demonstrated conclusion which is *per se* inherent in a certain genus; 2) axioms; 3) the subject genus whose properties and essential affections are made manifest by the demonstration. Thus from a knowledge that the essence of man is *rational animal* and what it is to be artistic it *necessarily* follows that being artistic is necessary of every man. There is a caution to be exercised though in demonstration: we should not attempt to demonstrate a conclusion in one genus from another co-ordinate genus; we cannot demonstrate a geometrical problem by arithmetic. However, if the one genus is subordinate to the other then it is possible, as in optics from geometry and in harmonics from arithmetic.

The changeable as such is incapable of demonstration. The highest type of demonstrated science is found in Metaphysics, because here the conclusion is deduced from absolutely ultimate and prior principles. In each genus of things there are principles which must be accepted to be since they cannot be demonstrated, being principles, and from which demonstrations are made in that science. The absolutely first principles are common analogously to every science. Proper principles would be like 'a line is what is between two points'; common or general principles would be like 'if equals are taken from equals the remainders are equals.' So a scientist does not argue about the principles in his science; he accepts them and draws conclusions from them. The essential definitions are assumed, too, as regards a science. Yet they, both principles and definitions, may be demonstrated from the common principles of the highest science, metaphysics, whose function it is to examine *the* fundamentals of being *qua* being, of reality in so far as it is real.

When distinguishing the meanings of *hypothesis, axiom* and *postulate* Aristotle insists that the subject-matter discussed in demonstration does not concern external speech. The demonstrative activity and its result, which is science, deals with what is in the soul (en te psyche) as does every syllogism. I mention this in opposition to a postulate of certain contemporaries that Aristotle was not concerned with a so-called internal thought activity or soul-function but rather only with purely formal linguistic expressiveness. Aristotle says quite the contrary. Often times when Aristotle steps out of the strict continuity of the discussion and looks at the matter as a whole he will make such expressions which confirm the position assumed in the *Categories,* that there is a definite relationship of *thing, thought* (or thinking about thing) and the linguistic expressions of the *thought-thing. Hypothesis* and *postulate* are different from *axiom* in that they do not assert necessity or *per se* existence and it

44

is not necessary to accept them. What is capable of proof but assumed without demonstration is *hypothesis* if the learner accepts it; to be sure it is hypothesis relative to that pupil. If the pupil has no opinion or a contrary opinion the same assumption is a *postulate*. Definitions, then are not hypotheses because definitions do not assert that something is or is not; but hypotheses are contained in the premises of syllogisms and they assume that some things are from which the being of the matter is inferred.

It is quite evident in Aristotle's mind that demonstration is impossible unless one thing is predicated of many, for demonstration depends upon the universal, as explained before. That this is so follows from his conception of the middle term as the cause of the conclusion. However, this does not mean that there are forms (Eide) or ideas in the Platonic sense. The univocal term, which serves as the middle, must be universal otherwise there is no *middle*. This term is understood by the activity of induction from singulars, which are the proper subjects of existence. That the universal is so derived is possible, ultimately, because of the separative activity or, as the medieval philosophers termed it, abstractive activity of the mind. All sciences possess the general principles in common and all sciences employ dialectic as a common procedure of investigation.

Scientific knowledge is not gained through sense directly, nor is sensation science because by sense we apprehend the individual whereas science is conversant with the universal. Sense perception is confined within the limits of time and place; science is true always and in every instance. Yet, because of the foundation of science in sense, scientific knowledge can be deficient through the deficiency of sense.

Science is different from opinion, also. Science concerns the universal and the necessary and its principle is intellect (nous) since science depends on axioms. It is always true. Opinion is concerned with the non-necessary and may be true or false. Hence the same man cannot have science and opinion about the same thing at one and the same time.

45

In summary, discourse is a movement of intellect from premises to conclusion; intellect (nous) is called the principle of understanding as well as the understanding itself; science is demonstrated knowledge; art is the principle of what is to be made; prudence is the principle of what is to be done; wisdom is the vision of truth in relation to *the* first principles; shrewdness, ready-wit or sagacity is a felicitous ex tempore conjecture of the middle term.

In Book 2 the subject-matter of scientific investigations is shown to be four-fold: *that* a thing is, *why* it is, *if* it is, *what* it is. When we know the *that* of anything, as, for example, *that* the sun is eclipsed, we then inquire as to the *why* it is eclipsed. If we know *that* something is, we then investigate *what* it is. In regard to experience the *that* and the *if* may refer to the same thing, the former as regards the actual sense experience and the latter as regards a problem. In either case, upon the positive experience of the existence or the proof of existence the subsequent questions concern the *why* as regards its extrinsic causes and the *what* in relation to the intrinsic causes. In the dianoetic procedure the middle is the *why* of the conclusion but we do not inquire into a middle if the thing and its cause are sensibly perceived, as, if we were above the moon we would not inquire about the *if* or the *why* of an eclipse, for sense would show us that the earth is now opposed and it would be clear that there is now an eclipse and from this we would grasp the universal cause.

There cannot be definition and demonstration of the same thing. For definition is of substance and *what* a thing is whereas demonstration assumes *what* a thing is and from it demonstrates that this thing is or is not of that. The definition cannot be demonstratively derived but it is acquired through induction. There are two types of definition: nominal (what a name signifies) or real (what a thing is) i.e. in terms of its cause: formal, material, efficient or final. In definition the thing defined must be located within a broad general classification or genus and then discriminated from

46

others within that class either by a remote or proximate difference. Division helps in this procedure because a division of things according to extension helps us to discriminate, and all the divided parts must be equivalent to the thing defined.

In conclusion Aristotle summarizes the activity of generating knowledge of the principles of demonstration. There is an innate sense power in all men whereby we perceive sense objects and they become permanent in the soul. This is brought about through memory, for from sense, memory is produced and from repeated memories of the same thing we get experience. As a result we have the universal "at rest" in the soul, "the one beside the many" which "one" is the principle of art and science; art if it concerns making, science if it concerns being. Thus by induction we acquire the universal from sense: first, sense (aisthesis) then, memory (mneme), then experience (empeiria), then, induction (epagoge). "As when a flight occurs in battle, if one soldier makes a stand, another stands, and then another until the fight is restored. . . . When one of a number of the same kind remains, the universal is first present in the soul. For the sense, indeed, senses the singular but the content is of the universal, of man, not of the man Callias. Again it stops in these until the universal is formed, as from a certain kind of animal, animal is derived and so on for others." Thus we apprehend the primary principles by intuition, which is the truest and most accurate activity of the soul; next is scientific knowledge.

Topics

Having finished his discussion of scientific demonstration, science in the strict sense, which involves a syllogistic conclusion derived necessarily in virtue of formal structure (*Prior Analytics*) and involving necessary matter (*Posterior Analytics*) Aristotle now investigates arguments concerning matter or content that is probable. The structural schemata remain the same but the matter is such as all or most men or the wise or the especially renowned or illustrious may be willing to accept as tenable opinions. The treatise, composed of eight books of 82 chapters, concerns dialectics, i.e. the method of syllogizing about any problem from probabilities, or, from another point of view, the personal ability of conversational disputation. Dialectic is the art of disputing by means of question and answer, of opposing or defending a proposition by the use of opinions generally accepted. The general principles of probability are called *topoi*; hence the title.

Aristotle feels it important to make several definite distinctions at the very beginning. The *syllogism* is a form of speech in which certain things being laid down something else results necessarily in virtue of what is laid down. A *demonstrative* syllogism consists of things true and primary but the *dialectical* is collected from probabilities. And those things are said to be probable which seem to be or appear to be to all or to most men, or to the wise, either all or a greater number, or to such as are especially renowned and illustrious. The sources of probable arguments are opinions generally held or authoritative pronouncements. A *contentious* syllogism (eristikos) is made up of apparent but not real probabilities. *Paralogisms* consist of what is appropriate to certain sciences and this kind of syllogism involves assumptions appropriate to science yet they are not true. The author, also, cautions us that he plans to give a general, brief resume of the matter and not a thorough scientific analysis of its contents.

The precise purpose of the treatise is to outline a method by which one may reason probably about any question that may come up. Any question will be concerned either with the genus of the subject, its specific difference, its property or its accidents. By dealing with them one acquires facility in argumentation, conversational proficiency and philosophical perspicuity for by such exercise one can learn to argue on every subject, converse with others from appropriate topics and learn to sift the true from the false. In philosophy dialectic is a procedural preliminary to a resolution of the problem in terms of scientific argumentation.

Since all questions and problems are concerned with genus, property, difference and accident it is essential to understand what they are, how they differ and how they are related. The definition of anything is a form of speech signifying what it is. The perfect definition will include genus and specific difference; the less perfect is made up of genus and property and the least accurate consists of an enumeration of accidents with the genus. Genus is a broad general classification referring to that part of the essential make-up possessed in common by different species, as animal in reference to man, ox and mule. Species is the total essence shared in common by those things which differ only accidentally, as man in regards to John and Joe, etc. The specific difference, as the name indicates, distinguishes one species from another in the same genus. The property is not of the essence but it is so connected with the essence that it necessarily accompanies it, as grammatical in reference to man. To overthrow a definition we must attack it from the point of view of genus or difference.

Definition must be the same as the thing, yet we should realize that *same* is predicated in a threefold way: in number, species and genus. Something may be the same numerically though designated by different terms, as garment and vestment; as regards the definition, the sameness in species is completely so, that of genus only partially so. And that all arguments concern genus, difference, property or accident may be shown either by induction or by syllogism (reasoning). By means of the latter it is clear that any predicate either reciprocates with the thing or not. If it reciprocates and signifies what the thing is, it is definition; if it reciprocates but does not signify what it is, it is property. If it does not reciprocate it will either be a part of the definition (genus or difference) or outside the definition and therefore accident. Again, either of these fall

49

into one of the ten categories for if it signifies what the thing is (definition) it will be substance, and, if not, one of the types of accidental determinations explained in the first work in the *Organon.*

In dialectics we distinguish between a dialectical proposition and a dialectical problem. The proposition is an interrogation probable to all or to the most renowned, provided it is not contrary to general opinion. It may resemble the probable or be contrary to those which appear probable, being advocated through contradiction, or may include the opinions upheld in the arts. A dialectical problem is a subject of inquiry concerning choice and avoidance (the ethical) or truth and knowledge, and that either for itself or as a preliminary to a solution of some other problem. A *thesis* is a paradoxical judgment, i.e. a supposition of someone eminent in philosophy that conflicts with general opinion or when we ourselves have an opinion based on reasons contrary to general opinion. Though a thesis is a problem, not every problem is a thesis, though, as a general matter of fact, almost all dialectical problems are called theses. It is not necessary to investigate all problems, but only those which are neither too easily nor too difficultly demonstrable and those not resolvable by simple perceptive experience.

Just as scientific demonstration included both induction and deduction so does the dialectical. Of these induction is more apt to persuade, is clearer, more known according to sense and more applicable to the general run of men; syllogistic reasoning is more forceful and more efficacious against our opponents in arguments. The means by which we shall become proficient in dialectics are four: securing the proper propositions (invention); having the ability to distinguish the different meanings of common expressions (acuteness); knowing the differences of things (discrimination); knowing the likenesses of things (penetration). A proposition or problem will concern either the ethical, physical or logical. When treated dialectically we will discuss them with an eye to public opinion. But when we consider them philosophically we will be interested in the truth. From the omission of the metaphysical as a branch of problems one may infer that the metaphysical itself cannot be treated dialectically but only insofar as the truth is discoverable. Of course, the dialectical investigation may be made as a procedural preliminary, as he has said before and as he himself proceeded, for example in the *Physics* and *Metaphysics*. In all cases of dialectical discussion the propositions are to be assumed as universal as possible in content.

The remaining Books of the *Topics* deal with the details of applying the general method discussed in Book I to the particular problems of disputation concerning the basic subject-matter of probable argumentation. Book II discusses the 'Topics' mainly related to genus; Book II concerns the 'topics' connected with the more eligible and the better; Book IV, 'topics' of species, similitude and relation; Book V concerning property; Book VI 'topics' related to definition; Book VII, identity, confirmation and subversion of definition; Book VIII, a digest-hand-book of summarized practical rules for dialectical disputations.

Sophistical Refutations

The Greek word 'elengxos' was originally a legal term relating to the procedure of arguing against a position or of refuting a case or position assumed by an adversary. Its precise translation would be, I presume, 'argument.' In our context, as qualified by the adjective 'sophistical' in its pejorative connotation, it is usually translated as *refutation*. Yet, in truth, a sophistical elenchus is not a real but only an apparent refutation. It leads to an opposite conclusion but does so by spurious means. Hence it is a *sophistical* refutation or a *sophistical* argument. Aristotle defines an elenchus as a syllogism involving a contradiction of a conclusion. As such it appears to be a valid bit of reasoning but it is deceitful because of fallacies of language or fallacies of matter.

51

The most natural and most popular source of fallacies is language. We cannot discourse about things by presenting the things in their existential status; we must use names as symbols of things. The fallacies would arise whenever we think that what happens in names also happens in things. Sometimes we use the same name for different things; at other times we use different names for the same thing. So we must be careful in the employment of terms in discourse as he has discussed in the *Categories* and mentioned elsewhere in passing. Another source of fallacies is probably psychological. Some men prefer to appear wise rather than to be wise. They are sophists or traders in apparent wisdom. Their main purpose is to win an argument for personal prestige or pecuniary enrichment. A study of sophistical arguments is a useful investigation because by it we may learn how to avoid fallacies in our own reasoning activities and how to discern the fallacies in our opponent's argument against us.

There are five objects aimed at by the contentious or sophistic disputant: an elenchus, the false, the paradox, the solecism and repetition. So the sophist will try to refute an adversary by an argument which contradicts his conclusion either through fallacies of diction or fallacies of matter. Failing this he tries to induce the opponent to state a manifest falsehood or to make an assertion which opposes generally accepted opinions. If one is led to employ barbarous expressions, or blunders in speech or any ungrammatical expression he may be apparently refuted. The least satisfactory procedure is to lead the opponent to trifling speech by repetition or tautologous expressions which are nugatory or worthless as regards the main argument. Each of these is taken up in detail throughout the thirty-four chapters along with the proper solutions to them. The most important of the fallacies are concerned with the first category. There are six fallacies of language: equivocation (use of the same word with different meanings), ambiguity or amphiboly (ambiguity in phrases or grammatical structure), composition and division (combining in the conclusion what was separate in the premises or vice-versa), fallacy of accent (when the meaning of a word differs according to a different accentuation), and figure of speech (which involves, among other possibilities, an expression in one category interpreted as belonging to another: judging all qualities to be quantities). The greatest safeguard against such fallacies would be a careful distinction of terms by definition, proficiency in grammar, alertness in speech, awareness of differences of accentuation and a precise knowledge of the distinctions in the categories and the predicables.

Fallacies apart from diction or those involved in the matter of the discussion are seven in number: accident (confusing the accidental with the essential), relative confused with absolute, ignorance of the issue or the argument (refuting a point that is not *the* point in question), fallacy of consequent (assuming that the acceptance of the consequent entails acceptance of the antecedent in an hypothetical or conditional argument), petitio principii (begging the question), false cause (post hoc ergo propter hoc) and complex question (have you stopped beating your wife?).

In concluding the treatise Aristotle reminds the reader that his purpose was to investigate reasoning in matters probable so that we may understand the sophistic art and avoid the fallacies involved in it. However, unlike matters involved in the rhetorical art which have a long history of development and many discussions by eminent rhetoricians, this matter of dialectic has no real predecessors. True, the schools of sophists have constructed treatises in the art but these have been merely manuals of instruction adapted to certain practical problems. No one, according to Aristotle, has treated the matter scientifically in reference to the general principles involved. As a matter of fact Aristotle was the first to prepare such a thorough consideration of all the elements involved in reasoning scientifically, dialectically, peirastically and sophistically. In regard to the scientific arrangement of the formal structure of syllogistic reasoning

Aristotle was *the* pioneer and, although much has been accomplished subsequently in the whole field of Logic, it is, perhaps, true to maintain that no one has made such a perfect contribution to the science and art of correct reasoning as Aristotle.

Rhetoric

The treatise on *Rhetoric* is divided into three Books. The first, in fifteen chapters, explains the nature of rhetoric, its similarity and dissimilarity with Logic and, also, the definite sciences, the end or purpose of Rhetoric in general, the means of achieving its end, the three kinds of rhetoric, the sources of arguments in each, the subject-matter of each. Book Two, in twenty-six chapters, considers the basic modes of persuasion, the topics common to all three types and the common matter out of which speeches are constructed. Book Three, in nineteen chapters, discusses the elements of style and the arrangement and contents of the physical parts of a speech.

Rhetoric, like Logic, is mainly a formal discipline which is not, in itself, a distinct science but rather a method of which all men should have knowledge. His predecessors have had much to say on the subject but generally, they have omitted discussions of the essential elements and concentrated more on undue appeals to the passions. The fundamental goal of rhetoric is persuasion, not absolute, but relative to the means of persuasion inherent in the particular subject. Rhetoric is "the ability of considering all the possible means of persuasion on every subject." Its means are either artificial or inartificial. The latter include laws (written and adapted to a particular case or universal), witnesses, deeds, torture, and oaths. The former include anything devised by human art which can be applied persuasively to the point at issue. Most oratory is fabricated for oral delivery and contains three species of means of persuasion: the character of the speaker revealed in his speech, the disposition of the hearers by an appeal to emotions and the speech itself. The persuasion is effective by means of the moral character of the speaker when the oration is spoken in such a way as to render the speaker worthy of confidence. Hence it must arise from the speech and not from any preconceived notion of the character of the orator. The second means is effective when the audience is brought to a state of appropriate emotional excitement under the influence of the speech. The content of the speech and its persuasive make-up will be mentioned later.

It is quite clear that a good rhetorician must understand the principles of dialectic and be able to reason logically on any subject-matter. He must, also, be something of a psychologist and know human nature in general and in regard to particular groups in order to devise the appropriate means of arousing the emotions requisite to a desired goal. For the latter, Aristotle goes into detail discussing the emotions that stir men, the predominant emotions in various age groups, the general and particular goals of men and the virtues and emotions relative to both. The rhetorician must be something of an ethician and politician, too, since rhetoric is not only an off-shoot of Logic but, also, of that branch of moral philosophy called the science of social life.

The means of persuading relative to the proving of a point are both inductive and deductive; the former is example and the latter enthymeme. He discussed both in great detail in Book II where he distinguishes example into the real and the fictitious, which is either an illustration, as found in the Socratic discourses, or a fable. Enthymemes are adduced from probabilities and signs, as we may argue that a certain mother loves her child because most mothers do or that a person is guilty of an alleged crime because he is trembling. An enthymeme is a general type of syllogistic reasoning having two species: the confirmative or refutative.

All rhetoric presupposes a speaker, a subject spoken about and an audience of one or more. Since rhetoric is the art of persuasion, the types of rhetorical argumentation will be determined by the audience. One may be either simply an observer or a judge who must make a decision about the past or the future. Thus the three classes of oratory are: 1) the political or deliberative in which the subject-matter concerns the future expedient or inexpedient relative to the finances of the State, war and peace, national defense, imports and exports, and legislation. The political orator urges that something be accepted because it is good or rejected because it is bad for the State. It is essential for him to know the four types of governments (democracy, oligarchy, aristocracy, monarchy) and the means of preserving or destroying each. 2) the forensic or judicial oratory concerns the past; one is accused in reference to something already done. In this type the aim concerns establishing the justice or injustice of an action. This is the task of the lawyer who must be familiar with the proper and general laws involved since injustice is "an evil voluntarily committed contrary to the law." There are two causes of injustice: depravity and incontinence (moral weakness). The things which men do they do either of themselves or by chance, by compulsion or by nature; and what they do of themselves and of which they are the cause is done either through custom or through natural desire influenced by reason or unaccompanied by reason. The forensic orator must know all this and be able to put the knowledge to work for either defendant or plaintiff. 3) The third type of oratory or rhetoric is the ceremonial or demonstrative and its purpose is to praise or blame someone in the present. It is the type heard at banquets and ceremonials during which the character and personality of a person is held up for commendation. Such an evaluation of character requires a knowledge of the end or purpose of man, which is happiness, and of the means to acquire it. The ingredients of happiness are noble birth, good offspring, wealth, honor, health, beauty, strength, stature, good fortune and virtue, i.e. moral excellence. All or any of these may be the basis of ceremonial oratory.

Book III treats of the speech itself both as regards the

56

style of its composition and delivery and the physical arrangement of the parts. Style is very important in relation to the goal of rhetoric: persuasion. The proper modulation of the voice is conducive to the arousal of certain emotions; harmony and rhythm are important. Excellence of style consists in its clarity, appropriateness, beauty, proper employment of figures of speech such as metaphors, similes, personification and hyperbole, warmth and euphony. The written style should involve facile readability, avoid long parentheses, include familiar expressions and correct grammatical structure. Of course, these general requirements must be variously adapted to the divergent requirements of the different branches of rhetoric. The same style is not appropriate for the political and the judicial. The written style is more precise; that of disputation more involved in emotion and more expressive of feeling. Some declamations appear ridiculous when read.

As to the physical make-up of a speech the essential parts are statement and proof because whoever proves, proves something and the statement is made with a view to subsequent proof. In most cases there are two other parts added to make the speech complete: exordium and peroration. The exordium is to the speech what the prologue is to a poem and the prelude to a musical composition. In ceremonial rhetoric the exordium arises from praise, blame, exhortation, dissuasion and appeals to the hearers. In judicial rhetoric the exordium should be like the prologue to a play and set forth the object of the speech like an insight into the plot. Besides putting the audience into the proper frame of mind the exordium should elevate the character of the orator and the one he is defending, cast aspersions on the adversary, conciliate the good will of the audience, arouse anger in his favor, win the attention of the hearer or, on occasion, distract the attention of the audience from a point by laughter e.g. The exordia of the political orators are derived in a manner similar to the judicial.

Between the exordium and the peroration are the two

essential elements of a rhetorical composition. There must be a statement of the case which involves narration during which the subject becomes clear, the speaker wins over the audience, conveys a notion of character, stirs up some emotions and involves the facts in feeling. Then comes the proof. In judicial oratory this would concern four topics: demonstration of the fact, whether harm has been done, the degree of importance of the action involved, the moral character of the action. In the ceremonial speech amplification is usually all the proof that is needed. But in deliberative or political rhetoric the proof must show that a proposal is not practicable, or, if practicable, unjust or not beneficial or not in such a degree as proposed. He must be on guard as to whether any falsehoods appear in the observations of his adversary. Enthymemes are best adapted to the judicial; example is more proper to the political.

The peroration is made up of four elements: rendering the audience favorable to oneself and ill-disposed toward the adversary, amplification or extenuation, excitation of passions of audience and an awakening of memory concerning the main points of his proof. The peroration should begin with a statement that what was proposed in the beginning has been accomplished. This can be done by direct juxtaposition with the adversary's position or by indirect comparison or by rhetorical interrogations: "what has this man established?" It is essential that the pertinent facts and proofs be recalled to the mind of the audience. A disjointed style is suitable to the conclusion of the peroration: "I have finished. You have heard. The facts are before you. Give your decision."

Poetics

The *Peri Poietikes,* as we have it today, is an extensive philosophical reflection upon poetry in general and its distinct species, especially, tragedy, upon the pragmatic aspects of poetic composition and upon the relationship between

58

epic and tragic poetry-making. Apparently the treatise originally contained another major section devoted to Comedy, which is no longer extant. Of the total twenty-six chapters, cc. 1-5 are of a general introductory type; cc. 6-18, except 17, deal explicitly with tragedy; cc. 17 and 19-22 appear to be a manual of practice relative to tragedy-making and its dictional ingredients; cc. 23-26, except 25, develop an explicit comparison of tragedy and the epic; c. 25 is concerned with general problems of criticism in poetry.

The precise purpose of the work is two-fold: 1) to examine reflectively the essence of poetry, generically considered, and the proper characteristics of the different species of poetry; 2) to inquire into the structure of plot and the essential elements of poetry-making. From the philosophical point-of-view the treatise involves a search for generalizations to be derived inductively, as was Aristotle's method, from the individual instances found in human experience. As regards the case at hand the individual facts were the actual historical poetry-making that was found in the near and remote history of Greece up to and including the major part of the fourth century B.C. This point is important and is quite evident from the treatise itself. It protects the work from the accusation of being an a priori canon of arbitrary rules imposed upon poetry from without and determining by some magical insight into "pure forms" what poetry must be or what tragedy must be. What is the activity called poetry? How does it differ from other human activities? To answer those questions we must examine the facts of history.

Not only must one beware of any purely a priori judgments in this matter but we must, also, be aware of the broader philosophical setting (also derived from and based on experience) in which the treatise on poetry is to be examined. The whole Organon must be kept in mind as regards methods of investigation and the Physics, Metaphysics, Ethics and Politics, especially, must be viewed as the ingredients of the tapestry that serves as a meaningful back-drop for the Poetics. This is absolutely essential if we are to appreciate, for example, the meaning attached by

59

Aristotle to the term *imitation.* (mimesis) Most students, professional and amateur, are aware that Aristotle said, "art imitates nature"; yet, it is only in the context of the *Physics*, at least, that this expression becomes clear and pure. Someone has remarked that whatever Aristotle meant by the expression he did *not* mean mere copying. But more of this later.

He begins with the general consideration that poetry, in its broadest application, in its genus as it were, is really synonymous with *making.* Any kind of making can be called poetry. As such it is really identical with *art,* the work-making activity of man, who, in addition, also performs a theoretical or speculative activity and an ethical or practical activity. The speculative concerns knowledge for its own sake; the practical is knowledge for doing; the poetical is knowledge for making. Since art considered as an intelligently directed activity concerning making may be called *know-how,* the type of art and the value of the making, as, also, the dignity of the imitation, will vary in proportion to the emphasis on *know* or on *how.* In no case can there be a human making which does not involve intelligence in action. The predominant proportion of intelligence may lead to an emphasis on *know* whereas a predominance of habit or manual dexterity may emphasize the *how,* a distinction fundamental in Plato's view but scarcely understood by those who interpret him solely from the tenth book of the *Republic.* Hence poetry or art or imitation always involves a making intelligently directed, but the dignity of the art varies with the qualitative preponderance of intelligence. Some arts were just useful; they imitate nature by filling up its deficiencies and administering solely to practical needs. Art's humblest function is to satisfy a want or alleviate a pain. Here the *how* may predominate. In addition there are the *liberal* arts, such as *Logic* and *Rhetoric,* whose making does not involve external matter but is more closely allied to the speculative activity of man. *Know* is emphasized. Then there are what have come to be called

60

the *fine* arts, which involve making in matter but the end is not merely utility. They give pleasure and relaxation. They are more closely allied to the notion of the beautiful. *Know-how* may be equally proportioned. It appears quite clear that in the predominantly useful and fine arts, or, more exactly, in those activities of making considered as such, there were *degrees* of imitation ranging from *almost* just copying to *almost* purely formal construction. I say *almost* because poetry, art, imitation as a human activity must involve elements of both *know* and *how*, or, you may prefer to call it intuition and technique in a certain contemporary setting.

Species of poetry were epic poetry, tragedy, comedy, dithyrambic poetry, instrumental music, painting, sculpture, rhapsodic-reciting and vocal mimicry. All are modes of imitation which differ among themselves according to the specific differentiation of medium, object and manner of imitation. The precise medium in painting is color, in sculpture it is form, in instrumental music it is melody. In epic, tragedy, comedy and lyric poetry the medium of imitation is rhythm, language and harmony (melody). As a matter of fact rhythm is common to them all; they differ because of a combination of rhythm with language and/or harmony, or by the use of rhythm alone as in the dance. In instrumental music of the type found in Greece there was rhythm with melody. Language and rhythm are found in the Socratic dialogues and iambic meters, for example. Tragedy is qualified by language, rhythm and melody, epic omits the last. An awareness of the basis of denominating these as arts will help us realize that it is the fact of imitation that makes a poet a poet and not the fact that he composes verses in whatever kind of meter it may be. And one will be a tragic poet or epic poet depending on the medium of imitation employed.

The objects of imitation are *men in action* and, as such, they will be either morally good or morally bad in varying degrees. A man in action as man cannot be considered

morally indifferent, as is evident from the ethical considerations of Aristotle. Here we catch another insight into his
meaning of imitation. In painting and the dance, in sculpture and in music, as well as in epic and tragedy, the object
of imitation is human action, which proceeds from character
(ethe) and thought (dianoia) and is indicative of the
morally good or bad. A landscape or seascape, somewhat
like Plato's allusion to a painting of a bed, would be improper subjects of imitation, to judge from this section, and
such a product would be almost pure copying, unless inanimate and lower animate forms of nature were presented
as directly involved in relation to men in action and, by
that I mean, essential to the active aspect of the man. Poly-
gnotus, the painter, and Homer, the epic poet, represented
men as nobler than the general run of individuals; Pauson
the painter, and Nichochares, the poet, portray them as
worse; Dionysius drew them as representative of the average
and Cleophon presented them similarly in his poems. Thus,
according to objects imitated you can have different varieties
of artistic compositions. There appears to be no possibility
of an artistic portrayal of ideas as such or of character as
such. They must be involved in human action and it is the
action which is fundamental. This thought is closely allied
with Aristotle's understanding of human life and the good-
life for man.

The manner of imitation employed in poetry as a fine
art was either pure narration, pure dramatic delivery or a
combination of both, the latter found in a preeminent way
in Homer. Tragedy uses the dramatic manner and the
intrusion of narrative detracts from the total effect. Remembering some of the historical examples of the distinct types
according to medium, object and manner we see that the
poems of Sophocles and Homer, though different because
of manner and medium, are similar as regards objects imitated: higher types of character manifested in action.

The activity of poetry seems to have arisen in man due
to two deeply ingrained causes: 1) the natural instinct for

imitation found in all men coupled with pleasure, which is a natural 'overtone' of action well done, and 2) the sense of rhythm and harmony which is natural to all men. Realistic representation in art excites a natural delight in such works of imitation. The pleasures associated with learning are stimulated by art products and, even when learning is not formally or explicitly present, we delight in the execution or the coloring or some other such ingredient. Here, as well as in a previous statement concerning the medium of painting and sculpture as involving color and shape, we see that Aristotle would be quite receptive to certain 'modern' trends in painting and sculpture. The natural endowments of men are basic. Starting with these two fundamentals certain individuals with additional aptitudes developed by degrees until the preliminary improvisation, at first quite crude, flowered into poetry. And, due to those special aptitudes different types of poetry resulted, whether epic, tragedy or comedy. Tragedy has gone through several stages of development. Aeschylus was the first to introduce a second actor, diminish the importance of the chorus and concentrate on the dialogue. Sophocles increased the number of actors on the stage at one time to three and also added painted scenery. The original short plot was replaced by one of greater compass and the diction went through several stages of polishing and improvement. A multiplication of acts and other accessories were gradual accretions. Whether tragedy has as yet reached its perfect form is an open question. As a matter of actual fact it has reached an advanced stage in which the dramatist attempts to curtail the action within the space of a day, though this was not always the case. (The only explicit reference to the external unities of a play found in Aristotle's works.)

Examining the dramas that have been composed, the extant plays as it were, Aristotle arrives at a definition of tragedy: "An imitation of an action that is serious, complete and of a certain magnitude; in language embellished with each kind of artistic ornament, the several kinds being found in separate parts of the play; in the form of action, not narrative; through pity and fear affecting the proper purgation of these emotions." "Embellished language" involves rhythm, harmony and song and some parts of the play are rendered with song and others without it. Some scenery is useful in the staging because of the fact that a human action is involved and it requires an appropriate setting or circumstance. Song and diction are the media. Again, because tragedy is an imitation of human action there are personal agents with distinctive types of character and thought involved. Thus every tragedy has a plot, the soul or formal essence of the action, character, in virtue of which certain qualities are assigned to the agents, thought, the source of proofs and generalizations, diction, song and spectacle in their order of importance. All the poets to a man have employed these elements. The spectacle depends more on the staging than the poetry-making and is not essential, especially since a play may be read without losing its effect. The most important element is the plot, the structure of the incidents, since tragedy is an imitation of action, not men nor ideas nor character simply. Character is for the plot and is a subsidiary of the action.

Tragedy involves an action that is "serious," that is, of grave consequence and it may concern whatever may take place as probable or necessary. It must be complete, with beginning, middle and end, a total unit, self-sufficient in itself. The size or extent of the action is, of course, relative and has varied over the years. From the point of view of the ingredients of beauty it should be of such a magnitude as to be embraced within the span of facile memory. It should be a size that can be grasped as a complete unit by the spectator. Like a natural object there is both a minimum and maximum size relative to the type involved. All things considered, the proper size is such as to allow a certain sequence of events, according to the law of probability or necessity, which will permit a change from bad fortune to good or from good to bad, the latter preferred by Aristotle.

The plot is the essential element of a tragedy. Its unity does not depend upon the fact that there is only one hero involved since the infinite variety of human actions in one man's life cannot be reduced to a unity. The action itself imitated must be one, not absolutely simple but complex and the parts must be integrated in terms of probability or necessity. Recall here, too, the fact that the beginning of a plot must not follow by causal necessity from something else, that the middle must so follow from the beginning and that, although the end necessarily or regularly follows from the middle, nothing necessarily follows from the end. It is structurally complete and so unified that if any part be removed the whole will be so much disjointed and disturbed. "For a thing whose presence or absence makes no manifest difference is not an organic part of the whole." The plot does not concern what has happened as an isolated incident. An account of such belongs to history not poetry. The poet presents what may happen as probable or necessary. The hero is the concrete vehicle for the presentation of a generalization and so the poet is closely akin to the philosopher and poetry to philosophy. This is further clarified when he discusses the pragmatics of plot construction. Poets have generally made use of the same historical characters, though this is not necessary to tragedy as such. The plot itself is not a descriptive account of a hero but an artistic construction, a creation depending upon the individual insight and genius of the poet.

Plots are either simple, when the change of fortune results without Reversal (peripetia) and without Recognition (anagnorisis), or complex, when the action involves both Reversal and Recognition. In a complex plot, which Aristotle considered the best tragedy, the Reversal must arise necessarily out of the structural elements of the plot so that the antecedents actually cause the downfall of the hero and are not merely antecedents. Remembering the fallacies, he means here that there must be a case of *propter hoc* and not just *post hoc*. In this element, as probably in every other one, Oedipus Rex is the perfect model. Recognition is a change from ignorance to knowledge and it should be coincident with the Reversal, as in Oedipus.

The tragic hero should pass from happiness to misery. The most effective tragedy would present the hero as being above the average type of man, as preeminently noble and yet marred by some serious flaw of character and/or judgment. When Aristotle demands a noble person for the tragic hero he has in mind the general practice of Greek poets but, also, the fact that the tragic action must be of some great importance or serious magnitude. The greater the nobility of the hero, compatible with a serious flaw, the greater the impact of the Reversal and, thus, the greater the appeal to the emotions of the audience. Obviously a perfect character would be out of place because a reversal of fortune would not necessarily result or be probable and the audience would not feel pity and fear but, rather, indignation. At the opposite extreme the downfall of a vicious individual would excite, perhaps, joy and satisfaction. The simple unhappy ending is best and along these lines Euripides is consistently the most tragic of the poets.

The goal of the tragedy is to arouse the emotions of pity and fear so that they may undergo a purgation or catharsis. As we have noticed the type of character is essentially related to this purpose. The incidents of the plot are the direct vehicle for the excitation of these emotions. The action itself must be such as to play upon these emotions and lead to their purgation. As defined in the *Rhetoric* "pity is a sort of pain occasioned by an evil capable of hurting or destroying, appearing to befall one who does not deserve it, which one may himself expect to endure or someone connected with him will and this when it appears near" whereas "fear is a sort of pain or agitation arising out of an idea that an evil capable either of destroying or giving pain is impending on us." What Aristotle means in this context by catharsis has been hotly debated. Surely he would not mean that by arousing the emotions a dangerous excess is produced, for, unlike some remarks in Plato, he looked upon tragedy as a beneficial element in human life. He does not mean, either, that the *painful* element in these emotions is removed, since they are species of pain and the purge would eliminate them completely. Some have judged that by means of the tragedy these emotions are purified of their "self-regarding" elements and rendered altruistic. Others interpret the catharsis as ceremonial in the religious sense of purification. Others consider it medically. Perhaps the poetic or tragic catharsis is an analogy drawn from both the ceremonial-religious context for its psychological connotation and from the medical for its physical counterpart with an admixture of the ethical in relation to his theory of the mean. I personally think that the expression does have an analogous reference to the religious, medical and ethical but, like every analogy, there would be a proper element of difference. That is the esthetic. As a result of the arousal of the emotions by the incidents of the plot excess of emotion is removed, or more is acquired, so that a proper balance would result; they (the emotions) are directed to proper objects in a proper way, the good exercise of these emotions gives an emotional purification within the context of an aesthetic experience.

Concerning the delineation of the characters in the play Aristotle thinks that there are four things to keep in mind: 1) any character must be presented as good in performing the proper function of his character; 2) it must be true to type presented (slave should act like a slave); 3) it must be true to life (not necessarily as an actual person but consistent with human life); 4) it must be consistent throughout (even if the character is inconsistent it should be presented as consistently inconsistent).

In the pragmatic aspects of actual construction of a tragedy the poet should try to visualize the scenes as actually parts of the action so as to avoid possible inconsistencies in staging. Aristotle had in mind the blunder of Carcinus who presented Amphiaraus entering the temple at one wing of the stage at the end of one scene and then had him leave the temple in a subsequent scene by emerging from the opposite wing; he mislaid the character. The poet should be able to put himself *in* his characters and know how one will react in a certain circumstance. This implies either a happy gift of nature or a strain of madness. In the first a poet can take the mold of any character; in the second he is lifted out of his proper self. The poet should, also, draw up an outline of the plot containing only the essential parts in their general aspect and then fill in the episodes later.

The general observations on diction are prefaced with a reference to what has been said on the same topic in the *Rhetoric*. The statements about letters, syllables, noun, verb, sentence, etc., are consistent with similar discussions in the *On Interpretation*. In general there should be a clarity of expression without vulgarity, achieved by an appropriate use of the ordinary and the unfamiliar, of foreign words and native expressions. The practical sign of genius in poetic composition is the mastery of metaphor.

Tragedy and epic have many similarities and differences. Each must be about a serious object, noble and of importance, complete in its action, possessing beginning, middle and end and resembling in its unity a living organism. Epic does not have melody and spectacle but the other parts are the same. They employ the same type of thought and diction. The epic is as a matter of current fact longer but was not always so. The epic meter is dactylic hexameter; the style includes narrative mainly but also dramatic presentation. There is more room for the marvelous and improbable in epic. Tragedy can be acted as well as read; it is more concentrated and more effective; it has greater unity. In addition it has all the perfection of the epic. Tragedy is the highest form of the poetic art.

The treatise has one chapter on criticism in poetry. After giving some of the condemnations of tragedy expressed probably by the Platonists Aristotle lays down in order his own observations. The poet should not be expected to be scientifically accurate in everything he portrays. Apparent inconsistencies are permissible if they serve the purposes of poetry and are somehow probable. The poet need not be literally true to fact for he may be treating the subject as it *ought* to be or as some say it is. There is room in Aristotle's theory for pure creativity. Don't blame the poet for errors in the speech of his characters. That may be the way he envisages the characters. Above all try to discover what the author intended by his presentation; if that is not possible we must use the criterion of a person of intelligence.

In the *Poetics,* outside of what has been mentioned above, there is no explanation of what imitation (mimesis) means. If, however, we reflect upon it within the context of his other writings, we come to understand its essential and proper meaning and the multiple elements that contribute to its extensive connotations. In our analysis of the *Posterior Analytics* we have already pointed out how art as a principle of making is developed in the intellect as one of the by-products of induction. Art, like knowledge of the principles of demonstration, is basically derived from experience of nature as regards its content. It is a symbolic re-presentation of nature which could be called an imitation. Yet it is not just a mechanical "holding a mirror up to nature" because there is involved the dynamism of intellectual intuition. Art, as a formal directive principle of making, is creative within the limitations of all the multiple aspects of nature: colors, sizes, shapes and forms, either the obvious concrete sense ones or the abstract mathematical ones. Even metaphysical forms derived from nature are imitable by the artist. Hence art imitates nature as regards the subject matter of the imitation. In a more important way art imitates nature when we see that nature is the sum-total of material entities, each of which involves a productive dynamism as constitutive of its nature. The nature of anything is the inner principle or source of its activity. Art as a dynamic principle of productivity is analogous to this concept of nature; it imitates nature in this way. Another aspect of the nature's dynamism is the fact that it involves an activity towards an end, goal or purpose. Such is true of art as an intelligently directed activity of making. It reaches out to a goal, the art-product. So art is the intrinsic principle of a person's artistic activity. Again, just as the nature is properly the formal substantial determination of a thing's essence so art is the formal accidental determination of an artist's activity *qua* artist. Art involves forms just as nature does. Matter limits forms in both nature and art. The nature of anything is its formal principle of unity; so is art. Order in nature depends upon form; so in art. In nature you find human actions which involve emotions, so in art. Natural objects have a definite size, so in art. Just as in nature an agent strives to produce an effect like itself, which requires a plasticity of the material acted upon, so art moves to the reproduction of itself (a formal perfection) in a concrete medium that is variable in each of the arts. Thus the imitation is multiple and on the level of analogy.

Beauty is associated with art just as it is with nature. In no sense is the beautiful merely the pleasant. The objects of nature and art are beautiful in both a metaphysical and aesthetic sense. The objective beauty of anything is a result of its unity, harmony (proportion, symmetry) and formal perfection; or, again, "the chief forms of beauty are order, symmetry and definiteness." It is really identical with its goodness but there are relative differences. The good is an end to be desired, to be possessed. There is no necessary desire for possession in regard to the beautiful; it is, in itself as beautiful, the subject-matter of contemplative delight. Beauty is based on form as looking to its effulgent perfection. The good is related to doing, to conduct, to acting for an end to be acquired; the beautiful is found also in motionless things, such as the mathematicals. Thus from the psychological-aesthetic viewpoint anything is called beautiful because it delights when contemplated. The psychological-aesthetic response is rooted in the objective constitutive elements of the object contemplated and the subject con-

70

templating. The aesthetic experience is the harmonious resultant of the confrontation of the dynamic object with the dynamically responding percipient.

THE PHYSICS

Aristotle's discussions about nature and motion in general have been compiled into eight books of seventy-one chapters. Book One is mainly concerned with the nature and number of the basic principles found in every object in nature. Book Two explains the conditions of change and the types of cause found in nature. Book Three treats of motion and the infinite. Book Four explains the fundamental concomitants of motion: place and time. Book Five and Six, types of movement, being-in-motion, the mover, moved and other relational aspects of motion. Book Seven comparison of movements, proportions of movements, moved mover. Book Eight, eternal character of movement and the existence of the prime mover.

At the very beginning of this work Aristotle is seen as putting into practice the elements of the method of philosophical investigation explained in detail throughout the *Organon*, especially the *Posterior Analytics*. He admits that he is in quest of scientific knowledge about Nature and points out the way to proceed in order to acquire the basic principles. He incorporates ideas about the psychological development of knowledge found in the work *On The Soul* and the *Posterior Analytics*.

In the actual philosophical quest Aristotle proposes the problem of the number and nature of the principles, elucidates the problem dialectically and then investigates it by means of the historical results at hand. Others have investigated this matter; what are their conclusions? He examines the conclusions of the early physicists, as he calls them, applies logical arguments to show in what way they erred or hit upon the truth and sets up his own answers to the

71

problem. The fundamental criterion for this latter evaluation is agreement with the facts. He proves from the fact of substantial variation that all things in nature are essentially composed of two elements or principles, philosophically viewed. They are matter (ule) or the capacity for becoming an object of a different kind and form (morphe) which is the nature-determining principle, the intrinsic structure-principle in a non-physical sense. The result is the Aristotelian hylomorphism, a theoretical explanation of the absolute ultimates in natural objects.

The discussions in Book One have fanned out and touched many other related problems. So we have certain explicit clarifications of what he really means by 'nature,' 'the natural,' 'by nature' and how they differ from 'art,' 'the artificial' and 'by art.' He clarifies the function of the philosopher of nature as distinct from the mathematician and the metaphysician. The philosopher of nature studies all material objects insofar as they are involved in mobility. The mathematician studies the same insofar as they are abstractly considered as quantities. The metaphysician studies them insofar as they are real, are beings or entities. It is this formal aspect which differentiates one science from another. Also, the essential conditions of all change are elaborated and he shows how the facts of change demand not only matter and form as intrinsic principles in each nature but also two extrinsic principles of change: the initiator or efficient cause and the goal or final cause. Whatever changes is changed by something and for something. The existence of regularity in nature, the same things regularly produce the same results, proves the teleological character of the universe. In the elucidation of these concepts Aristotle uses many analogies from the field of art. The bronze of the statue is the material cause, the figure or form or shape is the formal cause, the sculptor is the efficient cause, the statue to be made is the final cause of his sculpting activity.

The fundamental principles of all variation in nature are these four, no more and no less. They are universal in applicability because they are understood by induction to be essential to change as such, and not solely tied in with isolated factors of certain individual instances as such. Substantial change is absolute coming-to-be or passing-away, i.e. generation and corruption. Every natural object is generable and corruptible and, therefore, hylomorphic in essential constitution. Objects in nature change quantitatively (become heavier or lighter), qualitatively (alteration of formal accidental characteristics) and locally. These are types of accidental or incidental change since the object involved in it remains substantially the same kind. They are, also, kinds of motion in the strict sense of that term.

What is motion? A knowledge of the answer to this is quite essential, too, since nature is the principle of motion and if we do not know what motion is we cannot understand nature. So actually this is a central concept in his physics. He defines motion as "the actuality of what exists potentially insofar as it exists potentially." The last phrase is the most important element in the definition. 'The actuality of what exists potentially' is the valid designation of change in general. To agree with the facts designated as motion there is the additional element of successive continuity. Whatever is in motion is *on the way to*. It is neither at the *from which* nor at the *to which*, but in between and the *in between* is not static. It is process. The element of successive continuity is stressed by the phrase: "insofar as it is in potentiality." Viewed in terms of potentiality and actuality it is quite easy to see that being-in-motion requires some dependence on an external efficient cause and that the motion is in the moved. What about projectiles? In this case, the original mover imparts motion to the medium, say the air, and the air keeps the projectile moving until the unnatural motion is overcome by the natural and the projectile comes to rest in its natural place.

Motion is obviously relative to magnitudes as well as to places and times and the void. Now in spite of what have been the conclusions of certain of his predecessors (they have been logically inconclusive or fallacious in argumentative content) there is not and cannot be an infinite magnitude actually existing. If 'bounded by a surface' is the definition of a body, it is quite obvious that there cannot be a sensible or intelligible body that is infinite. Nor can number be infinite, for number or that which has number is numerable and what is numerable cannot be infinite. If there were an infinite body it would be either simple or complex. Not complex because the elements would be finite; not simple because if a simple body were infinite it would be everywhere in every direction and, therefore, no room for anything else. No one of the four elements, earth, fire, air, water can be infinite. Furthermore, the concept is quite repugnant to his previously proved hylomorphism.

A discussion of local movement obviously relates to an understanding of place. A body is locally moved when it goes from place to place. What is place? It is not a body, certainly; it is not matter or form. A body is in a place. A place cannot be in a place. Place is a container. Place is not a part of the thing contained. The immediate place of a thing is neither greater than nor less than the thing. Place can be left behind and is separable from the thing. All things considered, place seems to be "the innermost motionless boundary of what contains." If we draw a distinction between place and space, then space is not actually any real thing. It is not a body nor a part of a body and we cannot talk about space as really around things or in things. When we think of the extended dimensions of a body abstractly, i.e. when we think of extension as empty, as it were, then we have a concept of space. We apply this concept in our experience to designate that between one thing and another thing there is not a continuity of either. Therefore there is space between them. Outer space, from this point of view, would be a conception of our mind that there is an indefinitely extended receptacle into which we can hurl satellites or what have you. We must be careful,

74

though, not to hurl them into other objects *in* space. That space wouldn't really be a space because it is full.

Time is, also, very closely related to motion. Motion involves a magnitude (a body) traversing another magnitude. The magnitudes are natural bodies continuously extended. The parts of the magnitude traversed are measurable according to length, breadth and depth. Now, one object crossing over another extended magnitude obviously crosses part after part. The motion of the crossing object is designatable, also, in terms of its parts relative to the parts of the magnitude crossed. Just as the magnitude is measured from a prior part to a posterior part so the motion is numbered as regards its first part, second part, and so on. The name given to this aspect of motion is 'time.' Time is "the number of motion according to before and after." The 'number' referred to is the numbered number, the concrete part of motion, not an abstract number used as a principle of numbering. The numbered parts of motion are, of course, continuous, not existing in separation from each other, just like the parts of the continuum traversed. The latter is a stable and directional continuity; time is a fluid continuity. Just as a line is not made of indivisible points, so time is not made of indivisible *nows*. The nows of time are abstract designations we fabricate mentally in order to refer to the parts of time in static isolation. All motions take place in time and all moving things are in time. Furthermore, there is no motion of substance, because it has no contrary, nor of relation, nor of action and passion, nor of any category other than quantity, quality and where. There are only three kinds of motion: in quantity it is called increase and decrease; in quality it is alteration; in where it is locomotion. They are generically different and each admits of many specific varieties. No matter what the motion there must be a mover, and, to explain motion ultimately, there must be an unmoved mover, which, since the fundamental kind of motion (locomotion) is eternal, must be eternal.

This first mover has no parts, is not a body, is completely immovable, one and eternal.

ON THE HEAVENS

The *peri ouranou* contains four books with forty chapters. The first two deal with the heavenly bodies in general and the last two with sublunary bodies. It is generally concerned with the notion of body and local motion. A body is that which is divisible in every way and, hence, a continuum whose parts are always capable of subdivision. In contrast, a magnitude divisible in one way is a line, if in two ways, a surface. Since there are only three dimensions, there are no other kinds of magnitudes than the ones mentioned. And, just as body is complete in three dimensions, motion is complete in three forms: upwards, downward and about a center. This motion is locomotion and is due to a body because of its nature or principle of motion within. This is true whether it is a simple body, one possessing a principle of movement in its own nature, such as fire and earth, or a compound, one made up of simple bodies. The natural movement of fire and air is upward, of water and earth downward; natural movement that is circular would be the movement of a fifth something, simple and primary, neither heavy nor light because it is neither centripetal nor centrifugal, exempt from alteration and decay because it has no contrary. Our ancestors perceiving the unchangeableness of the primary bodily substance gave it the name of aither.

Could this primary body be infinite? Several reasons are brought up to show that such is not the case. A body which moves in a circle must be finite in every respect both from the point of view of the body and the time traversed in a complete orbit. Moreover, the infinite cannot move, since the smallest conceivable movement of it must take an infinity of time. As a matter of fact the heavens revolve in a finite time. None of the four elements could be infinite because there is no infinite heaviness or lightness possible. No magnitude can be infinite since every magnitude is in movement and if it were infinite there would have to be another place, infinite like itself to which it will move, which is impossible. The infinite cannot be acted upon by the finite; an infinite magnitude cannot act on the finite and there is no interaction between infinites. There cannot be more than one heaven because the natural movements and natural places of the elements demand a natural center and natural extremity, which is one as regards all.

Taking *heaven* to mean the substance of the extreme circumference of the whole it must include all physical and sensible body, since a simple body cannot be naturally or unnaturally outside the extreme circumference and mixed bodies are composed of simple bodies. "The world as a whole, therefore, includes all its appropriate matter, which is, as we saw, natural, perceptible body. So that neither are there now, nor have there ever been, nor can there ever be formed more heavens than one, but this heaven of ours is one and unique and complete." As a corollary there would follow that there is no place or void or time outside the heaven. No place, because of his definition of place as the *outermost immobile surface of the containing body;* no void because the void is that in which the presence of body is possible; no time because no movement.

Is the heaven generated or ungenerated, destructible or indestructible? All agree that the world was generated. But some assert that, once it is generated, it is eternal, others that it is destructible like any other natural formation. To assert that it was generated and yet is eternal is to assert the impossible. Human experience shows us that generated things are always seen to be destroyed. If the world came into being then it was capable of change and, hence, not eternal. If the world is believed to be one, it is impossible to suppose that it should be as a whole first generated and then destroyed, never to reappear. Neither what always is or what always is not is either generated or destructible;

and what is ungenerated and in being must be eternal. What is either generated or destructible is capable of being and not being for a definite time. The heaven as a whole neither came into being nor can it be destroyed; it is one and eternal with no beginning or end of its total duration, containing and embracing in itself the infinity of time. It moves with a regular movement without acceleration or retardation and is perfectly spherical in shape.

The stars are not composed of fire, as some have asserted, but the warmth and light which proceeds from them are caused by the friction set up in the air by their motion. This is a generalized induction from experience concerning the production of fire in wood, stone and iron by friction and also the phenomena concerned with the firing of missiles. The stars themselves are at rest but they move with the circles to which they are attached, the star in the greater circle moving with a swifter movement than those in lesser circles, the movement of the various circles becoming slower as they approach the earth which is at rest in the center. The movement of the stars depends for its speed on the distance of each from the extremity. The outermost revolution of the heavens is a simple movement and the swiftest of all; the movement of all other bodies is composite and relatively slow for the reason that each is moving on its own circle with a motion reverse to that of the heavens.

There have been many theories of the position of the earth, whether it is at rest or in movement and, concerning its shape. For Aristotle the earth is immobile, is at rest at the center of the universe so that the center of the earth coincides with the center of the whole. Its shape must be spherical because of the facts discerned in eclipses of the moon. That the earth is of no great size is evident from the fact that different stars are seen as we move a slight distance north or south on the surface of the earth.

After a consideration of the first heaven, the stars and their movement within revolving spheres and the earth as a heavenly body, he proceeds to a discussion of the four elements: earth, fire, air, water, beginning with the question as to whether generation is a fact or not. He reviews the theories of Melissus and Parmenides in contrast with those of Heraclitus and refutes especially the contention of Timaeus the Pythagorean, and perhaps, his friend Xenocrates, that all bodies are subject to generation by means of the composition and separation of planes. This latter theory would reduce all bodies ultimately to indivisible points deprived of all weight and lightness, which would be to make body no body at all. Each of the simple bodies must have a natural movement of its own either upward or downward, i.e. either a centripetal or centrifugal movement. This is due to their nature which is the principle of their ordered movement. If force, or a source of movement in something other than it, acts upon something it may either cooperate with the natural movement and accelerate that movement or constrain it by an unnatural movement due to the force alone. In either case air is instrumental to the movement and the force is transmitted to the air first and to the body mediately. In the case of projectiles the projectile continues to move without continued contact with the originating force through the instrumentality of the moved air.

An element is a body into which other bodies may be analyzed, present in them potentially or actually, and not itself divisible into bodies different in form. That such exist is evident from experience relative to generation and corruption, when mixed bodies are broken down into simple ones and built up from simple ones. Such elements cannot be infinite since body is distinguished from body by appropriate qualitative differences which are finite and limited. The atomic theory is also untenable from many viewpoints, the least of which is that, if the elements are atomic and of different sizes, they cannot be generated out of one another. If the atoms differ in figure there must be a finite number of them, not an infinite one. Moreover, the number of elements can not be infinite because there are only a finite number of simple movements. There cannot be just one element either as Thales, Anaximenes and Heraclitus have contended, whether it be water, air or fire. The primary objection to these theories is that they allow for only one natural movement which is contrary to experience.

The elements cannot be eternal for, if so, the time occupied in the processes of analysis and synthesis, which are mutually exclusive, would be two mutually exclusive infinites which is impossible. So the elements must be subject to generation and destruction. They are not generated from something incorporeal, because that presupposes the existence of an extra-corporeal void, already rejected. Nor are they generated from some kind of body which would require a body distinct from the elements and prior to them possessing no weight or lightness, with no tendency to movement and not in a place. Hence, the elements are generated from one another by changing into one another, which is a conclusion derived from the facts of experience on the unimpeachable evidence of the senses. The elements are the material for composite things and they can put off their qualitative distinctions and pass into one another. The foundation for this is, of course, prime matter, as explained in *the physics,* the first substrate of substantial variation. The basis of distinction of corporeal things depends upon the property, function and power, since every natural body has its own functions, properties and powers. This is related to an analysis of 'heavy' and 'light,' which are powers of bodies whose activities may be called *impetus.*

Why is it that some bodies move always and naturally upwards and others downward and others, again, move both upward and downward? The local movement of a body is analogous to what happens in other forms of change. In the first place, it is never the case of a change of any chance subject in any chance direction, since the relation of the mover to its subject is never fortuitous. What produces local motion and what is moved are not fortuitously related. What produces upward and downward motion produces weight and lightness; what is moved is potentially

80

heavy or light. The movement of each body to its own place is motion towards its form. Since the place of a thing, which is the natural goal of its movement, is the limit of that which contains it and the container of things that move upward and downward is the extremity and the center, the boundary comes to be, in a sense, the form of that which is contained. The question, then, as to why fire moves upward and earth downward is analogous to the question as to why what is healable when moved qua healable attains health and not some other quality. The only difference is that in the case of heavy and light the bodies are considered to have a source of change within themselves. When they are moved they move upward or downward according to their nature as being fire or earth, due to the potentiality of their being and the original creative force.

Fire, provided there is no extrinsic hindrance, moves upward, when generated, earth moves downward. The heaviness and lightness of bodies which combine these qualities is relative to the difference of their compounded parts. Fire is absolutely light; earth is absolutely heavy. The heaviness or lightness of wood or lead is relative to the medium; one is heavier in one medium, lighter in another. There is a center or goal toward which heavy things move and away from which light things move, because no movement can continue to infinity and the upward movement of fire and downward movement of earth make equal angles on every side of the earth's surface.

There are four elemental kinds of matter: earth, water, air and fire. But since they are able to change into each other there is a common matter for them all, which is different *in being* in each; and there is no reason why there cannot be, as it were, intermediary compounds of these contraries, possessing characteristics of several. The shape of bodies does not determine the movement absolutely, though it does have a relation to a body's speed of movement. Why does an object float or sink? Since there are two factors involved: the force responsible for the downward motion of the heavy body and the resisting force of the continuous surface, these must be in some ratio. In proportion as the force applied by the heavy thing exceeds the resisting force in the continuum the quicker it will force its way down. If the force of the heavy thing is less, it will float on the surface.

ON GENERATION AND CORRUPTION

The relatively short treatise *peri geneseos kai phthoras* is divided into two books of ten and eleven chapters respectively. Since the generation of the elements was mentioned in the *peri ouranou* here we find a follow up in which Aristotle distinguishes coming-to-be and passing-away from alteration and from increase and decrease. The difference between generation and corruption and local movement is evident from the *Physics* and *On The Heavens*.

In discussing the first problem: whether there is a distinction between alteration and generation and corruption, Aristotle reviews in detail the theories of his predecessors, the physici (The Presocratics) and presents the arguments which show that all of them, in failing to distinguish alteration from coming-to-be and passing-away in the absolute sense, actually fail to reach a philosophical solution to the problem of radical change. In one way or another they postulate the permanence of an underlying type of body which would be subject to change only in the sense that there is a condensation or rarefaction, a variation of position of ultimate indivisible particles, a change basically one of locomotion. The great variety of kinds of things, qualitative distinctions and mutations, and even growth become inexplicable philosophically.

All corporeal beings are indefinitely divisible in virtue of their status as quanta, even though 'through and through' division may not be an actual fact. There is a minimum beyond which a kind of corporeal thing cannot persist without disintegration into something of another kind. This fundamental change is absolute coming-to-be and absolute ceasing-to-be, which are temporally concomitant. The generation of one *is* the corruption of the other and vice-versa. This is possible because, as was developed in *the Physics,* there is a primary matter, the common substrate in all material beings. This shared principle of substantial variation makes generation and corruption possible and accounts for the fact of the continuity of natural developments. It is the potentiality principle of intrinsic variability even as regards the reciprocal mutations of the four elements. Yet, it alone does not explain the facts of such changes. In addition there is an actuality principle, too: the positive determinant of substantial diversity in any instance. This is the hylomorphism developed in *the Physics* when he discussed the four causes operating in nature. Here he repeats the observations again and stresses the necessity for an extrinsic movement and a final cause to adequately explain the facts. At the end of the treatise there is a linking up of all generation with the fundamental first mover through the intermediary of the heavens moved in an eternal circle and the activity of the sun acceding to and withdrawing from things in its cyclical path along the zodiac.

Generation and corruption are quite different from alteration. In alteration the being undergoing the change remains numerically and essentially the same while undergoing a mutation of its qualitative characteristics, which we have already seen to be susceptible of variations of degree as well as replaceable by their contraries. The principle of potentiality operates here, too, but not all potentiality is of the 'same piece.' Here it is a question of the material body, e.g. having some one quality actually and its contrary potentially, like being actually hot and potentially cold. The qualitative change leaves intact the kind of being undergoing the change. It remains generically, specifically and numerically the same; it becomes qualitatively different. In generation and corruption the basic kind of being, the substantial make-up, is changed.

Growth and diminution are, also, quite different from coming-to-be and passing-away and from alteration. It is evident that what is altered and what is coming-to-be need not change as regards place, whereas what is growing changes locally at least as regards the parts that are increasing over an ever-expanding area. Moreover, growth is not a change out of something which though potentially a magnitude, actually possesses no magnitude. It is an increase and diminution of a magnitude which is already there. Any and every part grows or becomes smaller by the accession or departure of something corporeal. Thus, three characteristics are involved: 1) any and every part changes; 2) by the accession or departure of something; 3) in such a way that the growing or decreasing thing is preserved and persists. The organic parts grow by the growth of the tissues and they have both a material and formal constitution. Every part can grow qua *form* but it is not necessary that fresh matter accedes to every particle of flesh, e.g. for some matter may flow in fresh while some other matter flows out. In growth there is an accession to every part of the flesh in respect to its form but not in respect to its matter, the whole, however, has become larger. Now this is only possible if the second characteristic is kept in mind: there is the accession of something, i.e. the food. In one sense the food is like and in another sense unlike the growing body. It is actually different but potentially alike. Growth involves the passing away of the actual-other and the coming to be of flesh. This is not just generation, for the food has not been simply transformed into flesh alone by itself. The growing thing grows *by* the food, by converting the food into itself as flesh, somewhat like fire lays hold of the inflammable and converts it into fire. In so far as the food acceding is potentially *so much* flesh it results in growth. In so far as it is potentially *flesh* it nourishes. This is why nutrition may continue as long as something is alive even when diminishing in its bulk. The form referred to before is a kind of

84

power in matter like a duct. When matter which is potentially a duct and, also, possesses potentially a determinate quantity, accedes to a duct, the duct becomes bigger and the food has been integrated into the form of the living thing.

Coming-to-be in the material realm requires an agent and a patient which are opposed formalities of the same matter. They are somehow like and somehow unlike. The patient is potentially other because of its basic matter; the agent strives to reproduce in the matter of the patient a new being formally like itself. This requires contact and as a result there is a mutual action and reaction so that each agent is somehow, also, a patient and each patient is somehow an agent. Because of this relationship the resultant generation may become formally like the predominant or there may arise something that is a mean type, if there is no predominant. This would explain the transmutation of species. Also, different parts of bodies are susceptible of different mutations because of a variation of intensity or degree of the potential possession of a quality, which is a step along the way to substantial change. By the mutation of proper qualities the underlying substance can no longer remain; it changes into another.

Earth, water, air, fire have predominant qualities viewed in terms of the dry, the cold, moist and hot respectively. Actually earth is cold and dry; water is cold and moist; air is hot and moist; fire is hot and dry. There is no possible combination of hot and cold together and moist and dry, because they are contrarily opposed. Due to the combination of pairs of qualities and the predominant, any of the elements can be converted into any other though the production is easier along the direction of the complementary qualities. The change of fire into water and of air into earth is more difficult because it involves the change of both qualities. More complex beings are produced in nature out of the elements insofar as they are combined in a variety of proportions. Not that the elements persist as elements actually in the compound; this would be in opposition to the unity of the hylomorphic structure. The potentialities of the elements are actualized along the lines of greater or lesser intensities of the fundamental qualities and, so, out of the elements are generated flesh, bone, etc. The compound contains the elements potentially just as, in reverse, the elements were potentially the compounds formed out of them. In addition to the matter-form complex required for such transformations, the sun in its cyclical elliptic movement enters in as the originative source. This explains the occurrences of such generations and corruptions and, also, the ceaseless alteration found in nature.

METEOROLOGY

Having discussed the basic causes of nature and all physical motion in the *Physics*, the heavens, motions of the stars and the elements in the *On The Heavens*, and coming-to-be and passing-away in the *On Generation and Corruption* Aristotle enters on a study of clouds, the relative spheres of the elements, comets, the milky way, rain, mist, hoarfrost, snow, hail, winds, rivers, seas, earthquakes, thunder, lightning, rainbow, the properties of compound bodies etc. in the *Meteorologikon*. At the beginning he counsels us that the subject-matter includes events that are natural but their order is less perfect than that of other things studied in the physical treatises. All puzzle us; some admit of explanations in some degree. And a satisfactory explanation of such phenomena, which are inaccessible to observation and experiment, is considered to have been given when the account is free from impossibilities. This reflection may enable us to appreciate what he says in the context of the fourth century B.C.

Throughout the Four Books of 41 chapters he is searching for an understanding of what meteorological phenomena basically are and what are their efficient causes. The posi-

86

tion of the air relative to fire is important for an understanding of meteors and kindred phenomena which are really caused by the friction generated by the movement of the heavens and the various spheres of the stars. The passage of the sun causes the evaporation of rivers and seas and this moisture makes up clouds and mist which are precipitated in the form of rain, dew, hoar-frost, hail, snow, according to the degree of union with the cold. From the experience of men we can discern certain cyclical patterns and variations within the patterns for diverse localities. There is a constant exchange of dry land and flooded land due to the inner growth and expansion of the earth.

There are many theories about the origin of the seas but he prefers the one that considers the seas as the residue of all waters. All rivers and all waters flow into the sea. All the light and sweet water is carried off quickly by the absorbing action of the sun. The remainder is the sea and it is salt by the admixture with the undigested residue of all living things, which is salty. By evaporation salt water is purified of varying amounts of salt, which he knows by experiment, yet only parts of the sea water are purified by the action of the sun.

Winds are also formed by the evaporative activity of the sun. There are two kinds of evaporation, one moist, the other dry. The former is vapor, the latter is the source and substance of all winds. This dry evaporation is aided by the earth's warmth stored up from the action of the sun. The accession and recession of the sun determined the movement of the winds. The origin of the motion is from above, the matter and the generation of wind come from below since wind is "a quantity of dry evaporation from the earth moving round the earth." Calm is due to two causes: either cold quenches the evaporation or excessive heat wastes it. Earthquakes are fundamentally due to winds, that is, to the violent inrush of the external evaporations into the earth. At times the air is broken down and becomes fire within the earth. The earth rises into a mound which bursts and live ashes and coals are spewed out along with a noisy burst of wind. This was witnessed taking place near Heracleia and in the neighborhood of Lipara in Italy.

There is an interesting explanation of thunder and lightning. When the sun warms the earth evaporation is either moist or dry. The heat that escapes disperses to the upper region. If any of the dry exhalation is caught in the process as the air cools it is squeezed out as the clouds contract and collides with the neighboring clouds. The sound of this collision is thunder. It usually happens that the exhalation is inflamed and burns with a thin fire. This is lightning. Other theories are also presented which maintain that lightning is a reflection, or fire shining through the clouds (thunder is its extinction). He claims that the same stuff is wind on the earth, earthquake under it and thunder in the clouds: dry exhalation. When secreted in a body we get a hurricane. A sort of undigested hurricane is a whirlwind. When there is a great quantity of exhalation and it is rare and squeezed out in the cloud itself we get a thunderbolt. Thunder splits things by the force of the exhalation.

Halos, mock suns, rods and rainbows are all reflections but are distinguished by the surface from which and the way in which the reflection takes place. The halo is due to the reflection from the mist that forms round the sun or moon and they are more common round the moon because the greater heat of the sun dissolves the condensation of the air more rapidly. When the air is in the process of forming into raindrops but the rain is not actually there, if the sun is opposite and bright enough to make the cloud a mirror the reflection renders the color of the object, i.e. the sun, without its shape. Because each mirror is so small what we see is a continuous reflection of color which is a rainbow. A mock sun is caused by reflection of sight to sun. Rods are seen when there are clouds near the sun that are uneven in density.

The Meteorologica concludes with a discussion of the properties of compound bodies. Two of the qualities of the elements are active (the hot and the cold) and two (the dry and the moist) are passive. Heat and cold moisten, dry hardens and softens things. In virtue of the dry and the moist things are said to be easy or difficult to determine or change. When hot and cold are in control they generate a thing, if they are not then there is the opposite result. Putrescence is the end of all natural objects except such as are destroyed by violence, e.g. burning flesh. The qualities set up certain processes in natural objects. Concoction is due to heat and its species are ripening, boiling and broiling. Concoction is "a process in which the natural and proper heat of an object perfects the corresponding passive qualities which are the proper matter of any given object." Inconcoction is an imperfect state due to lack of proper heat, i.e. cold. Only those bodies can be boiled that contain moisture which can be acted on by the heat contained in the liquid outside and thus become denser, smaller or heavier. Broiling is concoction by dry foreign heat.

Of the elements earth is especially representative of the dry, water of the moist. Thus all determinate bodies involve water and earth and every body manifests the quality of the element that predominates. Hardness and softness are qualities of things made up of the dry and the moist. Something is said to be absolutely hard whose surface does not yield into itself; soft that which does yield but not by interchange of place. Water is not soft for its surface, does not sink in but there is an interchange of place. Things are, also, called relatively hard and soft when compared with each other. We call that hard which exceeds the sense of touch; soft, that which falls short of it. A body must be either hard or soft, solid and determined. Drying takes place by a process of heating due to external or internal heat. Even when things are dried by cooling, e.g. a garment, it is the internal heat that carries off the moisture being driven off by the surrounding cold.

Liquefaction is either condensation into water or the melting of a solidified body. Bodies solidified by dry-hot are liquefied by the moist-cold (water). Bodies solidified by cold are dissolved by hot. If a body contains more water than earth, fire thickens it; if it contains more earth fire solidifies it. Water and earth are the constituents of homogeneous bodies both in plants and animals and metals. All mixed bodies are distinguished by the qualities proper to the various senses, i.e. by their capacities of acting. A thing is white, sweet, hot, etc. by virtue of a power of acting on sense. They are, also, distinguished by affections which express their aptitude to be acted upon, e.g. melting point, solidifying point, bending point, the aptitude for being softened by heat or water, to bend, break, be comminuted, impressed, moulded, squeezed, to be tractile, malleable, fissile, aptitude to be cut, to be viscous, compressible, combustible and their opposites. Homogeneous bodies, like the metals and bodies extracted from them, flesh, bones, hair in animals, wood, bark, leaves, etc. in plants are made up of water and earth and the agents are the hot and the cold. The homogeneous are made up of the elements and all the things of nature are made up of the homogeneous bodies as their definition. Matter is pure matter and the essence is pure definition but the bodies composed of them are matter or definition in proportion as they are near to either, e.g. the form is more difficult to discern the more it is immersed in matter. What a thing is is always determined by its function and it really is itself when it can perform its function. Yet it is not always easy to specify the proper function of things like fire, flesh, the parts of plants and inanimate bodies. So we cannot state what their form is accurately and we cannot always tell when a precise thing is there or not unless the body is thoroughly corrupted and its shape alone remains. We know something when we know the causes of it, the material and formal which express the definition and the efficient cause of its generation and corruption. After explaining the homogeneous bodies in terms of the qualities of their elements we must consider the non-homogeneous things such as plants, animals and man.

THE SOUL

Aristotle treats of living things, their powers, functions and formal essence in the *peri psyches* composed of three books distributed into thirty chapters. As is his customary procedure he discusses the subject in general by way of introduction and points out the value of such a scientific analysis, its usefulness and difficulties. He examines dialectically the opinions of various thinkers about the soul and elaborates his own conclusion as a result of induction from the facts of human experience. In general, we find here an application and elaboration of his fundamental theory of hylomorphism, actuality and potentiality and the doctrine of the four causes.

Knowledge of any kind is highly prized; the knowledge of the soul would be especially desirable by reason of the superior dignity of its nature and the greater exactness discovered in its investigation. Such knowledge contributes to a better understanding of nature since the soul is in some sense the principle of animal life. Yet its acquisition is one of the most difficult things in the world. The question of method of investigation is an important one here. It is quite evident that there is no single method concerning the essential whatness of all things as there is one method of demonstration. The method must be adapted to the subject-matter under investigation. There is a method for the mathematical disciplines and also metaphysics. We have seen that there are different methods of proceeding as regards the probable and the necessary. In this treatise, in addition to the historical survey and the dialectical discussions, which are common propaedeutics, Aristotle insists that the essential nature of the soul is discovered as a result of an analysis of the properties of a thing manifested in operation. In this method we actually begin with the object of the functions, proceed to an investigation of the powers producing the various functions, then to the properties characteristic of the thing and finally reach the essence. In what category of being are we going to place the soul? Is it in the order of the potential or the actual? Is it divisible or without parts? Is it everywhere homogeneous or not? Are its types different generically or specifically? Are the properties manifested by living things functions of the soul alone or of the complex of body and soul? The majority seem to involve the total complex and that is why we study the soul in natural philosophy. If any way of acting or being acted upon is proper to the soul it will be capable of existing separate from the body. To begin with a review of the opinions of his predecessors is considered useful for the avoidance of their errors and the acceptance of the truth.

In all the theories two characteristics have been considered as distinctive of soul: movement and sensation. There are two senses in which anything may be moved: indirectly, when it is contained in something which is moved, as a sailor in a ship, and directly, owing to itself. There are four species of movement: locomotion, alteration, diminution and growth. So if the soul is moved it must be moved in one or several of these ways. Plants show evidence of diminution and growth whereas animals are, also, involved in alteration and locomotion, the latter in the more highly developed animals. Historically, the soul has been defined in three ways: that which is originative of movement because it moves itself, that which is the most subtle and incorporeal and that which is composed of the elements. The opinions of the ancients concerning movement as relative to the soul interpret it as connected with one or other of the physical elements and therefore equate the soul with a kind of body. Yet this cannot be. For if soul originates movement it is through intention or a process of thinking. There is no necessity that what originates movement should itself be in movement. The soul is not a spatial magnitude. It has no place like a body. Moreover, the soul is not a harmony of the body. Harmony is a blend or composition of contraries and the soul cannot be such, since a harmony cannot be originative of movement nor can a harmony have active and passive affections. Indeed, it is not exact to say that the soul pities, learns or thinks. It is the man who does this with or by his soul. Soul need not be composed of the elements in order to be sentient of sensible things. Although, in one sense, it is correct to say that like is known by like, in another sense, like is known by unlike. The soul is potentially responsive to the actual characteristics of things. When the sensible object acts upon the sense the sense becomes like the sensible. The sensible in act is the sense in act. Thus the soul is not actually any one or any combination of the elements. Sometimes movement terminates in the soul, as in sensation, other times it starts from the soul, as in reminiscence, and terminates in the organs of the body.

Mind seems to be an independent substance implanted within the soul and to be incapable of being destroyed. If it could be destroyed it would be under the influence to old age parallel to what happens in case of sense. If the old man could recover the proper kind of eye he would see just as well as a young man. Intellectual apprehension declines only through the decay of some inward part; mind itself is impassible.

Soul is not a self-moving number. It is not in movement, as already shown. It is not a number. How can a unit be moved? By what agency? What sort of movement can be attributed to what is without parts or internal differences? If it originates movement and is capable of being moved it must involve a duality. Its movement would be like a line since a moving point generates a line. A number subtracted from a number is a number; in some cases a plant and animal when divided continue to live and each segment retains the same kind of soul. Calling a soul a number cannot account for its affections.

Soul is not made of an element or elements in order to be able to know all things as proposed by the "like is known by like" theory. Elements are not the only things soul knows but also compounds, God, man, flesh, bone. Nothing will be gained by the presence of elements in soul unless there be present also the various formulae of proportion constituting different things. If soul is a quantum, e.g. how will it know a quale, etc. Earth, bone, and sinews are insensitive, how will a being made of them be sensitive? There is nothing which human beings do not know. Moreover, why don't bodies formed of elements know their corresponding elements if like is known by like? Then, too, not all souls originate local movement.

Of bodies some have life in them, i.e. self-nutrition, growth and decay and, hence, living things will be compounds of body and a source of life. According to the general aspects of hylomorphism every body is essentially composed of primary matter and substantial form. The substantial form of a living thing will be its soul. Soul, then, is a substance in the sense of a form of a natural body having life potentially in it. Substantial form is actuality and soul is the actuality of a natural body. Actuality can mean either like knowledge possessed or knowledge in exercise. The soul is an actuality in the sense in which actual knowledge is knowledge possessed. The living body is organic and the organs are unified in virtue of the soul which is their actuality. The soul is the essential whatness of a living body. The soul plus the body constitute the living thing. The two are one in the fundamental sense of a relation of an actuality to that of which it is an actuality.

From another point of view, living is a predicate used to designate that which manifests locomotion, vegetation, sensation, intellection, appetition. Hence, soul would be defined functionally as that from which these activities proceed. Since it is the soul whereby something primarily lives, perceives and thinks, the soul must be the form rather than the matter or subject. And there are three species of soul: the nutritive in plants, the sensitive in animals and the intellective in man. Animals, also, vegetate by means of the sensitive soul and the sense of touch is the most fundamental and essential of all the senses. Without it an animal cannot naturally be or survive. A small minority of animals possess calculation and thought, and, likewise have all the characteristics of vegetation and sensation. In regard to every living body the soul is the originative source of movement, the end of the body and its formulable essence.

The essential and functional definitions of soul given so far are expressive of what soul is, generically considered. We must now strive to understand each specific type: nutritive, sensitive and intellectual. This requires a prior consideration of what nutrition, sensation and thinking are, for the question of what an agent does precedes the question as to what enables it to do what it does. Then, logically, we must go another step back and have some clear view of the objects of each activity, e.g. food, the perceptible and the intelligible.

Nutrition and reproduction are due to the same psychic source. It is by the absorption of food that this psychic power is distinguished from all the others. To be food for another, something must be transformed into the other and in the process it may increase the bulk, as was previously explained. Taking food in the sense of undigested matter, it is the contrary of what is fed by it; as digested it is like what is fed by it. What is fed is the besouled body and simply because it has soul in it. Insofar as the besouled body is a quantum, food may increase its quantity; insofar as the living body is a particular kind of substance the food is related to it as a nutritive object and by its assimilation of food the activity of the vegetative thing is a type of self-maintenance. What *does* the feeding is the vegetative soul; what is fed is the besouled body; the food is that wherewith it is fed. Since the end of this soul is to generate another being like that in which it is, it may be rightly called the reproductive soul. In any living thing which has reached its normal development, which is unmutilated and sexually reproductive its most natural act is the production of another like itself in order that it may partake in the eternal and divine insofar as its nature permits.

Sensation depends upon a process of movement from

without; it is some sort of qualitative alteration. What is sensitive is parallel to what is combustible. The combustible never ignites itself; the sense never stimulates itself. There must be an agent which has the power of stimulating the sense and reducing it from the potentiality of sensing to the actual possession of sensation. What is apprehended by actual sensation is the individual existing thing insofar as it is sensible, i.e. capable of acting upon the sense. The objects of sense are either proper sensibles, common sensibles or incidental (accidental) sensibles. The proper sensible is a special object relative to one and only one sense, such as color to seeing, sound to hearing, etc. Each kind of special sense has one kind of sense object relative to which it never errs. The common sensibles are sensed by more than one sense. In this category are movement, rest, magnitude, shape, number and unity. The incidental sensibles are the substantial realities in nature. It is incidental that the patch of white which is seen is the son of Diares. The son of Diares is accidentally seen by the sense.

The object of sight is the visible and the visible is color as found in a material surface. The material surface contains in itself the cause of visibility since there is in it the power to set in movement what is actually transparent. That is why an object is only visible with the help of light. Light is, as it were, the proper color of what is transparent and it exists whenever the potentially transparent is excited to actuality by the influence of fire or something resembling it. Color sets in movement what is transparent, e.g. the air, and that, extending continuously from the object to the organ, sets the organ in movement. If the colored object is placed in immediate contact with the eye, it cannot be seen. There must be some continuous medium intervening between the visible object and the sense. The stimulus is transmitted through this medium up to the sense and the sense responds with the sensation of the colored object. Relatively the same holds for sound and smell, and, possibly, taste, which requires a liquid medium. Touch, alone, may be in immediate contact with the object sensed, but even here the external envelope of flesh may be the appropriate medium.

There is both actual and potential sound. Things are said to have a sound because they can generate actual sound between themselves and the organ of hearing. Actual sound requires two smooth and solid bodies and a medium since it is generated by impact. In other words, there must be an impact between two bodies in a medium, preferably the air, which is not dissipated by the blow. An echo occurs when the air impinged upon is contained within the walls of a vessel and having been struck rebounds like a ball from a wall. It is analogous to what happens in the case of light which is always reflected from an object though the reflection may not be strong enough to cast a shadow by which we would recognize the presence of light. That has the power of producing sound which has the power of setting in motion a continuous mass of air from it to the organ of hearing. In the organ of hearing the air is contained within a chamber so that the animal may hear accurately all varieties of the movement of air outside. This is why we hear even when submerged in water. Both the striking and struck body sound, each in its different way. Acute and grave sounds are so named because the difference in the qualities is due to their respective speeds. Voice is a kind of sound emitted by what has soul in it, i.e. by an animal with a special organ. Nature employs the breath for two purposes: as an indispensable means of regulating the inner temperature of the living body, which is required for the living thing's being, and as the material of articulate speech, in the interest of the thing's well-being. In the strict sense, voice is a sound with a meaning and it is accompanied by imagination.

Smell and its object are more difficult to determine because our power of smell is less discriminating and it is bound up with and confused by pleasure and pain. Taste is more discriminating because it is a modification of touch

97

and in touch we actually surpass all other animals in discrimination. That is why man is the most intelligent of all animals and differences between men in respect of natural endowment are due to differences in this area. Smell has for its object the odorous and smelling takes place through a medium, air or water. The object of taste is flavor and what acts upon the sense of taste must be actually or potentially liquid. Tasting means being affected by what can be tasted as such, that is, the sweet and bitter, the succulent and saline, the pungent, harsh, astringent and the acid.

It is a disputed question as to whether touch is a single sense or a group of senses. In any case its object is the tangible as such, the hot and cold, dry and moist, hard and soft, rough and smooth, etc. Flesh is the medium between the object touched and the sense, with this clarification: that we are affected not *by* but *along with* the medium. There is a maximum and minimum threshold of the sensing of tactile qualities and the sense is actually a mean between the extremes, e.g. of hot and cold.

Summarizing the results of his investigation it is clear that 1) by a sense is meant *what has the power of receiving into itself the sensible forms of things without their matter;* this reception occurs in a way like a piece of wax takes on the impress of a gold signet ring without the gold; what alone matters is that the thing sensed has a quality whereby it can affect the sense; the quality depends upon the ratio in which the constituents of the object are combined; 2) by an organ of sense is meant *that in which a sense power resides.* The sense and its organ are factually the same but their essence is not the same. The sense is a ratio *in* a magnitude. It is due to the fact of the organic magnitude that excessive stimulation prevents a sense from responding afterwards to a lesser quality. He will show later that, because there is no similar impediment found in the area of intelligent thought, thinking does not involve a power *in* an organ. The power of intellect is *separate* from the body.

In addition to the five external or special senses described above Aristotle is forced by the facts of sense experience in its total ambit to conclude to the existence of certain internal senses. The first of these is a sort of *common* sense, i.e. a sense that is responsive to all the activities and objects of the external senses. We do, as a matter of actual fact, perceive the operations and objects of the presently active senses, distinguish the operations and objects of one sense from those of another and unite these operations and objects into a sense awareness of a unified response to one object, sensible in different ways by the different senses. Such an activity could not be an action of any one of the special senses since each is restricted to an action within the limitation of its own formal object. Seeing, for example, is a movement of both the acting (the colored object) and the acted upon (the sense) in the acted upon. And the response of the sense of seeing is limited to a colored surface. Hence, by the power of seeing we cannot sense sound, odor, savor or texture nor could we discriminate between them and unify them in relation to a single object by means of any one external sense. What perceives, distinguishes and synthesizes several different sense objects must be another sense common to them all. The same would apply to the perception, distinguishing and synthesizing of the activities of each of the other senses. No special sense can sense its own sensing, because a special sense is restricted to a special sensible quality of a magnitude. Seeing is not a colored surface; hearing is not a sounding body, etc. The activity of a sense is a psychic response, not a sensible magnitude.

In addition to the *common* sense there is another movement which results from the actual exercise of a sense power and this is called phantasy or imagination. It is different from actual perception since it lies somewhat within our power even when an object of perception is absent. Yet it is not found without any sensation and, in man, judgment does not take place without it. It is a sort of medium between actual sensing and subsequent thinking about the objects of prior sense experience. The function of imagination is to be that in virtue of which an image arises for us and without it there is no judgmental activity of thinking. Closely allied to phantasy and yet quite different from it are two other sense functions discussed later in connection with appetitive desire. The one is instinctive discrimination of the useful, suitable, harmful or unsuitable characteristics of the sensed object. Without this sense evaluation no animal would desire or experience aversion for a perceived object. An animal goes after a perceived object because it is evaluated as good for the percipient. These values are stored up in memory and in terms of them and their recognition as being present in the past an animal learns and profits from experience.

We turn now to knowing and thinking. Since everything is a possible object of thought the mind could not know unless it were free from all admixture of physical elements. It can have no nature other than a certain capacity or potentiality. Before we think the mind is not actually any intelligible object. It cannot be blended with a body, otherwise it would have some sensible quality and, also, an organ. It is the potential place of all forms. It is a sort of intellectual primary matter having no actual form of its own but capable of being actualized by any form. The potentiality of the thinking mind is quite different from that of the senses. As was said before, a sense is debilitated by an excessively strong stimulation whereas thought about a highly intelligible object renders the mind more capable of thinking about less intelligible objects. The reason is: "the faculty of sensation is dependent upon the body, mind is separate." When we have acquired knowledge of a set of intelligible objects, the mind is now in a state of potentiality but with a difference. We have habitual knowledge (science) and can exercise this knowledge on our own initiative. The mind can also think about the mind itself; a reflective activity impossible in a body or in anything using a bodily organ. Again, because the realities it knows

100

are known as separated from matter, as in the case of the mathematical and metaphysical, so these powers of mind must be separate from matter.

There is a problem if mind is considered as potentially all that it thinks and as actually none of them before it thinks, like a writing tablet on which nothing is actually written. Must there be an action of the intelligible on this potentiality in order to make the mind and the intelligible actually one, as in the case of the sense and the sensible? Well, there is a proportional resemblance. It seems that in every class of things, as in nature as a whole, there are the two factors of potentiality and actuality involved. To the potential there corresponds a cause that is productive of an actuality like art is related to its matter. These must be found *in* the thinking soul. Besides the mind, which is what it is by *becoming* all things there is the mind which is what it is by *making* all things. The latter is a sort of habit or character like light which makes potential intelligibles to be actual intelligibles and, at the same time, makes potential mind (intellect) to be actual mind. The *making* mind, essentially active, is separate from matter, impassible, unmixed. When mind is set free from its present condition it is immortal and eternal and we do not remember its former activity because in that situation it was dependent upon the imagination, which is destructible because organically involved.

The thinking activity involves two different classes of intelligible objects: the simple and the complex. Thinking in the area of the incomplex, there is no possibility of falsehood. This is the area of intuitive perception or simple apprehension discussed in the *Categories*. In the area of the complex the mind acts by either composing or dividing the incomplex objects of thought. This is the activity of judging, positively or negatively. Here there is a possibility of error. The dianoetic activity is a combination of intuitive perception and judgment. In it there is no possibility of falsehood, apart from the judgments involved; as was discussed in the *Prior Analytics*, there is only a question of the validity of the conclusion.

101

Perception is like asserting or knowing but, in addition, when the object is pleasant or painful the soul makes a sort of evaluation and pursues or avoids the object. The passions and emotions are tied in with this estimative power, as is the movement of pursuit or avoidance. As regards the thinking soul images serve as the contents of perception and when it evaluates them as good or bad it pursues or avoids them. That is why the soul never thinks without an image. Actually the power of thinking thinks the forms in the images, since the objects of thought are in the sensible form. And this includes abstract objects and all the states and affections of sensible things. Hence no one can learn or understand anything in the absence of sense and when the mind is actively aware of anything it is aware of it along with an image. The images are like sensible contents with the exception that they contain no matter. The soul is in a way all things: all sensible things by the activity of the senses; all intelligible things by mind.

We have seen that animals (including man) evaluate things by sense and thought. What is the power of originating local movement? It cannot be the nutritive power or powers since local movement is accompanied by imagination and appetite which are not present in the nutritive soul. It cannot be the sensitive power, as such, since some animals have it but not locomotion. It cannot be the discursive activity of speculative thought since that is never concerned with the practicable, whereas movement is always in terms of pursuit or avoidance. Even practical knowledge does not always and necessarily lead to such movement, as in the case of the medical art. Appetite in itself does not suffice since we realize that at times, although we desire something, we can successfully resist the desire and refuse to act for what we desire. When we do move to pursue or avoid something there is the combined activity of discrimination and desire; there is both sense evaluation and appetite in some movements and practical thought and intellectual appetite in others. The object of appetite stimulates practical thought and thereby starts a movement of the mind out towards the object. In man the appetite (sense) can originate movement contrary to calculation as in the case of desire. To produce movement the object must be such as to be brought into being by action and, hence, is in the realm of the contingent. The object originates movement through apprehension by thought or imagination. The realizable good moves the appetite so that the animal is moved to acquire the good desired. To sum up: because the animal possesses appetite it is capable of movement; it is not capable of appetite without imagination and, in man, this is either sensitive or calculative (deliberative). In man, acting in a human way, movement proceeds as a result of a practical syllogism of which the major premise is universal and the minor a particular application to an individual object as related to the calculating individual.

The nutritive soul is possessed by every living thing in nature. By means of it living things assimilate food, grow, decay and reproduce themselves. The sensitive soul is found only in animals. By means of it animals perform nutrition and reproductive functions as well as all sensitive and appetitive activities. The intellectual soul is the most perfect. By it men reason, judge, intuit meanings, desire the good abstractly apprehended as well as perform all the activities of animals and plants. The most basic sense in animals and men is that of touch. Without it their existence is impossible. Excess in intensity of tangible qualities leads to the destruction of the animal itself.

PARVA NATURALIA

After his investigation of soul in general and the proper characteristics of its three specific types, nutritive, sensitive and intellectual, Aristotle makes a survey of living things, especially animals, in order to discover what functions are common to all and what are peculiar to the different classes.

Sensation, memory, passion, appetite, pleasure and pain are common to all animals. Waking and sleeping, youth and old age, respiration, life and death are peculiar to certain classes of animals. All these characteristics belong to the complex of soul and body; some are affections of sensation, others are means of safe-guarding it, others involve its destruction. Hence, sensation is fundamental to every animal as such and we distinguish between what is and what is not an animal by its presence or absence. Of all the senses discussed in the *On The Soul* touch and taste are seen to be necessary, touch for the actual being of an animal and taste for its nutrition. Smelling, hearing and seeing are found in all animals possessing locomotion and they are a means of preservation of the animal. In man they are also means for the attainment of the highest perfection: knowledge of the truth. In this latter regard hearing takes precedence over the others since rational discourse is a cause of instruction in virtue of its being audible. This audibility pertains directly to words, each of which is a thought-symbol. The remainder of the seven chapters of the *De Sensu et Sensibili* involve a discussion of the nature of the sense organs relative to the four elements and the nature of the sense object relative to each sense.

The visual organ proper is composed of water yet vision pertains to it because it is translucent. Just as vision is impossible without external light it is impossible without light within the organ, which requires an interior translucent medium. The part of the organ immediately concerned with sound is air, the organ of smell is potentially fire, the organ of touch is of earth, the faculty of taste is a form of touch. As regards the objects of the special senses color is the limit of the translucent in a determinately bounded body. The translucent is a common 'nature' and power residing in bodies to varying degrees and light inheres in the translucent without determinate boundary. When it is in a determinate body its limit is the color. Savor is an affection imparted to an object due to the fact that the dry and earthy is washed in the moist by the filtering action of the heat. The savor belongs to an object as nutrient. The basic savors are sweet and bitter and intermediate savors depend on their mixtures. Odor consists of the sapid dry diffused in the moist and that is why odor is perceived in both water and air, whereas savor is in water alone. Sound and texture were sufficiently discussed in the *On The Soul*.

Each object of sense is a quantum and since a quantum as such is indefinitely divisible its sensible characteristics will be, also, in virtue of the division of the quantum. The fact that the infinitesimally small is not actually perceived is understandable in virtue of the general statements about potentiality and act. The quantum is not actually divided into its parts but only potentially so. Below a certain level of division the resulting parts would not be actually sensed but they are potentially sensible. A ten-thousandth part of a grain of millet is not actually seen but it is potentially perceptible. When united with a larger amount of grain sight, e.g. embraces the whole amount.

Do the objects of sense-perception or the movements proceeding from them through a medium always arrive at a mid-point? This seems obvious in the case of odor and sound. What about color? Empedocles claimed that light from the sun arrives first in the intervening space before it comes to the eye, which seems to be the case. But light has its reason in the being, not the becoming of something; it is not a movement but a qualitative change which can take place simultaneously over a large area. Hence Aristotle rejects the theory of Empedocles because it equates light with motion from place to place whereas it is qualitative in nature.

In the treatise *On Memory and Recollection* (2 chapters) Aristotle explains that memory relates to the past whereas perception is of the present and expectation of the future. Whenever one exercises the power of remembering he says within himself, "I heard this before" or "I had this idea before." Memory implies a time elapsed and memory is

105

possible only to those things which experience time. Since time is perceived by the *common sense,* memory will be essentially the activity of the same power and accidentally related to the power of intelligence. In the act of perception there is a sort of stamp of the impression made and this impressed affection is stored up somehow in the soul. When we remember, this impression is brought into consciousness and considered as a likeness of the object originally perceived. Regarded in itself the impression is an object of contemplation; considered as a likeness of something else it is a mnemonic token. Memory is an activity which will not occur until the original experience has undergone a lapse of time. Recollection is not the same as memory, though recollection implies it and the end result of an activity of recollecting is an actualized memory. Recollection is due to the fact that one movement has by nature another that succeeds it in regular order. When we recollect we experience certain antecedent movements until we experience the one after which comes what we seek. In other words, recollection is a process undergone in order to remember something definite. We may exercise recollection in a definite planned way by consciously starting with a member of a series whose conclusion will be what we desire to remember or the process may go on without conscious attention to a member of the series selected as such. There is a natural order of recollection as well as an artificial one (a mnemonic device). In general the middle point of a series is a good starting point, though at times we may proceed in several directions. A point of capital importance is to cognize correctly the time-relation of what one wants to recollect. Another difference between recollection and memory is that recollection involves a sort of inference and it is not found in any animals below man. The affection itself is corporeal, since it is a search for an image and, at times, we cannot control it completely since it is a process in a material part.

In the work *On Sleep and Waking* (3 chapters) it is

shown that sleeping and waking pertain to the same aspect of an animal, sleep being a privation of waking. The criterion by which we distinguish the two situations is sense perception. When awake anyone perceives either some external movement or some movement in his own consciousness. Waking may be called a state of exercising sense perception; sleeping the opposite. No animal capable of both is either always awake or always asleep. Sleep is really a sort of inhibition of the function of sense-perception by the special senses. Sleep does not occur merely from the fact that the special senses do not function or that one does not employ them or in the inability to exercise sense perceptions. Swooning and certain other cases of unconsciousness are instances of the latter. Rather it takes place in regard to the primary sense perception ability and is a rest from the movement implied in sense perception in general. Its end is the conservation of the animal. It arises from the evaporation attendant upon the process of nutrition and that is why periods of drowsiness come after meals. It also comes after certain forms of fatigue since fatigue acts as a solvent and dissolved matter acts like food prior to digestion. Sleep results from a sort of concentration, or natural recoil of the hot matter inwards so that the passages and tracts in the head are cooled as the evaporation ascends to it. A person awakes when digestion is completed. Sleep is a seizure of the primary sense organ rendering it unable to actualize its powers.

As regards dreaming (3 chapters) it is not by merely sense perception that we perceive a dream, nor by opinion, nor by intelligence. When the external object of sense perception has departed the impression it made persists and the impression may become an object of perception. Also, causes within the body are productive of sensory impressions. When a person is asleep these impressions (images) present themselves. The phantasms which are involved in dreams are lying within the soul potentially and become actualized while we are sleeping. Thus each dream image

107

is a remnant of sensory impression arising during sleep. It is a presentation based on the movement of sense impressions taking place in sleep.

Aristotle does not think that we should dismiss lightly divination through dreams nor should we give it implicit confidence. It is not improbable that some of the dream presentations may be preparatory causes of actions performed later, analogously to the way in which dreams are prepared by sense movements while we are awake. Dreams may be tokens and causes of future events. Yet most prophetic dreams may be mere coincidences. That familiar friends should have foresight in a special degree respecting one another is due to the fact that such friends are more solicitous on behalf of one another. The most skillful interpreter of dreams is one who is proficient in the art of observing resemblances.

The work on duration of life (6 chapters) calls attention to the facts of experience concerning the length of life in plants and animals generally and the longevity of particular types. What is the cause of the fact that some natural objects are long-lived and others short-lived? In general the length of life varies with the region of habitation; those in warm countries live longer than those in colder climates. Differences among individuals in the same locality would also be directly related to wamth and cold. Since fire and water are reciprocal causes of generation and decay, everything composed of them share in the same result. Because living things are composed of contraries, hot-cold, dry-moist, certain changes occur. The environment acts on all natural objects either favorably or unfavorably and the changes lead gradually to the destruction of living things. This may occur in a shorter or longer time and the length of duration seems to be related to size. Keeping in mind that living involves a constitution humid and warm, when living things become dry and cold they persist. As long as a suitable proportion of hot-cold, dry-moist persists they continue to live. The increase of cold and dry leads to their destruc-

108

tion. A lack of food also leads to the destruction of plants and animals because they consume themselves by using up their nutriment. Large plants have the longest life because they are less watery and, hence, less easily frozen.

On Youth and Old Age, On Life and Death and *on Respiration* extend over twenty-seven chapters most of which are devoted to discussions of the biological constitution of animals elaborated in more detail in *The History of Animals* and *The Parts of Animals*. The soul of animals is not a body or composed of the physical elements. Yet it does reside primarily in a special part of the animal: the heart in sanguineous animals and a corresponding organ in the non-sanguineous. The reason for this is considered to be the anatomical structure (the veins issue from the heart), the dependence of life on the seat of warmth in the organism (the heart being the first organ developed) and the need for a centrally located source of locomotion. This may be quite evident as regards nutrition but the reason assigning the heart as the primary organ of sensation (the common sensorium) is not too conclusive: if life is always located in this part, the principle of sensation must be there for it is qua animal that an animal is said to be living and it is called animal because endowed with sensation. Another reason considering the central position as the best for the exercise of the dominating power is not too satisfying in view of the position assumed in the *On The Soul* concerning the soul as the essential act of an organic body.

Youth is the initial stage of the development of an organism due to the growth of the primary organ of refrigeration and old age is the period of its deterioration. Life is coincident with the maintenance of heat, and death is its destruction. Death is, also, closely allied with respiration in some animals. When these are unable to breathe they die. In all cases life in animals is a function of heat which can be extinguished by its opposite or exhausted by its excess. It would seem that living involves a constant struggle between heat and cold for the possession of the organism;

an excess of either will cause its destruction. Nutriment is required for the continuation of the processes of living and refrigeration is a preventive against drying. Violent death occurs due to external causes, natural death involves internal decay, which in animals is called senility. Probably it is not heat as such which is the cause of death (when present in excess) but dryness which accompanies it. And cold prevents death by refrigeration not because of cold but its concomitant, the moist.

Three other lengthy treatises, *The History of Animals*, *On The Parts of Animals* and *The Generation of Animals* are elaborate developments of the facts of anatomy, physiology, general biology, genetics and animal psychology as discovered by Aristotle and his research assistants. They constitute a helpful background for an appreciation of the enormous wealth of information the Stagirite had at his disposal. Within this area he has developed his more pertinent theories as found in the analysis of the previously mentioned works. A reading of them in their entirety would be profitable for a more extensive understanding of his basic conclusions concerning all the ingredients of the philosophy of nature. *The History of Animals* and the natural sciences in particular are types of knowledge distinct from philosophy yet they are helpful for background references and factual confirmation.

METAPHYSICS

The study of physical objects in nature is followed by the *meta ta physika,* an enquiry into the highest science available to man, one which will fulfill his natural curiosity to its utmost and satisfy his deepest wonder. In fact, as the *Divine* Science, *First* philosophy is the highest *Wisdom*. It is a divine science because it investigates those things which exist separately from matter and are immovable such as God. It is first philosophy since it is concerned with the most fundamental and basic principles of being qua being, the real as such. It is wisdom since it treats of the highest speculative knowledge available to man. The nature, subject-matter, utility and dignity of such a science is clarified in fourteen books of 142 chapters.

Beginning with the obvious fact of human experience that all men desire naturally to know, he explains the procedure involved in the acquisition of wisdom. From sense awareness, which delights us in itself, memories are formed and from memory a single experience is produced. Experience is like science and art but differs from them in the fact that it is confined to the individual instances whereas they involve universal judgment. When the judgment is in view of things to be made, or of production, art is involved. When it is a question of contemplative understanding in a special field the universal judgment pertains to science. When the judgment relates to the *first* causes and principles of all science there is wisdom. The latter stage of human development is the fulfillment of wonder and it requires a great amount of leisure. The wise man is considered to be the one who knows things in general, is able to learn the most difficult things, is more exact and capable of teaching these causes, is able to put all knowledge into its proper order and delights in it for its own sake. Wisdom is the supremely free science for it alone exists for its own sake and is most like the divine activity.

The earliest philosophers perceived in a vague sort of way the task of philosophy but they did not succeed very well in rising beyond a consideration of the physical, which he shows by an historical survey of their opinions. For the most part they did not progress beyond the material cause and efficient cause. The formal cause was investigated by the Pythagoreans and the Platonists but the final cause was not explained with the clarity expected of a wise man. Plato's doctrine of the Forms can scarcely explain objects in the physical universe since the Forms are considered to be outside the things to be explained. His theory is a tapestry of poetic imaginings but hardly a scientific explanation. In general Aristotle's predecessors sought the four causes of all natural objects in a vague way but their explanations were more like the initial efforts of a juvenile. He would like to investigate the problems in a more mature and scientific fashion. This is a difficult task, because so very abstract and no one man can expect to attain the total truth adequately. Yet, taken collectively, a considerable amount of truth has been amassed. The basic principles of eternal things must be most true since each thing is related to the truth as it is in respect of being. We cannot grasp it completely because, like bats, our eyes are blinded by the brightness of the truth. We must realize that in this matter of finding the ultimate principles of all things it is impossible to proceed *ad infinitum*. If it were, this would mean that actually everything is unknowable. There cannot be an infinite progression upwards or downwards in the realm of material, formal, efficient or final causes because such a series cannot be traversed in order to account for the existence of anything or its intelligibility.

After these preliminary remarks Aristotle proposes a sketch of the general problems of philosophy in order to be clear about the ground to be covered. Can one science really treat of all four causes in their total extent? Can it treat of all kinds of substance and the attributes of substance? Are there immaterial substances? What are first principles? Do Forms exist apart from individual things? Are the objects of mathematics substances? Are the first principles individuals, etc.? His presentation of the problems shows that he is aware of the various philosophies that have attempted to satisfy the wonder of every man. What does he think a philosopher should study about?

The goal of his investigation should be a knowledge of being as being and of its fundamental attributes, viz. unity, truth, goodness, beauty and their opposites. It should include an analysis of the primary axioms of all thought and being, especially the law of non-contradiction, which is employed by all men since it is an expression of being qua being. No inquirer in a special science investigates the validity of this and kindred principles. The metaphysician must do so. The first principles cannot be demonstrated but we can "prove" them negatively by assuming the opposite and recognizing that the opposite is self-refuting. Substance is the basic type of being, the other nine categories are attributes or characteristics of substance. We must study all types of substances, immaterial as well as sensible, and actuality and potentiality in all their applicability. But before embarking on such a rough journey we must be clear about the meanings of the fundamental terms to be employed. The whole of Book Delta is a philosophical lexicon including the varieties of meanings associated with such terms as: beginning, cause, element, nature, necessary, one, many, being, substance, same, other, different, like, unlike, opposite, contrary, other in species, the same in species, prior, posterior, potency, capable, incapacity, possible, impossible, quantum, quality, complete, relative, limit, that in virtue of which, in virtue of itself, disposition, having or habit, affection, privation, have or hold, be in, from, part, whole, total, all, mutilated, genus, false and accident.

The science of metaphysics concerned with being qua being, is quite different from other sciences which deal with particular aspects of being and do not inquire into the essence of the things of which they treat. Nor do they concern themselves with the question as to whether what they deal with exists. Moreover, it is one of the speculative sciences, the most speculative, as a matter of fact, dealing with the highest aspect of things. Like natural and mathematical philosophy it is neither practical nor productive. But unlike them its object includes things which exist separately from matter and are immovable. Natural philosophy studies the sort of substance which has the principle of motion and rest in itself and hence, substance as involving matter in its definition. The object of *physics* cannot exist nor be defined without matter. The object of mathematics does not exist without matter but mathematics studies it without movement in an abstract way, quantitatively. Some of the mathematical disciplines, like geometry and astronomy, deal with particular aspects of quantified being whereas universal mathematics applies alike to all. If there were no substance other than physical substances, natural science would be the first science. But if there is an immovable substance, the science of this would be prior and first in a universal way.

Metaphysics is the science of being qua being. Now being has several meanings: relative to the *is* in a judgment, the accidental, substance, quality, quantity, where, when, etc., as well as potentially or actually being. As regards the accidental there is no science. So metaphysics will be concerned primarily with substance and only secondarily with the others insofar as they are related to substance. The notion of *is* as found in a judgment concerns combinations and separations in thought rather than things and does not pertain directly to this science. Substance is primarily *being* in definition, in the order of knowledge and in time. None of the other categories can exist independently of substance and the definition of them all requires a reference to substance. We know a thing most fully when we know its substance. Substance belongs most obviously to animals, plants and natural bodies composed of the elements. Some think that Forms and the objects of mathematics are, also, substances. We must examine all these opinions.

The word 'substance' is applied to the essence and universal and the genus of each thing and the substratum. This latter is sometimes called matter, sometimes form and sometimes the compound of both. By matter is meant "that which in itself is neither a particular thing nor of a certain quantity nor assigned to any other of the categories by which being is determined." Matter cannot be substance in the basic sense because "thisness" is thought to belong chiefly to substance. The compound of matter and form is the object of physics. This leaves substance as form as the object of metaphysics and it will be a genus or species, i.e.

have an essence expressible by a definition which is the formula of its meaning. In a secondary sense the essence of an accident will be considered as a formal perfection, too. We will know a thing fully when we know its essence and the essence is identical with a thing in its fundamental substantial reality.

The generation of natural objects and the production of things by art will help us understand what the form of a natural thing is and why it does not exist apart from the physical object as Plato imagined. The form is produced out of the potentiality of the material substratum by the causal influence of the efficient cause. In natural generations the embodied forms tend to reproduce another like themselves due to the tendency in the natural object. The form of the agent is the determining principle of its productivity. Like produces like out of the potentiality of the substrate. In a similar fashion art is the formal principle in the artist directing his productivity as regards the formation of the plastic material. The form that arises in the matter is an embodiment of the art in the artist. As regards the production of substances, matter is not produced, form is not produced but a substance is produced when some substance existing beforehand in complete reality causes another substance like itself to be actualized out of the potentiality of the substratum existing under another actuality. The generation of the new substance is the corruption of the old, brought about by some other agent-substance.

The universal is not a substance in the strict sense because it is not a "this particular thing." If the universal were a substance, since the genus is predicated of the individual as being in it, as animal is said to be in man, there would be more than one substance in each substance and no substance would be one. If the universal were a substantial reality existing in things it would be both one and many simultaneously. Animal would be one in horse and Socrates and yet many because horse and Socrates are two different animals. Moreover, how could animal exist apart from the types of animals and be just animal and not a particular kind of animal? How can the form of a thing exist apart from the thing of which it is the form? If so, each one thing would be more than one substance, since it participates in animal, a substance, and horse, another substance. Again, that which is one substance cannot be in many places at the same time. But what is common, i.e., the universal, is present in many places at the same time. Therefore no universal is substance in the sense of existing apart from its individuals as a unit in itself, nor as existing as a part of an individual in the individual.

The substance investigated in this type of science is the form, which is the actuality of the natural body existing in it. Since sensible substance has matter as a substratum, it, too, will be called substance but in potentiality. The complex is a generable and destructible substance composed of potentiality and actuality. Only those things subject to generation and corruption are composed of matter and form. Of things which have no matter either intelligible, i.e., mathematicals, or perceptible, each is by its nature essentially a kind of unit as it is essentially a being.

Having discussed being as regards natural substances and their accidental characteristics, and having explained in what way matter and form and the complex is being, how essence is related to being and why the universal is not being, Aristotle investigated actuality and potentiality. He has already shown that matter is potentiality and form actuality and why the complex is an unit. But here there is a fuller discussion of act and potentiality beginning from an analysis of motion in which the terms are realized fundamentally. The word potency is derivatively related to potent, which refers to the power to originate change in another. By reciprocity, potency refers to what can be acted upon. The prior potency (power) is in the agent; the latter is in the patient. The power of producing something may be innate, like the senses, or acquired either by practice or learning. But the same is not the case with passive potency, which is a capability of being acted upon because there is a privation involved. The actual is just the opposite. There is no privation, relatively or absolutely; there is no movement; there is just completion. Every movement is incomplete, since potentiality and actuality are both involved. But the actuality here is like *being* built or the buildi*ng* rather that built or the building. It is incomplete and along the way. It is in process. The actual is the complete. A thing is potential when it is not but can be. It is actual when it is. The actual is prior to the potential. In formula it is prior because the potential is potential because it can become actual. It is prior in time in one sense and posterior in another. What is identical in species is actually prior to the individual generated by the parent. But the newly generated individual was in potentiality prior to its generation by which it became actual. From the potentially existing the actually existing is always produced by an actually existing thing, e.g. man from man. There is always a first mover and the mover already exists actually. Actuality is prior in substantiality in the sense that the actuality is the end or that for the sake of which something is done, e.g. animals have sight in order that they may see. The form is actuality as regards the potency and prior to it in this way. Eternal things are prior in actuality to perishable things and so the actual is absolutely prior to the potential.

Metaphysics also studies unity and its opposite, plurality. As was explained in his philosophical lexicon, the one is either one by accident as "musical Coriscus," or one by its nature. The latter is primarily of interest in this science and it has four meanings: 1) the naturally continuous; 2) the whole; 3) numerically one, as the individual; 4) one in kind (the universal). All are called one because in each case there is a designation of something insofar as it is undivided in itself. The concept of unity was probably derived from the measure of quantity and, then, applied analogously to other areas. Measure is that by which quantity is known and quantity qua quantity is known basically by number;

117

and all number is known by one. In regard to length, breadth, depth, weight and speed the measure is something one, i.e. a unit taken as undivided. Anything is called one because it is undivided.

Unity seems to have just as many meanings as being; it is not a separate substance (a subsistent form) but a predicate indicating the indivision of being. In every category unity is identical with being: substance, quantity, quality, etc. and, since it is not restricted to any one category of being it may be called a transcendental attribute of being. From this it is clear that the many is contrary to the one and will have different designations according as it is opposed to the one. To the one belong the same, like and the equal whereas to plurality belong the other, unlike and the unequal.

Book Kappa is a recapitulation of parts of Books Beta, Gamma and Epsilon combined with extracts from the *Physics*. He reiterates the difficulties associated with the subject-matter of metaphysics and seems to imply that the final cause is properly included or mainly investigated in metaphysics. He again disagrees with the separate existence theory of Forms and of mathematicals placed between Forms and sensible substances. Neither separately existing Forms nor separated mathematical realities nor material substances as involving movement are the subject-matter of this science. Being qua being, or substance qua substance is primarily investigated and, if there are any immaterial and immovable substances he will investigate them later in the aspect of metaphysics called theology. That metaphysics can be one science is clear if being is taken analogously; every being is being, yet each being is a different being; they are all proportionally the same. Each is said to be because it is a modification of being qua being or a permanent or transient state or a movement of it or something else of the sort.

The first principle of being is "that the same thing cannot at one and the same time be and not be"; it is not demonstrable, but one can show that whoever denies it is actually asserting its validity. If one had questioned Heraclitus about the signification of words and the validity of judgments he would have been forced to admit this principle, though it is not at all certain that Heraclitus asserted its opposite. The saying of Protagoras, "that man is the measure of all things" would imply that, since what seems to each man is so, the same thing both is and is not. His statement is likewise self-refuting. This first principle of being and thought is absolutely certain and is grasped as such by an intuitive vision of being.

The early philosophers investigated substance as *being* in the fundamental sense but they restricted their study to the individual sensible substance. Unlike them, contemporary thinkers rank the universal, primarily genus, as substance. We must recognize that there are three kinds of substance: sensible perishable substance, sensible eternal substance and immovable substance. The latter includes the Forms *and* mathematicals for some; others restrict it to the object of mathematics; others identify the Forms and the mathematicals. Sensible substance is changeable in four different ways: by generation and corruption, increase and diminution, alteration and as regards place. Each involves the actuality of what exists in potentiality; the latter three are types of motion. Eternal material substances are not generable and corruptible but they are susceptible of motion from place to place. There is no need for the separate existence of Forms as regards objects generated in nature. Man is begotten by a previously existing man, an individual by an individual. The forms pre-exist in the generators and are produced by them. To explain change or local motion in the eternal non-generable substances separated Forms or mathematical ideas are quite useless. Since the universe is eternal and involves eternal movement it is impossible that it should have come into existence or cease to be. This eternal movement, however, must be accounted for, if not by an efficient cause, at least in terms of a final cause. This *first* cause is a separated immovable substance whose essence is actuality. It moves the first heaven by an attractive force so that the first heaven is endowed with an eternal movement. In itself this immovable substance is necessarily existent; its life is the activity of self-thinking thought. This is God, a living, eternal being, most good and in no way a magnitude. The existence of this first mover is necessary in order to explain the motion of the first heaven, moving with an eternal circular movement. Now, since there are other spheres also moving circularly there must be a plurality of first movers, their number depending on the number of all the spheres. According to astronomers there are either 55 or 47 spheres; hence, there will be 55 or 47 unmoved movers, each causing the respective movement as a final cause. All in all the universe is so constituted that everything in it is interconnected or ordered together to one end, the supreme good.

The Metaphysics has two final chapters constituting a sort of unit of subject-matter. In them Aristotle discusses dialectically and in grand detail the claims of Platonists that the Ideal Forms are the separate substances and the contemporary point of view that would make them mathematicals. ("mathematics has come to be the whole of philosophy for modern thinkers.") He is of the opinion that there is no valid way in which you can justify the position that the objects of mathematics either exist separately in a realm of ideal numbers, points, planes, solids, etc. or that they exist in mathematical abstractness in sensible things. The objects of mathematical speculation are constructed by the mind as a result of abstracting all the manifold aspects of quantitative relationships from materially extended things. Even when the mathematical sciences demonstrate in the area of order, symmetry and definiteness no separate realm is required. If the separate absolutes are numbers, in what way can they be considered as the causes of sensible things? If the substance of things is mathematical, what is the source of movement? Is it a number, plane or solid? If

120

the objects of mathematics exist separately, how can one avoid a process *ad infinitum* in mathematicals? If there are separate solids corresponding to sensible solids, would there have to be separate planes for separate solids and separate lines for the separate planes and separate points for the separate lines? If so, we would have two sets of solids (one sensible and one separate), three sets of planes, four sets of lines and five sets of points. With which will mathematics deal?

The theory of Ideas was fabricated in order to avoid the apparent cul-de-sac implied in the Heraclitean teaching that all sensible things are involved in a continual flux. If knowledge or thought is to have an object it cannot be anything in the realm of sense. There must be some other permanent, eternal, immutable realities. Socrates developed the proper method for acquiring a knowledge of such realities (induction) and the proper way for expressing them (definitions of universal essences). But Socrates did not assign these realities a separate existence. His followers did just that and called such entities by the name of Ideas or Forms. To them it seemed to follow that there would be an Idea corresponding to everything spoken of universally; for every universal term there is a separate Ideal-Form. Wherever there are many there must be an Ideal One. But this can lead to absurdities. There would be Forms of negations, privations, of perishable things, relations, etc. The theory, also, leads to the argument of a "third man," which would express a relationship between the sensible man and the Ideal Man and so on *ad infinitum*, as in the previous argument against the existence of separate solids, planes, lines and points. What does the existence of such forms contribute to the world of sensible things and our knowledge about it? They don't cause local movement or generation and corruption. Since the Ideal-Forms are separate from sensibles they can't account for the order of things or their qualitative characteristics. How can they be the principles of knowledge of those things from which they are separate? To say that the Forms are patterns and that other things participate in them "is to use empty words and poetical metaphors." It would seem impossible that substance and that whose substance it is should exist apart.

NICHOMACHEAN ETHICS

Aristotle's basic work in the field of purposeful human conduct is presented in ten books of 133 chapters. Working forward from the facts of human experience in the fields of art, science and, indeed, as regards every human act and pursuit he traverses the areas of the moral and intellectual virtues, examines friendship and pleasure and terminates in happiness. His method is historical, dialectic, inductive and deductive, within the whole range of the social life of man. The science of the whole field of human life, since man is by nature a social being, is called politics or political science. It embraces all the activities of the citizen of the polis as such. *The Nichomachean Ethics* is generally conceded to have been the work of the Master. Eudemus of Rhodes is regarded in the first century A.D. as the author of the compilation which is classified as the *Eudemian Ethics* and the *Magna Moralia* may be an epitome of both, current as far back as Marcus Aurelius (121-180 A.D.). The shorter treatise *On Virtues and Vices* is quite definitely from a later hand. *The Eudemian Ethics* contains 7 Books of 79 chapters (84 in Bekker) including Books 4-6 which are the same as Books 5-7 in the *Nichomachean Ethics*. The *Magna Moralia* is only two Books with 51 chapters.

If we examine everything that man does qua man we recognize immediately that he always aims at some end which is good because it terminates or fulfills intellectual desire or purposive choice. Further, some of these goods are objects produced or obtained by activities, others are the activities themselves desired for their own sake. There is a hierarchy of means and ends which would be completely empty and vain were our desire to fail to reach toward a goal desired for its own sake purely as an end. Such a good would be the ultimate and chief good the knowledge of which would have a great influence on human life. Aristotle will attempt to indicate roughly what such an end is within the limits of the subject-matter involved. Mathematical exactitude should not be expected in the realm of human conduct just as one should not expect to find probable reasoning in the field of mathematics. The affairs of human life form the data and subject-matter of this science and men young in character, who follow passion rather than knowledge, are somewhat inept in this field of investigation. Those who direct their desires and action by right reason (prattein kata ton orthon logon) will profit much from a knowledge of the matter discussed in this treatise. Each man is a good judge of what he knows; the man of universal education is a good judge without any qualification.

All men agree that the good which is desired by all as the end of all their human activities is happiness (eudaimonia), which may include the notion or overtone of prosperity, as we shall see. But, though all men desire happiness, there does not seem to be such a universal agreement as to what constitutes happiness. To judge from the lives that men lead some consider it to be pleasure, being quite slavish and brutish in their tastes. Others think of it in terms of honor, which is too superficial, actually dependent upon the bestower rather than the receiver and easily lost. Others consider it relative to a certain condition of life: health when in sickness, wealth when in poverty. Wealth is completely inadequate because it is always a means; health is too transitory. Virtue is better than any of those named and is actually preferred by the nobler type of man. But it, too, does not hold up under scrutiny because one may have virtue and be inactive or completely miserable in life. Happiness cannot be a state; it must be dynamic because human life is such and man is happy in living the full life. Furthermore, happiness is the ultimate end for we always choose it for its own sake, never for anything else, and we choose everything else we choose for the sake of happiness. The same conclusion is reached if we approach the question from the point of view of self-sufficiency. Happiness by itself makes life desirable and it is in want of nothing to make life completely successful and eminently prosperous.

To find out what constitutes man's happiness we must discover what is the proper activity of man qua man, since by analogy it appears that a thing's good lies along the lines of its proper function, whether it be the good of a flute player or a sculptor or the practiser of any art. Just as a carpenter or cobbler each has a proper function qua carpenter or cobbler, man qua man, because of his specific nature, must have a proper function. This could not be the common activities of nutrition and growth nor those of animal sensibility. It must be the precise function of his intellectual nature either in itself or as directing his other activities, that is, the life itself of exercising reason. Human happiness will consist in an exercise of vital powers in accordance with the best and most complete virtue. A rough outline which will be filled in with details as he goes along.

The end of man, thus envisaged, is the starting point of enquiry into the good life of man on earth. In terms of it we must evaluate the rightness and wrongness of all human activities. He has reached this conclusion by induction from the data of human living. He now re-examines the conclusion dialectically and historically in relation to current opinions on the subject. Here we find a distinction of the good into three classes: external goods, goods of the body and goods of the soul, the latter considered goods in the fullest sense. The exercise of vital powers is certainly a good of the soul, as is reason, and his point is confirmed. Another opinion claims that happiness is "living well" and "doing well." Again, a confirmation. All the characteristics assigned by others to happiness seem to belong to happiness as defined by him, whether it be that happiness is an excellence of man, or involves pleasure (of the noblest kind) or requires external goods, friends, wealth, political influence, good birth, the blessing of children and personal beauty. These are related to human happiness in this life as aids or instruments or perhaps necessary conditions although they may not be the essential notes or characteristics of it. Though the life of man needs these things it is the excellent use of his highest power that constitutes happiness. The happy man will preserve his good character all through life, after reaching maturity, and he will be occupied almost continually with excellent deeds and excellent speculations. He will take fortune in the noblest fashion and bear himself always "foursquare without a flaw." A happy man is "one who exercises his powers in accord with perfect excellence, being duly furnished with external goods, not for any chance time but for a full term of years and who continues to live so and shall die as he lived."

Since happiness involves the activity of the powers of the soul in accord with perfect excellence, he now inquires about the various kinds of excellences in man. We must know that there is an irrational as well as a rational aspect to the human soul. Of the irrational part one is common to plants and not specifically human; moreover, it is more active in sleep which is a cessation of those activities in virtue of which a man is judged good or bad. There is another aspect of the irrational soul, the power of appetite or desire which partakes of reason in a manner, when it "listens" to reason. The ordering of this involves the excellencies of the soul which are termed moral virtues, such as temperance. The excellencies of reason itself are termed intellectual virtues and they are wisdom, understanding and prudence. Intellectual excellence owes its birth and growth mainly to instruction while the moral is a result of habit or custom. The word for moral character (nthos) is a derivative of the name for custom (ethos). It is further plain that moral virtues are not implanted in us by nature

125

but that nature gives the capacity for acquiring them and this capacity is developed by training. We acquire the virtues by doing the act repeatedly, just as we acquire the arts by doing the activity associated with them. If the acts are not done well, vice results. It makes all the difference in the world, then, how one is trained from his youth.

His enquiry here is not purely speculative. He is not searching merely to know what virtue is but in order to become good. Of what kind must the acts be by which virtue is formed? They must be in accord with right reason and what constitutes right reason is discussed later in connection with the intellectual virtues. In matters of virtue *falling short* and *excess* are alike incompatible with the excellence involved. By analogy this is evident in the matter of exercise relative to health; it is similar in regard to temperance and courage. To fear everything shows a defect of confidence; to fear nothing is the excess of foolhardiness. To abstain from no pleasure or shun all are equally deficient states. By abstaining from pleasure we become temperate; when we have become temperate we are best able to abstain. In general, he who abstains from pleasure and delights in the abstention is temperate; the presence of vexation in such a case would indicate the absence of temperance. Every act is accompanied by pleasure or pain. Pleasure indicates that the action is being performed well. It is the overtone of an act well done.

Here a difficulty is proposed: how can it be said that man becomes virtuous by doing what is virtuous? If the act is virtuous is not the man already virtuous? Well, three things are required in order to be in a virtuous state: a man must know what he is doing, he must choose it for itself, and the act must be the expression of a formed and stable character. For the possession of virtue mere knowledge is of little avail whereas the other two conditions are all-important. If a man does an act which is an act of virtue but he does not know that it is an act of virtue, he is not therefore virtuous. If he knows that it is an act of virtue

126

and does not choose it for itself, he is not considered to be virtuous. He must know that it is an act of virtue and choose it for itself. By so doing he builds up the excellence of habit of a formed and stable character. Therefore when he acts by the habit he is designated as a man of virtue acting in accord with his firmly established character.

What is the precise nature of moral virtue? It is either a passion (motion) or a power (*faculty*) or a state of character (habit), since things in the soul are one of these. A passion is like anger, fear, joy, love, hate, etc., feelings accompanied by pleasure or pain. A power is that in virtue of which we are said to be capable of being affected. A habit is that by which we are disposed well or ill in regard to our affections. Certainly a moral virtue is not an emotion since we are not called good or bad in respect to them, not praised or blamed for them; they do not involve deliberate choice and they are not dispositions. Similarly moral virtue is not a power of the soul; the powers of the soul are natural whereas moral virtue must be acquired. Thus it must be habits of powers which cause the powers to be in good condition and able to perform their function well. This is the generic nature of virtue and by it every virtue is at an extreme from any vice. Specifically moral virtue consists in a mean between excess and defeat, the mean relative to the individual involved and to the passions and actions. In the case of all the passions it is possible to be affected pleasantly or painfully either too much or too little. To be affected pleasantly or painfully at the right time, on the right occasion, towards the right person, and with the right object and in the right fashion is the Mean and best course and characteristic of virtue. Virtue, then, "is a habit or trained power of choice whose characteristic lies in observing the mean relative to the person concerned, and which is according to the judgment of the prudent man." Specifically, or essentially, virtue is a moderation or mean but generically it is an extreme of perfection. So not all actions or passions admit of moderation: those which are evil in themselves, such as envy, malevolence, adultery, theft and murder. No one can be right in them. The rightness or wrongness of adultery does not depend on whether it is the right person, occasion and manner. It is wrong in itself. Contrariwise, there can be no excess nor deficiency in prudence or temperance or any of the virtues.

Descending from the general to particular instances, courage is the mean between cowardice and foolhardiness; temperance is the mean between insensibility and profligacy; liberality is the mean between illiberality and prodigality; magnificence the mean of meanness and vulgarity; proper pride the mean of undue humility and empty vanity; gentleness is the mean of wrathlessness and wrathfulness; truthfulness the mean of irony and boastfulness; wittiness, the mean of boorishness and buffoonery; friendliness the mean of peevishness and flattery; modesty the mean of shamelessness and bashfulness, etc., etc.

In the actual acquisition of virtue we must realize that it is a very difficult task to achieve the mean and that the completely virtuous man is a rarity. Since one of the extremes is more dangerous than the other we should be safer if we veer in the direction of the less evil. We should also consider what we are prone to by our individual natural propensities, an indication of which is the pleasure we find in certain actions and things. We must be especially on guard against pleasant things for in them it is difficult to be an unbiased judge.

Virtue deals with feelings and actions. Praise and blame are given only in the case of an action that is considered voluntary. It is necessary to understand when an action is voluntary. In general we see that the voluntary refers to an act proceeding from an intrinsic source with knowledge of the circumstances. The involuntary is what is done under compulsion or through ignorance, i.e. not originated by doer and through ignorance of the circumstances. In the case of someone throwing a valuable cargo over the side of a floundering ship in order to save the ship and his life, the action is both voluntary and involuntary from different points of view. The action is involuntary in itself but voluntary as a means to another end. The determining factor is the state of mind of the agent at the time. What is done through ignorance is always not-voluntary, but it is involuntary when the act involves a change of mind, i.e. the agent willing to act, not seeing the true nature of it at the time, is sorry afterwards when he sees what he has really done. Acting *in* ignorance is different from acting *through* ignorance. A drunken man does not act through ignorance but *in* ignorance. Furthermore, the term involuntary is not applied in regard to ignorance of the fitting. It is not ignorance of the principles, which should determine preference which is the ignorance that makes an act involuntary; not ignorance of the universal but ignorance of the particular occasion and circumstances of the act. The particulars of an act are: the doer, the deed and the circumstances of the deed, sometimes the instrument, the purpose and the manner of performance. It is impossible to be ignorant of all of these but a man may be ignorant of some of the circumstances, especially the result and the precise nature of the deed.

The voluntary is the generic classification and willing is an instance of the voluntary in man. But willing and choice are not the same. We may properly be said to will the end but we choose the means. Choice requires will, as appetite and movement toward the good in general and, in addition, deliberation as regards the means. Choice deals with what is in our power to do or not to do and our choice makes us morally good or bad. The distinguishing difference between will and choice is the element of previous deliberation which characterizes choice. Matters of deliberation and, hence, of choice exclude the eternal and unalterable, the necessary as such, matters of chance and generally, things that one himself cannot bring about. Positively, we deliberate about matters of conduct that are within our control. In such matters there are general rules but the individual result is unpredictable in virtue of them. There is an element of uncertainty and so we deliberate and seek counsel about the appropriate means as regards the end. Choice terminates the deliberation as regards practical action. This choice is *deliberate desire* for something in our power. The object of desire is the real good even though what appears good may be the object of the will for the individual; a distinction between the objective and psychological good. It is due to purposeful choice that virtue and vice depend upon ourselves and this is basically a matter of common experience. We are masters of our acts when we know the particular circumstances and we are masters of the beginnings of our habits of character which grow by almost imperceptible and gradual steps. Inasmuch as it is in our power to employ or not employ our natural powers the resulting character is voluntary.

The virtues of the irrational part of the soul are courage, with respect to feelings of fear and confidence, and temperance, as regards pleasures of the body, especially touch and taste. Liberality is the virtue of a free man as regards wealth. Highmindedness exhibits itself in matters of honors and dishonors, a sort of crown of virtue in the educated man. Gentleness is a virtue related to anger. Friendliness is a social virtue as regards living and conversing with others as involving the field of pleasure and pain. As regards the truth-value of this speech and action the virtue is truthfulness. As to relaxation in conversation, wittiness is the mean between buffoonery and boorishness.

Justice is that habit or stable state of character which renders a man apt to do what is lawful and fair. Injustice is its opposite. We can learn a lot about justice by examining the opposite since we consider one unjust who breaks the law and takes more or less than his due share. There are two types of justice then: deliberate action in accordance with the law, which has as its end the happiness of the community; this may be called general or complete or political justice, because it involves all virtue relative to

130

the members of the community; and, secondly, particular justice or fairness, which has to do with the distribution of honor, wealth and the other things divided among the members of the body politic. Considered as distributive justice it concerns the division of the goods of the state among the citizens according to a geometrical proportion, i.e. according to merit. Another branch of particular justice is called remedial since it concerns the restitution of proper balance in private transactions. Remedial justice may be either voluntary or involuntary insofar as it deals with contracts entered into voluntarily, such as buying, selling, lending at interest, hiring, etc. or it concerns actions that are secretly or openly violent, such as theft and adultery or assault, murder, rape, etc. The civil and criminal law deal with such remedial situations of justice and justice is meted out according to an arithmetical proportion, since the law makes no distinction between a good or bad man in the case of fraud, adultery, etc. The only question is the difference created by the injury and the determination of the damages done or suffered. The role of the judge is to make the parties equal by penalizing the offender and thus subtracting from his gain and making recompense for the sufferer's loss. Thus the fair of the just is a mean between excess and defect and the judge is a *mediator,* determining the mean.

As regards the proper proportion between goods and services of different kinds of people, e.g. a builder and cobbler, each must be evaluated in relation to some common factor. For this reason money was devised as a medium of exchange and by it we can figure out the number of shoes that would be equivalent to the work of building a house. The value of each is determined while each is still in possession of his wares. And the more common determinant is the need each has for the other's product. But, even if we have no need at the moment, money is a guarantee that we shall be able to make the exchange when we are in need. There would be no society were there no exchange and no exchange without equality and no equality without a com-

131

mon measure. In general, justice is a mean between excess and defect and each of these is unjust or the instance of a single vice. The justice between individuals is called commutative justice.

A man acts justly or unjustly when he does a just or or unjust act voluntarily. When he does them involuntarily he is not said to be just or unjust nor is he to be praised or blamed in such. To be voluntary it must be not only in the doer's control but be done knowingly without the intervention of accident or constraint. So justice is that habit in virtue of which the just man is apt to do deliberately that which is just, i.e. in dealings between two citizens justice is what fits them to apportion things so that each gets his fair share or proportionate share. As regards doing or suffering injustice, suffering injustice is a lesser wrong than doing it. The difference between doing an unjust act and doing it unjustly, i.e. as an unjust man, lies in the state of mind not in the external act. The unjust man acts from deliberate purpose and so one may commit a theft without being a thief and is not an adulterer though he commits adultery, etc. In general, justice implies that there are citizens, free men, on an equal footing of some kind, living under the law. The administration of law is the discrimination of the just from the unjust.

We cannot speak of injustice between master and slave, or between father and child or toward what is part of one's self. Though we can speak of justice between a man and his wife it is not on the same level as between citizens not in the same immediate family. Between citizens justice is partly natural and partly conventional, the natural being valid everywhere and it does not depend on the individual's acceptance or rejection. The conventional varies among individuals and is prescribed for a definite circumstance, such as measures of corn and wine.

What is just and what is equitable are generically the same but the equitable is better. The reason is that every law is laid down in general terms and in accord with what

132

holds for the majority of cases, whereas in concrete circumstances a particular case may be an exception and so the just must be amended. As amended we have the equitable in that particular case. An equitable man is willing to take less than his due even when the law is on his side.

After this analysis of the moral virtues Aristotle proceeds to a study of the intellectual virtues since virtue implies a mean as prescribed by right reason according to some standard. What is *right* reason and what is its *standard*? To answer this we must remember that the soul involves both rational and irrational activities and that the rational part of the soul involves both a scientific or demonstrative power and a calculative or deliberative power. Moreover, the powers that guide us in action and the grasp of the truth are sense, reason and desire. Sense cannot originate action and, of the other two, reasoning has two modes, viz. affirmation and negation, and desire involves pursuit and avoidance. Since moral virtue is a formed power of choice and choice is desire following deliberation, the calculation or reasoning must be true and the desire right and this regards the practical rather than the speculative. So purpose is either desiring reason or reasoning desire about what is to be done or avoided.

The mind arrives at truth by means of art, science, prudence, wisdom and understanding. Scientific knowledge is invariable and its object is necessary, eternal and invariable. Science can be taught. Induction is the process toward universal principles; syllogism (scientific reasoning) starts from these and proceeds to scientific conclusions. Hence, science is a formed habit of demonstration as explained in the *Posterior Analytics*. What is variable includes what man makes and what he does. The habit of making according to right reason is art, the habit of acting according to proper calculation is prudence. Prudence cannot be science because the sphere of prudence is action concerning what is variable; it cannot be art because it deals with doing rather than making. So prudence is a habit of calculative reason

133

which issues in action in the domain of human good and evil. Wisdom is the union of intuitive reason with scientific knowledge concerning the noblest of objects and it is the same for all men, whereas prudence is relative to the matters of deliberation concerning the variable in matters of practice. Wisdom deals with the general, prudence with the particular facts, for it issues in action. Prudence may be called practical wisdom. Its types relate to the proper management of a household (oekonomia), the legislative faculty and statesmanship, either deliberative or judicial. Just as understanding (intuitive reason) deals with primary principles which cannot be demonstrated, prudence deals with particular facts which cannot be scientifically proved.

What is this calculation or deliberation which prudence involves? It is not science or happy guessing or sagacity or just any kind of opinion but rather a correctness of reasoning (dianoia) by which we come to right conclusions in the correct manner and at the right time as to what ought to be done concerning the means to an end. It implies the exercise of intelligence, good judgment or discernment and correct reasoning. So intuitive reason is basic to both ultimate scientific truths and the principles of correct conduct. In virtue of our apprehension of the fundamentals of morality we deliberate about the proper means to our end. The conclusions of our deliberation are intuitively understood as the principles of conduct. We understand that the good is to be done, that such and such is good in such and such circumstances and therefore, we understand that it is to be done here and now. Prudence, as a virtue of the practical intellect, does not give us just a knowledge of the good but it produces the good act as ensuring the rightness of the means as moral virtue guarantees the rightness of the end. For, e.g. just acts involve both a knowledge that the acts are just and the performance of them by deliberate purpose for their own sake. "It is impossible to be prudent without being morally good," and virtue is a habit implying right reason. So if Socrates held that moral virtues are forms of reason he was partly right, if he meant that they imply reason. He is wrong if he meant simply that all virtues are forms of prudence. And prudence does not rule wisdom but "rules in its interests."

There are three types of moral states to be avoided: vice, whose opposite is virtue, incontinence, the contrary of which is continence, and brutishness, whose opposite is god-likeness. Having discussed virtue and vice he will now consider incontinence and softness and their opposites which are not vices and virtues but dispositions of a different kind. The usual method of dialectical discussion of current opinions is carried out so that all error can be wiped out and truth left in possession of the agora. Continence and hardiness are considered good and praiseworthy; incontinence and softness are bad and blameworthy. This is quite evident but in what sense can a man judge rightly and act incontinently, as some contend taking incontinence to mean "uncontrolled by reason"? The self-indulgent man is carried along by deliberate purpose to pursue the pleasure of the moment; the incontinent man does not agree that what is pleasant at the moment is always to be pursued but he pursues it just the same. Thus he acts against his knowledge or his firmly adhered-to opinion. How could this be? Well, knowledge may mean knowledge possessed habitually and not now in use or knowledge presently active and effective. It would not be strange to act against knowledge in the first sense but quite odd to do so in the second. Then, too, it is quite easy for someone to have knowledge in the sense of a universal principle and lack the knowledge of a particular instance. Again, one may have knowledge and be asleep or mad or drunk, in which case he may be mouthing demonstrations without actually knowing what they mean. It seems that the incontinent man is in this sort of condition. He knows what he should do or not do but under the influence of passion he is like one asleep or mad or drunk, uncontrolled by reason. When there is a universal judgment forbidding one to taste, a universal judgment that "all sweet things are pleasant" and a particular judgment "this is sweet," present with the appetitive desire for the sweet, then appetite moves the incontinent man to take what is sweet. Here it is the desire that is opposed to right reason and the action follows from the desire. The incontinent man must get out of his ignorance like one gets out of being drunk or asleep. The incontinent man is said to be incontinent *simply* as regards bodily pleasures carried to excess in the pursuit of pleasure and avoidance of pain, but he is considered to be *relatively* incontinent when there is a question of excess as regards victory, honor, wealth and such, which are good and pleasant in themselves. In both cases the act is done contrary to his deliberate choice and under the influence of passion. When excess of pleasure and avoidance of pain is done without desire or with a moderate amount of passion one is called self-indulgent rather than incontinent. He who succumbs to what the generality of men can and do resist is considered soft and luxurious. If one gives way to violent and excessive pleasures or pains we are prone to pardon him. We wonder when someone gives in to and cannot resist what the generality of men withstand, unless the cause be hereditary or a result of disease. People of keen and excitable temperaments are most liable to incontinence. An incontinent man is like one who gets drunk quickly and with a small amount of wine, i.e. less than most men. He does what a man of vice does but not with a deliberate purpose. He has knowledge like one drunk but he acts voluntarily, since he knows what he is doing, and, yet, he is not bad or vicious, since his purpose is good. The incontinent man is compared with a state that has good laws but never carries them out; the bad man is compared to a state that carries out its laws but they are bad.

Since moral virtue and vice concern pleasures and pains and since most people consider that happiness implies pleasure, he now takes up an investigation of pleasure and pain. First, we must realize, in contrast with certain common opinions, that pleasure is a concomitant of the natural exercise of a power, and, that no power is impeded by the pleasure proper to its exercise, but only by other ...ures. Secondly, pleasure itself is good and there is no reason why a certain kind of pleasure cannot be the supreme good, since a happy life is a pleasant one. The life of a good man would be no pleasanter than others unless the exercise of his powers were pleasanter. It is not pleasure which is bad but the proper amount of pleasure in the exercise of proper and fitting activities of the natural powers. The highest and best pleasure will be the resultant of the highest and best activity, as he will develop later after an analysis of friendship and love.

All men seem to need friends: the rich rely on them for a display of benevolence and the maintenance of their position; in poverty and all other misfortunes friends are considered the only refuge; when we are young friends keep us from error; when old age takes over we need friends to help us overcome our weakness in carrying out our plans; in the prime of life they help us in noble deeds; friendship is a natural bond between parents and offspring, between hosts and guests, between members of the same group, between citizens of the same State. Friendship is a beautiful and noble thing admired by all.

Friendship is based upon love and love is specified by the different types of the good: the useful, the pleasant and the befitting. In all cases of friendship there must be an awareness and return of mutual affection with the result that it is a relationship between men exclusively. Of the three types of friendship the lowest is based on mutual utility and it endures only so long as there is a mutual profit. Such friends love and wish each other well insofar as each receives some good from the other. When one fails to receive the expected good the friendship is terminated. It exists mainly between elderly people, business associates, host and guest. The second type is founded on the pleasant so that friends find each other a source of pleasure. This is especially the case with young people, who live mainly by pleasure. They are quick to make friends and quick to change them according to the pleasure derived. They fall in and out of love "many times a day." They enjoy each other's company and desire to be with each other constantly. The lover delights to look upon the beloved; the beloved likes the attention paid to him. When the bloom of youth is gone the friendship sometimes vanishes, for the one misses the delight derived from the contemplation of the beauty of the beloved and the other misses the attentions. However, the friendship could last if they have developed a love for each other's character. The most perfect kind of friendship is between those who resemble each other in virtue. They wish well to each other for the sake of each other and their friendship lasts as long as their virtue. Of course they are useful to each other in the order of virtue and bring pleasure thereby to each other. Such friendships imply mutual trust because each is convinced that the other will never wrong him. True friends desire to live together and will do so whenever possible. Because this type of friendship is between people eminently virtuous, which is not a common state of affairs, one will not have true friendship for many at the same time. Moreover, there is an intensity of love between friends which cannot be felt as regards many simultaneously. Between persons unequal, such as father and son, an elderly and younger person, man and woman, ruler and subject the friendship is based on a proportional love, i.e. the better of the two, the more useful and more pleasurable should receive more love than he gives. When love is proportioned to what is deserved there is established the proportional equality which is a necessary condition of friendship.

Every association of individuals gives some occasion for friendship. Partners on a voyage or in a campaign, brothers and comrades, fraternity brothers at a dinner, citizens at a festival, spectators at games are joined for some sort of mutual advantages. All are associations of citizens but the most basic ones are those determined by the various constitutions of States. Of such there are three basic kinds: kingship, aristocracy and timocracy, the perversion of each being tyranny, oligarchy and democracy respectively. Kingship is the best absolutely speaking and tyranny is the worst, because the tyrant seeks his own useful good whereas the king wishes the good of his subjects. Aristocracy degenerates into oligarchy because of the vice of the ruling class, who distribute honors and property not on the basis of merit but for their own personal gain of wealth. Democracy is the least bad of the corrupted forms. Likenesses of these forms of government are found in families: when the father rules for the good of the family there is a kingly type of rule but it may degenerate into tyranny when the father treats his offspring as slaves; the association of husband and wife is aristocratic because the husband rules in proportion to his merit and he intrusts to the wife matters of which she is especially capable. This relationship may degenerate into an oligarchy when the husband takes over complete control in everything. If a woman rules because of wealth or other influences there is also an oligarchy. The association of brothers is a timocracy but it can easily degenerate into a democracy where there is no master or where the head of the household is of a weak character. In these good family associations there is a relative superiority and, hence, a proportional friendship. In the degenerate forms there is little room for friendship.

The friendship between husband and wife is natural for human beings since they are impelled by nature to join together in couples for the propagation of the species and the nurture and education of the offspring. Such a friendship brings profit and pleasure but it will be based on virtue if each is good and each wills the good of virtue to the other. The conjugal union is the most basic for human beings; children are a special bond holding man and woman

139

together. The conjugal union is more natural than the union of civil society, which is, also, a natural institution since man is by nature a social being.

In friendship a man's relationship with his friends is built upon his relationship with himself since a friend is another self. The good man is of one mind with himself and wishes what is good for himself for his own sake, i.e. for the sake of his *self*. He loves himself in the proper sense. He wishes existence for himself; he wishes to live with himself; he sympathizes with himself in sorrow and rejoices with himself in joy. The bad man is self-loving in an improper sense since he desires money, honors, profit and pleasure out of due proportion to his merit. The good man will even surrender wealth, honor, profit and pleasure for the sake of his friends.

Does the happy man need friends? Since he is blessed with a sufficiency of goods and has acquired virtue in a high degree he will not need friends if by friends one means useful people. Also, his life is pleasant and he does not need adventitious pleasure. If happiness is a certain exercise of human powers which is good and pleasant in itself, a happy man will need friends as a source of contemplative pleasure in the good life they lead. Moreover, the solitary life is hard since one finds difficulty in being continuously active by himself. Again, living with good men will give him a sort of practice in virtue. Since the friend is an *alter ego* the good man will delight in the consciousness of the existence of his friend, will have delight by living with him and by conversing with him on noble things. The friend is desirable for him and he ought to have friends in order to be complete. The number of friends should be proportional to the ability of love and the possibility of communal living. The most appropriate number would be one at a time or a few at most.

Before giving a general summary of the good life for man Aristotle enters into a very detailed analysis of pleasure, occasioned by the widespread interest in the opinion of Eudoxus that pleasure is *the* good. The reasons for this opinion were, first, that all things strive after pleasure. What is desirable is good; what is most desirable is the best. The fact that all things incline to pleasure would seem to indicate that it is the best. Secondly, pain is the opposite of pleasure. Pain is the object of aversion for all. So its opposite is desirable for all. Thirdly, that is most desirable which we choose for its own sake. This is the case with pleasure. In opposition, such cannot be the case because pleasure is neither an object of desire nor an activity nor the objective perfection of an activity. Pleasure may be best understood in comparison with vision, e.g. like vision pleasure is something whole and entire at any moment and it is impossible that duration should make pleasure complete. Pleasure is not a motion. Every motion is incomplete at any moment, it requires duration in time and its whither and whence are specifically different. Any sense exercises itself upon its proper object and exercises itself completely when it is in good condition and its object is the best of those within its scope. This exercise is not only the most complete but also the most pleasant, for the exercise of any power is accompanied by pleasure and the most complete exercise gives the most pleasure. So pleasure is a completion of the exercise of a power, not as a habit completes it nor as the object and the power complete the exercise of the power, but as a superaddition to the exercise like the "grace of youth." Pleasure is the *overtone* of an activity well performed. It accompanies all activities so long as the power operates as it should and in regard to its proper object. Well, why then can't we be completely capable of continuous pleasure? Perhaps, because pleasure exhausts us and because no human power is capable of continuous exercise. Since pleasure accompanies the exercise of powers properly functioning and since life is an activity, pleasure will complete the life which men desire and it, too, is desirable because men find in it the completion of life.

Pleasures differ in kind, for specifically different things

141

are completed by specifically different things, as seems the case in products of both art and nature. Intellectual pleasures differ from sense pleasures. The several kinds of each are different from each other; since the activities are different their completions are different. The exercise of a power is increased by its proper pleasure, as one is more likely to understand something if the exercise of understanding is pleasant when applied to it; one is more apt to penetrate to the depths of understanding if pleasure is involved. The exercise of one power is impeded by the pleasure proper to another, as when a lover of the flute is hindered from following an argument when he hears someone playing, since he takes more delight in it. Also, when anything gives us intense delight we cannot do anything else at all. The goodness or badness of a pleasure is dependent upon the goodness or badness of the activity of the powers involved. Ultimately the test of the goodness of pleasure is virtue or, more concretely, the virtuous man. Of the good pleasures, the proper pleasures of man will be those of the exercise of his proper activities: intellect and will.

In summary, happiness is not a habit or a trained power. It resides in the exercise of a power that is desirable in itself and completely sufficient in itself and, hence, excellent and noble. The exercise of the trained powers which are proper to man are most desirable to man and the perfect man finds the exercise of virtue most desirable. That is truly valuable and pleasant which is so to the perfect man. Amusement is not considered as valuable and pleasant in itself but it is a sort of recreation which we need because we cannot work continuously and it is a means to the exercise of our powers. The enjoyment of bodily pleasures is within the reach of everybody, of children as well as slaves; it, too, is a means rather than an end. If happiness is the exercise of virtue it will be the exercise of the highest virtue, the excellence of the best part of which is reason. Hence happiness is the speculative contemplation of the best object by the noblest power in man. Such is the most

142

pleasurable of activities, the most self-sufficient. The necessities of life are needed in suitable quantities as conditions for the exercise of the contemplation of the truth. Above all leisure is required during a complete extent of time. It is reason which is man in the truest sense; the contemplative activity of a life of reason is the best and most pleasant and, therefore, the happiest. The exercise of moral virtue is happiness in a secondary analogous sense and it is this aspect of happiness which requires the necessities of external goods: so that man's happiness be complete for the *whole* man. All this is confirmed by the test of truth in practical matters, i.e. the facts of life.

Knowledge of what constitutes human happiness is not enough. We must endeavor to acquire it by our own efforts. This requires a basic natural endowment bestowed on a man by nature or some divine agency. Training in the habits of character must be undergone from the earliest times so that one will not become accustomed to live solely by pleasure of the passions. This demands a body of suitable laws for the guidance of youth in temperate living and the continuance of the development of virtue in adult life. Education in the principles of correct living must be carried on, also, from the beginning so that reason may be perfected, too, as regards proper conduct. A proper organization of law is needed for the well-being of all the citizens of the State but, perhaps, individuals are educated better under a system of private education. For the mastery of any science or art the individual must advance to its general principles and become acquainted with them in the proper method. The molding of character can be done best by one who has knowledge of man and of the State and can discriminate about the utility of laws for the common happiness of the citizens. Such a man would be a statesman in the proper sense of the term. The enquiry into the good life for man will be completed when we inquire into the matter of legislation. This will be accomplished by examining any valuable utterances of our predecessors, by looking

143

into the collection of Constitutions of States, by investigating what tends to preserve or destroy states and the several kinds of constitutions, by deciding what are the causes of good and bad governments. In conclusion we will be able to decide what system of laws and customs are best suited to each kind of constitution.

POLITICS

Aristotle's incomplete treatise on the political life of citizens united for the common good is presented in 103 chapters divided into 8 Books. His aim seems to be to understand what constitutes the ideal political organization absolutely and relatively, and how the ideal may become a practical reality. The method of investigation is historical, both from the viewpoint of the natural genesis of communities in general and from the actual examples of established governments in particular. It involves conclusions from inductive generalizations and it is dialectical in terms of the evaluation of various theories about the nature and formation of States. The education of citizens is a necessary aspect of the formation of the ideal community and the treatise concludes with a consideration of the proper method of education and the proper subject-matter to be stressed to insure the good life of men in the State. Unfortunately the education procedures are incomplete. The intellectual and moral development, though considered as most important and most essential to the ultimate goal, is merely skimmed over in passing. The treatise is clearly unfinished or else a major portion has been lost in the process of transmission to us. Yet from this and other treatises we do not have too much difficulty in drawing up a satisfactory curriculum involving the liberal disciplines of literature, rhetoric, logic, arithmetic, geometry, astronomy and music as a basis and with natural philosophy, moral philosophy and the divine science of metaphysics composing the superstructure. The

144

educative process is quite clear, too, from the discussions in the *Organon* concerning method and from the actual procedures followed in each investigation he undertakes in separate works. One may consider the *Politics* as a goal to which all the other discussions are suitable means.

It is quite evident that every *polis* is a community of free men whose aim is the highest good of the citizens which constitute it. In the natural order there is a progressive development of communities from the original state of a simple household of husband, wife, children and slaves, through the intermediate stage of villages, composed of many households, to the relatively complete organization which is a State. The family is the fundamental unit established by nature for the alleviation of men's daily needs, and the village was probably, in the beginning, a colony formed by the expansion of the family under the kingly rule of the eldest. The State comes into existence as a group of colonies united together to supply the necessities of life and it continues in existence for the sake of the good life: human happiness. Hence the State is a natural community of men who are by nature political animals united by the bond of justice. The precise type of organizational unity, of course, results from the constructive artistic ability of the citizens. The family is temporally prior to the State but the State is by nature prior to the family and to the individuals that compose it, since a whole is naturally prior to a part, the end is prior to the means and the perfect (self-sufficing) is prior to the imperfect.

Property is an element of the household and the art of acquiring and utilizing it is a part of the art of managing the household. Included in the property required for the provision of the necessities of life are living instruments, the slaves, who take precedence over all other properties since they are ministers of action rather than just instruments of production, like a shuttle in weaving. The slave belongs to the master wholly, and by nature is the type of being who should be ruled since he participates in the

145

intellectual principle only to the extent of apprehending what he should do as commanded by the master. He is strong in body and well-fitted for servile labor but incapable of the higher activities of reason required for the political life as such. Such a natural slavery is both expedient and right whereas slavery by right of conquest without respecting the natural differences of men is wrong, since it is based on the law of force and violence. The natural type of slavery is really a kind of friendship with a common interest whereas slavery by law or force is an unnatural relation between enemies. Master and slave are, also, related in a way proportional to the relation between soul and body.

The art of managing the household includes, too, the necessary and honorable type of wealth-acquiring, i.e. the procurement of the physical necessities of life from nature. Another type of wealth-getting is retail trade and it is justly censured because it involves the accumulation of money for its own sake. Trade which consists in a sort of natural barter is not reprehensible but commercial trading for the sake of money is. The most reprehensible type of such trading is that of usury which makes an unnatural use of an instrument of exchange in order to breed money. The useful aspects of household management involve the knowledge of live-stock, husbandry, including tillage and planting, the keeping of bees, fish, fowl or any animals useful to man, lumbering and mining. In all these pursuits the master controls the slaves with a monarchical rule. His relationship with his offspring is royal by virtue of love and respect; over his wife he exercises a constitutional rule for, although there may be exceptions, the male is generally more capable of command than the female. In these relationships appear the main concern of the management of the family: the acquisition of human excellence more so than that of wealth. The master ought to have moral virtue in perfection absolutely, the wife, children and slaves should have it relatively to their proper status. Since every family is a unit in the State the perfection of the whole depends upon the perfection of the family; women and children must be educated "with an eye to the constitution." The children grow up to be citizens and half the free persons in the State are women.

From a consideration of the household Aristotle goes on to an historical investigation of the ideal State. Beginning near at hand he evaluates the communities proposed by Plato in the *Republic* and the *Laws*. In the first, the abolition of private property and the family will harm rather than aid the State by the increase of dissension and the destruction of the affection naturally felt for wives and offspring. Private property is a means to individual happiness and helps in the cultivation of the virtue of liberality. It is quite impractical to advocate a communism of women and children, and Socrates' principle, *the greater the unity of the State the better* is self-defeating and self-destructive of the very nature of the State. Pluralistic differentiation is essential and the only feasible unity is a proportional one. The self-sufficiency of a State requires lesser rather than a greater degree of unity. Furthermore, that which is common to the greatest number has the least care bestowed upon it. Each one will expect the other to fulfill a common duty. Each citizen will have a thousand sons and yet no son since anybody is equally the son of anybody. How will the guardians control the acts of homicides, unlawful loves and slanders which are especially evil when committed against fathers, mothers and near relatives? In the *Laws* Plato abandons the common status of women, children and property but leaves the Ideal State otherwise quite the same. The increase in the number of the citizens makes it really impractical, there is no limit to private property, no restrictions on the population increase and no provisions for proper foreign relations. The constitution implied is too oligarchical.

The regulation of property seems to be a problem in all states. Phaleas of Chalcedon thought that the citizens of a State ought to have equal possessions which would not

147

be too bad if the possessors were living in neither luxury nor penury. The regulation of moderation in possessions is not the central point. It is the desires of men which must be moderated and this requires an equal education for all, which is not feasible. It is quite impractical to expect all men to be satisfied with numerical equality. Hippodamus of Miletus divided the land into three parts and the citizens into three groups: artisans, husbandmen and warriors. But the artisans were allotted no land, the first portion being given over to the worship of the gods; the husbandmen had no weapons. Hence, both classes could easily become the slaves of the warriors. Only these latter would have an actual share in government. And, who would cultivate the land of the warriors? If they do it they are husbandmen. If the husbandmen do it they will cultivate their own land and the warrior's land too: how will they supply the quantity of produce needed for two households? Hippodamus, also, reduces the judges to arbiters since he desires them to confer about the decision to be rendered. He proposes such a readiness to change existing laws that laws would lose all requisite force and become enfeebled. The most praiseworthy of existing States, those of Sparta, Crete and Carthage have serious imperfections. The Spartans have trouble controlling the slaves; their women are too influential, they control the wealth and live in a state of intemperance and luxury; there is a gross inequality of property; the legislators are notably open to bribery. The Cretan constitution is like the Spartan, a narrow and faction-ridden oligarchy. It dispenses too much without written law. The Carthaginian constitution is an oligarchy with certain democratic features. It lays too much stress on wealth and is not concerned about positions which involve conflicts of interest being held by the same men. The greatest offices can be bought; wealth is of more account than virtue. Solon is held up for respect because he was considered to have been a good legislator who emancipated the people, established the Athenian democracy and harmonized the various ele-

148

ments in the State. About other legislators little more need be said.

A knowledge of the essence and attributes of different kinds of governments depends upon a knowledge of what makes a citizen a citizen since the state is a composite of individual citizens. One is not a citizen because he lives in a certain place; nor is one a citizen because he has no legal right except that of suing and being sued; nor one too young or too old to perform state duties. His special characteristic is that he shares in the administration of justice and in offices. From the point of view of democracy a citizen is one who has the power to take part in the deliberative or judicial administration of the State. And a state is a body of citizens sufficing for the purpose of life. From another point of view, the State is a partnership of citizens in a constitution. The function of a citizen will be relative to the constitution.

As to the problem whether the virtue of a good man and a good citizen is the same or not one must first investigate what the virtue of a citizen is. If there are many forms of government it is clear that there is not one single political virtue which is perfect virtue, and the good citizen need not be the good man. Every citizen must have the virtue of a good citizen, otherwise the State cannot be a perfect organization of citizens. But they will not have the virtue of a good man unless it is assumed that the citizens be good men as well as good citizens. Taking States under a random consideration the virtue of a citizen is not always identical with the virtue of a good man. According to Aristotle's concept of the *Ideal State* the virtue of a good man would render him both capable of ruling and being ruled, of administering justice, of living temperately and courageously with his fellow-men and, thus, give him the virtue of a good citizen. Good men are good citizens; good citizens are good men in Aristotle's Utopia. Because mechanics and laborers cannot practice virtue while leading the life of mechanics and laborers they will not be included in the

149

category of citizens. In oligarchies no laborer can be a citizen because the qualifications are too high; a mechanic may be since the actual majority of them are rich.

There are three types of governments, each of which is a true form because the good is the common interest of all. To each true form corresponds a perversion in which the goal is a private rather than a common interest. When the rule is in the hands of one, the good form is kingship and its perversion is tyranny. When the control is in the hands of the few, the good form is aristocracy, and its perverse form is oligarchy. When the rule is in the hands of the many, the true form is a constitutional government and its perversion is a democracy. Absolutely speaking, the best form of government is the kingly and its opposite, tyranny, is the worst. Relatively, democracy seems to be the least offensive of all perverted forms of rule. It is considered as perverted because its goal is not the common good of all but the interest of the needy. Actually the essential distinction between oligarchy and democracy is not based on numbers, for the many could be rich and the few poor, but on the fact that whenever rule is based on wealth there is an oligarchy, when it is based on poverty there is a democracy.

There are five types of monarchy: 1) according to law, which may be called a generalship for life; some are hereditary and others elective; 2) legal and hereditary, almost a tyranny, as found among Barbarians; 3) Dictatorship, a legal and elective tyranny; 4) heroic, exercised over willing subjects but limited to certain functions of general and judge; 5) absolute monarchy similar to the control of the household. The last is, perhaps, the best. It arose somewhat naturally to satisfy the needs of primitive society; it is now out of fashion and objectionable in many ways, such as, it tends to become hereditary and thus incompetent men become rulers and no single man can attend properly to all the aspects of government.

States are composed of many different elements: husbandmen (the food-producing class), mechanics (who practice the arts), traders, serfs or laborers, the military, politicians, wealthy, magistrates and officers (rulers). There may be combinations of these in the same men but the distinction between rich and poor is mutually exclusive. Hence arises the opinion that there are two kinds of governments: oligarchy and democracy. Of the latter there are five types: 1) based on equality—all share alike in government; 2) based on a low property qualification; he who loses his property loses his rights; 3) all citizens under no disqualification share in government but the law is supreme; 4) every citizen is admitted to government and the law is supreme; 5) the multitude has supreme power even over the laws. This last form easily degenerates into a tyranny of the many. The different kinds of oligarchies are: 1) property qualification is such that poor have no share in the government; 2) a high qualification and vacancies are filled by election; if the election is made out of all qualified persons it tends to aristocracy, if out of a privileged class, oligarchy; 3) son succeeds father; 4) hereditary but magistrates are supreme and not the law; this becomes a dynastic sort of rule. In many States the constitution may not be democratic but because of education and the habits of people it can be administered democratically. Or the constitution may be democratic and administered in an oligarchical spirit. This happens mostly after a revolution. Aristocracy is a government by the best who alone are citizens. In this type the good man is absolutely the same as the good citizen. If the magistrates are chosen according to wealth and merit you have one sub-type and, another, if according to wealth, virtue and numbers. There are two parts of any good government: the actual obedience of the laws and the goodness of the laws which they obey. In actual fact, the admixture of rich and poor is called a constitutional government and the combination of freedom, wealth and virtue is called an aristocracy. A constitutional government arises from a combination of elements found in both democracy and oligarchy. It is a sort of mean between them. In oligarchies they fine the rich if they do not serve as judges and give no pay to the poor; in democracies they pay the poor and do not fine the rich. Democracy requires no or a small property qualification from members of the assembly; oligarchies require a high one. The appointment of magistrates by lot is considered democratic and their election is oligarchical. Assuming a medium position would be the mark of a polity or constitutional government. In a tyranny the arbitrary power of an individual is supreme, he is responsible to no one, governs all alike, against their will with a view to his own advantage.

What is the best constitution for most states and the best life for most men, neither assuming a standard of virtue above the ordinary, nor an exceptional education, nor an ideal state, but a form of government which states in general can attain? It will be neither the rule of the poor nor of the rich but the rule of the middle class, for it is the mean condition in which men are most ready to follow the rational principle. Those who have too much of the goods of fortune are neither willing nor able to submit to authority; those who are very poor are too degraded and are unable to rule. Those in the middle class do not covet others' goods nor do others covet theirs. When the middle class is also larger and stronger than both the other classes or at least either singly, the state is most likely to be administered well.

All constitutions must make appropriate provisions for three aspects of government: the legislative, executive and judicial. Under the legislative will come matters concerning war and peace, passing laws, electing magistrates and auditing their accounts. How these powers are assigned will depend upon the type of constitution. Under the executive branch are included all the offices whether of priests, political officers, masters of choruses, heralds, ambassadors, superintendents, inspectors, etc., as to how many there should be, how and where set up, the duration of the terms of office, etc. The judicial branch is set up as to the number of courts, the source of the judges, the manner of selecting the judges according to the requirements of the constitution.

Revolutions may arise in any kind of state. The universal and chief cause of revolutions is the desire of equality or inequality. Inferiors revolt in order to become equal; equals revolt in order to become superior. The motives of revolutions are the desire for gain and honor or the fear of dishonor and loss. Causes of revolutions are insolence, fear, excessive predominance, contempt, disproportionate increase in some part of the state, election intrigues, carelessness, etc. Revolutions are effected either by force or fraud. Revolutions in democracies are generally caused by the intemperance of demagogues resulting in a persecution of the rich or the inciting of the mob by oratory to put power into the hands of the few. In oligarchies the oppression of the people and the internal rivalry of the oligarchs may bring on a revolution. Aristocracies are overthrown when the mass of the people have a notion that they are as good as their rulers or an individual wants to rule alone. In order to guard against the overthrow of a government we must know the causes which destroy constitutions and be on our guard against them. In particular there must be a careful watch over obedience to the laws, more especially in small matters. Guard against the beginnings of change. All citizens must be treated with a proportional equality. Tenure of offices should be restricted. The citizens should be kept aware of the dangers, proximate and remote, which could overthrow the government. Contentions and quarrels should be controlled. The power of individuals and the opportunities for personal aggrandizement should be moderated. A strict supervision should be maintained over all revenues and expenditures; accounts should be audited regularly and publicly. Special qualifications should be demanded for the holding of the highest offices: loyalty to the established constitution, the greatest administrative

153

capacity, virtue and justice proper to the form of government. In the choice of a general skill should be more important than virtue, if both cannot be found in the same man. In an office of trust more than ordinary virtue is required. What contributes most to the permanence of a constitution is the adaptation of education to the form of government. The best laws will be useless unless the youth are trained by habit and education in the spirit of the constitution. In a democracy the two fundamental principles are government by the majority and freedom. But freedom is not license, i.e. acting according to individual fancy. It is relative to the rule of the constitution. Royalty is preserved by the limitation of its powers so that it does not degenerate into a tyranny. Tyranny is preserved by loping off those who are superior; men of spirit are put to death; common meals, clubs and education are forbidden; anything calculated to inspire courage or confidence in the subjects is outlawed; literary assemblies and meetings for discussion are prohibited; means must be taken to prevent the subjects from becoming friendly with each other; close supervision by means of spies must be maintained over the subjects as regards their place of habitation, their occupations and utterances. Fear of informers prevent people from speaking their minds. Quarrels should be stimulated between friends and different classes of people to prevent unity. Subjects should be kept impoverished, dependent and in need. State projects should be instituted in order to keep everybody at hard work and thus prevent conspiracies. Multiply taxes, keep the state at war. In summary, a tyrant preserves his power by the humiliation of his subjects, the creation of mistrust among them and the prevention of unified action whereby power to overthrow him is accumulated. The tyrant must play the game of being a benevolent ruler by pretending to have a care of the public monies by avoiding all waste and publishing an account of the use of all revenues. He should appear to be dignified, kind and not harsh in order to inspire reverence rather than fear.

He should avoid any public display of vice or over-indulgence in pleasures, such as drunkenness. He should adorn and improve the state as if he were its guardian. He should appear to be earnest in the service of the gods since this inspires reverence for him and avoids the condemnation of injustice. Men of merit should be honored by the tyrant personally whereas all punishment should be inflicted by courts of law. In all the forementioned causes of revolutions, reasons for the breakdown of states and the methods for their preservation Aristotle has displayed an extensive knowledge of history and he uses it copiously to illustrate his points. His judgments are conclusions drawn from the facts of historical experience.

In order to set up a democracy one must realize that there are different species of it, depending on the differences of populations and the precise continuation of the properties and characteristics of a democracy. The basic property of a democratic state is liberty. One principle of it is for all to rule and to be ruled. Justice depends upon numerical equality and thus the poor, because they are more numerous, will have more power than the rich. The will of the majority is supreme. The second principle is that each man lives as he likes, whence arises the claim of men to be ruled by no one, if possible. If this is not possible then they desire to rule and be ruled in turns. Of democracies the best is an agricultural democracy. The next best is the pastoral, then the commercial, and the worst is that in which all share alike, all offices are open to all. This will not last unless well regulated by laws and customs. Extreme poverty should be avoided because it lowers the character of a democracy. Each citizen should be allotted enough out of the public revenue to enable him to purchase a small farm or make a beginning in trade or husbandry. The nobility should, among themselves, give the poor the opportunity of securing work. The poor should be prevented from plundering the rich.

The last two books of the *Politics* investigates the positive aspects of the best form of a state and the educational procedures in order to insure its development and preservation. Assuming that the best form of a constitution would be the one which would assure the living of the best life for all, he repeats his conclusions about the good life found in the *Ethics*. The best life for man would be a contemplative life of wisdom along with the moral virtues and an appropriate amount of both external goods and goods of the body. So the best form of government is one under which every man can act best and live happily. The first consideration in such a state would concern the population. Since a state must be relatively self-sufficient the actual number of the inhabitants cannot be too small nor too large. Just as in the case of all natural and artistic objects there is a relative maximum and minimum. If the population is too small it cannot be self-sufficient; when it is too large constitutional government is rendered impossible and no one is capable of achieving order out of such a multitude. If offices are to be distributed according to merit as judged by the citizens who elect the holders of the offices, the citizens must know each other's character. An impossible situation with a large multitude.

The territory of the state should be as near as possible self-sufficing. In size and extent it should be such as to permit the inhabitants to live temperately and liberally in the enjoyment of leisure. It should be difficult of access to the enemy and easy of egress by the inhabitants. For protective purposes it should be only large enough to be taken in at a single view, well situated as regards sea and land. Communication by sea is desirable for reasons of trade but a port in the center of the city might be detrimental because of the influx of foreigners and undesirables.

In character the citizens should possess a happy combination of high spirits and intelligence, and, thus, they should be a combination of Europeans and Asiatics. There must be husbandmen to produce food, artisans to construct the instruments of proper living and traders for the barter of necessary goods. These will not be citizens. The class of warriors will be citizens in the strict sense. In their youth they will actually function as such; in middle age they will be rulers and magistrates; in old age some will be selected as priests. They alone will be owners of land and each will have two parcels of it: one plot near the city and one near the frontier to insure an interest in the defense of the total state. Although the land is divided into public and private property there will be a friendly consent about an appropriate common use of private property for the common good.

The land should be in a healthy location with a natural abundance of springs and fountains of pure water. The streets and houses should be laid out according to a plan which would insure both beauty and adequate defense against an enemy. There should be a protective wall around the whole city. When a state is well-prepared defensively no enemy even thinks of attacking it.

By far the most important aspect of a state concerns the education of the citizens in the proper means for the attainment of happiness. Three things make men good and virtuous: nature, habit, rational principle. By nature one must be a man and, then, he learns by habit and instruction. He who would learn to command must first learn how to obey. From youth onward one should be accustomed by habit to obey and to live in accord with the laws of the constitution according to which peace is the goal of war and leisure the goal of toil. The virtues of temperance and courage, prudence and justice will develop gradually under direction and habitual exercise. The care of the body precedes the care of the soul and is ordered to it. Education should deal with development of the body, control of appetites and the development of the intellect. To ensure that the bodies of the future citizens be as fit as possible the age of marriage must be regulated so that those who are too young or too old do not beget children. The offspring of the too young tend to be small and badly developed; those of the too old are defective in body and mind. The age of marriage should be arranged so that both husband and wife are at the prime of life and thus better prepared to produce the best offspring. Women should marry when they are about 18; men when they are about 37. When the male has reached the age of about 55 the couple should cease having a family and should cohabit for the sake of health or some reason other than having children. Women who are with child should be careful of their diet and take a certain amount of exercise every day. Deformed children should not be permitted to live; when couples have children in excess, let abortion be procured before sense and life begin. After children have been born they should be supplied with milk for food and should be accustomed gradually to the cold and other hardships in order to strengthen the body. Up to the age of five there should be no demand of study or labor lest growth be impeded. Games should be cultivated, loud crying and screaming should be permitted in order to strengthen their voices. A strict supervision by the directors of education must be maintained over the stories told to the young, for all such are designed to prepare the way for the later life. The young should never be allowed to repeat or hear any indecency of speech. All indecent pictures, images and speeches should be banished from the stage. Youth should be kept strangers to all that is bad and, especially, to anything which would suggest vice or hate.

The education of children is the common interest of the state since it is for the good of the state that the children are trained in the way required by the constitution. From the age of seven education should be public, regulated by law and an affair of the state. The usual branches of education are: 1) reading and writing; 2) gymnastic exercises; 3) music and 4) drawing. With the exception of gymnastic exercises these are branches of learning we study with a view to leisure spent in intellectual activity. Reading and writing are also useful in household management and the political life. Drawing is helpful for developing a critical

158

judgment of artistic works and of the beauty of the human form. Gymnastic exercises of the lighter kind should be used in the education of children up to the age of puberty and 3 years after, but the physique must not be developed at the expense of the intellectual training, as in Sparta. Music not only relaxes, amuses and conduces to intellectual enjoyment but has a power of forming character. Therefore, it has a very precise role in the education of the citizen. But should children be taught to play and sing music? It seems impossible for those who do not perform to be good judges of the performance of others. Thus, those who are to be judges must be performers, beginning to practice at an early age and learning to appreciate and delight in what is good. They need not acquire the fantastic marvels of execution displayed by professionals. Any musical instrument intended only to give pleasure to the hearer, and, which requires extraordinary skill of hand should be rejected. Music should be studied for education, purgation and intellectual enjoyment. He promises to explain in his discussion of poetry (*Poetics*) what he means precisely by purgation. Unfortunately, if he kept his promise, we do not have any record of it, as is clear from the analysis of the *Poetics*. Melodies expressive of ethical conduct should be cultivated by children; melodies of action and passionate or inspiring melodies give pleasure and are conducive to the over-all development of all men.

OECONOMICA

After the incomplete *Politics*, Bekker's edition of the Aristotelian works include a treatise called *Economics*, made up of two books, the first of which contains 6 chapters and the second a continuous recital from page 1345-1353. Though Aristotelian in spirit there is evidence that the Master did not actually compose them. In some Latin versions there is a third book added concerning the duties of a wife in the household.

The science of Economics, as presented here, concerns the prudential management of the household as contrasted with *Politics*, the science of the city. The components of the household are man and property, as developed in the *Politics*. The union of male and female is a natural one whose goal is the propagation of the species and the achievement of the good life of happiness. Husband and wife cooperate, each in his or her own way, to achieve this two-fold purpose. Nature has made the male stronger in order to protect the family physically and educate the offspring; the female is better equipped to nurture the children. A man must avoid doing any wrong to his wife. Husband and wife ought not to approach each other with false affectation in their person or their manners, "for if the society of husband and wife requires such embellishments, it is no better than play-acting on the tragic stage." The proper management of the household also includes the apportionment of work, punishment and food for the slaves. As regards wealth, the economist ought to possess four qualities: to be able to acquire it and guard it; to order his possessions and use them properly. The house should be physically arranged for the health and well-being of its inhabitants.

Book Two is mainly concerned with examples of the various means employed by noteworthy men of history to provide themselves with money for the management of various types of economies: the Royal, Satrapic, Political and Personal. As such it seems a little out of place in the present treatise. The third Book is more pertinent since it concerns the duties of a wife regarding the management of the internal affairs of the household.

A good wife should be the mistress of the home, responsible for the care of all within it including the expenditure of funds on such festivities, dress and ornamentation as are approved by her husband. Her excellence derives from self-control, and an honorable and well-ordered life

160

rather than from the costliness of raiment or an abundance of wealth. In all matters she should aim to carry out the wishes of her husband, dread above all things the gossip of gadding women, endure difficulties with patience and gentleness, and rule the home without complaint and criticism. If there seems to be a reason for charging her husband with wrong let her rather attribute the unpleasantness to his ignorance, sickness or accidental errors. The wife should remember that she is a partner in his life and in the procreation of children than which nothing can be greater or more divine. While praying that her husband may be spared adversity, if trouble should come, she should consider that here a good woman receives her highest praise. In times of stress they should be faithful and dutiful. "To find partners in prosperity is easy enough; but only the best women are ready to share in adversity."

The husband will treat his wife in a similar way since she is the partner of his life and parenthood. He should expect nothing more divine than to beget children by a noble and honored wife, assist her in the proper rearing of them in virtuous living, be faithful to her, love and trust her as his own. To a wife nothing is of more value than honored and faithful partnership with her husband. Between a free woman and her lawful spouse there should be a reverent and modest mingling of love and fear; fear such as is felt between righteous and honorable partners. There is no greater blessing on earth than when husband and wife rule their home in harmony of mind and will, each vying with the other in the effort to contribute most to the happiness of the home and to excel in virtue and righteousness.

The preceding presentation of the contents of the *Aristotelian Corpus* was compiled as an appropriate background for the *Aristotle Dictionary* which follows. As is quite evident to the reader, very little attempt has been made to "interpret" or evaluate the ideas discussed by Aristotle

161

himself or to correlate them with the development of logic, the physical sciences, ethics, aesthetics, politics, metaphysics, etc. since his time. This does not mean that there have been no worthwhile contributions made to these areas of intellectual curiosity since the fourth century B.C. Quite the contrary. But I have judged that an analytical presentation of what Aristotle is supposed to have taught about these many subjects would be more suitable to this type of book. The analysis or paraphrase or simple repetition of his words should supply us with an agreeable environment for an appreciation of his definitions, conclusions and 'bold statements' presented in a somewhat out-of-context fashion in a dictionary.

In the dictionary itself references are made to the appropriate *loci* of the quotations in accord with the generally accepted method of giving the precise page, column and lines in the Bekker edition of the Greek published in 1831. This is of practical value since there have been many translations of the works of Aristotle and most of them include some references to the Bekker *loci*. No matter what the translation, if it has been made in consultation with that monumental work, any reader can find the actual context from which the definitions, etc. have been extracted. By way of illustration of the method of reference: if the quotation in the dictionary is followed by DE A 2.7.419a 15-20, that would mean that in the Bekker edition of Aristotle's works in the treatise entitled *De Anima* (peri psyches) Book 2, chapter 7, page 419, column a, lines 15-20 you will find that statement. Actually the pages of the Bekker text are numbered consecutively in the first two volumes of a four volume set, the last two devoted to commentaries and other related works. Hence the absolutely essential parts of the reference numbers are the page numbers, column designation and line reference. Some Aristotelian works are divided merely into chapters rather than books. In that case the first number is the chapter, the next is the page, etc.

162

EXAMPLE   DE A–2. 7. 419a15-20

DE A – De Anima (peri psyches—on the Soul).
2. – Book 2
7. – Chapter 7
419 – page 419 in the Bekker edition
a – column a, i.e. left hand column of 2
columns
15-20 – lines 15-20.

REFERENCES

ARISTOTELIS OPERA EDIDIT ACADEMIA REGIA BORUS-
SICA. Vol. 1-2. Aristoteles Graece ex recognitione Immanuelis Bek-
keri. Berolini, 1831. Pp. 1-1462.

ARISTOTELES. ARISTOTELIS OPERA OMNIA. GRAECE ET
LATINE. Aemilius Heitz, Parisiis, 1848.

THE WORKS OF ARISTOTLE. Translated into English under
the editorship of W. D. Ross. Oxford University Press, 1908-1931.

LOEB CLASSICAL LIBRARY. Greek and English texts published at various times by Harvard University Press, Cambridge,
Mass.

ARISTOTLE'S PHYSICS. Translated by Richard Hope. University of Nebraska Press, 1961.

ARISTOTLE METAPHYSICS. Translated by Richard Hope. Ann
Arbor Paperbacks. The University of Michigan Press, 1960.

ARISTOTLE'S POETICS: THE ARGUMENT. By Gerald F.
Else. Harvard U. Press, 1957.

Theodore E. James

Manhattan College.

ARISTOTLE

DICTIONARY

KEY OF REFERENCES

Many of the treatises that constitute the generally accepted Aristotelian canon are commonly designated by Latin titles.

Organon (O. F. Owen) comprising:

CAT—Categories
DE I—De Interpretatione
P A—Prior Analytics
PO A—Posterior Analytics
T—Topics
S E——Sophistici Elenchi

C—Constitution of Athens (J. S. Dymes)
POL—Politics (E. Walford)
ECO—Economics (E. Walford)
RH—Rhetoric (T. Buckley)
P—Poetics (T. Buckley)
N E—Nicomachean Ethics (R. W. Browne)
E E—Eudemian Ethics (T. Taylor)
M M—Magna Moralia (T. Taylor)
H A—Historia Animalium (T. Taylor: H. E. W.)
PHY—Physics (T. Taylor)
DE A—DE Anima (H. E. W.: T. Taylor)
ME—Metaphysics (J. H. M'Mahon)
DE V—De Vita et Morte (Taylor)

DE R—De Respiratione (Taylor)
DE IN—De Incessu Animalium (Taylor)
DE M A—De Motu Animalium (Taylor)
DE C—De Caelo (Taylor)
DE M—De Meteorologia (Taylor)
DE G ET C—De Generatione et Corruptione (Taylor)
DE P A—De Partibus Animalium (Taylor)
DE S ET S—De Sensu et Sensibili (Taylor and H. E. W.)
DE M ET R—De Memoria et de Reminiscentia (Taylor)
DE SOM—De Somniis (Taylor)
DE S—De Somno (Taylor)
DE DIV—De Divinatione per somnum (Taylor)
DE L ET B—De Longitudine et Brevitate Vitae (Taylor)
DE G A—De Generatione Animalium (Taylor)

A

Abstinence

He who avoids all pleasures, like a boor, is an insensible sort of person.

N E–2. 2. 1104a24-25

Accent, Fallacy of

But concerning accent . . . it is not easy to frame an argument except in writings and poems as, for instance, some defend Homer against those who accuse him of having spoken absurdly: to men ou kataputhetai ombro, for they solve this by accent saying that ou is to be marked with an acute accent.

S E–4. 166b1-6

Accident

Now those things which are not predicated of a subject I call per se, but those which are so predicated I call accidents.

PO A–1. 4. 73b8-10

I call accidents those that are neither inherent in all nor per se, as musical or white is said to be in an animal.

PO A–1. 4. 73b4-5

But whatever do not signify substance, but are predicated of another subject, which is neither the thing itself, nor something belonging to it, are accidents, as white is predicated of man, since man is neither white, nor anything belonging to white. . . . Such as do not signify substance it is necessary should be predicated of a certain subject.

PO A–1. 22. 83a24-31

Accident is that which is not any of these, neither definition, nor property, nor genus; yet it is present with a thing and may not be present.

T–1. 5. 102b4-6

That was said to be accident which is neither definition, nor genus, nor property, yet is present with a thing.

T–1. 8. 103b17-19

We must especially have regard to the definition of accident . . . we designate that an accident which may be or may not be with a certain thing.

T–4. 1. 120b30-35

Of all things the easiest to establish is the accident, for it is enough to show that it belongs to something. . . . On the other hand, the hardest to overthrow is the accident . . . it is impossible to subvert it except by showing that it does not belong to something.

T–7. 5. 155a28-36

That is said to be an accident which can be present or not present in a subject, or that in whose definition is included a relation to that in which it is.

PHY–1. 3. 186b18-21

Still from these it is manifest that there is nothing to prevent accident sometimes, and relatively from becoming a property, as to sit being accident, when someone alone sits it will then be a property . . . however, it will not be a property simple.

T–1. 5. 102b20-26

An accident is denominated as that which is inherent in something, and which it is true to affirm is so, yet not either necessarily, or for the most part.

ME—4. 30. 1025a14-15

Whatever may be neither always nor for the most part this I call accident.

ME—5. 2. 1026b31-33

An entity subsists according to accident . . . either because both are inherent in the same entity, or because they are inherent in that entity, or because they are the same with that in which the accidents are inherent, and of which the thing itself is predicated.

ME—4. 7. 1017a8-22

No accident is either always or very frequently produced.

DE DIV—1. 463a2-3

Accident, Fallacy of

Fallacies which arise from accident are when something is attributed to a thing because it is attributed to one of its accidents . . . Thus if Coriscus is different from man, he is different from himself, for he is a man.

S E—5. 166b28-33

Accident, Fallacy of, refutation of

With respect to those arguments which are from accident, there is one and the same solution for them all, for since it is uncertain when an assertion can be made of a thing because of accident . . . it must be said that the conclusion is not necessary.

S E—24. 179a26-31

Accidents (misfortunes)

Now accidents are whatever things happen against all calculation, and proceed not from criminal principle.

RH—1. 13. 1374b6-7

Accidents, no demonstrative Knowledge of

Of accidents, however, which are not per se after the manner in which things per se have been defined, there is no demonstrative science, since it is not possible to demonstrate the conclusion of necessity, because accident may not be present.

PO A—1. 6. 75a18-22

Act

Hence from what we have stated it is clear that whatever exists of necessity is in act, so that if eternal natures are prior in existence, act is prior to potency, and some things, as the first substances, are in act without potency, but others are in act with potency, namely those which are prior by nature but posterior in time; lastly there are some which are never in act but are in potency only.

DE I—13. 23a21-26

Vide ENERGY.

Acting Unjustly

The voluntary commission of hurt in contravention of law.

RH—1. 10. 1368b6-7

Action (As One of the Categories)

Action, for example, 'cuts,' 'burns.'

CAT—4. 2a3; T—1. 9. 103b23

Action

If to be able is to be disposed, and if the use of anything is action; to use is to act and to have used is to have acted.

T–4. 4. 124a31-34

Ability to suffer or to act would be a property of being.

T–5. 9. 139a7-8

Both action and passion admit of contraries and more and less, for to make warm is contrary to making cold; to be warm, contrary to being cold . . . they are also capable of more and less, to be heated, more or less, to be grieved, more or less; wherefore to act and to suffer admit the more and less.

CAT–9. 11b1-10

Action is motion.

E E–2. 3. 1220b26-27

Action is always particular.

N E–6. 9. 1141b16

Moral purpose then is the origin of action, i.e. the original motive, but not the final cause.

N E–6. 2. 1139a31-32

The end or character of an action depends upon the choice made at the moment of performing it.

N E–3. 1. 1110a13-14

It is actions as we have said that determine the character of the resulting moral states.

N E–2. 2. 1103b30-31

He who performs any action, not knowing what the action is, nor to what end it will lead, nor about whom such action is conversant, acts from ignorance essentially, and therefore acts involuntarily.

E E—2. 9. 1225b5-7

An action which is due to ignorance is always non-voluntary; but it is not involuntary, unless it is followed by pain and excites a feeling of regret.

N E—3. 2. 1110b18-22

Action always consists in two things: when that for the sake of which the action is exists, and that which acts for the sake of this.

DE C—2. 12. 292b6-7

All things whatsoever which men do not of themselves, they do either by chance, or from compulsion, or by nature.

RH—Bk. 1. 10. 1368b33-36

A man's actions are signs of his habit.

RH—Bk. 1. 9. 1367b31-32

Actions of Man

It is not correct to say that the soul is angry . . . it is better to say that man pities, or thinks or learns with or by the soul.

DE A—1. 4. 408b11-15

Active Intellect

(Besides the mind that is potentially all things) there is mind such that it makes all things; and this is like a habit, for example like light; for light also makes colors which are in potentiality to be in some way actual colors. And this (intellect) is separable and impassible, unmixed, since it is in its substance actuality; for that which is act is always more noble than that which suffers.

DE A—3. 5. 430a13-19

172

Activity

Activity implies action and good action.

N E—1. 9. 1099a3

No activity is perfect if it be impeded.

N E—7. 14. 1153b16

Nothing is so pleasant or so lovable as the exercise of activity.

N E—9. 7. 1168a14-15

Actual

Every thing is able at one time to be actual, and at another not.

PHY—3. 1. 201b7-8

Actuality and Capacity

That which is hot in actuality, is cold in capacity; and that which is cold in actuality is hot in capacity.

DE G ET C—2. 7. 334b21-23

Actuality and Potentiality

In all the productions of nature and art what exists potentially is brought into entity only by that which is in actuality.

DE G A—2. 1. 734a30-31

Actually Infinite

Nothing is actually infinite.

DE G ET C—1. 3. 318a20-21

Adversity

Adversity renders those who are true friends apparent.

E E—7. 2. 1238a19-20

Affection, Examples of

'To be lanced,' 'to be burned' are affection.

CAT—4. 2a4

Affection

Dissimilarity of manners is most apt to interrupt affection.

ECO—Bk. 1. 4. 1344a18

There are two things which principally inspire mankind with care and affection, namely, the sense of what is one's own, and exclusive possession.

POL—Bk 2. 4. 1262b22-23

Affections

Vide passions.

Affirmation

Affirmation signifies something of something, and this is either a noun or anonymous, but what is in affirmation must be one and of one thing.

DE I—10. 19b5-7

Affirmation is the enunciation of something concerning something.

DE I—6. 17a25

Now each of the above (the ten categories), considered by itself is predicated neither affirmatively nor negatively, but from the connexion of these with each other affirmation and negation arises.

CAT—4. 2a4-7

Still without a verb there is neither affirmation nor negation, for 'is,' or 'will be,' or 'was,' or 'is going to be,' etc., are verbs, . . . since in addition to their meaning they signify time.

DE I—10. 19b12-14

Affirmation is prior to negation; just as the hot is to the cold.

DE C—2. 3. 286a25-26

Affirmation and Negation

The affirmation and negation are one, which indicate one thing of one, either of a universal, being taken universally, or in like manner if it is not.

DE I—8. 18a13-15

For every affirmation and negation seems to be either true or false.

CAT—4. 2a6

Affirm and Deny

To affirm and deny something of many, or many of one, is not one affirmation nor one negation, except that it is some one thing which is manifested from the many.

DE I—11. 20b13-15

Affirmative

It is necessary in every syllogism that one of the premises be affirmative and one universal.

P A—1. 24. 41b6-7

Agent

Such agents, therefore, as have not a form in matter, these are impassive; but such as have, are passive.

DE G ET C—1. 7. 324b4-6

Agriculture

Agriculture should be ranked first because it is just.

ECO—Bk. 1. 1. 1343a27-28

Agriculture contributes much towards fortitude.

ECO—Bk. 1. 2. 1343b2-3

Air

Air is naturally moist.

DE S ET S—5. 443b5-6

Thus, since he who says the property of air is that it is breatheable, assigns property in potentiality (for a property of this kind is that which is capable of being breathed) but also assigns the property to that which is not; for although an animal should not exist, which is naturally capable of breathing the air, yet the air may exist, though if animal is not it is not possible to breathe; hence a thing of such a kind as that it may be breathed will not then be the property of air.

T—5. 9.138b30-35

Since he who asserts the property of air to be the respirable, asserts the property of a certain thing of similar parts, but assigns such a thing as is verified of a certain air, but is not spoken of all air (for all is not respirable), the respirable would not be the property of air.

T—5. 5. 135a33-135b1

The air which is emitted by expiration is hot, but that which is received by inspiration is cold.

DE R—5. 472b34-35

The air co-impels the natural motion of every thing.

DE C—3. 2. 301b22

The air flows circularly, because it is drawn along together with the circulation of the universe.

DE M—1. 3. 341a1-2

176

Air produces hearing.

DE A–2. 8. 419b34

The air in itself has no sound, because it is too easily divisible.

DE A–2. 8. 420a7

Wind is not air; vide WIND.

Aliment

Aliment belongs to matter.

DE G ET C–2. 8. 335a15-16

All

Things are able either to act or suffer, either to be or not to be, either in an infinite, or in some definite time.

DE C–1. 12. 283a7-9

Alliation

Alliation is a motion according to quality. Vide: ALTERATION.

DE C–1. 3. 270a27

Alter ego

A friend is another I.

M M–2. 15. 1213a13

Alteration

For alteration is the mutation of quality.

CAT–14. 15b11

Of motion there are six species: generation, corruption, increase, decrease, alteration, and change of place.

CAT–14. 15a13-14

177

Ambidexterous

Of all animals man is the only one that can use both hands equally.

H A—2. 1. 497b31-32

Ambition

It seems that ambition makes most people wish to be loved rather than to love others.

N E—8. 9.1159a12-14

Men are guilty of the greatest crimes through ambition, and not from necessity.

POL—Bk. 2. 7. 1267a12-14

Amphiboly (Equivocation)

As then in deceptions from equivocation, which mode of paralogism seems to be the most usual, some are manifest to every one, for almost all absurd sentences are from diction, for instance 'which of the cows will deliver before?' 'Neither, but both from the rear.'

S E—33. 182b13-18

Of refutations which are from equivocation and ambiguity some have a question with several meanings, others a conclusion with different meanings; for instance, 'he who is silent, speaks.'

S E—19. 177a9-12

Amphiboly, Fallacy of

Such arguments as these are from amphiboly: 'I wish that you the enemy may take' . . . also 'there must be sight of what one sees'; 'he sees the pillar, does the pillar have sight?'

S E—4. 166a6-10

Analogous

I call it analogous when the relation of the second term to the first is similar to that of the fourth to the third; for then the fourth is used instead of the second or the second instead of the fourth.

P—21. 1457b16-19

Analogy

Bone is analogous to the spine, the nail to the horn, the hand to the claw, the feather to the scale, and so on.

H A—1. 1. 486b19-21

According to analogy are things one, as many as are disposed as one thing in relation to another.

ME—4. 6. 1016b34-35

Anger

Desire for vengeance on account of apparent contempt.

T—8. 1. 156a32

A desire accompanied by pain of a revenge which presents itself, on account of an apparent slight from persons acting toward one's self, or some of one's friends, unbecomingly.

RH—2. 2. 1378a31-33

Is in the irascible part of the soul.

T—2. 7. 113a36-113b1

Anger is productive of heat.

DE P A—2. 4. 650b35

Anger possesses a certain pleasure; since it is accompanied with the hope of vengeance.

E E—3. 1. 1229b31-32

179

Through the medium of anger and excited feeling arise acts of vengeance.

RH—Bk. 1. 10. 1369b11-12

Animal

An animal is defined because of the possession of sense perception.

DE S—1. 454b24-25

Animals, in so far as each is an animal, have sensation necessarily, for it is thus that we distinguish what is animal and what is not.

DE S ET S—1. 436b10-12

A man and an ox are both animal and are so named univocally, since not only the name but also the definition is the same; if a man should state in what sense each is an animal the statements would be the same.

CAT—1. 1a8-10

All animals are less wise than man.

DE P A—4. 10. 686b22-24

It seems that animals possess a certain natural power about each of the passions of the soul, with respect to wisdom and folly, fortitude and timidity, mildness and asperity, and other habits of a similar kind.

DE H A—9. 1. 608a13-17

Animals are viviparous, oviparous, or vermiparous.

H A—1. 5. 489a34-35

In some species, there is neither male nor female.

H A—1. 2. 489a12-13

The function of animals is hardly anything other than to produce young which in plants corresponds to seed and fruit.

DE G A—1. 4. 717a21-22

Many animals have no voice: for example, animals that are bloodless.

DE A 2. 8. 420b9-10

Animals therefore are composed from both similar and dissimilar parts; but the similar are for the sake of the dissimilar parts.

DE P A—2. 1. 646b10-12

Fat animals are barren. For that which ought to pass from the blood into the genital seed, this is consumed into fat and suet.

DE P A—2. 5. 651b13-14

Animals do not live prosperously at the same seasons, nor are they similarly happy in all excesses of heat and cold.

H A—8. 18. 601,23-25

Some animals have gills, and others have lungs, but no animal has both.

DE R—10. 476a6-7

Larger, for the most part, live longer than smaller animals.

DE L ET B—4. 466a13-15

Animate and Inanimate

The living being appears to differ from the inanimate being in two respects particularly: movement and feeling.

DE A—1. 2. 403b25-27

Antithesis

Vide CONTRADICTION.

Appetite

Appetite is a desire for what is pleasant.

RH—Bk. 1. 11. 1370a17-18

The appetite is desire, passion and will.

DE A—2. 3. 414b2

Appetite is divided into three things, viz. into will, anger and desire.

E E—2. 7. 1223a26-27

It is evident that this faculty of the soul that is called appetite is the cause of motion.

DE A—3. 10. 433a31

All such things as appear pleasant are produced in action on the impulse of appetite.

RH—Bk. 1. 10. 1369b15-16

I call all those appetites irrational which men desire not from any conception which they form: of this kind are all which are said to exist naturally, as those of the body; thirst or hunger, in the case of sustenance; objects of touch generally, etc.

RH—1. 11. 1370a19-24

Appetites attended by reason are all those whatsoever which men exercise from a persuasion.

RH—1. 10. 1370a25

Aporema

A dialectical syllogism of contradiction.

T—8. 11. 162a17-18

Arguments

In disputation, there are four genera of arguments, the

182

didactic, the dialectic, the peirastic (or tentative), and the contentious.

S E—2. 165a38-39

An argument is most clear in one way, and that the most popular, if it be so concluded as to require no further interrogation.

T—8. 12. 162a35-37

We ought to make universal records of arguments, even if that discussed be particular; for thus it will be possible to make one argument many.

T—8. 14. 164a3-5

There are five reprehensions of an argument per se, the first, indeed, when from the questions asked nothing is concluded, neither the proposition, nor, in short, any thing; all or the greatest part of those from which the conclusion arises, being either false or improbable; and neither things being taken away, nor being added, nor some being taken away, but others added, the conclusion is produced. The second is, if there be not a syllogism against the thesis from such things, and in such a way, as was mentioned before. The third, if there is indeed a syllogism, from certain additions, but these should be worse than those questioned, and less probable than the conclusion. Again, if certain things are taken away, for sometimes men assume more than is necessary, so that the syllogism does not result from these being granted; further, if from things more improbable and less credible than the conclusion, or if from things true indeed, but which require more labor to demonstrate than the problem.

T—8. 11. 161b19-33

Aristocracy

A state that is governed by more than one, but by a few only, we call an aristocracy: either because the govern-

183

ment is in the hands of the most worthy citizens, or because it is the best form for the city and its inhabitants.

POL—Bk. 3. 7. 1279a34-37

A state governed by the best men, upon the most virtuous principles, and not according to any arbitrary definition of good men, has alone a right to be called an aristocracy. For it is there only that the good man and the good citizen are identified; while in other states men are good only relatively to their own country. Moreover, there are some other states, which are called by the same name, that differ both from oligarchies and free states, wherein they choose men for office, not only according to their wealth, but according to their merit.

Now this polity differs from both of the above and is called an aristocracy; for in those governments wherein virtue is not their common care, there are still men of high worth and approved merit. Whatever state, then, as at Carthage, favors the rich, the virtuous, and the citizens at large, is a sort of aristocracy; but when only the two latter are held in esteem, as at Lacedaemon, and the state is jointly composed of these, it is a virtuous democracy. These are the two species of aristocracies over and above the first, which is the best of all governments. There is also a third, which is to be found whenever any one of what are called free states inclines to the dominion of a few.

POL—Bk. 4. 7. 1293b5-21

Aristocracy is a form of government in which those hold office who can conform to the constitutional plan of education. By such education I mean that established by law.

RH—1. 8. 1356b33-35

All aristocracies are free oligarchies.

POL—Bk. 5. 7. 1306b23-25

Virtue is the object of an aristocracy.

POL—Bk. 4. 8. 1294a10-11

The end of aristocracy is the institutions relating to education and the principles of law.

RH—1. 8. 1366a5-6

It is evident that an aristocracy is to be preferred to a monarchy.

POL—Bk 3. 15. 1286b5-6

Aristocrats

Those who are naturally framed to bear the rule of free-men, whose superior virtue makes them worthy of the management of others.

POL—Bk. 3. 17. 1288a9-12

Army

He who will not bear arms injures the community.

RH—1. 1373b24

Art

Art must be the same thing as a productive state of mind under the guidance of true reason.

N E—6. 4. 1140a10

Art is the reason of the work without matter.

DE P A—1. 1. 640a31-32

Art is form.

ME—6. 9. 1034a24

From Art are generated those things of whatsoever there is a form in the soul.

ME—6. 7. 1032a32-1032b1

Art has to do with creation.   N E–6. 4. 1140a20

The end of art is production and not action.

                                                N E–6. 4. 1140a16

Art imitates nature.   DE M–4. 3. 381b6

Art imitates nature in this respect (i.e. evolving har-
monies out of dissimilars). The art of painting by joining
in the picture the varicolored elements brings about a
representation corresponding to the original object; so also
in music.   DE MUNDO–5. 396b11-15

The arrangement of anything through art is merely
incidental or accidental, not of the nature.

                                                PHY–2. 1. 193a14-16

Epic poetry and tragic poetry, and comedy and dithyrambic poetry, and the greatest part of the art pertaining
to the flute and the lyre, are entirely imitations.

                                                P–1. 1447a13-16

From sense, memory is produced, but from repeated
remembrance of the same thing, we get experience, for
many remembrances in number constitute one experience.
From experience, however, the universal now established in
the soul, the one beside the many which is a single unit within them all, the principle of art and science arises: if it is
conversant with coming-to-be you have art; if with being,
it is science.   PO A–2. 19. 100a3-9

An art comes into being when, out of many conceptions
of experience, one universal opinion is evolved with respect
to similar cases.   ME–1. 1. 981a5-7

Nothing comes from the carpenter to the matter, i.e. of the wood, nor any part of the carpenter's art into that which is made, but the form and species are given to the matter by the motion coming from him; and the soul in which the form is contained and also his knowledge move his hands or some other member with a motion of a certain quality varying according to what is to be created, the hands and the instruments move the matter.

DE G A–1. 22. 730b11-19

A bed, a coat and other things of the same kind in so far as they are by art have no innate impulse to change.

PHY–2. 1. 192b16-19

Art products require the pre-existence of a homogeneous cause, such as the art of a statue which precedes the statue; this cannot be spontaneous or produced automatically.

DE P A–1. 1. 640a28-30

Art and Experience

Experience is a knowledge of singulars, whereas art is of universals.

ME–1. 1. 981a15-16

Art (Medical)

Art is a cause of health.

RH–Bk. 1. 5. 1362a4

Article

A sound without signification which shows the beginning or end or distinction of a word.

P–20. 1457a6-7

Assembly

Of all magistracies a popular assembly is best suited to a democracy.

POL–Bk. 6. 2. 1317b28-30

187

Aspiration

All beings are naturally adapted to aspire after good.

M M—2. 7. 1205b35-36

Attorney

The pleader's business is nothing more than to prove the matter of fact, either that it is, or is not the case; that it has, or has not happened.

RH—Bk. 1. 1. 1354a26-28

Awake

To be awake is defined as loosening of sense.

DE S—1. 454b26-27

Axiom

What he who intends to learn any thing must necessarily possess, that I call an axiom.

PO A—1. 2. 72a16-17

B

Bad

The bad man is continually at war with, and in opposition to, himself.

M M—2. 11. 1211b3

Baldness

Man is manifestly the most bald of all animals.

DE G A—5. 3. 783b9

Baseness

It is pleasure which makes us do what is base.

N E—2. 2. 1104b9-10

Beauty

The chief forms of beauty are order, symmetry and limit, which the mathematical disciplines demonstrate in a special way.

M E—13. 3. 1078a36—1078b2

Beauty seems to be a certain symmetry of the members.

T—3. 1. 116b21-22

Beauty is different according to the several ages. The beauty of youth is having a body useful in enduring toils, whether those of the course or of personal exertion, himself being pleasant withal to look upon with a view to delight

189

. . . But the beauty of one who has attained life's prime is the fitness adapted to the fatigues of war with an aspect to be looked upon with pleasure tempered by awe. That of the old consists in the body being capable of the fatigues which it needs must undergo and exempt withal from pain by reason that it has none of the afflictions by which an old age is disfigured.

RH—1. 5. 1361b7-15

Some people are beautiful due to their native beauty while others seem to be so due to decorations.

S E—1. 164b20-21

The beautiful consists in magnitude and order.

P—7. 1450b36-37

Neither can any very small animal be beautiful . . . nor yet a very large animal.

P—7. 1450b37-39

The painter will not allow the foot of a figure, howsoever beautiful, to be out of proportion with the rest.

POL—3. 13. 1284b8-10

Beauty of words consists, as Licymnius observes, in the sound or in the idea conveyed or in their delicacy of application.

RH—3. 2. 1405b6-11

Beautiful things, however, are the virtues, and the works proceeding from virtue.

E E—7. 15. 1248b36-37

Beauty and Its Appearance

Some are beautiful on account of beauty, but others appear so from ornament.

S E—1. 164b20-21

Becoming

A just man becomes just by doing what is just and a temperate man becomes temperate by doing what is temperate.

N E—2. 3. 1105a17-19

Bees

It remains that bees generate the drones without coition; and that so far as they generate they are females, but that they have among themselves, in the same manner as plants, the female and the male.

DE G A—3. 10. 759b28-30

Bees have a foreknowledge of tempestuous weather and rain.

H A—9. 40. 627b10-11

Bees derive their wax from the gum of trees.

DE H A—5. 22. 553b28

Begging the Question

If then begging the question is to prove by itself what is not of itself manifest, this is not to prove, since both what is demonstrated and that by which the person demonstrates are alike dubious, either because the same things are assumed present with the same thing, or the same thing with the same things.

P A—2. 16. 65a26-29

Being, Analogy of

Now, being is spoken of in various senses, indeed, but in reference to one and to one certain nature, and not equivocally; but in like manner also, as everything conducive to health is termed so in reference to health, partly, indeed, in its preservation of that state, and partly in giving rise to it, and partly in being an indication of health, and partly in

191

being receptive of it . . . Thus is entity spoken of in various ways; but every entity in reference to one first cause; for some things because they are substances are styled beings; but others because they are affections of substances; but others because they are a way to substance, either as corruptions or privations, or qualities, or things formative or generative of substance or of those which are spoken of in reference to substance or the negations of any of these or of substance.

ME—3. 2. 1003a33-1003b10

Being

Being is multifariously predicated.

PHY—1. 3. 186b12

It is not possible that there should be one genus of beings or that unity or being should be such; for it is necessary that the differences of each genus both exist and that each should be one.

ME—2. 3. 998b22-24

That which is primarily being and not any particular being, but being simply or absolutely, will be substance.

ME—6. 1. 1028a30-31

If unity and being be a genus neither will being or unity constitute any difference.

ME—2. 3. 998b26-27

Being is not a genus.

PO A—2. 7. 92b14

Being must of necessity be when it is, and non-being, not be, when it is not; but it is not necessary that every being should be, nor that non-being should not be.

DE I—9. 19a23-24

192

It is better to be than not to be.

DE G ET C–2. 10. 336b28-29

Their being is living for the beings that live.

DE A–2. 4. 415b13

Being, Property of

Ability to suffer or to act would be a property of a being.

T–5. 9. 139a7-8

Being, as a Copula

Signifies a certain composition which is impossible to understand without the composing members.

DE I–3. 16b24-25

Vide ENTITY.

Being and Non-Being

It appears that it is possible for the same thing both to be and not to be, for every thing which may possibly be cut or may possibly walk, may also possibly not be cut, and not walk, and the reason is that every thing which is thus possible is not always actual, so that negation will also belong to it, for that which is capable of walking may not walk, and the visible may not be seen.

DE I–12. 21b12-17

Being and Truth

As each thing is disposed in regard to being so also is it in regard to truth.

ME–1a. 1. 993b31

Being from Anything

The 'being from anything' is said in one way to be that from which a thing is as from matter; and this in a twofold respect, either according to the first genus, or according to the last species.

ME–4. 24. 1023a26-28

Belief

We believe all things either through syllogism or from induction.

P A–2. 23. 68b13-14

Now there are three causes of a speaker's deserving belief; and these are prudence, moral excellence, and having our interests at heart.

RH–Bk. 2. 1. 1378a6-9

Things which have not yet been done, we do not yet believe to be possible; but it is evident that things which have been done are possible.

P–9. 1451b16-18

Belief never belongs to the brute animal, while imagination very often belongs to him.

DE A–3. 3. 428a20-21

Beneficence

Beneficence relates either to the safety, and the causes, whatever they are, of the existence of its object, or to his wealth, or to any other goods whose acquisition is not easy.

RH–Bk. 1. 5. 1361a30-31

Black

Black is a privation of white.

ME–9. 2. 1053b30-31

Blackness

Blackness is as it were a negation of seeing.

DE M–3. 4. 374b12-14

Blame

It is ridiculous to lay the blame of our wrong actions

194

upon external causes, rather than upon the facility with which we ourselves are caught by such causes.

N E—3. 1. 1110b13-15

Blood

The essential concoction of the blood is suet and fat.

DE P A—2. 6. 652a9-10

Blood also is hotter to the touch than water or oil; but is more rapidly congealed than either of these.

DE P A—2. 2. 648b32-33

According to age, the blood is different in quantity and quality.

H A—3. 19. 521a31-32

Boastfulness

Exaggerated humility is a form of boastfulness as well as excess.

N E—4. 13. 1127b26-27

Body

That which in every way and in three directions is divisible according to quantity is a body.

ME—4. 6. 1016b27-28

It is the bodies especially that appear to be substances, and particularly the natural bodies, which are, in fact, the principles of the other bodies.

DE A—2. 1. 412a11-12

Body could not be soul: for the body is not one of the things that can be attributed to an object.

DE A—2. 1. 412a17-18

Just as the eye is both pupil and sight, so the soul and the body are the animal.

DE A–2. 1. 413a2-3

The fully developed man has the upper parts of the body smaller than the lower parts . . . In infancy, man has the upper part greater than the lower.

H A–2. 1. 500b26-34

Earthly bodies tend downward to the middle.

DE C–1. 2. 269a27

It is evident that the first of bodies is perpetual, and that it has neither increase nor diminution, but is undecaying, unchanged in quality, and impassive.

DE C–1. 3. 270a12-15

It is evident that there cannot be an infinite body.

DE C–1. 6. 273a21-22

It is not possible, therefore, that there can be any simple body beyond the heavens. But if no simple, neither can any mixed body be there; for mixed body existing it is also necessary that there should be simple bodies.

DE C–1. 9. 278b35-279a2

I call those bodies simple which have a principle of motion according to nature, such as fire and earth, and the species of these, and also things allied to these.

DE C–1. 2. 268b27-29

Bond-Slaves

The poor were in a state of bondage to the rich, both themselves, their wives, and their children, and were called Pelatae (bond-slaves for hire) and Hektemori (paying a sixth of the produce as rent).

C–2

196

Bone

The nutriment is consumed into the bones.

DE P A–2. 6. 652a12

The bones of males are harder than those of females, and the bones of carnivorous animals than of those that are not carnivorous.

DE P A–2. 9. 655a12-13

Two bones, each of which is concave, are connected by an astragalus as a medium, which is convex in each extremity, and which enters into the concavity of each bone and thus conjoins it like a nail.

DE P A–2. 9. 654b19-21

There is no bone that is isolated and separated.

H A–3. 7. 516a9-10

Boundary

It is necessary that the boundary *from which,* and the boundary *to which* a thing is naturally adapted to be moved should be specifically different.

DE C–1. 8. 277a13-15

Brain

Man, however, has the most brain of all animals, in proportion to the magnitude of his body.

DE P A–2. 7. 653a27-28

The brain of man, being very large and moist, requires the most abundant defense.

DE P A–2. 14. 658b8-10

The brain is bipartite in all animals.

DE P A–3. 7. 669b21-23

197

The brain itself, in all animals, has no blood.

H A–3. 3. 514a18

The brain is naturally the coldest of all the parts in the body.

DE P A–2. 7. 652a27-28

Nature has fashioned the brain opposite to the seat of the heart, and the heat it contains.

DE P A–2. 7. 652b20-21

Instead of large and few veins, frequent and thin veins surround it; and instead of abundant and thick blood, these veins contain thin and pure blood.

DE P A–2. 7. 652b31-33

Bravery

Nor is he a brave man who exposes himself to danger knowingly, in consequence of anger.

E E–3. 1. 1229a24-25

If he should endure danger without fearing it, he will not be brave.

M M–1. 20. 1191a29-30

Breathing

Not all animals breathe.

DE A–1. 5. 411a1

Brutality

Brutality is not so bad a thing as vice, but it is more formidable.

N E–7. 7. 1150a1-2

Brutality is found chiefly among the barbarians, although it is sometimes the result of disease and mutilation.

N E—7. 1. 1145a30-32

Brutes

Brutes lack reason.

N E—7. 7. 1149b34-35

Buffoon

The buffoon is the slave of his own sense of humor.

N E—4. 14. 1128a34

C

Castration

All castrated animals are changed into the female nature.

DE G A–1. 2. 716a5-6

Categories

These are ten in number: what a thing is, quantity, quality, relation, where, when, position, possession, action, passion.

T–1. 9. 103b21-24
CAT–4. 1b25

Causes

All causes are principles.

ME–4. 1. 1013a17

The modes of causes, however, are many in number.

PHY–2. 3. 195a27-28

There are four causes.

ME–11. 4. 1070b26

Causes are denominated under four different heads, the first of which we assert to be the substance and the essence of a thing . . . and the second cause we affirm to be the matter and the subject, and the third is the source of the first principle of motion; and the fourth, the cause that is in opposition to this, —namely both the final cause and the good.

ME–1. 3. 983a26-32

Causes are four, one indeed as to the essence of a thing, another that which from certain things existing this necessarily exists, a third that which first moves something, and a fourth on account of which a thing exists.

PO A–2. 11. 94a20-22

A cause is as the end, this is the final cause, as for instance, health is the end of walking.

ME–4. 2. 1013a32-34

The form and exemplar are regarded as causes.

ME–4. 2. 1013a26-27

After another manner cause is form and paradigm (and this is the definition of the essence of a thing) and the genera of this.

PHY–2. 3. 194b26-27

That constitutes a cause from whence is the first principle of change or of rest.

ME–4. 2. 1013a29-31

In one way that is called cause from which, as inherent, anything is produced as for example the brass of a statue.

ME–4. 2. 1013a24-25

Cause, therefore, is after one manner said to be that, from which, being inherent, something is produced.

PHY–2. 3. 194b23-24

That which is a cause through itself is always prior to that which is a cause through another.

PHY–8. 5. 257a30-31

There are naturally two causes of action, thought and moral habits, and through these actions all men obtain or fail of the object of their wishes.

P–6. 1450a1-3

All things whatever which men do, they necessarily do from seven causes: by chance, compulsion, nature, custom, reason, anger, or appetite.

RH–Bk 1. 10. 1369a5-7

It is the cause that is sought in all questions.

PO A–2. 2. 90a6-7

Causes, Four

There are four causes, first, the final cause, second, the formal cause (which are as it were one), third, matter and fourth, the efficient cause, or source of the motion.

DE G A–1. 1. 715a4-7

Vide KNOWLEDGE, SCIENTIFIC.

PO A–2. 11. 94a20-22

Cause, First

That whence the principle of motion is derived to all things, must be considered as the first cause.

DE M–1. 2. 339a23-24

A different cause subsists where the subject is different, and the first cause constitutes, as it were, that which imparts motion, and is different according as the subject is different.

ME–11. 4. 1070b26-27

That cause, however, appears to be the first for the sake of which we say a thing is effected.

DE P A–1. 1. 639b14

202

Cause, Essential

Essential cause therefore is definite; but cause, according to accident, indefinite.

PHY—2. 5. 196b27-28

Censure

How far and in what way a person must deviate from the mean in order to be censurable is a question which it is not easy to decide theoretically.

N E—4. 11. 1126b2-3

Celestial Body

A celestial body is perpetual, and has no end of its local motion.

DE M—1. 2. 339a24-26

Chance

Things proceed from chance which are of such kind that their cause is not definite, and are produced in the absence of any final motive, and that neither invariably nor usually, nor in any prescribed order.

RH—1. 10. 1369a32-34

Chance is a cause of those goods which baffle all calculation.

RH—Bk. 1. 5. 1362a6-7

Not everything which is from chance is also from fortune.

PHY—2. 6. 197a37-197b1

Chance, Mind and Nature

Even if chance or spontaneity be a cause of the firmament, prior as a cause will be mind and nature.

ME—10. 9. 1065b3-4

Change

Everything undergoes a change from its contrary, as from heat into cold.

ME—10. 10. 1067a6-7

Everything which undergoes a change is changed from that which is an entity in potentiality into that which is an entity in act.

ME—11. 2. 1069b15-16

Changes are four in number: either according to quiddity, or quality, or quantity, or to place where; simple generation and corruption according to quiddity; increase and diminution according to quantity; alteration according to quality; motion according to place.

ME—11. 2. 1069b9-13

That which undergoes a change is changed either from a subject into a subject, or from that which is not a subject into a subject, or from a subject into a non-subject or from a non-subject into a subject; but I mean by a subject that which is made manifest by affirmation.

ME—10. 11. 1067b15-18

That which is changed may be changed in a fourfold respect: for it may be changed either from a subject into a subject; or from a non-subject into a non-subject; or from a non-subject into a subject; or from a subject into a non-subject.

PHY—5. 1. 225a3-6

There must be a subject in every change and this, although it is one numerically, in form it is not one.

PHY—1. 7. 190a14-16

Any change in regard to quality, quantity or place must have an end.

DE C—1. 7. 274b13-15

204

Character

The end or character of an action depends upon the choice made at the moment of performing it.

N E—3. 1. 1110a13-14

A person's character depends upon the way in which he exercises his powers.

N E—3. 7. 1114a7

Not every man is good or evil or just or unjust; but also there are shades of character intermediate between these.

ME—4. 22. 1023a5-7

Characteristics, Acquired

Children are produced similar to their parents not only in natural things but in acquired also.

DE G A—1. 17. 721b29-30

Choice

It is demonstrated that it is possible to do many things willingly without deliberate choice; for we do many things willingly suddenly. But no one deliberately chooses any thing suddenly.

E E—2. 8. 1224a2-4

Deliberate choice consists of deliberative opinion.

E E—2. 10. 1226b9

Anger, therefore, and desire are inherent indeed in brutes, but deliberate choice is not.

E E—2. 10. 1225b26-27

Chorus

It is necessary to conceive the chorus to be one of the players, and a part of the whole, and that it cooperates with the players.

P—18. 1456a25-26

Circle

A plane surface whose circumference is at all points equidistant from the center.

RH—3. 6. 1407b27-28

The circle ranks among things perfect.

DE C—1. 2. 269a20

Citizen

Whoever has a right to take part in the judicial and executive part of government in any state, him we call a citizen of that place: and a state, in one word, is the collective body of such persons, sufficient in themselves for all the purposes of life.

POL—Bk. 3. 1. 1275b17-21

It is not residence which constitutes a man a citizen; for in this point sojourners and slaves are upon an equality with him. Nor will it be sufficient that he have the privileges of the laws, and may plead or be impleaded; for this point belongs to all who have a mutual agreement upon which to associate; for these privileges are theirs also; and withal it very often happens that sojourners have not perfect rights therein, but are obliged to apply to some patron; and this shows that their share in the community is incomplete. In like manner, with respect to boys, who are not yet enrolled, or old men who are discharged from service, we admit that they are in some respects citizens, yet not completely so. But we add some qualification, for the one are not of full age, and the others are past service. Nor is there any difference between them. But what we mean is sufficiently clear; we want a complete citizen, one in whom there is no such defect as needs to be corrected in order to make him fully so. As to those who are banished or degraded, there may be made the same objections, and the same answers. There is nothing that more characterizes a complete citizen than having a share in the judicial and executive part of the government. With respect to offices, some are fixed to a particular time, so that no person on any account is permitted to fill them twice, or else not till some certain period has intervened; others are not fixed, as that of a juryman, or a member of the popular assembly.

POL—Bk. 3. 1. 1275a7-26

With respect to citizens, although different from each other, yet they have one common care, the safety of the community: and for this reason the virtue of a citizen has necessarily a reference to the state.

POL—Bk. 3. 4. 1276b27-31

He who is called a citizen is most truly a citizen of a democracy.

POL—Bk. 3. 1. 1275b5-6

For common use, men define a citizen to be one who is sprung from citizens on both sides, not on the father's or the mother's only.

POL—Bk. 3. 2. 1275b21-23

A man who is an excellent citizen need not possess that virtue which constitutes a good man.

POL—Bk. 3. 4. 1276b34-35

It is a great recommendation to know how to command as well as to obey; and to do both these things well is the virtue of an accomplished citizen.

POL—Bk. 3. 4. 1277a25-27

The citizens of the same state ought to be affectionate to each other, or at the least not to treat those who have the chief power in it as their enemies.

POL—Bk. 6. 5. 1320a14-16

City

A great city and a populous one are not the same thing.

POL—Bk. 7. 4. 1326a9-10

The most obvious division of the city is into two parts: the poor and the rich.

POL—Bk. 4. 4. 1291b7-8

Classes

In every state the people are divided into three sorts: the very rich, the very poor, and, thirdly, those who are between them.

POL—Bk. 4. 11. 1295b1-3

Climate

Those nations that dwell in warm climates have a longer life.

DE L ET B—1. 465a9

Cloud

Clouds are condensed laterally with reference to the course of the sun.

DE M—2. 4. 360a2-3

Cold

Cold is a certain nature, and not a privation in those things, the subject of which is hot, according to passive quality.

DE P A—2. 2. 649a18-20

Color

Every color is motive of what is actually transparent.

DE A—2. 7. 418a31-418bl

Every color is in a body.

CAT—2. 1a27

Color is in the extremity of bodies.

DE S ET S—3. 439a30

Color is not visible without light, but every color is seen in light.

DE A—2. 7. 418b2-3

Colors are produced by the mixture of the white and the black.

DE S ET S—4. 442a12-13

The light red, the purple, the green, and the blue are between the white and the black; and the other colors are mingled from these.

DE S ET S—4. 442a23-25

Color also may be produced from reflection, when a mirror is of such a kind as not to receive figure but color.

DE M—1. 5. 342b11-13

Combustion

Bodies which are more moved, and more swiftly, are more rapidly set on fire.

DE M—1. 3. 341a34-35

Comedy

Comedy aims at representing men as worse than in actual life.

P—2. 1448a17-18

Comedy originated from those who sang the phallic verses.

P—4. 1449a11-12

Comedy is an imitation of bad characters, yet it does not imitate them according to every vice.

P—5. 1449a32-33

Comets

We have already said that the outermost part of the air which is accustomed to be considered as endowed with fire, when it is moved by a discrete motion, separates off a concretion which is called a comet.

DE M—1. 8. 345b32-35

Commendation

Commendation is language exhibiting greatness in the case of virtue.

RH—1. 9. 1367b26-27

Commotion

A state is liable to commotions, when those parts of it which seem to be opposite to each other approach close to an equality, as the rich and the common people.

POL—Bk. 5. 4. 1304a38-1304b2

Community

The most perfect political community must be amongst those who are in the middle rank.

POL—Bk. 4. 11. 1295b35

Competence

Everybody is competent to judge the subjects which he understands, and is a good judge of them.

N E—1. 1. 1094b27-28

Competition

Those contending with each other for superiority do not remain friends.

M M—2. 11. 1211a14-15

Complex

Whatever changes is complex.

PHY—1. 7. 190b10-11

Complex Speech

Vide SPEECH.

CAT–2. 1a7-19

Composition, Fallacy of

The following belong to composition: he who sits can walk and he who does not write may write. For it does not signify the same if a person speaks separately and conjointly, that it is possible that a person sitting, may walk, and that one not writing may write.

S E–4. 166a23-27

Compulsion

All things originate in compulsion which are produced through the instrumentality of the agents themselves contrary to their inclination and reason.

RH–1. 10. 1369b5-6

Compulsory

An act is compulsory, if its origin is external to the agent or patient.

N E–3. 1. 1110a1-2

What is not compulsory is pleasant; for compulsion is contrary to nature.

RH–Bk. 1. 11. 1370a10

Conceit

Conceited people are foolish and ignorant of themselves, and make themselves conspicuous by being so.

N E–4. 9. 1125a27-28

Conception

As in the soul there is sometimes a conception which does not involve truth or falsehood and at other times those which do, so also in speech, for truth and falsehood are involved in composition and division.

DE I–1. 16a9-13

Conclusions

Conclusions are infinite, but terms finite.

PO A–1. 32. 88b6-7

Conduct

To act rightly in many things, or frequently, is difficult.

DE C–2. 12. 292a28-29

It would be wrong to suppose that there can be a mean state or an excess or deficiency in unjust, cowardly or licentious conduct.

N E–2. 6. 1107a18-20

Wise deliberation will be correctness in matters with reference to a particular end, of which prudence is a true conception.

N E–6. 10. 1142b32-33

Confirmation

It is more difficult to confirm than to subvert definition.

T–7. 5. 154a23-24

Conjunction

A sound void of signification which neither impedes nor produces one significant sound adapted to be composed from many sounds and which may be placed either at the beginning or the end of the period, unless something requires that it should be placed by itself at the beginning.

P–20. 1456b38-1457a3

Consequent

Things are consequent in two ways; either they may be consequent simultaneously or subsequently. Knowledge is a

212

consequent upon learning subsequently; life is so on health simultaneously.

RH–1. 6. 1362a28-31

Consequent, Fallacy of

The refutation on account of the consequent is from fancying that the consequence reciprocates. For when from the existence of that thing, this necessarily is, they fancy that if this is, the other necessarily is, whence also deceptions from sense about opinion occur. For often men take gall for honey, and since it happens that the earth when it has rained becomes moist, if it be moist, we think that it has rained, yet this is not necessary.

S E–5. 167b1-8

Consequent, Fallacy of, Solution to

Those fallacies which prove from the consequent we must show from the argument itself. Now there are two types of such: it is either as universal to particular, as animal to man, for it is taken for granted, if this is joined with that, that also with this; or according to opposition, for if it follows that, the opposite also follows the opposite. Hence also the argument of Melissus, for if what was begotten had a beginning, he requires it to be granted that the unbegotten had not a beginning, wherefore if the heaven is unbegotten, it is also infinite, yet this is not so, for the consequence is vice versa.

S E–28. 181a22 30

Contact

Things are said to be in contact with each other when their extremities exist together.

ME–10. 12. 1068b27

Contentious (Argument)

An argument will be contentious in so far as its aim is apparent victory.

S E–11. 171b32-33

Contentious arguments are those which infer, or seem to infer, from the apparently, but not really, probable.

S E–2. 165b7-8

Contentious Syllogism

Vide SYLLOGISM, CONTENTIOUS.

Continence

Continence is not a virtue, but a sort of mixed state.

N E–4. 15. 1228b33-34

Continence is preferable to steadfastness.

N E–7. 8. 1150a36-1150b1

The continent is not the temperate man.

M M–2. 6. 1203b23

Both the incontinent and continent man, therefore, act according to nature simply, yet not according to the same nature.

E E–2. 8. 1224b35-36

Contingent

Vide POSSIBLE.

Contingent Propositions

In contingent propositions (since contingency is multifariously predicated, for we call the necessary, and the not necessary, and the possible contingent) in all affirmatives, conversion will occur.

P A–1. 3. 25a37-40

Continuous

Nothing continuous is without parts.

PHY–6. 1. 231b4-6

It is also evident that every thing which is continuous is divisible into things always divisible.

PHY–6. 1. 231b15-16

Every thing continuous is divisible to infinity.

PHY–6. 8. 239a22

That is called continuous of which the motion is one essentially, and also which it is not possible should be otherwise.

ME–4. 6. 1016a5-6

Color is continuous to light, and light to the sight.

PHY–7. 2. 245a6-7

Continuous Motion

There is not any motion that is continuous save that which is local and to this belongs the motion that is circular.

ME–11. 6. 1071b10-11

Continuum

A thing is called continuous when the extremity of either of the parts by which they are in contact and in continuity are one and the same.

ME–10. 12. 1069a6-7

Contradiction

Contradiction is an opposition which has no medium in respect to itself.

PO A–1. 2. 72a12-13

Neither is it possible that there is any mean between a contradiction.

ME–3. 7. 1011b23-24

Of contradiction there is nothing intermediate.

ME–9. 4. 1055b9

Contraries

Those things are called contraries, both those which cannot be present in the same subject at the same time, of things that differ in genus; and those things are called contraries which involve the greatest amount of difference, of those that are in the same genus, and things that widely differ of those under the same capacity, and those of which there is the greatest difference, either simply, or according to genus, or according to species.

ME–4. 10. 1018a25-31

Contraries are first principles of entities.

ME–1. 5. 987b2-3

It is impossible that contraries should be inherent in the same subject at the same time.

ME–3. 6. 1011b17-18

All contraries are in the same genus.

DE G ET C–1. 7. 324a2

Of contraries also, if one is definite, the other likewise will be definite.

DE C–1. 6. 273a9-10

Contraries act upon, and suffer from each other, and are corruptive of each other.

DE C–2. 3. 286a33-34

It is evident that true opinion can neither possibly be contrary to true opinion, nor true negation to true negation, for those are contraries which concern opposites; but about the same things the same may be verified, but contraries cannot possibly be inherent in the same thing at one and the same time.

DE I–14. 24b6-9

Contrariety

The first or chief contrariety consists in habit and privation.

ME—9. 4. 1055a33

I term a difference of genus diversity which makes the very thing to be diverse; therefore, will this constitute contrariety.

ME—9. 8. 1058a7-9

In quality there is also contrariety.

CAT—8. 10b12

There is contrariety in relatives.

CAT—7. 6b15

The contrarieties of change are according to the contrarieties of place.

DE C—1. 4. 271a3-4

Not all the contrarieties of body make forms and principles, but those alone which subsist according to the touch.

DE G ET C—2. 2. 329b8-10

The contrarieties of place are upward and downward, before and behind, on the right hand and on the left.

DE C—1. 4. 271a26-27

Convention

'By convention' (we have said that a noun is significant 'by convention') because nothing is a noun or name by nature but only when used as a symbol.   DE I—2. 16a27-29

All persons ought to endeavor to follow what is right, and not what is established.   POL—Bk. 2. 8. 1269a3-4

217

Conversion

Nouns and verbs, when transposed, have the same signification as "man is white" and "white is man."

DE I–10. 20b1-2

Conversion of Propositions

Vide PROPOSITIONS.

Coordinate Genera

Vide Genus.

Copulation

In all sanguineous animals that are viviparous and pedestrious, the males have organs adapted to such a generative act, yet all of them do not similarly approach to the female.

DE H A–5. 2. 539b19-21

Crustaceous animals copulate . . . when the one being supine and the other prone, they apply their tails.

DE G A–1. 14. 720b9-11

Fishes copulate in a prostrate position, and are rapidly freed from each other.

DE G A–1. 6. 718a1-2

With respect to insects, those which do not hide themselves copulate in the winter, and are produced when the weather is tranquil and the wind southern; such, for instance, as flies and ants.

DE H A–5. 9. 542b27-30

The mollia copulate with the mouth, thrusting against each other, and expanding their folds.

DE G A–1. 15. 720b15-16

218

Serpents copulate by involution.

DE G A–1. 7. 718a17

Correlatives

Correlatives seem to exist simultaneously by their nature. This is true of the generality of them, for double and half are simultaneous . . . and the existence of the master and slave are simultaneous. . . . It does not however, appear to be true of all relatives, for the object of knowledge may be prior to knowledge since, for the most part, we derive knowledge from things pre-existing.

CAT–7. 7b15-25

Corruptible

Whether any thing formerly was but afterwards is not, or may not exist, we say it is corruptible.

DE C–1. 11. 280b20-22

Corruption

Corruption, therefore, is produced in all living beings from a defect of heat.

DE R–17. 478b31-32

The greatest and the most rapid corruptions therefore are produced from war, but others from diseases, and others from sterility.

DE M–1. 14. 351b13-15

Vide: GENERATION.

Courage

Courage (is that virtue) by which men are ready to achieve honorable exploits in the midst of danger, conformable to the direction of and in subservience to law.

RH–1. 9. 1366b11-13

He who faces dangers with pleasure, or at least without pain, is courageous.

N E—2. 2. 1104b7-8

It is by habituating ourselves to despise and face alarms that we become courageous, and, when we have become courageous, we shall be best able to face them.

N E—2. 2. 1104b1-3

Courage is a mean state in regard to sentiments of fear and confidence.

N E—3. 11. 1116a10-11

It would seem that experience of particular things is a sort of courage.

N E—3. 11. 1116b3-4

The temperance of a man and of a woman are not the same, nor their courage, nor their justice, as Socrates thought: for the courage of a man consists in commanding, the women's in obedience. And the same is true in all other particulars.

POL—Bk. 1. 13. 1260a21-24

Courageous Man

Derives his name from the word 'courage.'

CAT—1. 1a15

Creation

Everything that is produced always comes from a being who exists in all reality, in actuality.

DE A—3. 7. 431a3-4

Crimes

Crimes are whatever things, not falling out contrary to calculation, proceed from criminal principle; for the things

which are done through desire, proceed from criminal
principle.

RH—1. 13. 1374b8-10

Criminality

For the criminality and injustice of the act stands essentially in the deliberate principle on which it is done.

RH—1. 13. 1374a11-12

Criticism

He who knows what is a good or bad tragedy, knows the same in respect to epic poetry.

P—5. 1449b17-18

D

Dancing

The arts pertaining to dancing imitate by rhythm, without harmony.

P—1. 1447a26-27

Death

We call death the destruction of the heat (of the body).

DE VITA ET MORTE—469b19-20

Old men die without any violent passion happening to them.

DE R—17. 479a20-21

Death and corruption subsist similarly in all imperfect living beings.

DE R—17.478b28-29

Nothing is so fearful as death.

N E—3. 9. 1115a26

If to die were a delectable thing, the lascivious would frequently die through intemperance.

E E—3. 1. 1229b34-36

Decay

If the whole body should become fat and suet, it would perish.

DE P A—2. 5. 651b2-3

Deeds

Deeds are said to be just and temperate, when they are such as a just or temperate person would do, and a just and temperate person is not merely one who does these deeds but one who does them in the spirit of the just and the temperate.

N E–2. 3. 1105b5-9

Defect

Defect, which is an evil, has excess as its contrary which is also an evil.

CAT–11. 14a1

Definition

A definition shows what a thing is.

PO A–2. 3. 91a1

The definition is proper to what is defined and is predicated in respect of what it is.

PO A–2. 4. 91a15-16

Definition is a sentence signifying what a thing is.

T–1. 5. 101b39

Definition is said to be a statement of what a thing is; one kind of definition will be a nominal one another of what the name signifies.

PO A–2. 10. 93b29-31

Another kind of definition is a sentence giving the cause of the existence of something.

PO A–2. 10. 93b38-39

That definition is a discursus or description of the very nature or essence of a thing, and that the essence or formal principle belongs either to substances only, or especially both primarily and simply, is manifest.

ME–6. 5. 1031a12-14

A definition is of that which is universal.

ME–6. 10. 1035b34-1036a1

Every definition is universal.

PO A–2. 13. 97b26

Definitions then are not hypotheses, for they are not asserted to be or not to be.

PO A–1. 10. 76b35

Definition is a sentence that is composed from the things that are differences, and from the last of these that is drawn up in accordance with a correct classification, at least.

ME–6. 12. 1038a28-30

In definition one thing is not predicated of another.

PO A–2. 3. 90b34-35

Hence it is evident that the easiest thing of all is to destroy a definition; but to confirm it is the hardest.

T–7. 5. 155a17-18

In the definition of everything there is a necessity that the definition of substance be included.   ME–6. 1. 1028a35-36

If any one were to define *what* a certain man is, he would define it appropriately by giving the species or the genus; and he will do it more clearly by the former than the latter. Whatever else he may introduce is, in a manner, foreign to the purpose.

CAT–5. 2b34-36

224

Degenerate

Very degenerate men are prescient, and clearly see future events in dreams, as not being sent by divinity.

DE DIV—2. 463b15-16

Deliberation

Deliberation is a certain syllogism.

DE M ET R—2. 453a13-14

Wise deliberation necessarily implies the exercise of reason.

N E—6. 9. 1142b12

Wise deliberation is, as we conceive, the principal function of the prudent man.

N E—6. 10. 1142b31-32

We deliberate not about ends but about the means to ends.

N E—3. 5. 1112b11-12

The matters about which we deliberate are practical matters lying within our power.

N E—3. 5. 1112a30-31

The business of deliberation is partly exhortation, partly dissuasion.

RH—Bk. 1. 3. 1358b8-9

There is never any deliberation about such as either has or will have an existence of necessity; such again, as it is impossible should exist or be produced; neither in fact is there about every one even of contingent subjects; for of goods which may or not accrue, some exist naturally, others are produced by chance, on the subject of which it is not worth while to deliberate; but evidently deliberation is of

225

those about which men resolve, of which character are all such as are of a nature to be referred to ourselves, and the first principle of whose creation is in our power; for in deliberation we carry on our investigation until we ascertain whether the achievement be possible to us or not.

RH—1. 4. 1359a32-1359b2

A slave can have no deliberative faculty, a woman but a weak one, a child an imperfect one.

POL—Bk. 1. 13. 1260a12-14

Democracy

When the husbandmen and those only who possess moderate fortunes have the supreme power, they will govern according to law; for as they must get their livings by their labor, they have but little leisure for public business: they will therefore establish fit laws and call public assemblies when there is a necessity; and they will readily let every one partake with them in the administration of public affairs, as soon as they possess that fortune which the law requires as a qualification. For to exclude any class would be a step towards oligarchy, and for all to have leisure to attend unless they have a subsistence would be impossible. This form of government, then, is one species of democracy. Another species is distinguished by the prevailing mode of electing magistrates, in which every one is eligible to whose birth there are no objections, provided he is able to find leisure to attend. For this reason, in such a democracy the supreme power is vested in the laws, as pay is not given. A third species is where all freemen have a right to a share in the government, but where they will not accept it for the cause already assigned; for which reason here also the supreme power will be in the law. A fourth species of democracy is the last established in point of time in the states. For as the cities have been enlarged far beyond their original size, and as the public revenue has become considerable, the populace, on account of their numbers, are admitted to share in the management of public affairs, and even the poor are at leisure to attend to them, as they receive pay; nay, they have the greatest leisure of all, as they are not hindered by having any care of their own property, as is the case with the rich, who on this account often take no part in the public assembly and the courts of justice; thus the supreme power is lodged in the poor, and not in the laws.

POL–Bk. 4. 6. 1292b25-1293a10

Democracy is a form of government in which men apportion out the magistracies to themselves by lot.

RH–1. 8. 1365b31-32

A democracy is a state where the freemen and the poor, being the majority, are invested with the power of the state.

POL–K. 4. 4. 1290b17-19

Among equals it is neither advantageous nor right that one person should be lord over all, either where there are no established laws, but where his will is the law, or where there are laws: neither is it right that one who is good should have rule over those who are good; or one who is not good over those who are not good.

POL–Bk. 3. 17. 1287b41-1288a4

The most pure democracy is that which is called so principally from the equality which prevails in it.

POL–Bk. 4. 4. 1291b30-31

There are two things which seem to be the limits of a democracy, that the people in general are supreme, and enjoy freedom.

POL–Bk. 5. 9. 1310a28-30

In a democracy the poor ought to have more power than the rich, as being the greater number, and that which is decreed by the majority is supreme.

POL—Bk. 6. 2. 1317b8-10

A democracy considers only the poor.

POL—Bk. 3. 7. 1279b8-9

The last and worst form is that which gives a share to every citizen.

POL—Bk. 6. 4. 1319b1-3

A democracy is a government in the hands of men of low birth, poverty, and vulgar employments.

POL—Bk. 6. 2. 1317b40-41

A kingdom may degenerate into a tyranny, an aristocracy into an oligarchy, and a state into a democracy.

POL—Bk. 3. 7. 1279b4-6

A democracy is where it is in the hands of those who are worth little or nothing.

POL—Bk. 3. 8. 1279b18-19

Where the majority live by tillage or pasturage.

POL—Bk. 6. 4. 1318b9-10

Democracy, Its End
The end of democracy is liberty.

RH—1. 8. 1366a4

Demagogue
Where the power is not vested in the laws, there demagogues abound.

POL—Bk. 4. 4. 1292a10-11

The one flatter the few when they are in power. The others are those demagogues who have a share in the oligarchy and flatter the people.

POL—Bk. 5. 6. 1305b34-36

Demonstration

For there are three things in demonstrations, one, the demonstrated conclusion, and this is that which is per se inherent in a certain genus; another are axioms, but axioms are they from which the demonstration is made; the third is the subject genus, whose properties and essential accidents demonstration makes manifest.

PO A—1. 7. 75a39-75b2

I call demonstration a scientific syllogism, and I mean by scientific that according to which, from our possessing it, we know.

PO A—1. 2. 71b17-19

Demonstration is from what is more certain and is prior.

P A—2. 16. 64b32-33

Demonstration is when a syllogism consists of things true and primary or of such a kind as assume the principle of the knowledge concerning them through certain things primary and true.

T—1. 1. 100a27-29

The beginning of every demonstration is the definition of the quiddity; wherefore those definitions are said to be dialectical and useless by which accidents cannot be perceived or conjectures easily made about them.

DE A—1. 1. 402b25-403a2

But I term demonstrative even those common opinions from which all derive their demonstrations; for instance, that everything must needs be either an affirmation or negation, and that it is impossible for the same thing to be and not to be at the same time, and whatsoever other such propositions there are.

ME–2. 2. 996b27-31

(In a demonstration) the conclusion is not in the form of a question nor does it follow from a concession, but it must follow necessarily even if the respondent does not acknowledge it.

PO A–2. 5. 91b16-18

Every demonstration proves a predicate of a subject.

PO A–2. 3. 90b33-34

Without affirmative there is no negative demonstration.

PO A–1. 25. 86b38-39

Denial

The proposition which removes something from something.

DE I–6. 17a25-26

Dense

A thing is said to be dense from having its parts near each other.

CAT–8. 10a21

Derivatively

Things are said to be named derivatively which derive their name from some other name different in termination.

CAT–1. 1a12

Desire

Desire is the appetite for what gives pleasure.

DE A–2. 3. 414b5-6

230

The active exercise of the desire augments its native strength, until the desires, if they are strong or vehement, actually expel the reasoning power.

N E–3. 15. 1119b9-10

Desire is contrary to moral purpose.

N E–3. 4. 1111b15-16

It seems that some desires are universal and others are individual and acquired.

N E–3. 13. 1118b8-9

There are three things which influence us to desire them, viz. the noble, the expedient, and the pleasant.

N E–2. 2. 1104b30-31

The object of desire, then, and the object of the will, are either real or apparent good.

E E–7. 2. 1235b25-26

It appears that they experience pain and pleasure; and if these two emotions exist in them, it follows necessarily that there is desire.

DE A–3. 11. 434a2-3

The desires devoid of reason are anger and appetite.

RH–Bk. 1. 10. 1369a4

Deviation
A small deviation to those who depart from truth becomes in its progress ten thousand times greater.

DE C–1. 5. 271b8-9

Dialectic
The dialectic problem is a theorem tending either to choice and avoidance, or to truth and knowledge, either per

se, or as cooperative with something else of this kind, about which the multitude either hold an opinion in neither way, or in a way contrary to the wise, or the wise to the multitude, or each of these to themselves.

T—1. 11. 104b1-5

A dialectic proposition is an interrogation, probable either to all, or to the most, or to the wise.

T—1. 10. 104a8-9

Dialectic propositions are both those which resemble the probable and which are contrary to those which appear probable, being proposed through contradiction and whatever opinions are according to the discovered arts.

T—1. 10. 104a12-15

This is peculiar, or especially appropriate to dialectic, for being investigative, it possesses the way to the principles of all methods.

T—1. 2. 101b2-4

Dialectic science is merely tentative of the knowledge of those things that philosophy has already actually reached.

ME—3. 2. 1004b25-26

This mode of arguing (i.e. purely verbal) is not appropriate to dialectic, wherefore a thing of this kind must be altogether avoided by dialecticians, viz. arguing against a name, unless any one should be otherwise incapable of discussing the proposition.

T—1. 18. 108a33-35

Dialectical arguments are such as collect contradiction from probabilities.

S E—2. 165b3-4

232

If then a dialectical question be the seeking of an answer either to a proposition or of one part of a contradiction . . . there would not be one answer to them, for neither is there one question. . . . "What is it?" is not a dialectical question, for a choice should be given by the question to enunciate this or that part of the contradiction.

DE I–11. 20b22-29

It is the business of the dialectician to understand through common propositions those from which is made a real refutation or an apparent one, or a dialectical one or a contentious.

S E–9. 170b8-11

Diction

Of all diction, the following are the parts: the letter, the syllable, the conjunction, the noun, the verb, the article, the case, and the sentence.

P–20. 1456b20-21

Didactic

Didactic arguments are those which syllogize from the proper principles of each discipline, and not from the opinions of him who answers.

S E–1. 2. 165b1-2

Difference

Differences in animals are manifested in their kind of life, their actions, their nature, as well as in their parts.

H A–1. 1. 487a11-12

Difference also is of the number of those things not in a subject.

CAT–5. 3a23

Vide GENUS.

233

Difficulty

Difficulty is defined in reference either to the pain, or length of time.

RH—Bk. 1. 6. 1363a24

Disagreement

Any trifling disagreement becomes the cause of seditions.

POL—Bk. 5. 3. 1303a20-21

Disposition

Disposition is styled an arrangement of that which has parts either according to place or to potentiality, or according to species.

ME—4. 19. 1022b1-3

Disputation

It is requisite still, not to dispute with every one, nor to exercise ourselves against any casual person, for it is necessary to employ bad arguments against some, since against him, who altogether tries to seem to elude us, it is just indeed, by all means, to try to draw a conclusion, yet it is not proper readily to engage with casual persons, since depraved disputation will necessarily occur; for even those who practice themselves, cannot forbear disputing contentiously.

T—8. 14. 164b8-15

Diversity

Things that are diverse in genus are at a wider interval from one another than those that are diverse in species.

ME—9. 10. 1059a14

Diverse are those things called of which either the species are numerous, or the matter, or the definition of the substance.

ME—4. 9. 1018a9-11

234

Division

Concerning division the arguments are these: five is two and three, therefore odd and even.

S E–4. 166a33-34

Division and Union

Division too and union are the same . . . but their essence is not the same.

PHY–4. 13. 222a19-20

Divisible

In every thing continuous and divisible, there are excess, defect, and a medium.

E E–2. 3. 1220b21-22

That which is divisible amounts either to magnitude or multitude.

ME–10. 10. 1066b4-5

All magnitude and all time are always divisible; so that they cannot be primarily in that in which they are.

PHY–6. 10. 237b20-21

Doctrine

All doctrine, and all intellectual discipline, arise from pre-existent knowledge.

PO A–1. 1. 71a1-2

Dog

It is by the teeth that we can recognize whether dogs are young or old.

HA–2. 2. 501b11-12

Double Question, Fallacy of

Those arguments which arise from making two questions one, when it escapes notice that there are many and one answer is given as if there were only one question. e.g. 'whether is the earth sea, or the heaven?'

S E—5. 167b38-168a1

Double Question, Fallacy of, Response to

Against those which make many questions one, we must employ definition immediately in the beginning, for the interrogation is one to which there is one answer, so that neither many things must be affirmed or denied of one thing, nor one of many, but one of one.

S E—30. 181a36-39

Doubt

It will contribute towards one's object, who wishes to acquire a facility in the gaining of knowledge, to doubt judiciously.

ME—2. 1. 995a27-28

Downward

Motion towards the center.

DE C—1. 2. 268b22

Drama

Both tragedy and comedy at first originated from extemporaneous efforts.

P—4. 1449a9-10

Dramatic Ability

A gift of nature and rather outside the province of art.

RH—3. 1. 1404a15-16

Dream

A dream is a certain phantasm, and that during sleep.

DE SOM—3. 462a15-16

We do not perceive a dream by sense, nor yet by opinion.

DE SOM—1. 458b9-10

As in moisture, if any one vehemently agitates it, at one time no image appears, but at another, it appears, indeed, yet perfectly distorted, and different from what it really is; but when the moisture is still, the image is pure and apparent; thus, also, in sleep, the phantasms and the other motions which happen from sensible perceptions, at one time, when the said motion is greater, are entirely obliterated; but at another time, being disturbed, visions and monstrous appearances, and unpleasant dreams, are produced.

DE SOM—3. 461a14-22

Dreams will not be sent from divinity . . . They are nevertheless divine; for nature is divinely arranged, but not itself divine.

DE DIV—2. 463b13-15

He is a judge of dreams according to the most consummate art, who is able to survey similitudes; for every one is capable of forming a judgment of dreams which manifestly indicate future events.

DE DIV—2. 464b5-7

Dreaming

That this passion, therefore, which we call dreaming, is neither the passion of one who opines, nor of one who acts dianoetically, is evident.

DE SOM—1. 459a8-9

Drought

The same places of the earth are not always wet or dry, but they are changed according to the generations and failures of rivers.

DE M—1. 14. 351a19-21

E

Ear

Large ears, protruding ears indicate loquacity and stupidity.

H A—1. 11. 492b2-3

Earth

As far as we know about the earth, the horizon changes with our change of location, which shows that the earth is round and bulging.

DE M—2. 7. 365a29-31

The earth also has necessarily a spherical figure.

DE C—2. 14. 297a9

Some parts of the sea always receding, and others always acceding, it is evident that the same parts of the earth are not always some of the sea, and others continent, but all these are changed in time.

DE M—1. 14. 351a21-26

It is evident that the earth is immovable.

DE C—2. 14. 296b25-26

Earthquake

Neither water nor earth is the cause of earthquakes but wind, rushing into the earth from the external evaporation.

DE M—2. 8. 366a3-5

238

When a violent earthquake happens, the shock neither ceases immediately, nor entirely; but at first, indeed, it continues for forty days; and afterwards shakes the same places for one or two years.

DE M—2. 8. 367b32-368a1

The greater part too, and the greatest of earthquakes, happen at night; but those which are produced in the day happen about noon.

DE M—2. 8. 366a12-14

Easily Done

Easy things are such as are done either without pain or in a short time.

RH—1. 6. 1363a23

Eclipse

A privation of light from the moon through the interposition of the earth.

PO A—2. 2. 90a15-17

Since the moon is eclipsed through the interposition of the earth, the periphery of the earth which is of a spherical figure will be the cause of this.

DE C—2. 15. 297b28-30

If the earth were not spherical the eclipses of the moon would not have such segments as they now have.

DE C—2. 14. 297b24-25

Education

It will be found to be education and morals that are almost the whole which go to make a good man, and that the same qualities will make a good citizen or good king.

POL—Bk. 3. 18. 1288a41-1288b2

It is evident that laws should be laid down concerning education, and that it should be public.

POL—Bk. 8. 1. 1337a22-24

As a state contains a multitude, it ought to be brought to unity and community, as we have already said, by education.

POL—Bk. 2. 5. 1263b36-37

Eel

Eels are neither generated from copulation, nor do they bring forth eggs, nor has any eel ever been caught which had either any genital seed or an egg.

DE H A—6. 16. 570a3-4

Efficient Cause

But with regard to generations, and actions, and every kind of change, we are in a way of understanding each when we understand the first principle of motion.

ME—2. 2. 996b22-23

Vide CAUSE.

Egg

Among the seeds that are complete, we call egg that which contains two parts: one that serves first of all to form the animal, and the other wherein it finds its nutriment, once it is generated.

H A—1. 5. 489b6-8

Elderly, Habits and Passions of

Doubtful, indecisive, cynical, suspicious, cowardly, illiberal, timid, tenacious of life, selfish, despise appearances, live in memory, weak in anger, but keen, live more by calculation, are apt to pity, querulous.

RH—2. 13. 1389b13-1390a28

Election

In a free state the whole community should not elect at the same time, but some out of the whole, or out of some particular rank; and this either by lot, or vote, or both. And they should elect either out of the whole community, or out of some particular persons in it, and this both by lot and vote.

POL—Bk. 4. 15. 1300a34-36

To elect a proper person in any line is the business of those who are skilled in it; as in geometry, it is the part of geometricians, and of steersmen in the art of steering. But even if some individuals do know something of particular arts and works, they do not know more than the professors of them; so that, even upon this principle, neither the election of magistrates, nor the censure of their conduct, should be intrusted to the many.

POL—Bk. 3. 11. 1282a8-14

Nor is it right for any one about to be elected to office to solicit a place; for every person who is fit to hold office, whether he chooses it or not, ought to be elected.

POL—Bk. 2. 9. 1271a10-12

Elements

An element is called that from which, as an inherent first principle and indivisible in species, something is compounded into a different species.

ME—4. 3. 1014a26-27

An element is that whereunto as inherent in a thing, as matter, a compound is divided, as for instance, of the syllable AB, A and B are the elements.

ME—6. 17 1041b31-33

The elements change into each other.

DE G ET C—2. 6. 332a1-2

It remains that they must be generated from each other.

DE C–3. 6. 305a32

It is necessary that the elements should be finite in number.

DE C–3. 4. 303a2-3

The elements, such as fire, air, water, and earth, are inodorable.

DE S ET S–5. 443a9-11

Air is nearer to fire than all the rest of the elements, and water is nearer to earth.

DE M–1. 2. 339a18-19

Since the bodies of all animals, and likewise of all plants, are composed from the four elements, in some of them earth predominates, as in plants; in others, water, as in aquatic animals; and in others air or fire, as in pedestrious and winged animals.

DE R–13. 477a27-30

Elenchus

Vide REFUTATION.

Emotion

By the emotions I mean desire, anger, fear, courage, envy, joy, love, hatred, regret, emulation, pity, in a word whatever is attended by pleasure or pain.

N E–2. 4. 1105b21-23

The irrational emotions seem to be as truly human as the reason itself and therefore we are as truly responsible for our emotions as for our reasoning.

N E–3. 3. 1111a34-1111b2

Thought, love, and hate are not qualities of the mind, but of the man that possesses the mind, in so far as he possesses it.

DE A—1. 4. 408b25-27

Vide PASSIONS.

End

The end is that for the sake of which a thing is done.

E E—2. 11. 1227b36

That with a view to which we act is the end; an end is that for the sake of which everything else is done.

RH—1. 7. 1363b16-17

All things in nature have an end or are the conditions of things that have an end.

DE A—3. 12. 434a31-32

There are different kinds of ends: some are actions, others are products of the actions.

N E—1. 1. 1094a3-5

The end or character of an action depends upon the choice made at the moment of performing it.

N E—3. 1. 1110a13-14

No one deliberately chooses the end, but things which contribute to the end.

E E—2. 10. 1226a7-8

The end is some good of the soul and not an external good.

N E—1. 8. 1098b19-20

End of Man

Every one individually and all men in general have some end at which directing every aim, they both choose and avoid; and this, to speak summarily, is happiness and its constituents.

RH–1. 5. 1360b4-7

Encomium

Encomium is language extolling what one has actually done.

RH–1. 9. 1367b28-29

Endurance

It is endurance of painful things, as has been said, that entitles people to be called courageous.

N E–3. 12. 1117a32-33

It is the mark of a lofty mind to show no signs of depression under great sufferings and injuries.

ECO–Bk. 1. 7. (Bk. 3. Loeb. p. 405)

Energy

It is evident that energy, or activity, is prior to potentiality.

ME–8. 8. 1049b5

That also energy is both superior and more excellent than potentiality, however excellent, is evident.

ME–8. 9. 1051a4-5

Energy is an end.

ME–8. 8. 1050a9

Corporeal activity has no communication with the actuality of intellect.

DE G A–2. 3. 736b28-29

244

Felicity, however, is either a habit, or an energy, since energy is better than disposition, and the best energy is the energy of the best habit.

E E–2. 1. 1219a28-33

Vide ACT.

Entelechy

The soul is the first entelechy of a natural body that has life potentially.

DE A–2. 1. 412a27-28

The soul is the entelechy of the body.

DE A–2. 1. 412a21

Enthymeme

Now an enthymeme is a syllogism from likelihoods (probabilities) or signs.

PA–2. 27. 70a10-11

A rhetorical syllogism.

RH–1. 2. 1356b4

Enthymemes are adduced from probabilities and signs.

RH–Bk. 1. 2. 1357a32-33

Are the very body of persuasion.

RH–1. 1. 1354a14-15

Entity

One signification of entity is 'the what a thing is' or quiddity, and this certain particular thing; and another is quality or quantity, or each of the rest of the things that are so predicated.

ME–6. 1. 1028a11-13

Entity is denominated partly as that which subsists according to accident, and partly as that which subsists essentially.

ME—4. 7. 1017a7-8

Enunciation

One first enunciative sentence is affirmation; afterwards negation, and all the rest are only by conjunction. It is necessary however that every enunciative sentence should be from a verb, or from the case of a verb.

DE I—5. 17a8-11

Envy

Men envy those with whom they are at rivalry.

RH—Bk. 2. 10. 1388a13

Those who are ambitious are more given to envy than those who are devoid of ambition.

RH—Bk. 2. 10. 1387b31-32

Vide JEALOUSY.

Epic Poetry

Concerning the poetry which is narrative and imitative in meter, it is evident that it ought to have dramatic fables (plots) in the same manner as tragedy, and should be conversant with one whole and perfect action, which has beginning, middle and end, in order that, like one whole animal, it may produce its appropriate pleasure.

P—23. 1459a17-21

It requires revolutions, discoveries, and disasters. Besides which, the thought and the diction should be well formed.

P—24. 1459b11-12

246

Epic

The epic differs from tragedy in the length of the composition and in the meter.

P–24. 1459b17-18

It is the peculiarity of the epic to possess abundantly the power of extending its magnitude. . . . In the epic, many events may be introduced which have happened at the same time, which are properly connected with the subject, and from which the bulk of the poem is increased.

P–24. 1459b22-28

The epic is an attendant on tragedy.

P–5. 1449b9-10

The epic differs from tragedy in that it has a simple metre, and is a narration. It also differs in length.

P–5. 1449b11-12

Epicheirema

A dialectical syllogism.

T–8.11.162a16

Episode

The episode is the whole part of the tragedy between two complete odes of the chorus.

P–12. 1452b20-21

Episodic

I call the plot episodic, in which it is neither probable nor necessary that the episodes follow each other.

P–9. 1451b34-35

Of simple plots and actions, the episodic are worst.

P–9. 1451b33-34

247

Equable Motion

That the heaven is moved with an equable motion is evident.

DE C—2. 6. 289a8-9

Equality

Nature has made all men equal, and therefore it is just, be the administration good or bad, that all should partake of it.

POL—Bk 2. 2. 1261a39-1261b2

Equitable

One who in his moral purpose and action aims at doing what is equitable, and does not insist upon his rights to the damage of his neighbors, but is content to take less than is his due, although he has the law on his side, is equitable.

N E—5. 14. 1137b35-1138a2

That which is equitable is just.

N E—5. 14. 1137b8-9

Equity

Equity is that idea of justice, which contravenes the written law.

RH—Bk. 1. 13. 1374a25-27

Equity, also, is the having a sympathy for human failings; and the having an eye, not to the law, but to the lawgiver; and not to the language, but to the intention of the lawgiver. And not to the conduct, but to the principles of the agent; not to his conduct in one particular, but to its whole tenor. Not what kind of person he has been in this instance, but what he has always shown himself or generally at least. The having, too, a remembrance of the good one has received, rather than of the ill; of the good one has

248

received, rather than what one has done; though injured, to endure it patiently; to prefer a decision by argument, rather than by recourse to action; a wish to proceed to arbitration, rather than to judicial decision, for the arbitrator looks to what is equitable, the judge to what is law; and in order to this it was that arbitration was introduced, in order, namely, that equity might prevail.

RH–1. 13. 1374b10-22

Equity is the common characteristic of all that is good in our relation to our neighbors.

N E–6. 12. 1143a31-32

Equivocally

Things are said to be named equivocally when the definition agreeing with the name is different for each although they have a common name.

CAT–1. 1a1

Equivocation, Fallacy of

Such arguments as these are from equivocation: those who know, learn, for grammarians learn those things they recite; for to learn is equivocal, signifying both to understand by using science and also to acquire science.

S E–4. 165b30-34

Eristic

Vide SOPHISTIC and CONTENTIOUS.

Err

If we think that a thing was done at a certain time, and this opinion is false, then memory deceives us, and we err.

DE M ET R–2. 452b24-26

Error
There is error both in deficiency and excess.

M M–1. 17. 1189b28-29

Erudition
It is the province of an erudite man to be able sagaciously to judge what is well or ill said by the teacher.

DE P A–1. 1. 639a4-6

Esse
Esse is not the substance of any thing.

PO A–2. 7. 92b13-14

Essence
The essence is the cause of being for all things.

DE A–2. 4. 415b11-12

It is not possible that essence, or quality, or a participated property should be infinite.

PHY–1. 2. 185a34-185b2

Each essence is able to generate many such things as itself.

E E–2. 0. 1222b16-17

Essences, Knowledge of
The accidents are a great aid in coming to know the essence of each thing; for when we are able to know the accidental appearances, whether some or all, then we can speak well concerning the substance.

DE A–1. 1. 402b21-25

Essences, Natural

All natural essences are either bodies, or are generated together with bodies and magnitudes.

DE C—3. 1. 298b3-4

Essential

The essential is expressed in many ways; in one way, the very nature of each thing or the formal cause; . . . secondly, whatsoever things are inherent in the essence; and, thirdly, a thing that has primarily been a recipient in itself, or a certain part of things that belong to itself; fourthly, that of which there is not any one other cause; fifthly, as many things as are inherent in some one particular thing alone, and as far forth as it is alone.

ME—4. 18. 1022a24-35

Essential Attributes (per se)

But I call those 'per se' which are inherent in what a thing is, as line is in triangle, and point in line, also those things which are inherent in their attributes in the definition declaring what a thing is, as the straight and the curved are inherent in a line . . . what are in neither way inherent I call accidents.

PO A—1. 4. 73a34-73b5

Essential Good

Essential is final good.

E E—1. 8. 1218b10

Eternal

It follows that the object of science is necessary. It is therefore eternal; for all such things as are necessary in themselves are eternal, and that which is eternal admits neither of generation nor of corruption, i.e. it has neither beginning nor end.

N E—6. 3. 1139b22-24

If, therefore, there are certain things that are eternal and immovable, there is in them nothing compulsory or contrary to Nature.

ME–4. 5. 1015b14-15

Eternity

The end of the whole heaven, and the end which comprehends the infinite time and infinity of all things is eternity.

DE C–1. 9. 279a25-27

Ethics

Scientific exactitude is impossible in reasoning upon particular ethical cases.

N E–2. 2. 1104a5-7

Eunuch

No eunuch becomes bald.

H A–9. 50. 632a4

Every

'Every' does not signify the universal but it signifies that the universal (term) is universally applied.

DE I–7. 17b11-12

DE I–10. 20a12-14

Evil

That which is evil is by the constitution of Nature subsequent to that which we term potentiality.

ME–8. 9. 1051a18-19

Evil is in its nature infinite.

N E–2. 5. 1106b29

Evolution

The evolution is for the sake of the thing and it is not the case that the thing is for the sake of evolution.

DE P A–1. 1. 640a18-19

252

Excess

Let excess be defined to be, as much and yet more: the thing exceeded, however, to be that comprised within the excess.

RH—Bk. 1. 7. 1363b7-9

All excess whether of folly, cowardice, incontinence, or savagery is either brutal or morbid.

N E—7. 6. 1149a4-7

Existence

That for the sake of which a thing exists is in the smallest degree evident, where matter mostly abounds.

DE M—4. 12. 390a3-4

Animals, too, only exist on earth and on water; but not in air or fire, because the former are the matter of bodies.

DE M—4. 4. 382a6-7

Exodus

The exodus is the whole part of the tragedy, after which there is no further melody of the chorus.

P—12. 1452b21-22

Exordium

The business of exciting attention is common to all the divisions of a speech, wherever it may be necessary.

RH—Bk. 3. 14. 1415b9-10

Experience

Repeated acts of memory about the same thing done constitute the force of a single experience.

ME—1. 1. 980b29-981a1

Experience accrues to men from memory.

ME–1. 1. 980b28-29

All experience harmonizes with the truth.

N E–1. 8. 1098b11

The peculiar principles in every science are many, hence it is the province of experience to deliver the principles of everything, for instance, I say that astronomical experience gives the principles of astronomical science, for from phenomena being sufficiently observed, astronomical demonstrations have thus been invented, so also is it in every other art and science.

P A–1. 30. 46a17-22

Expert

One is designated an expert because he possesses knowledge in a particular branch.

CAT–8. 10a35

Expiration and Respiration

It is impossible at one and the same time to expire and respire.

DE R–1. 471a17-18

Extremes

Among the extremes, if a person errs on the side of excess, he may be called passionate and his vice passionateness, if on that of deficiency, he may be called impassive and his deficiency impassivity.

NE–2. 7. 1108a6-9

Eye

In general, the white of the eye is identical in all men. But the part called black presents numerous differences.

H A–1. 10. 491b34-492a2

Only in man, or rather especially in man, does the color of the eyes vary so much. The other animals have one color only.

H A—1. 10. 492a5-6

Eyebrows

Extended toward the temples, they indicate a spirit of mockery, imitation, and raillery.

H A—1. 9. 491b16-18

Low eyebrows indicate an envious nature.

H A—1. 9. 491b17-18

When the eyebrows are straight, it is a sign of great gentleness.

H A—1. 9. 491b15

When they curve toward the nose, it is a sign of coarseness.

H A—1. 9. 491b15-16

Eyelashes

Of those animals that have hair man alone has eyelashes in each eyelid.

DE P A—2. 14. 658a14-15

F

Faculties

There are three faculties in the soul which determine action and truth, viz. sensation, reason, and appetite or desire.

N E–6. 1. 1139a17-18

I call those faculties in respect of which we are said to be capable of experiencing these emotions, e.g. capable of getting angry or being pained or feeling pity.

N E–2. 4. 1105b23-25

Fallacy

There are two types of fallacies, some depend on language and some are apart from language. Those which depend on language are six in number: equivocation, amphiboly, composition, division, accent and figure of speech.

S E–4. 165b23-27

The fallacies apart from language are seven: from accident; on account of what is asserted simply or not simply but in a certain respect, or place or time or relation; ignorance of the issue; fallacy of consequent; petitio principii; placing non-cause for the cause; double or leading questions.

S E–4. 166b20-27

False

He speaks falsely who, when either things are or when

they are not, makes assertions about them in a contrary way to that in which they actually subsist.

ME—8. 10. 1051b4-6

The false is denominated in one way as a false thing; and, in regard of this, partly in the fact of its not being composed, or in the impossibility of its being in a state of composition.

ME—4. 29. 1024b17-19

That which is false does not exist, nor does it amount to deception, but ignorance.

ME—8. 10. 1052a1-3

False Argument

An argument is called false in four ways: one when it appears to conclude, yet does not do so, which is called a contentious syllogism; another when it concludes indeed, that which does not pertain to the proposed problem, and this happens especially in arguments leading to the impossible; or it concludes pertinently to what is laid down, yet not after an appropriate method, and this is when a non-medical argument appears medical, or the non-goemetrical to be geometrical, or the non-dialectic to be dialectic, whether the result be false or true. Another way, if it concludes through falsities, and of this the conclusion will be sometimes false, and sometimes true, as the false is always concluded through falsities, but it is possible that the true may be so even from things not true, as was said also before.

T—8. 12. 162b3-15

False Cause, Fallacy of

That is (a fallacy) which is from what is not a cause, being assumed as a cause, is when what is causeless is taken as if the refutation were produced on account of it. Now such a thing happens in syllogisms leading to the impossible,

257

since in these it is necessary to subvert some one of the posita; if then it be reckoned in necessary interrogations for the impossible to result, the refutation will often appear to arise on account of this, as that the soul and life are not the same, for if generation be contrary to destruction, a certain generation will be to a certain destruction; but death is a certain destruction and is contrary to life, so that life is generation, and to live is to be generated but this is impossible, wherefore soul and life are not the same.

S E—5. 167b21-31

Falsehood

Falsehood in itself is base and censurable.

N E—4. 13. 1127a28-29

False Subsistence

That which subsists as false is nonentity.

ME—5. 4. 1027b18-19

Fame

When one is considered by all to be endowed with virtue or to possess what all desire or the generality, or the good or the prudent.

RH—1. 5. 1361a25-27

Familiars

That certain persons clearly perceive future events, and that familiars especially foresee things pertaining to familiars happens because familiars are particularly solicitous about each other.

DE DIV—2. 464a27-29

Family

A family is that society which nature has established for daily support, and those who compose it are called by

Charondas 'Feeders at the same manger,' and by Epimenides the Cretan 'Users of the same hearth.'

POL—Bk. I. 1. 1252b12-15

But as in every subject we should first begin with examining into its component parts, and as the first and smallest parts of a family are the master and slave, the husband and wife, the father and child, let us first inquire into these three relations, what each of them is, and what they ought to be; that is to say, the despotical, the conjugal, and thirdly the paternal; though these two latter relations have no peculiar established name. Let these then be considered as the three distinct parts of a family. Now there is a duty which some identify with the government of a family, while others regard it as constituting its most important part; I mean that of providing for its maintenance. Now we must inquire philosophically how the matter stands. But let us first speak of the master and the slave, that we may both understand what things are absolutely necessary, and also see if we can get to learn any thing better on this subject than what is already laid down. Some persons have thought that the power of the master over his slave is a certain science, and that the government of a family and a slave, political and regal government, are all the same things, just as we said at the beginning; but others think that despotic government is contrary to nature, and that it is custom only which makes one man a slave and another free, but that in nature there is no difference between them; for which reason that tie must be unjust, for it is founded in force.

POL—Bk. I. 3. 1253b5-23

Since every family is part of a state, and each of those individuals is part of a family, and the virtue of the parts ought to have regard to the virtue of the whole; it is necessary to instruct both the wives and children of the community, as to the nature thereof, inasmuch as it is of some

259

consequence to the virtue of the state that the wives and children herein should be virtuous.

POL—Bk. I. 13. 1260b13-18

Fear

A sort of pain or agitation, arising out of an idea that an evil, capable either of destroying or giving pain, is impending on us.

RH—Bk. 2. 5. 1382a22-23

Fear is sometimes defined as an anticipation of evil.

N E—3. 9. 1115a9

Those animals whose blood is very watery, are more timid; for fear refrigerates.

DE P A—2. 4. 650b27-28

Fearlessness

There are two ways in which men become dead to apprehension, either from never having experience, or from being possessed of resources against calamity.

RH—Bk. 2. 5. 1383a27-28

Feel

To feel is to experience some affection.

DE A—2. 11. 423b31-424a1

Feet

In all animals the number of feet is always even.

H A—1. 5. 489b22-23

Felicity

Felicity is the energy of a worthy soul.

E E—2. 1. 1219a33-34

It is acknowledged, therefore, that felicity is the greatest and most excellent of human goods.

E E—1. 7. 1217a21-22

Happiness is a certain action; for it is good action.

PHY—2. 6. 197b4-5

It is evident that all men consider felicity as subsisting in three lives, the political, the philosophical, and the voluptuous.

E E—1. 5. 1216a27-29

There are some things the lack of which must mar felicity, e.g. noble birth, a prosperous family, and personal beauty.

N E—1. 9. 1099b2-3

Vide HAPPINESS.

Female

That which generates in itself and from which is made what is generated.

DE G A—1. 2. 716a21-23

The female contributes the matter for generation and this is the substance of the menses.

DE G A—1. 19. 727b31-32

The animal that makes the emission in itself is called the female.

H A—1. 3. 489a11-12

In the female, there is less blood on the surface of the body, but within it there is more.

H A—3. 19. 521a21-22

Females are naturally libidinous, incite the males to copulation, and cry out during the act of coition.

DE H A—5. 2. 540a11-13

Woman is more compassionate than man, and has a greater propensity to tears.

DE H A—9. 1. 608b8-9

The female, when born, more rapidly acquires youth, acme, and old age than the male.

H A—7. 3. 583b26-27

The haughtiness of women has been the ruin of many tyrannies.

POL—Bk. 5. 11. 1314b26-27

The female is more dispirited, more despondent, more impudent, and more given to falsehood, than the male. She is likewise more easily deceived, and more apt to remember; and again the female is more vigilant, less active, and in short less disposed to motion, and receptive of less nutriment than the male.

H A—9. 1. 608b11-15

She is, also, more envious, more querulous, more slanderous, and more contentious.

DE H A—9. 1. 608b9-11

It is easy to find persons who will share prosperity, but, except a very few and very good ones, women are not willing to share misfortunes.

ECO—Bk. 1. 7. (Bk. 3. Loeb, p. 405)

Female Excellencies

The excellencies of females in regard to person are beauty and stature; in regard to mind, temperance and industry without meanness.

RH—1. 5. 1361a6-8

Ferocity

Females, therefore, when they have brought forth are first more ferocious, but the males are ferocious at the time of copulation.

DE H A—6. 18. 571b10-12

Fertility

Fat men and women are less fertile than thin, since the residue is concocted and changed into fat.

DE G A—1. 18. 726a3-5

Fibres

Fibres are solid and terrene; so that they become as it were the nourishers of heat in the blood, and cause anger to become fervid.

DE P A—2. 4. 650b36-651a2

Figures

Figures are infinite.

DE S ET S—4. 442b21

Figure of Speech, Fallacy of

Those arguments occur from figure of speech when what is not the same is interpreted after the same manner, as when the masculine is interpreted feminine, or the feminine as masculine . . . or again quantity as quality or quality as quantity.

S E—4. 166b10-13

Final

We speak of a thing as absolutely final, if it is always desired in itself and never as a means to something else.

NE—1. 5. 1097a33-34

Finite

That which is composed from things finite both in multitude and magnitude, is also finite in multitude and magnitude.

DE C—1. 5. 271b21-22

Finite Body

That it is necessary, therefore, that every body which is moved in a circle should be finite, is evident.

DE C—1. 5. 273a4-6

Fire

Fire is the excess of heat.

DE G ET C—2. 4. 331b25

The nature of fire is dry.

DE S ET S—4. 441b10

Fire tends upward in a right line.

DE C—1. 2. 269a17

Fire has no weight.

DE C—4. 4. 311b27

The corruption of fire is extinction and consumption.

DE R—8. 474b13-14

First Known

Those things are first evident and manifest which are more confused and then they become more known by their elements and principles.

PHY—1. 1. 184a21-23

First Principles

There are various ways of discovering first principles;

264

some are discovered by induction, others by perception, others by what may be called habituation, and so on.

N E–1. 7. 1098b3-4

Fish

All fishes scatter their eggs. . . . For if all the eggs were preserved, fishes of every kind would be too numerous.

DE H A–6. 13. 567a31-567b3

Flame

Flame is the boiling of a dry wind.

DE M–1. 4. 341b21-22

Flesh

This is the principle and the body of animals.

DE P A–2. 8. 653b21-22

The flesh of man is softer than that of other animals.

DE P A–2. 16. 660a11-12

It is impossible that the flesh can be the organ of the other senses.

DE P A–2. 8. 653b29-30

Men who have hard flesh are ill endowed with intelligence: those who have soft flesh on the contrary are well endowed.

DE A–2. 9. 421a25-26

Flowers

Man, as I may say, is the only animal that perceives and is delighted with the smell of flowers, and things of this kind.

DE S ET S–5. 444a31-33

Fluid

Every animal without exception has a fluid of which it

cannot be deprived, either naturally, or by violence, without dying immediately; and there is also a part wherein this fluid is contained.

H A–1. 4. 489a20-21

Flying

No animal is capable of flight simply.

H A–1. 1. 487b21

Among animals that fly, some have feathers, like the eagle and the hawk; others have membranes, like the bee and the cockchafer; others have wings resembling leather, like the flying-fox and the bat.

H A–1. 5. 490a5-8

Folly

When a man does not arrange his life with a view to a certain end, it is an indication of great folly.

E E–1. 2. 1214b10-11

Fondness

We are all most fond of such things as have cost us trouble.

N E–9. 7. 1168a21-22

Foolhardiness

The foolhardy person may be regarded as an impostor, and as one who affects a courage that he does not possess.

N E–3. 10. 1115b29-30

Foot

I use the term foot for a member employed for movement in place.

DE IN–5. 706a31-32

Forehead

Men who have a high forehead are slower than others.

H A–1. 9. 491b12

Those whose forehead is wide have extraordinary faculties.

H A–1. 9. 491b13

Those who have a narrow forehead are very quick.

H A–1. 9. 491b13

Those whose foreheads are round are hot tempered.

H A–1. 9. 491b14

Foresight

The cause, too, why certain persons in an ecstasy foresee future events is because the proper or appropriate motions did not disturb, but are expelled.

DE DIV–2. 464a24-26

Forgetful

Very young persons and old men are forgetful.

DE M ET R–1. 450b5-6

Form

By form I mean the essence or very nature of the thing.

ME–6. 10. 1035b32

I mean by form the essence or very nature of each thing, and the first substance.

ME–6. 7. 1032b1-2

Form, therefore, is nature.

PHY–2. 1. 193a30-31

It is according to form that we know all things.

ME–3. 5. 1010a25

Form is one principle, as, for instance, order, or music, or some one of other things which are thus predicated.

PHY–1. 7. 190b28-29

Form of Man

The form of man always appears in flesh and bones, and in such like parts.

ME—6. 11. 1036b3-4

Fortitude

The third kind exists through unskilfulness and ignorance . . . the fourth species subsists from hope . . . the fifth is that which arises from the impulse of the irrational passions.

E E—3. 1. 1229a16-21

Fortuitous

There is no science through demonstration of that which is fortuitous.

PO A—1. 30. 87b19

Fortunate

Nobody who is fortunate can become miserable; for he will never do what is hateful and mean.

N E—1. 11. 1100b33-34

Fortune

Simply considered, it is not the cause of anything.

PHY—2. 5. 197a10-11

Fortune is a cause by accident in things which rarely happen, according to the deliberate choice of those things which subsist for the sake of something.

PHY—2. 5. 197a5-6

Fortune itself is unstable; since none of the things which proceed from it can either have a perpetual or a frequent subsistence.

PHY—2. 5. 197a31-32

Fortune is indefinite.

PHY—2. 5. 197a8-9

Good fortune is the accession and actual possession, either of all, of most, or the greatest of those goods of which chance is the cause.

RH–Bk. 1. 5. 1361b39-1362a2

Good fortune is something of necessity different from happiness, as every external good of the soul is produced by chance or by fortune; but it is not from fortune that any one is just or wise.

POL–Bk. 7. 1. 1323b26-29

Freedom

Where the government is not vested in the laws, then there is no free state.

POL–Bk. 4. 4. 1292a32

Free Man

We say a free man exists who is such for his own sake, and not for the sake of another.

ME–1. 2. 982b24-26

Free Will

The first principle of things that are practical is free-will in the agent.

ME–5. 1. 1025b23-24

Friend

One who participates in another's joy at good fortune, and in his sorrow at what aggrieves him, is his friend.

RH–Bk. 2. 4. 1381a3-6

A true friend is one who is a true friend only on account of virtue.

E E–7. 12. 1244b16-17

A friend is to be preferred to things, and not things to a friend.

E E–7. 2. 1237b30-34

The greatest as it seems of all external goods.

N E–9. 9. 1169b9-10

Friends, Two

Two friends have a greater power both of intelligence and of action than either of the two by himself.

N E–8. 1. 1155a15-16

Friendliness

Let the bearing friendly feeling be defined to be 'the wishing a person what we think good, for his sake and not for our own, and, as far as is in our power, the exercising ourselves to procure it.'

RH–2. 4. 1380b35-1381a1

Friendship

One species, indeed, is defined on account of virtue; another on account of the useful; and another on account of the delectable.

E E–7. 2. 1236a31-33

Friendship is a kind of virtue or implies virtue.

N E–8. 1. 1155a4

Friendship resembles a moral state.

N E–8. 7. 1157b29

Friendship is measured by desert, and a certain equality.

E E–7. 4. 1239a8-9

No one honors wealth for itself but for something else, but friendship is honored for itself.

T–3. 1. 117a1-4

270

If people are friends, there is no need of justice between them.

N E–8. 1. 1155a26-27

It is indispensable to life.

N E–8. 1. 1155a4-5

The species of friendship are companionship, intimacy, relationship (kinship).

RH–Bk. 2. 4. 1381b33-34

It appears that friendship and justice have the same occasions and the same sphere.

N E–8. 11. 1159b25-26

Friendship looks for what is possible, not for what is proportionate or due to the merit of the friend.

N E–8. 16. 1163b15-16

It is only the friendship of the good which cannot be destroyed by calumnies.

N E–8. 5. 1157a20-21

Perfect friendship is in some sense an excess.

N E–8. 7. 1158a12

Friendship is the greatest good which can happen to any state, as nothing so much prevents seditions.

POL–Bk. 2. 4. 1262b7-9

Future

It is not possible to remember the future.

DE M ET R–1. 449b10-11

Nor is that which will be, and that which is about to be, the same thing.

DE DIV–2. 463b28-29

G

Generation

Of things that are being produced, some are produced by nature, and others by art and others by chance.

ME—6. 7. 1032a12-13

All things which are produced either by nature or art involve matter, for it is possible for each of them both to be and not to be and this capability is the matter in each.

ME—6. 7. 1032a20-22

One thing is generated from another . . . by something in act, which is either of the same genus or the same species.

DE G ET C—1. 5. 320b17-20

A thing is generated from that which is not.

DE G ET C—1. 3. 319a26

Simple generation is from that which is simply non-being.

DE G ET C—1. 3. 317b5

Only substances are said to be generated in the strict sense.

PHY—1. 7. 190a32-33

Of every substance there is generation.

ME—10. 2. 1060b18-19

Generations take place from opposites.

DE I–14. 23b14

Generation is into contraries, and from contraries.

DE G ET C–2. 5. 332b21-22

It is indeed universally evident that every thing is naturally adapted to be generated from everything.

DE G ET C–2. 5. 332b27-28

It is impossible that there be a production of anything if nothing may pre-exist.

ME–6. 7. 1032b30-31

Those elements which are changed from one into one, are generated from one thing being corrupted; but those which are changed from two into one, are generated from more than one thing being corrupted.

DE G ET C–2. 4. 331b35-36

It is evident that what is called form or substance is not generated but that the union which is said to take place according to this is generated, and that in everything which is produced matter is inherent and the one part is matter but the other form.

ME–6. 8. 1033b16-19

It is not possible that things more rare and more dense can be generated, if there is not a vacuum in the indivisibles.

DE G ET C–1. 8. 326a23-24

The principles of generation are male and female; the male as the efficient cause, the female as the material.

DE G A–1. 2. 716a4-6

The male supplies the form and motive principle but the female the body and the matter.

DE G A—1. 20. 729a9-11

Among those that have the faculty of generation, are distinguished the animal that makes the emission in itself, and the animal that makes it in another.

H A—1. 3. 489a10-11

Others generate animals, indeed, not such as are homogeneous; and these are such as are generated not from the coition of animals, but from putrid earth and excrements.

DE G A—1. 1. 715a24-25

To say that the world is generated, and that it is at the same time perpetual, is among things that are impossible.

DE C—1. 10. 279b17-18

Neither is it possible that any body can be generated beyond the world.

DE C—1. 9. 278b24

Generation, Mutual

Fire and air, water and earth, are generated from each other and each of these exists in each in potentiality.

DE M—1. 3. 339a36-339b1

Generation and Corruption

Generation is the corruption of non-being; and corruption is the generation of non-being.

DE G ET C—1. 3. 319a28-29

Every generation is a corruption of another and every corruption a generation of another.

DE G ET C—1. 3. 319a5-6

274

The passage to non-being simply is simple corruption; the passage to being simply, is simple generation.

DE G ET C–1. 3. 318b9-11

It is impossible that generation amounts to motion, for nonentity would be produced by accident . . . neither does corruption constitute motion, for motion or rest is a thing that is contrary to motion, but corruption is contrary to generation.

ME–10. 11. 1067b30-1068a1

Genus

Genus is that which is predicated of many things differing in species.

T–1. 5. 102a31-32

Genus and difference are apparently consequent so long as there is species.

T–4. 2. 123a18-19

Further, do we regard genus as that which first is inherent in definitions, which is predicated in the case of the essence of a thing the differences of which are called qualities.

ME–4. 28. 1024b4-6

Genus is styled so partly when there may be a continuous generation of things that possess the same species. . . . And it is that also from which things derive their being as the first disposing cause towards existence.

ME–4. 28. 1024a29-32

When I say genus, I understand, for example, bird and fish. These two animals have a difference of genus; and each one, in its particular genus, has other differences, since there are several species of fish and birds.   H A–1. 1. 486a23-25

275

I call bird a genus, but man a species, and I also denominate every thing a species which, according to universal definition, has no difference.

DE P A–1. 5. 645b24-26

In every genus of things, there is that which is in act, and that which is in capacity.

PHY–3. 1. 201a9-10

Genus (Pl. Genera)

The differences of different genera and of things not arranged under each other are diverse also in species, as of 'animal' and 'science.' For the differences of 'animal' are 'quadruped,' 'biped,' 'winged,' 'aquatic,' but none of these forms the difference of 'science,' since 'science' does not differ from 'science' in being 'biped.' But as to subaltern genera there is nothing to prevent the differences being the same, as the superior are predicated of the genera under them.

CAT–3. 1b16-21

Gentlemen

It belongs to a gentleman not to live in dependence on another.

RH–Bk. 1. 9. 1367a32

Geometrician

The geometrician carries on speculations relative to man neither as far forth as he is man, nor as far forth as he is indivisible, but as far forth as he is a solid.

ME–12. 3. 1078a25-26

Geometry

For neither are the lines that fall under the cognisance of the senses the same as the geometrician describes them; for nought of the things that are perceived by the senses is in this way strictly straight or round, for the circle touches the rule not in a point.

ME–2. 2. 997b35-998a3

Giving

It is easier to abstain from taking than to give.

N E–4. 1. 1120a17

Goats

Goats however when they are fat are less prolific.

DE H A–5. 14. 546a1-2

God

In this way is God disposed as to existence and the principle of life is inherent in God; for the energy or active exercise of mind constitutes life and God is this act and essential act belongs to God as his best and everlasting life.

ME–11. 7. 1072b26-28

God is happy and blessed not by reason of any external good but in himself and by his nature.

POL–7. 1. 1323b23-26

God and nature make nothing in vain.

DE C–1. 4. 271a33

It is clear, therefore that God is in the whole universe and moves everything, so, likewise God is in us and moves us.

E E–7. 14. 1248a25-27

God, who is the end of life, and in the contemplation of whom felicity consists, does not govern imperiously. And, as it is elsewhere shown, he is not in want of any thing.

E E–7. 15. 1249b13-16

He who bids the laws to be supreme makes God supreme.

POL–Bk. 3. 16. 1287a28-30

All men believe that there are gods.

DE C–1. 3. 270b5-6

Good

For the good is what all desire.

RH–1. 7. 1365a1

The good has been well defined as that at which all things aim.

N E–1. 1. 1094a2-3

Let good be defined to be: whatever is an object of choice for its own sake; and for the sake of which we choose something else; what every thing aims at, or every thing which has perception, or which has intelligence; or every thing would aim at were it possessed of intelligence; whatever intelligence would award to each; whatever the intelligence conversant with every instance awards to each, that to each individual is his good; that which being present one is well disposed and independent.

RH–1. 6. 1362a21-27

Good is multifarious, in fact as many as being.

E E–1. 8. 1217b25-26

Good in food is what produces pleasure; in medicine, what produces health; in the soul, it is a certain quality; sometimes it is what happens at a certain time, as what happens at the right time; frequently also quantity, as the right amount. So then, the term 'good' is equivocal.

T–1. 15. 107a5-12

There are three kinds of things good for man, namely, what is external, what belongs to the body, and to the soul.

POL—Bk. 7. 1. 1323a25-26

The good of man is an activity of soul in accordance with virtue or, if there are more virtues than one, in accordance with the best and most complete virtue.

N E—1. 6. 1098a15-17

All objects of determined choice are good.

RH—Bk. 1. 6. 1363a19

All men participate of a certain portion of good.

E E—7. 2. 1238b13-14

Virtue is a kind of good.

T—6. 4. 142b14

A person is not good, if he does not take delight in noble actions.

N E—1. 9. 1099a17-18

Good is finite.

N E—2. 5. 1106b30

Goods have been divided into three classes, namely, external goods as they are called, goods of the soul and goods of the body.

N E—1. 8. 1098b12-14

It is clear then that there will be two kinds of goods, some being absolute goods, and others secondary.

N E—1. 4. 1096b13-14

When one thing is a consequence of another, but that other thing is not a consequence of it; then that of which the other is a consequence is the greater good.

RH—Bk. 1. 7. 1363b27-30

Ideal good is indeed immovable.

E E—1. 8. 1218a22

The highest good is clearly something final.

N E—1. 5. 1097a28

Some philosophers have held that . . . there is an absolute good which is the cause of goodness.

N E—1. 2. 1095a26-28

Good, Simply

What is simply good is more desirable than what is good for someone; as to get well is better than to be cut. For the former is simply good, the latter to those who need an operation.

T—3. 116b8-10

But that is simply (honorable) which, when nothing is added, you may declare to be honorable or the contrary.

T—2. 11. 115b29-30

Goodwill

Goodwill may be said to be the germ of friendship.

N E—9. 5. 1167a3-4

Government

Government is a certain ordering of the state, which respects the magistrates as to the manner in which they are regulated, where the supreme power shall be placed.

POL—Bk. 4. 1. 1289a19-22

It is evident that every form of government or administration (for the words are of the same import), must contain the supreme power over the whole state, and that this supreme power must necessarily be in the hands of one person, or of a few, or of the many; and that when the one, the few, or the many direct their policy to the common good, such states are well governed: but when the interest of the one, the few, or the many who are in office is alone consulted, a perversion takes place; for we must either affirm that those who share in the community are not citizens, or else let these share in the advantages of government.

POL—Bk. 3. 7. 1279a25-32

There are four forms of government: democracy, oligarchy, aristocracy, and monarchy.   RH—Bk. 1. 8. 1365b29-30

When governments alter, they alter into the contrary species to what they before were and not into one like their former.   POL—Bk. 5. 12. 1316a18-20

It is a general maxim in democracies, oligarchies, monarchies, and indeed in all governments, not to let any one acquire a rank far superior to the rest of the community, but rather to endeavor to confer moderate honors for a continuance, than great ones for a short time.

POL—Bk. 5. 8. 1308b10-15

Domestic government is a monarchy (for every house is ruled by one head), but a political government is composed of freemen and equals.   POL—Bk. I. 7. 1255b19-20

A government has never, or very seldom, been established where the supreme power has been placed amongst those of the middle rank.   POL—Bk. 4. 11. 1296a37-38

281

Every legislator ought to establish such a form of government, as from the present state, and disposition of the people who are to receive it, they will most readily submit to, and persuade the community to partake of.

POL—Bk. 4. 1. 1289a1-3

It is evident that all those governments which have the common good in view are rightly established and strictly just; but that those which have in view only the good of the rulers are all founded on wrong principles, and are widely different from what a government ought to be; for they are tyrannical; whereas a state is a community of freemen.

POL—Bk. 3. 6. 1279a17-21

This is a proof of a well-constituted government, if it admits the people to a share, and still remains unaltered in its form of polity, without any popular insurrection worth notice on the one hand, or growing into a tyranny on the other.

POL—Bk. 2. 11. 1272b30-33

Governments are preserved, not only by having the means of their corruption at a great distance, but sometimes also by its being very near them. For those who are in continual fear keep a stricter hand over the state.

POL—Bk. 5. 8. 1308a24-27

An oligarchy and a tyranny are of all governments of the shortest duration.

POL—Bk. 5. 12. 1315b11-12

It is evident that a government according to written laws is not the best.

POL—Bk. 3. 15. 1286a14-16

282

The most perfect government is that which is formed of many parts.

POL–Bk. 2. 6. 1266a4-5

Grammarian

The grammarian derives his name from the word grammar.

CAT–1. 1a14

Grammatical Art

A certain grammatical art is in a soul as in a subject, but it is not predicated of a subject.

CAT–1. 1a25

Gravity

Gravity is both that which involves any weight and that which possesses a superabundance of weight.

ME–9. 1. 1052b28-29

All things, even air itself, have gravity in their own place except fire.

DE C–4. 4. 311b8-9

All things have gravity except fire, and levity except earth.

DE C–4. 4. 311b5

Gravity, Infinite

It is impossible that there should be bodies which have infinite gravity and levity. DE C–1. 6. 274a16-17

It is necessary that the gravity of an infinite body should be also infinite. DE C–1. 6. 273b26-27

Greatness

If a man has often succeeded in the same thing, this is a feature of greatness.

RH—Bk. 1. 9. 1368a13-14

Growth

No being decays or grows, in Nature, without self-nourishment.

DE A—2. 4. 415b26-27

H

Habit

Habit is considered to be a disposition according to which that which is disposed is disposed well or ill; and this either according to itself, that is, essentially, or in relation to another; as, for example, health is a certain habit, for it is a disposition of this sort. ME—4. 20. 1022b10-12

Habits are dispositions also, but dispositions not necessarily habits, for those who have habits are also, after a manner, disposed according to them, but those who are disposed are not altogether possessed of the habit.

CAT—8. 9a10

Habit differs from disposition in that it is a thing more lasting and stable. CAT—8. 8b27

In habit originates every thing which men do because they have often done it before. RH—Bk. 1. 10. 1369b6-7

Habit is denominated, in one way, as a certain act of the possessor and the possessed, just as it were a certain action or motion. ME—4. 20. 1022b4-5

Habits are such things as are the causes of these things being inherent in us rationally, or irrationally; such for instance as fortitude, temperance, timidity, and intemperance.

E E—2. 2. 1220b18-20

Neither does any one of the other sciences deliver to him who learns it the use and the act, but only the habit of that science.

M M–2. 10. 1208a33-34

It is easier to change habit than to change nature.

N E–7. 11. 1152a29-30

Habitation

Places in a low, were inhabited posterior to those in an elevated situation.

DE M–1. 14. 352a2-3

Habitus

As one of the categories.

Vide POSSESSION.

Hail

Hail is ice.

DE M–1. 12. 347b36

Hair

The color of the hair varies when the animal becomes old. In man the hair whitens with age.

H A–3. 11. 518a7-8

Halo

Halos cannot be produced opposite to the sun.

DE M–3. 6. 377b34

Happiness

An activity of perfect life in accord with perfect virtue.

E E–2. 1. 1219a38-39

The definition (of happiness) is in harmony with the view of those who hold that happiness is virtue or excellence of some sort; for activity in accordance with virtue implies virtue.

N E–1. 9. 1098b29-31

Happiness is something final and self-sufficient, being the end of all action.

N E–1. 5. 1097b20-21

Let happiness be defined to be good fortune in conjunction with virtue; or independence of life; or the life which is most pleasant, accompanied by security; or abundance of property and slaves, with power to preserve and augment it.

RH–Bk. 1. 5. 1360b14-17

A person is incapable of happiness if he is absolutely ugly in appearance, or low born, or solitary and childless, and perhaps still more so, if he has exceedingly bad children or friends, or has had good children or friends and has lost them by death.

N E–1. 9. 1099b3-6

Some people hold that happiness is virtue, others that it is prudence, others that it is wisdom of some kind, others that it is these things or one of them conjoined with pleasure or not dissociated from pleasure, others again include external property.

N E–1. 9. 1098b23-26

Much external assistance is necessary to a happy life; but less to those who are of a good, than to those who are of a bad, disposition.

POL–Bk. 7. 13. 1331b41-1332a2

Happiness consists in the perfect practice of virtuous activities.

POL–Bk. 7. 8. 1328a37-38

It belongs more frequently to those whose morals are most pure, and whose understandings are best cultivated, and who preserve moderation in the acquisition of external goods, than to those who possess a sufficiency of external good things, but are deficient in the rest.

POL—Bk. 7. 1. 1323b2-5

Happiness requires leisure.

N E—10. 7. 1177b4

What is the highest of all practical goods? As to its name there is, I may say, a general agreement. The masses and the cultured classes agree in calling it happiness, and conceive that 'to live well' and 'to do well' is the same thing as 'to be happy.'

N E—1. 2. 1095a16-20

But to be happy, and to live blessedly and well, will especially consist in three things which appear to be most eligible. For some say that prudence is the greatest good, but others virtue, and others pleasure.

E E—1. 1. 1214a30-33

A happy life must arise from an uninterrupted course of virtue.

POL—Bk. 4. 11. 1295a36-37

The masses define it as something visible and palpable, e.g., pleasure, wealth, or honor.

N E—1. 2. 1095a22-23

Ordinary or vulgar people conceive it to be pleasure and accordingly approve a life of enjoyment.

N E—1. 3. 1095b16-17

Perfect happiness is a species of speculative activity.

N E—10. 8. 1178b7-8

Happiness, its Constituent Parts

Noble birth, many and excellent friends, wealth, good and numerous offspring, a good old age; and moreover personal excellencies as health, beauty, strength, stature, athletic prowess, fame, honor, good fortune, and virtue, and its constituents: prudence, courage, justice, temperance.

RH–1. 5. 1360b18-24

Happy Life

It is admitted that a happy life must be an honorable one, and a pleasant one too.

POL–Bk. 8. 5. 1339b18-20

Happy Man

We may safely then define a happy man as one whose activity accords with perfect virtue and who is adequately furnished with external goods, not for a casual period of time but for a complete or perfect lifetime. But perhaps we ought to add, that he will always live so, and will die as he lives.

N E–1. 11. 1101a14-17

The happy man should live well and do well, as happiness, it has been said, is in fact a kind of living and doing well.

N E–1. 8. 1098b20-22

Harmonics and Optics

There is the same mode of reasoning in the sciences of harmonics and optics for neither are the speculations of either carried on as far forth as the power of vision or as far forth as voice is concerned, but as far forth as lines and numbers are the objects of inquiry.
ME–12. 3. 1078a14-16

Harmony

A ratio of numbers in sharp and flat.
PO A–2. 2. 90a18-19

Hatred

The efficient causes of hatred are anger, vexatiousness, calumny.

RH—Bk. 2. 4. 1381b37-1382a2

Have (to Have)

'To have' is predicated in many ways, either as habit and disposition or some other quality, for we are said *to have* knowledge and virtue; or as to quantity, as the size which anyone has; or as things about the body, as a garment . . . or as in a part, as a ring in the hand; or as a part, as a hand or foot; or as in a vessel, as a bushel has wheat; or as a possession, for we are said to have a house or land. A man is also said to have a wife . . . by this we mean nothing else than that she lives with a man.

CAT—15. 15b15-32

Head

Man is the only animal, as we have said, that, in his perfection, has this part in relation with the axis of the universe.

H A—1. 15. 494a33-494b1

Heads

Plants that have heavy heads live longer than those that have not.

DE L ET B—6. 467a34-467b1

Health

The excellence of the body is health and that in such a degree as for us to be exempt from sickness while we have the free exercise of the body.

RH—1. 5. 1361b3-4

Neither health nor sickness can subsist in beings lacking life.

DE S ET S—1. 436a18-19

Heart

The heart is the only one of the viscera, and in short is the only part of the body which is subject to any grievous malady.

DE P A—3. 4. 667a32-34

Those whose senses are dull have a hard and dense heart; but those that are more sensitive have a softer heart.

DE P A—3. 4. 667a13-14

Heat

Heat is a certain passive quality of sense.

DE M—1. 3. 341a15

Heat is a certain category and form.

DE G ET C—1. 3. 318b16-17

All heat naturally tends upwards.

DE M—1. 4. 342a15-16

Heat is motive.

DE G A—2. 1. 732a20

The hot and the cold generate when they vanquish the matter.

DE M—4. 1. 379a1

Boiling water heats more than flame.

DE P A—2. 2. 648b26-27

Heat contributes to the erectness of the body.

DE P A—3. 6. 669b3-6

Heaven

We call heaven the essence of the ultimate circulation of

291

the universe; or that natural body which exists in the ultimate circulation of the universe.

DE C–1. 9. 278b11-14

It is necessary that there should be only one heaven, and not many.

DE C–1. 8. 277a10-11

We see that the heaven is circularly moved.

DE C–1. 5. 272b14

In the whole of past time, according to successive tradition, no change appears to have taken place, either in the whole of the extreme heaven, or any of its proper parts.

DE C–1. 3. 270b13-16

It is evident that beyond the heavens there is neither place, nor a vacuum, nor time.

DE C–1. 9. 279a11-12

Heavy

What moves to the center naturally.

DE C–1. 3. 269b23

Highmindedness

In respect of honor and dishonor the mean state is highmindedness, the excess is what is called vanity, the deficiency littlemindedness.

N E–2. 7. 1107b21-23

It seems then that highmindedness is, as it were, the crown of the virtues.

N E–4. 7. 1124a1-2

Hind

The hind appears to excel in prudence.

H A–9. 5. 611a15-16

History

History and poetry differ in this, that one speaks of things which have happened, and the other of such as might have happened.

P—9. 1451a38-1451b2

Honor

Honor is an evidence of your having a character for beneficence.

RH—Bk. 1. 5. 1361a27-28

Whoever is prudent will not fail to remember with how much honor it becomes him to requite his parents, his wife, and his children, in order that he may gain the name of one who is just and upright in distributing to each their due.

ECO—Bk. 1. 8. (Bk. 3. Loeb, p. 409)

Cultivated and practical people identify happiness with honor, as honor is the general end of political life.

N E—1. 3. 1095b22-23

Excessive honors are also a cause of sedition.

POL—Bk. 5. 3. 1302b10-11

Honor the Gods

To honor the gods . . . is honorable simply.

T—2. 11. 115b33

Honorable

By the honorable I mean a thing of such a kind as that which is divine, and that which is more excellent, such as soul and intellect.

M M—1. 2. 1183b21-23

293

That is honorable which, while it is an object of choice on its own account, is commendable also; or which, being good, is pleasant, simply because it is good.

RH—Bk 1. 9. 1366a33-36

The upward is more honorable than the downward; the before than the behind; and the right than the left.

DE IN—5. 706b12-13

Homonymous

Things are termed homonymous, of which the name alone is common, but the definition is different.

CAT—1. 1a1

Homonyms

Vide Equivocal.

Hypothesis

Of thesis, that which receives either part of contradiction, as for instance, I mean that a certain thing is, or that it is not, is hypothesis.

PO A—1. 2. 72a18-20

Definitions then are not hypotheses (for they are not asserted to be or not to be) but hypotheses are in propositions. Now it is only necessary that definitions should be understood, but this is not hypothesis, except some one should say that the verb to hear is hypothesis. But they are hypotheses from the existence of which, in that they are, the conclusion is produced.

PO A—1. 10. 76b35-39

It is manifest that when there is a false and not impossible hypothesis, the consequence of the hypothesis will also be false and not impossible.

PA—1. 15. 34a25-26

294

I

Ice

Water congealed or condensed.

ME—7. 2. 1043a9-10

Ideas

The assertion that ideas are models or exemplars, and that other things participate in them is to speak quite at random and to assert what is mere poetic metaphor.

ME—12. 5. 1079b25-26

Ideas, Platonic

Farewell to the ideas for they are inane figments and even if they were they are irrelevant. For demonstrations concern those things which first fall under the senses.

PO A—1. 22. 83a32-35

Ignorance

Ignorance, considered not according to negation but according to a disposition of mind, is deception produced through a syllogism.

PO A—1. 16. 79b23-24

Ignorance is the error which makes people unjust and generally wicked.

N E—3. 2. 1110b28-30

He who performs any action not knowing what the action is nor to what end it will lead nor about whom such

295

action is conversant acts from ignorance essentially, and therefore acts involuntarily.

E E–2. 9. 1225b5-7

An action which is due to ignorance is always non-voluntary; but it is not involuntary unless it is followed by pain and excites a feeling of regret.

N E–3. 2. 1110b18-22

The corruption of ignorance is reminiscence and discipline.

DE L ET B–2. 465a22-23

Ignoratio Elenchi

Other fallacies arise from a lack of definition of what a syllogism is or an argument; to refute is to contradict one and the same thing.

S E–5. 167a21-25

Ignoratio Elenchi, Fallacy of

It is possible to resolve all fallacies into ignorance of what refutation is.

S E–6. 168a17-18

Illiberality

Illiberality is incurable; for it seems that old age and impotence of any kind makes men illiberal.

N E–4. 3. 1121b12-14

Imagination

A movement caused by sensation in action.

DE A–3. 3. 429a1-2

Imagination is a movement that could not take place without sensation nor elsewhere except in thinking beings.

DE A–3. 3. 427b15-16

296

Imagination is quite different from sensation and thought. It is not produced, it is true, without sensation, and without it there is no conception. But it is easily evident that imagination and conception are not identical.

DE A—3. 3. 427b14-17

Memory pertains to that part of the soul to which, also, imagination pertains; and those things are essentially objects of memory which are objects of imagination.

DE M ET R—1. 450a22-24

Animals have imagination just as well as man.

DE A—3. 10. 433a11-12

Imagination is not always present.

D E A—3. 3. 428a8

Imagination that extends to will is found exclusively in animals endowed with reason.

DE A—3. 11. 434a5-7

Imagination depends only on us and on our will.

DE A—3. 3. 427b17-18

Imitation

In the arts, all of them produce imitation in rhythm, words, and harmony.

P—1. 1447a21-22

Imitation consists in these three differences, namely, in the means, the object, or the manner.

P—3. 1448a24-25

It is necessary either to imitate those who are better than we are, or those who are worse, or such as are like ourselves.

P—2. 1448a4-5

297

Immortality

The actuality of good is immortality, and this is perpetual life.

DE C—2. 3. 286a9

Immortality appears to be a certain affection or accident of life.

T—4. 5. 126b35-37

Implication

Vide INFERENCE.

Impossible

The impossible and the false do not signify the same thing.

DE C—1. 12. 281b2-3

Impotentiality

Impotentiality is a privation of potentiality, and a certain removal of a first principle of such a sort, as has been mentioned, either entirely so, or from being by nature adapted to have such, or already to have such when it has been naturally fitted thereto also.

ME—4. 12. 1019b15-18

Impulse

Irrational impulse is that through which desire aspires after certain things, as good and delectable, without reason.

E E—7. 14. 1247b24-26

Inartificial

The proofs which are called inartificial, because they are peculiar to judicial oratory, are five in number, namely: laws, witnesses, deeds, torture, oaths.

RH—Bk. 1. 15. 1375a22-25

Incontinence

The incontinent are not unjust but they act unjustly.

N E–7. 9. 1151a10-11

It is not possible that the prudent man can be incontinent.

M M–2. 6. 1204a11-12

Incorruptible

We call that incorruptible, which is, indeed, but which cannot not be, or which once will not be but exists now.

DE C–1. 11. 280b27-28

That is most properly said to be incorruptible, which is indeed, but cannot be corrupted, so as to exist now, and afterwards not.

DE C–1. 11. 280b31-33

Increase

Increase is from the upward.

DE C–2. 2. 284b27-28

Indignation

Slaves, sorry fellows, and men devoid of ambition are not liable to feelings of indignation, since there is nothing of which they think themselves worthy.

RH–Bk. 2. 9. 1387b12-14

Individual

That which can not be predicated of many.

DE I–7. 17a40

Of all beings then, some are of such a nature as not to be truly predicated universally of anything else, as Cleon and Callias, that which is singular (individual) and that which

299

is sensible, but others are predicated of these. . . . That some things therefore are naturally adapted to be predicated of nothing is clear, for of sensibles each is almost of such a sort as not to be predicated of any thing except accidentally, for we some times say that that white thing is Socrates.

P A–1. 27. 43a25-35

Individuals partake also of genus and species.

T–4. 1. 121a37-38

Individuals, and whatever is one in number, are predicated of no subject, but nothing prevents some of them from being in a subject.

CAT–2. 1b5-8

Induction

Induction is a progression from singulars to universals.

T–1. 12. 105a13-14

Induction, then, and the syllogism through induction consists in showing one extreme of the middle through the other extreme; as if A is the middle of AC, and we show through C that A is with B, for thus we make inductions. . . . Induction proceeds through all.

P A–2. 23. 68b15-29

It never happens that we have a preexistent knowledge of particulars, but along with induction we receive the science of particulars as it were by recognition; since some things we immediately know, as the angles are equal to two right angles if we know that what we see is a triangle.

P A–2. 21. 67a21-26

In some way also induction is opposed to syllogism, for the latter demonstrates the extreme of the third through the

300

middle, but the former (demonstrates) the extreme of the middle through the third.

P A–2. 23. 68b32-35

The proving that such or such is the fact in many and similar cases is called in the other art (dialectic) induction, in this (rhetoric) it is called example.

RH–1. 2. 1356b12-15

For we accept all things either through syllogism or induction.

P A–2. 23. 68b13-14

Induction and Likeness

Speculation concerning the similar (likeness) is useful for induction and for hypothetical syllogisms and for the statement of definitions. For induction, because by the induction of similar particulars we deem it proper to infer the universal, since it is not easy to form induction when we are ignorant of similars.

T–1. 18. 108b7-12

Induction, in Rhetoric

(In rhetoric) the example is an induction.

RH–1. 2. 1356b5

Induction, Its Role in Science

Vide SCIENCE (KNOWLEDGE), PROCESS OF ACQUIRING.

Induction-Demonstration-Universals

It is clear that if any one of the senses be deficient the corresponding knowledge is deficient since we learn either by induction or by demonstration. Now demonstration is from universals, but induction from particulars, it is im-

301

possible to investigate universals except through induction, since things which are said to be from abstraction will be known through induction . . . it is impossible for those who have not sense to make an induction, for sense is conversant with singulars, as the science of them cannot be received, since neither (can it be received) from universals without induction, nor through induction without sense.

PO A–1. 18. 81a38-81b9

Inequality

Not only an inequality of possessions, but also of honors, occasions seditions, though in a contrary way in either case; for the vulgar will be seditious if there be an equality of goods, but those of more elevated sentiments, if there is an equality of honors; whence it is said:

When good and bad do equal honors share.

Homer *Iliad* 9.319.

POL–Bk. 2. 7. 1266b38-1267a2

Inexperience

Men are brave from the contrary to experience.

M M–1. 20. 1190b32-33

Inference

From true propositions we cannot infer a falsity, but from false premises we may infer the truth, except that not the why but only the fact is inferred; the why cannot be established from false premises.

P A–2. 2. 53b7-10

It is also manifest that we may infer a true conclusion from false premises.

P A–2. 15. 64b7-8

Infinite

The infinite either is that which it is impossible to pass through, in respect of its not being adapted by nature to be

302

permeated, or it is that which possesses a passage without end, or that which is scarcely so, or that which by nature is adapted to have, but has not, a passage or termination.

ME—10. 10. 1066a35-1066b1

The infinite is devoid of parts and indivisible.

ME—10. 10. 1066b17

Neither a square, nor a circle, nor a sphere, can be infinite, as neither can a line which is a foot in length.

DE C—1. 5. 272b19-21

If therefore every sensible body has an active or passive power, or both, it is impossible that there should be an infinite sensible body.

DE C—1. 7. 275b4-6

Neither is an infinite right line perfect; since, if it were, it would have a beginning and end.

DE C—1. 2. 269a21-22

An infinite time has no end.

DE C—1. 7. 275a22-23

The infinite has the power of a principle, and the greatest power in quantity.

DE C—1. 5. 271b14-15

It is not possible that the infinite can be moved.

DE C—1. 7. 274b29-30

It is impossible that an entity that exists in actuality should be infinite for it must needs be quantity.

ME—10. 10. 1066b18-19

The infinite has infinite power.

DE C—1. 7. 275b20-21

The infinite as infinite is unknowable.

PHY—1. 4. 187b7-8

Infinite Body

If there is in existence an infinite body, it will be infinite in every direction.

ME—10. 10. 1066b33-34

It is evident that there is not an infinite body in act.

PHY—3. 7. 207b10-12

Infinite Mutation

There is not any infinite mutation.

PHY—6. 10. 241a26-27

Infinite Progression in Causes

That there is at least some first principle and that the causes of entities are not infinite, either in a progress in a straight forward direction, or according to form, is evident.

ME—1a. 2. 994a1-2

Infinite Distance

An object cannot be seen at an infinite distance.

DE S ET S—7. 449a21-23

Infinites

It is impossible to cross over infinites.

PO A—1. 3. 72b10-11

Inflexion

There are, however, four modes of inflexion at the joints. For it is necessary that the inflexion both of the fore and hind legs should either be at the concave part; or, on the contrary, at the convex part; or conversely, not at the same part, but that the fore legs, indeed, should be inflected at the convex part, and the hind legs at the concave part; or in a way contrary to these, that the fore legs should have their concavity towards the anterior part, and their convexity behind, but the hind legs should have their convexity at the anterior part, and their concavity behind, so that their convexities should be diametrically opposite, and the concavities external.

DE IN—13. 712a1-8

Injured

To be injured is to suffer injustice at the hands of a willing agent; for commission of injustice has been previously defined to be a voluntary act.

RH—1. 13. 1373b27-29

Injustice

For the criminality and injustice of the act stands essentially in the deliberate principle on which it is done.

RH—1. 13. 1374a11-12

There is a difference between an act of injustice and that which is unjust. A thing is unjust by nature, or by ordinance; but this very thing, when it is being done, is an act of injustice.

N E—5. 10. 1135a8-11

The suffering of injustice is not voluntary.

N E—5. 11. 1136b5-6

A man cannot commit injustice in an absolute or strict sense against what is his own.

N E—5. 10. 1134b9-10

305

Injustice is not a part of vice but the whole of vice.

N E–5. 3. 1130a9-10

Vide JUSTICE.

Insatiability

The wickedness of man is insatiable. For though at first two obols might be sufficient pay, yet when once it has become customary, they continually want something more, until they set no limits to their expectations; for it is the nature of our desires to be boundless, and many live only to gratify them.

POL–Bk. 2. 7. 1267a41-1267b5

Insects

Are not generated from animals, but are produced spontaneously. . . . Some indeed are generated from the dews . . . others, again, are generated in putrid mud and dung, but others in wood . . . some likewise are generated in the hairs, but others in the flesh, and others in the excrements of animals.

DE H A–5. 19. 551a1-6

Instant

Neither is it possible for the same instant always to remain.

PHY–4. 10. 218a21-22

Instruction

All teaching and all learning grasped by reason proceeds from previous knowledge.

PO A–1. 1. 71a1-2

Instruction is imparted to all by means of advancing through those things that are less known to Nature to things that are more known.

ME–6. 4. 1029b4-5

Intellect

The intellect continues in perfection up to fifty years.

POL—Bk. 7. 16. 1335b32-35

Chance and fortune, therefore, are posterior both to intellect and nature.

PHY—2. 6. 198a9-10

The mere intellect has no motive power.

N E—6. 2. 1139a35-36

Intelligence

Intelligence is one and continuous, like thought.

DE A—1. 3. 407a6-7

Intelligence is critical, i.e. it makes distinctions.

N E—6. 11. 1143a9-10

It appears to be in the soul like a sort of substance and incapable of destruction. What would appear especially as if it could destroy it, is the decline that weakens man in old age.

DE A—1. 4. 408b18-20

The intelligence, applied to indivisibles only, cannot err.

DE A—3. 6. 430a26-27

The intelligence commands resistance on account of the future result, but the desire commands the need of being satisfied at once.

DE A—3. 10. 433b8-9

Of sanguineous animals, those that have a cold and thin blood are more intelligent than those that have hot and thick blood.

DE P A—2. 2. 648a2-4

Intelligence in Man

It is more rational to judge that (man) is gifted with hands as a result of his intelligence rather than that being endowed with hands is the cause of his superior intelligence.

DE P A—4. 10. 687a9-10

Intemperate

The intemperate is more depraved than the incontinent man.

M M—2. 6. 1203a17-18

Intercourse

Intercourse either is not an end or it is for the sake of friendship.

P A—2. 22. 68b5-6

Internationalism

It seems that friendship or love is the bond which holds states together.

N E—8. 1. 115a22-23

Interrogate

He who is about to interrogate should discover a ground whence he may argue; secondly, he should interrogate and arrange the several particulars to himself; thirdly and lastly, he should advance them against another person.

T—8. 1. 155b3-7

Intervals

The intervals are six in number by which animals are naturally adapted to be limited, viz. the upward and downward, behind and before, and besides these the right and the left.

DE IN—4. 705a26-28

Intuition

Of those habits which are concerned with learning, by which we ascertain truth, some are always true, but others admit the false, as opinion and reasoning; but science and intuition are always true, and no other kind of knowledge except intuition is more accurate than science, but the principles of demonstration are more known, and all science is connected with reason, there could not be a science of principles: but since nothing can be more true than science except intuition, intuition will be concerned with principles. . . .

PO A—2. 19. 100b5-15

Investigation

We investigate four things: *that* a thing is so, *why* it is so, *if* it is, *what* it is.

PO A—2. 1. 89b23-25

Involuntary

Acts done under compulsion, or from ignorance, are involuntary.

N E—3. 1. 1109b35-1110a1

He who performs any action not knowing what the action is, nor to what end it will lead, nor about whom such action is conversant, acts from ignorance essentially and therefore acts involuntarily.

E E—2. 9. 1225b5-7

Is

'Is' produces an affirmation always and completely in every case.

P A—1. 3. 25b22-23

When 'is' is the third element in predication there can be oppositions doubly; thus in the proposition "man is just" the verb 'is' is the third element.

DE I—10. 19b19-21

Without a verb there is neither affirmation nor negation for 'is' or 'will be' or 'was' or 'is going to be' and so forth are verbs . . . since they signify time.

DE I—10. 19b12-14

J

Jealousy

Pain at the apparent success of some worthy person.

T–2. 2. 109b35-36

Judge

In particular subjects it is a person of special education, and in general a person of universal education, who is a good judge.

N E–1. 1. 1095a1-2

As to whether a thing is important or trifling, just or unjust, whatever questions of this nature the legislator has not determined, on these the judge must somehow or other make up his mind for himself, and not take instructions on them from the parties at issue.

RH–1. 1. 1354a26-31

Judgment

From judgment proceed whatever appear to be useful, either as an end or as conducing to the end, when it is by reason of their usefulness that they are realized in action.

RH–1. 10. 1369b7-9

Judicial Decisions

Judicial decisions are made off hand; so that it is difficult under these circumstances to assign what is just and expedient.

RH–Bk. 1. 1. 1354b3

Just

That which is just then is, in a sense, a mean, as the judge is a mean.

NE—5. 7. 1132a24

The just is something equal.

E E—7. 9. 1241b12-13

A just man becomes just by doing what is just.

N E—2. 3. 1105a17-18

Just Act

Actions in accordance with virtue are not e.g. justly or temperately performed because they are in themselves just or temperate. It is necessary that the agent at the time of performing them should satisfy certain conditions, i.e. in the first place that he should know what he is doing, secondly that he should deliberately choose to do it and to do it for its own sake, and thirdly that he should do it as an instance of a settled and immutable moral state.

N E—2. 3. 1105a28-33

Justice

Now justice is the virtue by which each has his own as the law prescribes.

RH—1. 9. 1366b9-10

Now justice is a social virtue; for it is the rule of the social state, and the very criterion of what is right.

POL—Bk. I. 2. 1253a37-38

Justice is essentially human, i.e. it affects the mutual relations of men as men.

N E—5. 13. 1137a30

All men have some natural inclination to justice, but they proceed therein only to a certain degree; nor can they universally point out what is absolutely just. For instance, what is equal appears just, and is so, but not to all, only among those who are equals; and what is unequal appears just, and is so, but not to all, only amongst those who are unequals. This relative nature of justice some people neglect, and therefore they judge ill; and the reason of this is, that they judge for themselves, and almost every one is the worst judge in his own cause. Since then justice has reference to persons, the same distinctions must be made with respect to persons, which are made with respect to things.

POL—Bk. 3. 9. 1280a9-19

Justice, indeed, and the other virtues are entirely and in every respect eligible. M M—1. 2. 1183b39-1184a1

Justice, then, is complete virtue although not complete in an absolute sense but in relation to one's neighbors. . . . It is in the highest sense complete virtue, as being an exercise of complete virtue. It is complete too, because he who possesses it can employ his virtue in relation to his neighbors and not merely by himself. N E—5. 3. 1129b25-33

Collective justice will be the mean between profit and loss. N E—5. 7. 1132b18-19

Free states and aristocracies are mostly destroyed by a departure from justice in the administration itself.

POL—Bk. 5. 7. 1307a5-7

Justice, therefore, and friendship are either the same thing, or the one has something nearly allied to the other.

E E—7. 1. 1234b31

313

K

Kindness

That conformable to which he who has it is said to confer a benefit on one who needs it, not in return for anything nor in order that anything may accrue to him who so confers it, but that some benefit may arise to the object.

RH—2. 7. 1385a17-19

King

If it is an individual who shall happen so far to excel in virtue as to surpass all other persons in the community, then it is right that he should be king and lord of all.

POL—Bk. 3. 17. 1288a15-19

A king desires to be the guardian of his people, that those who have property may suffer no wrong, and that the people in general may live free from tyranny.

POL—Bk. 5. 10. 1310b40-1311a2

Nothing then remains but what indeed seems natural, and that is, for all persons quietly to submit to one who is thus eminently virtuous, and to let such men be perpetually kings in the respective states.

POL—Bk. 3. 13. 1284b32-34

A king is ambitious of honor.

POL—Bk. 5. 10. 1311a5

The object of a king is virtue.

POL—Bk. 5. 10. 1311a6-7

Kingdom

Now we usually call a state which is governed by one person for the common good, a kingdom.

POL—Bk. 3. 7. 1279a32-34

In the case of hereditary kingdoms, we must add one cause of destruction, namely, that many who enjoy it are proper objects of contempt, and that they are insolent.

POL—Bk. 5. 10. 1313a10-12

A kingdom is very seldom destroyed by any outward attack. But it has the greatest number of causes of subversion within.

POL—Bk. 5. 10. 1312b38-40

Kingships

The first is that of the heroic times; which was a government over a free people, with limited rights in some particulars: for the king was their general, their judge, and their high priest.

The second, that of the barbarians, which is an hereditary despotic government, regulated by laws.

The third is that which they call Aesymnetic, which is an elective tyranny.

The fourth is the Lacedaemonian; and this, in a few words, is nothing more than an hereditary generalship: and in these particulars they differ from each other.

POL—Bk. 3. 14. 1285b20-29

Know

All men by nature are actuated with the desire to know.

ME—1. 1. 980a22

To know is predicated in a threefold manner: either as universal knowledge or proper or actual exercise.

P A—2. 21. 67b3-5

It is not only however requisite that he who is to possess knowledge through demonstration should know in a greater degree first principles, and believe rather in them than in the thing demonstrated, but also that nothing else should be more credible or more known to him than the opposites of the principles, from which a syllogism of contra-deception may consist, since it behooves him who possesses knowledge singly to be unchangeable.

PO A—1. 2. 72a37-72b4

Knowledge

If a man conceives things which cannot be otherwise, as if he grasps the definitions through which demonstrations are formed he will not opine but he will know.

PO A—1. 33. 89a16-19

The knowledge of what a thing is, is identical with the knowledge of the why, and this is either simply or relatively as regards an attribute.

PO A—2. 2. 90a31-34

There is a difference between knowledge of the fact and knowledge of the reasoned fact. Within the same science, they differ in two ways: if the syllogism is not formed through immediate things (since the primary cause is not assumed which is prerequisite in knowledge of the reasoned fact) and when the premises are immediate yet not through the cause but through that which is more known of the things which reciprocate.

PO A—1. 13. 78a22-28

We judge that we know something when we know the first causes and the first principles even down to the basic elements.

PHY–1. 1. 184a3-5

Knowledge, as a genus, is explained by reference to something else for it is said to be knowledge of something, but individual instances of knowledge are not relative.

CAT–8. 10b25ff

This treatise is embarked on for the sake of acquiring knowledge; nor do we consider we know until we grasp the reason why for this is to grasp the prime cause.

PHY–2. 3. 194b17-20

Is in the soul as in a subject but it is predicated of a subject, viz. 'grammar.'

CAT–2. 1b1

We call that by which we know sometimes knowledge, sometimes intelligence, for we say that we know by one of them.

DE A–2. 2. 414a5-6

We can know what a thing is neither by definition nor by demonstration.

PO A–2. 7. 92b38

Knowledge is a consequent on learning subsequently.

RH–Bk. 1. 6. 1362a30-31

Upon the whole, a proof of a person's having knowledge is even the ability to teach; and for this reason we consider art, rather than experience, to be a science; for artists can, whereas the handicraftsmen cannot convey instruction.

ME–1. 1. 981b7-9

Knowledge is a principle of power.

RH—Bk. 1. 11. 1371b27-28

The object of knowledge would appear to be prior to knowledge, since, for the most part, we derive knowledge from things preexisting. . . . It is true that there can be no knowledge if the object of knowledge does not exist. It is equally true that an object may exist even though knowledge of it does not exist.

CAT—7. 7b24-32

One may ask, for example, how the intelligence knows evil or black. It knows them in a sense by their contraries.

DE A—3. 6. 430b21-23

He who knows what justice is, is not immediately just.

M M—1. 1. 1183b15-16

We do not wish to know what fortitude is, but we wish to be brave; nor what justice is, but to be just.

E E—1. 5. 1216b21-24

Knowledge, Demonstrative

If therefore demonstrative knowledge is knowledge of the necessary it must be obtained through a necessary middle term otherwise one will know neither why it is nor that it must necessarily be.

PO A—1. 6. 75a12-15

Knowledge, Reasoned

To know why a thing is is to know it through its cause, wherefore the middle must be inherent in the third and the first in the middle.

PO A—1. 6. 75a35-37

318

Knowledge, Scientific

It is impossible to have scientific knowledge through demonstration without a knowledge of first immediate principles. . . .

PO A—2. 19. 99b20-22

We think that we know scientifically when we know the cause; there are four causes: one as to the essence of the thing, another that which from certain things existing, this necessarily exists (material cause), the third, that which moves something (efficient) and a fourth, that on account of which (final cause).

PO A—2. 11. 94a20-22

Knowledge (Science)

It is necessary to say that knowledge is conception of the knowable.

T—6. 8. 146b5

Knowledge, Scientific, and Opinion

The object of scientific knowledge and science differs from the object of opinion, and from opinion, because science is universal and subsists through things necessary, and what is necessary cannot subsist otherwise than it does: some things however are true and subsist otherwise. It is evident then that science is not conversant with these (or else things which are capable of subsisting otherwise, could not possibly subsist otherwise). Yet neither is intellect conversant with such (I call intellect the principle of science) nor indemonstrable science, and this is the notion of an immediate proposition. But intellect, science and opinion, and what is asserted through these, are true wherefore it remains that opinion is conversant with the true or false which may be otherwise; opinion in fact is the grasp of a proposition which is immediate but not necessary . . . opinion is unstable. He thinks that he has an opinion when he thinks that a connection may be otherwise.

PO A—1. 33. 88b30-89a7

319

Knowledge, Scientific and Sense

It is not possible to have scientific knowledge through sensation, for, although, there is sensible perception of such a thing as this and not of this particular thing, yet it is necessary to have a sensible perception of this particular thing, somewhere and now. But it is impossible sensibly to perceive the universal and in all things, for it is not this particular thing, nor now otherwise it would not be universal, since we call the universal that which is always and everywhere.

PO A—1. 31. 87b28-33

As science stands to the object of science so is sense to the object of sense.

T—1. 17. 108a9-10

Knowledge of Particulars

For we know nothing of those things which fall under the senses once they have passed out of range, even though we perceived them before, except by means of universal and proper knowledge, which we are not actually using.

P A—2. 21. 67a39-67b3

Knowledge, Preexistent

The preexisting knowledge required (for learning and teaching) is of two kinds: in some cases we must presuppose that they are; in other cases we must understand the meaning of the term; in others we must understand both.

PO A—1. 1. 71a11-13

L

Labor

Such males as are more laborious, sooner grow old, on account of the labor they sustain. DE L ET B–5. 466b13-14

Language

Language is the cause of learning.
DE S ET S–1. 437a12-13

Law

Law, now, I understand, to be either peculiar or universal; peculiar, to be that which has been marked out by each people in reference to itself, and this is partly unwritten, partly written. I call that law universal which is conformable merely to the dictates of nature; for there does exist naturally an universal sense of right and wrong, which, in a certain degree, all intuitively divine, even should no intercourse with each other, nor any compact have existed. RH–1. 13. 1373b4-11

Law is either proper or common. Proper law I call that by whose written enactments men direct their city; the general or common law, whatever unwritten rules appear to be recognized among all men. RH–1. 10. 1368b7-9

The law is an agreement, and as the sophist Lycophron says, a pledge between the citizens of their intending to do

321

justice to each other, though not sufficient to make all the citizens just and good.

POL—Bk. 3. 9. 1280b10-12

It would be most admirably adapted to the purposes of justice, if laws properly enacted were, as far as circumstances admitted, of themselves to mark out all cases, and to abandon as few as possible to the discretion of the judge. And this because, in the first place, it is easier to get one or a few of good sense, and of ability to legislate and adjudge, than to get many: and next, legislative enactments proceed from men carrying their views a long time back: (or, from men who have reflected on the subject for a long time) while judicial decisions are made off hand; so that it is difficult for persons deciding under these circumstances to assign what is just and expedient; and, what is most of all to the point is this, that the award of the legislator is not particular nor about present circumstances, but about what is future and general; whereas the member of a popular assembly and the judge decide on points actually present and definite; and under their circumstances feelings of partiality and dislike and personal expediency will, in many instances, antecedently have been interwoven with the case, and to such a degree that one is no longer able, adequately, to contemplate the truth, and that personal pleasure or pain throws a shade over the judgment. In regard, then, the other particulars . . . it is right to leave the judge a discretion in as few as possible; but questions of fact, whether it has or has not taken place, will or will not happen, does or does not exist; all such it is necessary to abandon to the discretion of the judges; since it is not possible that the legislator ever should foresee them.

RH—1. 1. 1354a31-1354b16

All laws ought to be framed, and are framed by all men, with reference to the state, and not the state with reference to the laws.

POL—Bk. 4. 1. 1289a13-15

It is as much a man's duty to submit to command, as to assume it, and this also by rotation: for this is law, for order is law; and it is more proper that the law should govern than any one of the citizens.   POL—Bk. 3. 16. 1287a16-18

The universal law is derived from particular facts.

N E—6. 12. 1143b4-5

The administration of justice is the determination of what is just and unjust.   N E—5. 10. 1134a31-32

A law derives from custom all its power to enforce obedience, and this requires long time to establish; so that to make it any easy matter to pass from the established laws to other new ones is to weaken the power of law.

POL—Bk. 2. 8. 1269a20-24

Nor is it moreover right to permit written laws always to remain unaltered; for as in all other sciences, so in politics it is impossible that every thing should be expressed in writing with perfect exactness; for when we commit a thing to writing, we must use general terms; but in every action there is something particular in itself, which these may not comprehend; and hence it is evident that certain laws will at certain times admit of alterations.   POL—Bk. 2. 8. 1269a8-13

It is impossible that the same laws should be fitted to all sorts of oligarchies and democracies; for of both these governments there are many species and not one only.

POL—Bk. 4. 1. 1289a22-25

He who intrusts man with supreme power gives it to a wild beast, for such his appetites sometimes make him. Passion, too, influences those who are in power, even the

very best of men; for which reason the law is intellect free
from appetite.

POL—Bk. 3. 16. 1287a30-32

Law, Moral

The moral law is far superior to the written law.

POL—Bk. 3. 16. 1287b5-6

Law, Natural

A law of nature cannot be altered by habituation.

N E—2. 1. 1103a19-20

Lawful

Whatever is lawful is in some sense just.

N E—5. 2. 1129a34

Leadership

If there is any one superior to the rest of the community
in virtue and abilities for active life, him it is proper to
follow, and him it is right to obey; but he must have not
virtue alone, but also the power according to which he may
be capable of acting.

POL—Bk. 7. 3. 1325b10-12

Learn

To learn is accompanied by pain.

POL—Bk. 8. 5. 1339a28-29

Learning

All teaching and all learning grasped by reason proceeds
from previous knowledge.

PO A—1. 1. 71a1-2

Learning, Not Recollection

In like manner is the reasoning in the Meno that learning is reminiscence, for it never happens that we have a pre-existent knowledge of particulars, but along with induction we receive the science of particulars as it were by recognition; since some things we immediately know, as the angles are equal to two right angles if we know that what we see is a triangle. Also, in like manner as regards others.

P A–2. 21. 67a21-26

Legal Justice

The law looks only to the degree of the injury, it treats the parties as equals, and asks only if one is the author and the other the victim of injustice.

N E–5. 7. 1132a4-6

Legislation

The people may be allowed to have a vote in whatever bill is proposed, but may not themselves propose any thing contrary to it.

POL–Bk. 4. 14. 1298b30-32

Legislator

The legislator, and he who is truly a politician, ought to be acquainted not only with that which is most perfect in the abstract, but also that which is the best suited under any given circumstances.

POL–Bk. 4. 1. 1288b25-27

Leisure

Nature requires not only that we should be properly employed, but that we should be able to enjoy leisure honorably.

POL–Bk. 8. 3. 1337b30-32

Letter

A letter is an indivisible sound . . . from which an intelligible sound is adapted to be produced.

P–20. 1456b22-23

Liberal

Of all virtuous people none are so much beloved as the liberal; for they are benefactors, and their benefaction consists in their giving.

N E—4. 1. 1120a21-23

Liberality

Liberality appears to be the mean concerning properties.

N E—4. 1. 1119b22-23

Liberality consists in the moral state of the giver.

N E—4. 2. 1120b7-9

Liberality tends to benefit in pecuniary matters.

RH—1. 9. 1366b15-16

Disregard of self is a characteristic of liberality.

N E—4. 2. 1120b6-7

Liberty

The very foundation of a democratical state is liberty.

POL—Bk. 6. 2. 1317a40-41

Libido

Hairy men are more libidinous, and have a greater quantity of seed than such as are smooth.

DE G A—4. 5. 774b1-2

Licentious

He who enjoys every pleasure and never abstains from any pleasure is licentious.

N E—2. 2. 1104a22-24

Licentiousness

Licentiousness as a whole is not so voluntary, as nobody desires to be licentious.

N E–3. 15. 1119a32-33

Licentiousness deserves more severe reproach than cowardice; for it is easier to train oneself to meet its temptations as they frequently occur in life.

N E–3. 15. 1119a25-27

Temperance and licentiousness have to do with pleasures of such a kind as the lower animals generally are capable of, and it is hence that these pleasures appear slavish and brutish.

N E–3. 13. 1118a23-25

The licentious man then desires all pleasures, or the greatest pleasures, and is led to prefer these to anything else. He feels a double pain, viz. the pain of failing to obtain them and the pain of desiring them, as all desire is attended by pain.

N E–3. 14. 1119a1-4

Life

By life we understand these three facts: self-nourishment, developing, and decaying.

DE A–2. 1. 412a14-15

Life consists, as we said, in perceiving or understanding.

N E–9. 9. 1170a18-19

Life is the permanency of the soul.

DE R–18. 479a29-30

It follows necessarily that every living being has a nourishing soul and that it has it from birth to death: for it fol-

327

lows of necessity that what is once born grows, develops, and dies.

DE A—3. 12. 434a22-25

The preservation, therefore, of the vital heat is necessary to the existence of life.

DE V—4. 469b18-19

Life is a consequent on health simultaneously.

RH—Bk. 1. 6. 1362a31

Life and Nourishment

No being is nourished without having life also.

DE A—2. 4. 415b26-27

Light

Light is the actuality of the transparent in so far as it is transparent.

DE A—2. 7. 418b9-10

Light is always reflected.

DE A—2. 8. 419b29-30

What moves away from the center.

DE C—1. 3. 269b24

Why does light pass through a lantern? for necessarily that which consists of smaller particles passes through larger pores, if light is produced by transit. . . .

PO A—2. 11. 94b28-29

Lightness

The relatively light and lighter exist, when of two things possessing gravity, and equal in bulk, the one naturally tends downward swifter than the other.

DE C—4. 1. 308a31-33

Lightning

Lightning is produced after the percussion, and posterior to the thunder; though it appears to be prior to it, because the sight apprehends its object prior to the hearing.

DE M—2. 9. 369b8-9

Like

It is quite absurd to say that like is not affected by like.

DE A—1. 5. 410a24-25

Limit

A termination is called the last of each thing, and beyond which, as first, it is not possible to assume anything, and within which, as first, are comprised all things, and that, likewise, which may be a form of magnitude, or of that which is in possession of magnitude, and which is the end of everything.

ME—4. 17. 1022a4-6

Line

That which is divisible in one direction is a line.

ME—4. 6. 1016b26

A line is a continuous quantity for you may take a common term at which its parts meet, the point.

CAT—6. 5a1-2

Of magnitude indeed, that which is divisible in one way is a line.

DE C—1. 1. 268a7-8

Lips

Nature formed the tongue of man both for the sake of sapors and of speech; thus, also, she fashioned his lips both for the sake of speech, and the defence of the teeth.

DE P A—2. 16. 659b35-660a2

329

The lips, however, of men are soft and fleshy, and are capable of being employed to a twofold purpose, viz, for the defence of the teeth, as in other animals; and for a still better purpose, that of well-being.

DE P A–2. 16. 659b30-33

Locomotion

The principle from which locomotion originally arises is the soul.

DE A–2. 4. 415b9-10

Two causes of locomotion are intelligence and appetite.

DE A–3. 10. 433a9

Logic

Logic and rhetoric are both in an equal degree conversant about contraries.

RH–Bk. 1. 1. 1355a35

Longevity

The cause why quadrupeds are long-lived is their not having bile, but why birds live long, their being of a dry constitution or something else.

PO A–2. 17. 99b5-7

Love

To love is a certain act of pleasure, and is good.

M M–2. 11. 1210b6-7

This is a criterion of the commencement of love, when persons feel pleasure not only in the presence of the object, but are enamoured also of it when absent, on memory.

RH–Bk. 1. 11. 1370b22-24

Love is more a question of friendship than intercourse.

P A–2. 22. 68b4

He therefore who loves is beneficent, as far as he loves.

M M–2. 11. 1210b12

Lovers

Lovers sometimes, because they cannot endure the misery of the objects of their love, destroy both themselves and those whom they love. For they suffer more from their calamities than from their own.

E E–7. 12. 1246a22-23

Loved

To be loved is preferable in love to sexual intercourse.

P A–2. 22. 68b3-4

It would seem to follow that it is better to be loved than to be honored.

N E–8. 9. 1159a25-26

M

Magistrates

It is necessary that in small states the magistrates should be few, in large ones many.

POL–Bk. 6. 8. 1321b8-10

Magnanimity

Magnanimity is that virtue which is apt to confer important benefits.

RH–Bk. 1. 9. 1366b17

Magnificence

Magnificence is the virtue which produces grandeur in expenditures.

RH–Bk. 1. 9. 1366b18-19

Magnitude

Body will be the only perfect magnitude; for it is alone bounded by three things: and this is all.

DE C–1. 1. 268a22-24

That which is increased must necessarily have a certain magnitude, for growth is an increase and diminution is a lessening of the magnitude there.

DE G ET C–1. 5. 320b30-32

A right line and a circumference are the only simple magnitudes.

DE C–1. 2. 268b19-20

No magnitude is produced from intelligible elements.

PHY—4. 3. 209a15-16

Majority

It is very right that the many should have the greatest powers in their own hands. For the people, the council, and the judges are composed of them, and the property of all these collectively is more than the property of any person, or of a few who fill the great offices of the state.

POL—Bk. 3. 11. 1282a38-41

Male

By a male animal is understood that which can generate in another.

DE G A—1. 2. 716a20-21

The animal that makes the emission in another is called the male.

HA—1. 3. 489a12

The female always affords matter, and the male a fabricative power.

DE G A—2. 4. 738b20-21

But the male, as we have before observed, is more disposed to give assistance in danger, and is more courageous than the female.

DE H A—9. 1. 608b15-17

By nature and generally males live longer than females and the cause is because the male is warmer than the female.

DE L ET B—5. 466b14-16

The males of the human species have a larger brain than the females.

DE P A—2. 7. 653a28-29

333

Man

The definition of man is the definition of his soul.

M E–6. 11. 1037a28-29

A man and an ox are both animal and are so named univocally, since not only the name but also the definition is the same.

CAT–1. 1a8-9

Man is the only animal that is erect, because his nature and essence are divine.

DE P A–4. 10. 686a27-28

Man is an animal naturally formed for society.

POL–Bk. 3. 6. 1278b19

It is evident that a state is one of the works of nature, and that man is naturally a political animal, and that whosoever is naturally, and not accidentally, unfit for society, must be either inferior or superior to man; just as the person reviled in Homer,

'No tribe, nor state, nor home hath he.'

POL–Bk. I. 2. 1253a1-5

Man is naturally a social being.

N E–1. 5. 1097b11

The function of man then is an activity of soul in accordance with reason, or not independently of reason.

N E–1. 6. 1098a7-8

Man is generative of actions.

M M–1. 11. 1187b5-7

'Man' is predicated of the individual man; 'animal' is predicated of 'man'; it will, thus, be predicated of the individual man, too; for the individual man is both 'man' and 'animal.'

CAT–3. 1b7-11

Man, Individual

Lastly, some are neither in, nor predicated of, any subject, as 'a certain Man' and 'a certain horse,' for nothing of this sort is either in or predicated of a certain subject.

CAT–2. 1b3-5

Man, Good

We call a man good when he is of perfect virtue.

POL–Bk. 3. 4. 1276b33-34

Man, Peculiarity of

The inability to experience smell without inhaling is a peculiarity of the human race.

DE A–2. 9. 421b14-15

Man, Universal

'Man' is predicated of a subject, i.e. of the individual man, yet is in no subject.

CAT–2. 1a21

Mankind

The greatest part of mankind is desirous of riches rather than honor.

POL–Bk. 6. 4. 1318b16-17

Manners

Manners are a quality of the soul acquired by custom.

E E–2. 2. 1220a39-1220b1

Marriage

It is conducive to temperance not to marry too soon.

POL–Bk. 7. 16. 1335a22-23

The proper time for a woman to marry is eighteen, for a man, thirty-seven, a little more or less.

POL—Bk. 7. 16. 1335a28-29

Marrow

It is the concocted excrement of the sanguineous nutriment, contained in the concavities of the bones and spine, and distributed for the nutrition of them.

DE P A—2. 6. 651b22-24

Master

There would seem to be one sort of knowledge proper for a master, and another for a slave; that of the slave is such as the slave taught at Syracuse; for there a fellow at a stipulated sum instructed the boys in the routine business of a household slave. . . . The knowledge of the master, on the other hand, is the proper use of his slaves, for the office of a master lies in the employment, not in the mere possession of them.

POL—Bk. 1. 7. 1255b22-33

Mathematician

About what sort of entities are we to assert that the mathematician is engaged: for surely he is not engaged about those things that are here—that is, about sensibles—for none of these constitutes the description of entity which the mathematical sciences investigate. Neither is the science now under investigation—I mean Metaphysics—conversant about mathematical entities, for no one of these possesses a separable subsistence. Nor is it a science belonging to substances cognisant by the senses, for these are corruptible.

ME—10. 1. 1059b9-14

But as the mathematician institutes for himself an inquiry regarding abstract quantities—for he conducts his speculations by removing out of his consideration all sensible

336

natures, such as gravity and lightness, and hardness, and its contrary, and further, heat and cold and other sensible contrarieties, but he merely leaves remaining quantity and continuity. (He speculates into things) so far forth as they are quantities and continuous.

ME—10. 3. 1061a28-35

Mathematics

Mathematics speculates about a certain portion of matter, appropriating it to itself, as, for instance, about lines, or angles or numbers or something else pertaining to other quantities: not however as far forth as they are entities, but so far forth as each of them is that which is continuous in one, or two, or three dimensions.

ME—10. 4. 1061b21-25

The mathematical sciences are concerned with forms and do not regard one certain subject, for though the geometrical questions concern a certain subject yet not so far as they are geometrical are they in a subject . . . to know what a rainbow is pertains to the natural philosopher, but why it is pertains to the optician either simply or mathematically.

PO A—1. 13. 79a7-13

Mathematics uses definitions for its premises, never just accidents and in this the mathematical sciences differ from dialectical reasonings.

PO A—1. 12. 78a10-13

Mathematical Accuracy

Mathematical accuracy of language is not to be required in all things, but in those things that do not involve any connexion with matter.

ME—2. 3. 995a14-16

Mathematical Entities

That, indeed, therefore, neither are mathematical entities

337

in a greater degree existences than bodies, and that they are not antecedent in their essence to those objects that fall under the notice of the senses, but are so merely in point of definition, and that it is not possible that they should be made to involve a separate subsistence in any place, has been declared with sufficient clearness.

ME–12. 2. 1077b12-14

Mathematical Philosophy

And of mathematical science some are conversant about entities that are immovable, it is true, yet, perhaps, not separable, but subsisting as in matter.

ME–5. 1. 1026a14-15

Matter (Ule)

I call matter that which essentially is termed neither quiddity, nor quantity, nor anything else of those things whereby entity is defined.

ME–6. 3. 1029a20-21

Matter is unknown in itself. Now matter is partly sensible and partly intelligible; that which is sensible is such as brass and wood, and such as is movable; but intelligible matter is that which is inherent in things that are sensible, but not so far forth as they are sensible, as mathematical entities.

ME–6. 10. 1036a8-12

Matter

All sensible substances involve matter; I mean by matter that which is not this certain particular thing in act, but in potentiality is this certain particular thing.

ME–7. 1. 1042a25-28

Matter exists in potentiality because it may advance on to form; but when it exists in act, then it exists in form.

ME–8. 8. 1050a15-16

Of that which is being produced must there now necessarily exist something; and if, in short, it is undergoing corruption, there will subsist a certain entity; and if it is being produced there must needs be that from which it is produced and by which it is generated, and that this process does not go on to infinity.

ME–3. 5. 1010a17-32

Matter therefore as a principle is the cause in generated natures of the ability to be, and not to be.

DE G ET C–2. 9. 335a32-33

Matter, however, so far as matter, is passive.

DE G ET C–1. 7. 324b18

Matter, indeed, is non-being according to accident.

PHY–1. 9. 192a4-5

Matter is a medium insensible, and inseparable.

DE G ET C–2. 6. 332a35-332b1

Matter has immediately a contrary.

DE L ET B–3. 465b29-30

Matter and Form

Because the matter of singulars is a thing that is different, both your matter and form, and that which imparts motion and species differ in number from mine, though according to the formal principle of the universal they are the same.

ME–11. 5. 1071a27-29

Matter and Generation

It is necessary, therefore, that matter and generation should be prior in time, but that the essence and form of every thing should be prior in reason.

DE P A–2. 1. 646a35-646b2

339

Maxim

The maxim is an assertion . . . on some general subject, but not every general subject but respecting as many subjects as moral conduct is concerned about and as are objects of choice or avoidance in acting . . . both the conclusions of enthymemes and their premises, after the syllogistic form has been done away with, become maxims.

RH–2. 21. 1394a21-28

Maximum and Minimum

Since it is not possible for an animal or plant to be infinitely big or small neither can the parts or the whole be.

PHY–1. 4. 187b16-18

Mean

Where there is excess and deficiency, there is also a mean.

N E–4. 10. 1125b18-19

Virtue is a mean state, so far at least as it aims at the mean.

N E–2. 5. 1106b27-28

The mean state is everywhere laudable, but we ought to incline at one time towards the excess and at another towards the deficiency; for this will be our easiest manner of hitting the mean, or in other words of attaining excellence.

N E–2. 9. 1109b23-26

Everybody who understands his business avoids alike excess and deficiency; he seeks and chooses the mean, not the absolute mean, but the mean considered relatively to ourselves.

N E–2. 5. 1106b5-7

The mean states then in life are three, viz. friendliness, truthfulness, and wittiness.

N E—4. 14. 1128b4-7

Those who seek for what is just seek for a mean; now the law is a mean.

POL—Bk. 3. 16. 1287b3-5

Measure of Things

Every moral state has its own honors and pleasures, nor is there any point perhaps so distinctive of the virtuous man as his power of seeing the truth in all cases, because he is, as it were, the standard and measure of things.

N E—3. 6. 1113a31-33

Media

All media, and the things of which they are media, are contained in the same genus.

ME—9. 7. 1057a19-20

It is necessary that media should derive their being from contraries.

ME—9. 7. 1057a19

Meditation

Meditations preserve the memory by reminiscence.

DE M ET R—1. 451a14-16

Memory

From sense, therefore, as we say, memory is produced.

PO A—2. 19. 100a3

For no memory is a habit, but rather an action.

T—4. 5. 125b18-19

Memory, therefore, is neither sense for understanding but is either a habit or passion of some one of these, when time intervenes.

DE M ET R–1. 449b24-25

Memory will be of the intelligible accidentally, but essentially of that which is first sensitive.

DE M ET R–1. 450a13-14

Those animals only that have a perception of time remember, and this by that power by which they perceive.

DE M ET R–1. 449b29-30

Many animals besides man have equally the faculty of remembering and learning.

H A–1. 1. 488b25-26

Those also, who are very young, and very old, labor under a defect of memory, on account of motion.

DE M ET R–2. 453b4-5

Memory and Reminiscence

To remember, however, differs from reminiscence, not only in time, but because many other animals participate of the former, but no one of the known animals, as I may say, participates of the latter, except man.

DE M ET R–2. 453a6-9

Those who are of a slow genius excel in memory, and those who are of a rapid genius and docile, excel in reminiscence.

DE M ET R–1. 449b7-8

Metaphor

The greatest number of elegancies arise from metaphor.

RH–Bk. 3. 11. 1412a17-19

342

Our metaphors should not be far-fetched.

RH—Bk. 3. 2. 1405a35-37

Metaphysics

There is a certain science which makes as the object of its speculation being as being and the things which are essentially inherent in this.

ME—3. 1. 1003a21-22

It is the province of this science (first philosophy) to investigate being so far forth as it is being and respecting quiddity or the nature of a thing and respecting those things that universally are inherent in it, so far forth as it is being.

ME—5. 1. 1026a30-32

Metaphysics, or the First Philosophy, is conversant about entities which both have a separate subsistence and are immovable.

ME—5. 1. 1026a15-16

Meteorology

Is concerned with events that are natural, though their order is less perfect than that of the first of the elements of bodies; they take place in the region nearest the movement of the stars; they include the milky way, comets and meteors and all affections which we consider common to the air and water; we will expound, moreover, how many parts and species of earth there are and how many their affections; finally we will contemplate the causes of the motions of the winds and of the earth and all things resulting from such . . . and of the falling of thunder-bolts and of whirlwinds and firewinds and the other affections of bodies resulting therefrom. . . .

D M—1. 1. 338a26-339a5

Method of Reasoning

Vide REASONING, METHOD OF.

Middle-Aged, Dispositions of

Moderate, spirited with coolness, possessing all the virtues found in excess or defect in the young and those in old age.

RH—2. 14. 1390a29-1390b13

Mind

What is called the mind of the soul (and by mind I mean that by which the soul thinks and judges) is actually nothing of the existing things before it knows.

DE A—3. 4. 429a22-24

Because the mind is not actually any of the real things before it thinks, it cannot be reasonably considered as blended with the body; if it were it would acquire warmth or cold or even have an organ like the senses.

DE A—3. 4. 429a23-26

The thinking part while being impassible must be receptive of form and potentially such as its object without being it.

DE A—3. 4. 429a15-16

Because everything is a possible object of thought, mind, in order to know must be simple, i.e. unmixed with any other.

DE A—3. 4. 429a18-19

Mind does not at one time know and at another time not; when separated it is just what it is and nothing more; this alone is immortal and eternal.

DE A—3. 5. 430a20-23

The actual perception by mind of mind itself doth subsist in this way throughout all eternity.

ME—11. 9. 1075a10

The mind is perhaps something too divine, something impassible.

DE A—408b29-30

The mind is in its prime about the age of forty-nine.

RH—Bk. 2. 14. 1390b11

Mind (Nous)

It was well to call the mind the location of forms; but this applies only to the intellective soul and the forms are present only potentially.

DE A—3. 4. 429a27-29

Mind and Body

It is impossible for the mind and body both to labor at the same time.

POL—Bk. 8. 4. 1339a9-10

Mingling

Those things are mingled, which have a contrariety of agents.

DE G ET C—1. 10. 328a31-32

Among things divisible and passive, such as are easily bounded are capable of being mingled; for these are easily divided into small parts.

DE G ET C—1. 10. 328a31-34

Mobile

A thing is movable in so far as it involves a capability of having motion impressed upon it, and that which imparts motion does so from act.

ME—10. 9. 1066a29-30

Modesty

Although modesty is not a virtue, yet a modest person is praised as if he were virtuous.

N E—2. 7. 1108a31-32

Moisture

Hot moisture is the cause of increase, and of life.

DE L ET B—5. 466b21-22

When the moisture gradually descends it is called a drizzle, but when in larger parts rain.

DE M—1. 9. 347a11-12

All things receive increase from moisture.

DE P A—2. 2. 647b26-27

Monad

That which is indivisible according to quantity, and so far forth as it is a quantity (I mean what is in every direction indivisible, and is without position), this is called a unit or monad.

ME—4. 6. 1016b24-25

Monads when composed can neither produce body nor possess gravity.

DE C—3. 1. 300a18-19

Monarchy

There is a fifth species of kingly government, which is where one person has a supreme power over all things whatsoever, in the manner that every tribe and every state is supreme over those things which belong to the public; for as the master of a family has a kingly rule in his own house, so a king is master of his own state, and over one or more tribes.

POL—Bk. 3. 14. 1285b29-33

Those who are accustomed by nature to submit themselves to the political rule of a family eminent for virtue, are adapted to kingly government.

POL—Bk. 3. 17. 1288a8-9

Monarchy is that form (of government) in which one man is supreme; and of monarchies those which are held by conformity to some limitations are kingdoms, but the unlimited are tyrannies.

RH—1. 8. 1365b37-1366a2

A monarchy is a tyranny where one person has a despotic power over the whole community.

POL—Bk. 3. 8. 1279b16-17

It is a common preservative of all monarchies not to make one person too great.

POL—Bk. 5. 11. 1313a19-20

It seems absurd to suppose that one person can see better with two eyes, and hear better with two ears, or do better with two hands and two feet, than many can do with many; for we see that absolute monarchs now furnish themselves with many eyes, and ears, and hands, and feet; for they intrust those who are friends to themselves and their government with part of their power. If they are not friends to the monarch, they will not do what he chooses; but if they are friends to him, they are friends also to his government: but a friend is an equal, and like his friend: if then he thinks that such should govern, he thinks that those who are his equals and like himself should govern. These are nearly the objections which men usually urge in dispute against kingly power.

POL—Bk. 3. 16. 1287b26-35

Monarchy, Absolute

When the whole state is wholly subject to the will of one person.

POL—Bk. 3. 16. 1287a9-10

Money

Money is a sort of medium or mean; for it measures

everything and consequently measures among other things excess or defect.

N E–5. 8. 1133a20-21

Money therefore is like a measure that equates things, by making them commensurable.

N E–5. 8. 1133b16-17

Money has not a natural but a conventional existence because it is in our power to change it, and make it useless.

N E–5. 8. 1133a30-31

As regards the giving and taking of money, the mean state is liberality, the excess and deficiency are prodigality and illiberality.

N E–2. 7. 1107b8-10

Money-Making
The life of money-making is in a sense a life of constraint, and it is clear that wealth is not the good of which we are in quest.

N E–1. 3. 1095a5-7

Moon
The moon evidences . . . that she is spherical.

DE C–2. 11. 291b18-19

Morality
The pleasure or pain which follows upon actions may be regarded as a test of a person's moral state.

P–2. 1448a1-5

The motion of the moon is downward, but slow.

DE M–1. 3. 341a22-23

Since the objects of imitation are men in action, and

these men must be either of a higher or a lower type (for moral character mainly answers to these divisions, goodness and badness being the distinguishing marks of moral differences), it follows that we must represent men either as better than in real life, or as worse, or as they are.

N E–2. 2. 1104b3-5

Moral Purpose

Moral purpose is the origin of action, i.e. the original motive but not the final cause.

N E–6. 2. 1139a31-32

The moral purpose then may be defined as desiderative reason or intellectual desire.

N E–6. 2. 1139b4-5

Moral purpose implies reason and thought.

N E–3. 4. 1112a15-16

It seems to be a general law that our moral purpose is confined to such things as lie within our own power.

N E–3. 4. 1111b29-30

It is clear that moral purpose is something voluntary.

N E–3. 4. 1111b6-7

Nothing that is past can be an object of the moral purpose.

N E–6. 2. 1139b6-7

Moral Virtue

He who is to govern ought to be perfect in moral virtue (for his business is entirely that of a master artificer, and reason is the master artificer), while others want only that portion of it which may be sufficient for their station.

POL–Bk. I. 13. 1260a17-20

Morphe

That which is nourished is figure and form conjoined with matter.

DE G ET C–2. 8. 335a15-16

Vide FORM.

Motion

If the categories are divided by substance, quality, place, action, passion, relation, quantity, there must needs be three motions: of quality, quantity and of place; but according to substance there does not exist any motion on account of there being nothing contrary to substance; nor is there a motion of relation.

ME–10. 12. 1068a8-11

Of motion, there are six species: generation, corruption, increase, diminution, alteration, and change of place.

CAT–14. 15a14

There are four kinds of motion: transition, change of state, decay, increase: the soul must necessarily have either one of these motions, or several, or all of them.

DE A–1. 3. 406a12-14

All such things as subsist from nature appear to contain in themselves a principle of motion and permanency: some according to place, others according to increase and diminution; and others according to change in quality.

PHY–2. 1. 192b13-16

The act of that which exists in potentiality so far forth as it exists in potentiality.

ME–10. 9. 1065b16

350

The actuality of that which is potential so far forth as it is potential constitutes motion.

ME—10. 9. 1065b33

Motion is continuous.

E E—2. 3. 1220b26

Motion is one when it is indivisible, and indivisible according to time.

ME—4. 6. 1016a6

Every motion is imperfect.

ME—8. 6. 1048b28-29

The motion in a right line is the motion of simple bodies.

DE C—1. 2. 269a25-26

There is one natural motion of every simple body.

DE C—1. 2. 269a8-9

There is one motion of cach of the simple bodies.

DE C—1. 3. 270b28-29

Motion follows that which is moved.

DE G ET C—2. 10. 337a25-26

The motion in a right line is upward and downward.

DE C—1. 2. 268b20-21

Every motion is in time.
PHY—6. 2. 232b20

Motion is divisible in a twofold respect; in one way by time; in another, according to the motions of the parts of that which is moved.
PHY—6. 4. 234b21-23

All things cease to be moved when they arrive at their proper place.

DE C–1. 19. 279b1-2

If any thing moves being immovable, that indeed will touch the thing movable, but itself will not be touched by any thing.

DE G ET C–1. 6. 323a31-32

It is evident, therefore, that local motion is either solely or especially present with those animals which effect the mutation according to place with two or four marks (or members).

DE IN–7. 707a16-18

All things are perpetually in motion.

DE L ET B–3. 465b25-26

Motion has not a subsistence separate from things.

PHY–3. 1. 200b32-33

All motion is a certain mutation.

PHY–5. 1. 225a34

Motion and Magnitude

We measure magnitude by motion and motion by magnitude.

PHY–4. 12. 220b28-29

Motion, Alternate

That also which is moved progressively proceeds alternately from the right and left part; for thus the body becomes restored to its former situation.

DE IN–8. 708b16-19

Motion, Apparent

When we have beheld for some time a body in motion,

352

such as a river, and especially if it flows rapidly, things at rest will appear to us to be moved. DE SOM–2. 459b18-20

The land appears to be moved to those that are sailing, in consequence of the sight being moved by something else.

DE SOM–2. 460b26-27

Moved Requires Mover and Goal

Everything which has motion impressed upon it is put in motion by something and in the direction of something.

ME–10. 6. 1063a17-18

Movement

Movement is a sort of act, but an incomplete act.

DE A–2. 5. 417a16-17

Every moving object can move in two respects: either by another, or by itself. DE A–1. 3. 406a4-5

It is necessary that that which is moved in a circle from whatever point it begins should similarly arrive at all the contrary places. DE C–1. 4. 271a24-25

To be moved by violence is the same thing as to be moved contrary to nature. DE C–3. 2. 300a23

Movement partakes in its nature of plurality.

ME–3. 2. 1004b29

The function of movement to change position is performed by the feet, the wings, and the corresponding organs.

H A–1. 3. 489a26-29

Some animals, however, are moved while they sleep, and do many things which pertain to wakefulness, but not without a phantasm or sense-perception; for a dream is as it were a sense-perception.

DE S—2. 456a24-26

Mover, First

Since that which has motion impressed upon it and which imparts motion exists as a medium, there is therefore something which, not having motion impressed upon it yet imparts motion which is a thing that is eternal, being both substance and act; but in this way it imparts motion—I mean that which is desirable and that which is intelligible imparts motion whereas they are not moved themselves.

ME—11. 7. 1072a24-27

Of necessity must this Immovable First Mover constitute an entity.

ME—11. 7. 1072b10

It will happen that the first mover in all things which are moved is immovable.

PHY—8. 5. 258b5-6

There is something which always moves the things that are in motion, and the first imparter of motion is itself immovable.

ME—3. 8. 30-31

We shall assert that the first mover is necessarily without parts and has no magnitude.

PHY—8. 10. 267b25-26

The first mover produces a perpetual motion, and in an infinite time. It is evident, therefore, that it is indivisible, without parts, and has no magnitude.

PHY—8. 10. 267b24-26

354

The air is the first mover with respect to that which is moved.

PHY—7. 2. 245a8

Mover

The mover may be of two kinds—motionless, or mover and moved at the same time.

DE A—3. 10. 433b13-14

Moving Body

It is impossible that the body which is moved in a circle should have either gravity or levity.

DE C—1. 3. 269b29-31

No body non-movable can have a soul without sensation.

DE A—3. 12. 434b3-4

Moving Cause

The moving cause is prior in nature to that which is being moved.

ME—3. 5. 1010b37-1011a1

Multiple

The multiple is according to number in respect to one, but such as is not defined.

ME—4. 15. 1020b34-35

Multitude

Multitude is styled that which is divisible in potentiality into what is not continuous.

ME—4. 13. 1020a10-11

Multitude is a certain quantity if it may be numerable, but magnitude if it may be measurable.

ME—4. 13. 1020a8-10

Such things as are many in number involve a connexion with matter.

ME—11. 8. 1074a33-34

The multitude are less liable to corruption; as water is from its quantity, so are the many less liable to corruption than the few.

POL—Bk. 3. 15. 1286a31-33

The multitude fancy that they are able to use dominion and power and wealth, but they do not rightly form this opinion.

M M—2. 3. 1199b18-20

Mutation

All mutation is finite.

DE C—1. 8. 277a15-16

It is difficult by leaping to produce a continued mutation.

DE IN—14. 712a31-32

Mutation, Infinite

This much, therefore, has been said by us to prove that there is neither any infinite mutation nor any continued motion, except that which is in a circle.

PHY—8. 8. 265a10-12

Mutation of Contrariety

When therefore the mutation of contrariety is according to quantity, it is increase and diminution; when according to place, it is motion.

DE G ET C—1. 4. 319b31-33

Mute

That which even with the concurrence of the tongue has of itself no sound but becomes audible in conjunction with things which have a certain sound.

P—20. 1456b28-30

356

N

Name

The name signifies the existence or the non-existence of this particular thing. ME—3. 4. 1006a28-29

Vide NOUN.

Names as Symbols

Since we cannot discourse by adducing the things themselves we use names as symbols of things. SE—1. 1. 165a6-9

Narration

In deliberative speeches narration occurs least of all.
RH—Bk. 3. 16. 1417b11-12

Natural

What happens regularly is natural. DE G A—1. 19. 727b29-30

Natural Bodies

All natural bodies and magnitudes are essentially movable according to place. DE C—1. 2. 268b13-15

Natural Distribution

Nature, in the same manner as a wise man, always distributes to every thing that which it is able to use.

DE P A—4. 10. 687a10-12

Natural Knowledge, Way of

The naturally constituted way of acquiring knowledge of nature is to proceed from what is more knowable to us and advance to what is more knowable by nature.

PHY—1. 1. 184a15-18

Natural Objects in Motion

We must suppose that those that exist by nature are, all or some of them, in motion; which is evident by induction.

PHY—1. 2. 185a12-14

Naturally (by Nature)

All those things exist naturally whose cause is internal and ordinate; for they turn out either invariably or generally in the same way.

RH—1. 10. 1369a35-1369b2

Nature

Nature is merely one certain genus of entity.

ME—3. 3. 1005a34

The very nature of a thing is the essence of that thing.

ME—6. 4. 1030a3

The very nature of a thing appertains to those things the discourse respecting which is a definition.

ME—6. 4. 1030a6-7

Nature is styled the substance of things that exist by nature.

ME—4. 4. 1014b36-37

Of those things which exist some are by nature others are through other causes. By nature indeed, are animals and their parts, plants and simple bodies such as, earth, fire, air, water. For these and others of the like we say exist by nature.

PHY—2. 1. 192b8-12

The earliest nature, and that termed so with precision, is the substance—I mean of those things possessing the principle of motion in themselves.

ME—4. 4. 1015a13-15

The very nature of everything is that which is denominated as subsisting essentially or absolutely.

ME—6. 4. 1029b13-14

Nature is twofold, one kind being as matter, but another as form.

PHY—2. 8. 199a30-31

Nature is called, in one way, the production of things that are by Nature . . . and in another, as that from which, as being inherent, that which is being naturally produced is primarily formed.

ME—4. 4. 1014b16-18

Nature is the origin of the earliest motion in each of the things in itself subsisting by Nature, so far as it is this very thing.

ME—4. 4. 1014b18-20

Those things are said to be by nature as involve growth through another body by means of contact, and growth along with or growth beside as embryos.

ME—4. 4. 1014b20-22

The first principle of motion, in those things that by Nature subsist, is Nature, inherent as a first principle in a manner either potentially or actually.

ME—4. 4. 1015a17-19

Nature is a principle of motion and mutation.

PHY–3. 1. 200b12

Moreover, is that styled Nature from which, as its primary matter, there either is or arises anything of the things that subsist by Nature, being without regular motion, and unchangeable from the power which belongs to itself, as of a statue . . . the brass is called the nature.

ME–4. 4. 1014b26-30

Nature, however, is the primary matter.

ME–4. 4. 1015a7

We must first presuppose that in nature nothing acts on or is acted upon at random, nor may anything be made from anything else at random unless we assume that it is accidental.

PHY–1. 5. 188a31-34

Nature makes nothing in vain but always the best possible in each kind of living thing according to its essence.

DE IN–2. 704b15-17

Nature produces nothing in vain, but with a view to that which is better.

DE IN–12. 711a17-19

Nature does nothing contrary to nature.

DE IN–11. 711a7

The cause, however, why serpents are without feet is, that nature does nothing in vain, but looking in all things to that which is best, gives to every thing that which it is capable of receiving, and preserves its peculiar essence and characteristic property.

DE IN–8. 708a9-12

360

Nature does nothing casually.   DE C–2. 8. 290a31

Nature always makes the best of possible things.

DE C–2. 5. 288a2-3

Nature is accustomed to avoid the infinite, for the infinite lacks an end and nature always seeks an end.

DE G A–1. 1715b14-16

All things generated by nature are either contraries, or from contraries.   PHY–1. 5. 188b25-26

All corruptible and generable natures are changeable in quality.   DE C–1. 12. 283b19-20

Nature always contrives as an auxiliary against the excess of every thing, the association of its contrary that the one may equalize the excess of the other.   DE P A–2. 7. 652a31-33

Everywhere nature returns to another part what she has elsewhere received.   DE P A–2. 14. 658a34-35

Whatever is contrary to nature is not right.

POL–Bk. 7. 3. 1325b9-10

There is nothing which nature avoids so much as what is painful or desires so much as what is pleasant.

N E–8. 6. 1157b16-17

Necessary

That which does not admit of being otherwise than it is.

ME–4. 5. 1015a33-35

What is compulsory is styled necessary. ME—4. 5. 1015a28

That is necessary without which it is not possible for what is good either to subsist, or to arise, or to cast aside any evil, or that any evil should be exterminated.

ME—4. 5. 1015a22-24

Necessary is defined as that without which, as a co-operating cause, it is not admissible for a thing to exist.

ME—4. 5. 1015a20-21

The necessary subsists simply, indeed, in things eternal.

DE P A—1. 1. 639b23-24

What is necessary to be through itself and necessarily accepted is neither an hypothesis nor a postulate.

PO A—1. 10. 76b23-24

Necessity

Wherefore what is must be when it is, and what is not, must not be when it is not; but it is not necessary that every being should be, nor that non-being should not be, since it is not the same thing for every being to be from necessity when it is, and simply to be from necessity, and in like-manner as to non-being. DE I—9. 19a23-27

Necessity seems to be a something that is inevitable (correctly so), for it is contrary to the motion according to free-will, and according to the power of reasoning.

ME—4. 5. 1015a31-33

Necessity is two-fold; it may be in accord with a thing's nature or with violence and against its nature.

PO A—2. 11. 94b37-95a1

362

All things that will be, it is necessary should be generated, and hence there will be nothing casual nor fortuitous, for if it were fortuitous it would not be of necessity.

DE I–9. 18b14-17

It is evident, therefore, that the necessity which is in natural things is that which is denominated as matter, and the motions of this.

PHY–2. 9. 200a30-32

Necessity, Hypothetical

Hypothetical necessity is in everything generated as well as in art productions.

DE P A–1. 1. 639b24-25

Neck

A long neck is weak.

DE P A–4. 12. 693a4

Negation

Negation is the enunciation of something from something.

DE I–6. 17a25-26

Nerves

Some bones are bound together by nerves.

DE P A–2. 9. 654b25

Night

The air of the night is more undisturbed, because the night is more tranquil.

DE DIV–2. 464a14-15

Nihilo, Ex

Entity is spoken of in a twofold point of view; so that it is admissible in a way that something should arise from

363

that which has no being, and that it is in a way not admissible that it should be so; and that the same thing at the same time should be an entity and a nonentity, but not according to the same entity; for in potentiality, no doubt, is it admissible at the same time for the same thing to be contraries, but in actuality not so.

ME—3. 5. 1009a32-36

Nobility

It is worthy of a sensible and generous nobility to divide the poor amongst them, and to induce them to work by supplying them with what is necessary.

POL—Bk. 6. 5. 1320b7-9

Noble

I understand by noble, in speaking of animals, the one that comes of a well-endowed stock.

H A—1. 1. 488b18-19

Nobleness

Nobleness is a characteristic of all the virtues.

N E—4. 4. 1122b7

Non-Being

It will be true to say that non-being belongs to certain things.

DE G ET C—1. 3. 317b3

None

"Every" or "none" signifies nothing else than that affirmation or negation is applied of the name universally.

DE I—10. 20a12-14

Non-Existence

If any thing is corruptible in an infinite time, it will possess the power of not existing.

DE C—1. 12. 281b20-21

364

Noon

Noon is generally the most tranquil part of the day.

DE M–2. 8. 366a14-15

Noun

A noun is a sound signifying by convention, without time, no part of which is separately significant.

DE I–2. 16a19-20

A composite sound significant without time of which no part is of itself significant.

P–20. 1457a10-12

Nothing is a noun or name by nature but only when used as a symbol.

DE I–2. 16a29

Nouns and Verbs

Nouns and verbs of themselves resemble conceptions without composition and division . . . which are neither true nor false.

DE I–1. 16a13-16

Nouns and verbs, indeed, when transposed, have the same signification.

DE I–10. 20b1-2

Noun, Indefinite

'Not-man' is not a noun . . . since it is neither a sentence nor a denial. Let it be an indefinite noun because it exists in respect of every thing alike, both of that which is and of that which is not.

DE I–2. 16a30-33

Nourishment

There are three things: the being nourished, that by which it is nourished, and that which nourishes it.

DE A–2. 4. 416b20-21

Nouveau Riche

The having recently become rich is as it were an inexpertness in wealth.

RH–Bk. 2. 16. 1391a17

Now

The *now*, or an instant, is not a part of time.

PHY–4. 10. 218a6

Number

A discrete quantity. There is no common boundary at which the parts meet.

CAT–6. 4b23-30

Neither therefore does number constitute a cause in respect of production, nor does it as number exist at all, nor as such number as is of the nature of a monad, nor as matter, nor as the formal principle, and the form itself of things. But undoubtedly, neither does it constitute that on account of which a thing exists—I mean the final cause of things.

ME–13. 5. 1092b23-25

Has order in respect to another number but not position.

CAT–6. 5a30

We call number infinite, because there is not a greatest number.

DE C–1. 5. 272a1-2

That numbers do not constitute substances, and that they are not causes of form, is plain.

ME–13. 5. 1092b16-17

366

Nutriment

It is necessary that every thing which is increased should receive nutriment.

DE P A–2. 3. 650a2-4

Nutrition

Nutrition is indeed the same with increase, but in definition different.

DE G ET C–1. 5. 322a22-24

This function in particular distinguishes this faculty of the soul from all other faculties.

DE A–2. 4. 416a20-21

Nutriment

All things are nourished by that which is sweet, either simply or mingled.

DE S ET S–4. 442a2

O

Obesity

Those that are very fat become rapidly old; for they have but little blood, in consequence of the blood being consumed into fat.

DE P A–2. 5. 651b8-10

Objection

Objection is a proposition contrary to a proposition; it differs, however, from a proposition because objection may be partial, but proposition cannot be so at all, or not in universal syllogisms. Objection indeed is advanced in two moods, and through two figures; in two moods because every objection is either universal or particular, and by two figures, because they are used opposite to the proposition and opposites are concluded in the first and third figure alone.

P A–2. 26. 69a37-69b5

Objects

It will not be possible to perceive at one and the same time objects which are not contrary.

DE S ET S–7. 448a4-5

Obscenity

It is as much the business of the legislator, as any thing else, to banish every indecent expression out of the state.

POL–Bk. 7. 17. 1336b2-3

Obstinacy

People who are self-opinionated, or ignorant, or boorish, are all obstinate. Self-opinionated people are so from motives of pleasure or pain.

N E–7. 10. 1151b12-14

Offense

There are three ways in which people may hurt each other in society. An action done in ignorance is called a mistake. When the hurt done is contrary to expectation, it is a mishap. When the action is the result of deliberate purpose, the agent is unjust and wicked.

N E–5. 10. 1135b11-24

Old

Those who are advanced in life are apt to view things in an unfavorable light.

RH–Bk. 2. 13. 1389b19-20

Old Age

A good old age is an old age slow in approach, unattended by pain.

RH–Bk. 1. 5. 1361b26-27

Oligarchy

An oligarchy (is a form of government) in which those only who, from the valuation of property, are entitled (to hold office).

RH–1. 8. 1365b33

The first is when the greater part are men of moderate means, and have not too large property; for this gives each man of property leisure for the management of public affairs: and, as they are a numerous body, it necessarily follows that the supreme power must be in the laws, and not in the individuals; for in proportion as they are far from a monarchical government and have not sufficient fortune to neglect their private affairs, while they are too many to be supported by the public, they will of course determine to be governed by the laws, and not by each other. But if the men of property in the state are fewer than in the former case, and if their property is large, then an oligarchy of the second sort will take place; for those who have power will claim a right to lord it over the others. And, to accomplish this, they will associate themselves with some who have an inclination for public affairs, and as they are not yet powerful enough to govern without law, they will make a law for that purpose. And if they set themselves, as being fewer, to gain greater fortunes, the oligarchy will then alter into one of the third sort, because they keep the offices of state in their own hands by a law, which directs the son to succeed upon the death of his father. But as soon as they extend their strength further by means of their wealth and powerful connexions, such a dynasty nearly approaches to a monarchy, and the men will be supreme, and not the law; and this is the fourth species of an oligarchy, and it corresponds to the last-mentioned kind of democracy.

POL—Bk. 4. 6. 1293a12-34

When the people in general do not partake of the deliberative power, but certain persons chosen for that purpose, who govern according to the law, this also is an oligarchy.

POL—Bk. 4. 14. 1298a40—1298b2

An oligarchy is a state where the rich and those of noble family, being few, possess it.

POL—Bk. 4. 4. 1290b19-20

An oligarchy is where the supreme power of the state is lodged with the rich.

POL—Bk. 3. 8. 1279b17-18

The purest and best-framed oligarchy is one which approaches most nearly to what we call a free state.

POL—Bk. 6. 6. 1320b21

370

An oligarchy is liable to a revolution both in time of war and peace.

POL—Bk. 5. 6. 1306a19-20

An oligarchy will be destroyed when they create another oligarchy within it.

POL—Bk. 5. 6. 1306a12-13

Oligarchy, Its End

The end of oligarchy is wealth.

RH—1. 8. 1366a5

Oligarchy and Democracy

An oligarchy and a democracy differ in this form from each other, namely, in the poverty of those who govern in the one, and the riches of those who govern in the other; for when the government is in the hands of the rich, be they few or be they more, it is an oligarchy; when it is in the hands of the poor, it is a democracy.

POL—Bk. 3. 8. 1279b40-1280a3

One

Universally, whatever things do not involve division, so far forth as they have it not, so far are they styled one.

ME—4. 6. 1016b3-5

One is called that which subsists as such according to accident in one way, and in another, that which subsists essentially.

ME—4. 6. 1015b16-17

Of things denominated one essentially some are styled so on account of their being continuous.

ME—4. 6. 1015b36-1016a1

371

A thing is called one according to accident, for instance Coriscus and musical, and the musical Coriscus.

ME—4. 6. 1015b17-18

Those are more one which by nature are continuous than those things that are continuous by art.

ME—4. 6. 1016a4

In another way a thing is called one in respect of the subject being in species indifferent or destitute of a difference.

ME—4. 6. 1016a17-18

One and Many

In every genus of things the one is naturally prior to the many and the simple to the composite.

DE C—2. 4. 286b16-17

Oneness

Those are styled one the definition of whatsoever of which, denominating the essence of them, is indivisible, as far as regards another definition signifying the being of the thing, for every actual definition is essentially indivisible?

ME—4. 6. 1016a32-35

Those things are styled one, also, of which the genus is one, differing by opposing differences.

ME—4. 6. 1016a24-25

Some things are one according to number, but others according to species, and others according to genus, and others according to analogy.

ME—4. 6. 1016b31-32

Ontology

In every respect is the science of ontology strictly a science of that which is first or elemental, both on which the

372

other things depend and through which they are denominated.

ME—3. 2. 1003b16-18

If there is something that is eternal and immovable, and that involves a separate subsistence, it is evident that it is the province of the speculative, that is, of the ontological, science to investigate such.

ME—5. 1. 1026a10-11

Operations

All operations are either from art, or from potentiality, or the understanding.

ME—6. 7. 1032a27-28

Opinion

Opinion is conversant with the true or false, which yet may have a various subsistence . . . for both opinion is unstable, and its nature is of this kind.

PO A—1. 33. 89a2-3

It is clearly impossible to opine and know the same thing at the same time.

PO A—1. 33. 89a38-39

It is evident that true opinion can neither possibly be contrary to true opinion nor true negation to true negation, for those are contraries that subsist about opposites.

DE I—14. 24b7-9

The sphere of opinion is universal; it embraces things which are eternal or impossible as much as things which lie within our own power.

N E—3. 4. 1111b30-33

Vide PROBABILITY.

Opinion and Knowledge

No one thinks that he opines, but that he knows, when he thinks it impossible for a thing to subsist otherwise than it does, but when he thinks that it is indeed thus, yet that nothing hinders it being otherwise, then he thinks that he opines; opinion as it were being conversant with a thing of this kind, but science with what is necessary.

PO A–1. 33. 89a6-10

Opinion and Science

If the opinion is vehement, in consequence of being stable, and not to be shaken, it in no respect differs from science.

M M–2. 6. 1201b5-7

Opposition

One thing is said to be opposed to another in four ways, either as relative, or as contrary, or as privation and habit, or as affirmation and negation.

CAT–10. 11b16

Opposition, Correlative

Whatever things are relatively opposed are said to be what they are with reference to opposites, or are in some manner referred to them, as the double of the half.

CAT–10. 11b17

Opposition, Contrary

Those which are opposed as contraries are by no means said to be what they are with reference to each other, but are said to be contrary to each other. 'Good' is the contrary of 'bad'; white, the contrary of black.

CAT–10. 11b35

Opposition, Contrary with a Medium

In the case of those opposed contrarily in which it is not

374

necessary that one should be inherent, there is something intermediate. e.g. black, white; good, bad.

CAT—10. 12a2-4

Opposition, Contrary Without a Medium

Such contraries are of that kind (without a medium) that one of them must necessarily be in those things, in which it can be naturally, or of which it is predicated; these have nothing intermediate. e.g. health, sickness; odd, even.

CAT—10. 12a1-5

Opposition, Privation and Habit

Privation and habit are predicated of something identical, as sight and blindness of the eye, and universally in whatever the habit is naturally adapted to be produced, of such is either predicated. We say then, that each of the things capable of receiving habit is deprived of it, when it is not in that, wherein it might naturally be, and when it is adapted naturally to possess it; thus we say that a man is toothless, not because he has no teeth, and blind, not because he has no sight, but because he has them not when he might naturally have them, for some persons from their birth have neither sight nor teeth, yet they are neither called toothless nor blind.

CAT—10. 12a25-32

Opposition, Affirmation and Negation

Whatever things are opposed as affirmation and negation it is necessary that one should be true and the other false.

CAT—10. 13b1-3

Opposites

Things that are opposite are called contradiction, and contraries, and relations, and privations, and habit, and those things from which ultimate things arise, and those into which they are resolved; as for instance the generations and corruptions of bodies, and whatsoever things it is not admissible at the same time should be present in that which is receptive of both.

ME—4. 10. 1018a20-23

Oration

An oration is constituted of three things, of the speaker, and of the subject about which he speaks, and of the person to whom.

RH—Bk. 1. 3. 1258a38-1358b1

The greatest number of the divisions of a speech are exordium, statement, proof, peroration.

RH—Bk. 3. 13. 1414b7-11

The necessary divisions are the statement and the proof.

RH—Bk. 3. 13. 1414a30-31

Oration, Delivery of

The points in reference to which they conduct their inquiries are three, namely, the loudness of the voice, the fitness of its tones, and its rhythm.

RH—Bk. 3. 1. 1403b29-30

Orator

The time proper to the deliberative orator is the future. The time proper to a judicial pleader is the past. To the demonstrative orator the present time is the most appropriate.

RH—Bk. 1. 3. 1358b14-20

All orators effect their demonstrative proofs by allegation either of enthymemes or examples and in no other way whatever.

RH—Bk. 1. 2. 1356b6-7

Orator, Ceremonial

The aim of the ceremonial (demonstrative) orator is honor and disgrace; and these also refer other considerations to these two.

RH–1. 3. 1358b27-29

Orator, Judicial

The aim of the judicial (forensic) orator is justice and injustice; but he also embraces by the way those other considerations.

RH–1. 3. 1358b25-27

Orator, Political

The aim of the deliberative (political) orator is the expedient and inexpedient; for he who recommends, advises you to adopt a better measure; but he who dissuades, diverts you from the worse; the other considerations either of justice and injustice of honor and disgrace, he adjoins by the way in addition to these two.

RH–1. 3. 1358b20-25

Nearly all the questions on which the political (deliberative) orator harangues are five: questions of finance (ways and means), of war and peace, national defence, imports and exports and legislation.

RH–1. 4. 1359b16-23

Oratory

Three kinds of oratory are: the deliberative, judicial and demonstrative.

RH–Bk. 1. 3. 1358b6-8

Order

Of all things there is order, and every time and life are measured by a period; except that all are not measured by

377

the same period, but some things by a less and others by a greater.

DE G ET C—2. 11. 336b12-14

Ox-Flies

Ox-flies are generated from wood.

DE H A—5. 19. 552a29

P

Pain

Pain, however, is consequent to every thing which is done from compulsion.

M M—1. 12. 1188a2-3

It is pain which makes us abstain from doing what is noble.

N E—2. 2. 1104b10-11

Anger is attended by pain, hatred is not.

RH—Bk. 2. 4. 1382a11

Palpitation

The palpitation of the heart happens, as I may say, in man alone, because man alone entertains the hope and expectation of something future.

DE P A—3. 6. 669a19-21

Parados

The parados is the first speech of the whole chorus.

P—12.1452b22-23

Paralogisms

Besides all the above-named syllogisms, there are paralogisms, which consist of things peculiar to certain sciences, as happens to be the case in geometry, and those sciences allied to it.

T—1. 1. 101a5-8

Pardon

The people should be allowed the power of pardoning, but not of condemning.

POL–Bk. 4. 14. 1298b35-37

Paronym

Things are called paronyms which, though differing in case, have their appellation from some thing.

CAT–1. 1a12

Part

A part is said to be in one way that into which any quantity whatsoever may be divisible.

ME–4. 25. 1023b12-13

Those things into which the species of animal may be divided without quantity also are called parts of this species. Wherefore they say that species are parts of genus, We further call those things parts into whatsoever anything is divided, or those things whereof the whole is made up; moreover those things contained in the definition are also parts of the whole. Wherefore the genus is called part of the species and in other respects the species is called a part of the genus.

ME–4. 25. 1023b17-25

A part measures.

PHY–4. 10. 218a6-7

Parts, Dissimilar

All the dissimilar parts are composed of similar parts; the hand, for example, is composed of flesh, nerves, and bone.

H A–1. 1. 486a13-14

Participate

To receive the definition of what is participated.

T–4. 1. 121a11-12

380

Partridge

With respect to partridges, if the females stand opposite to the males when the wind blows, they become pregnant; and they frequently become pregnant even from the voice of the male, if they happen to be enflamed with the desire of coition.

DE H A–5. 5. 541a26-28

Passion

As one of the categories. Passion, for example, 'to be cut,' 'to be burned.'

CAT–4. 2a3-4

Admits of contraries and more and less.

CAT–9. 11b1-10

Passion is denominated, in one way, as quality according to which a thing admits of alteration.

ME–4. 21. 1022b15-16

The principle of all passions is condensation and rarefaction.

PHY–8. 7. 260b7-8

Passion being victorious causes the reasoning power to be at rest.

M M–2. 6. 1202a6-7

Hence it would seem that passion, when well disposed, is rather the principle of virtue than reason.

M M–2. 7. 1206b28-29

Vide: ACTION.

Passions of the Soul

Spoken words are symbols of passions of the soul.

DE I–1. 16a3

Just as letters are not the same for all neither are speech sounds and yet the passions of the soul are the same in all and the things signified are the same.

DE I–1. 16a5-8

Passions (Emotions)

Passions are all emotions whatsoever, on which pain and pleasure are consequent, by whose operation, undergoing a change, men differ in respect to their decisions: for instance, anger, pity, fear.

RH–2. 2. 1378a19-23

Passions and Actions

I call passions and actions, generation, increase, copulation, wakefulness, sleep, progressive motion, and such other particulars as belong to animals.

DE PA–1. 5. 645b33-35

Past

Memory is of the past.

DE M ET R–1. 449b15

Patriot

The true patriot in a democracy ought to take care that the majority are not too poor.

POL–Bk. 6. 5. 1320a32-34

Peculiarities

The speculation of peculiarities is posterior to that of things common.

PHY–3. 1. 200b24-25

Peirastic

Peirastic arguments are those which are conclusive from things appearing to the respondent, and which are necessary for him to know, who pretends to possess science.

S E–2. 165b4-6

382

Perceive

To perceive sensibly is not similar to learning, but to contemplation.

DE S ET S—4. 441b22-23

Perception

The sensible object is prior to the actual sensing.

CAT—7. 7b35

It is not possible to perceive two things by one sense at one and the same time, unless they are mingled.

DE S ET S—7. 447b15-16

Percussion

There is no percussion without movement.

DE A—2. 8. 419b13

Perfect

Perfect is denominated that beyond which it is not possible to assume anything or any one single portion.

ME—4. 16. 1021b12-13

Perfection

Nothing is perfect which has not an end: and the end is a bound.

PHY—3. 6. 207a14-15

The perfect is naturally prior to the imperfect.

DE C—1. 2. 269a19-20

Period

I call a period a form of words which has independently in itself a beginning and ending, and a length easily taken in at a glance.

RH—3. 9. 1409a35-1409b1

A period either consists of clauses or is simple.

RH—Bk. 3. 9. 1409b13

Peroration

The peroration is composed of four things—of getting the hearer favorable to one's self, and ill-disposed towards the adversary; and of amplification and extenuation; and of placing the hearer under the influence of the passions; and of awakening his recollection.

RH—Bk. 3. 19. 1419b10-13

Perpetual Motion

It is necessary that perpetual motion should be inherent in a divine nature.

DE C—2. 3. 286a10

Perpetuity

It is impossible that a thing which once was not should afterwards be perpetual.

DE C—1. 12. 283b7-8

The genus of men, animals, and plants always is.

DE G A—2. 1. 731b35-732a1

Per Se

Entities are said to subsist (exist) essentially whatsoever signify the figures of predication (categories); for as often as they are predicated, so often do they signify to be. Since, therefore, of the things that are predicated some signify what a thing is, or quiddity, and others quality, and others quantity, and others relation, and others action or passion, and some the place where, and others the when, to each of these the to be signifies the same thing.

ME—4. 7. 1017a22-27

Universals are per se but accidents are not per se but are predicated of singulars.

ME—4. 9. 1017b35-1018a2

Perspicuity

Proper words produce perspicuity.

P—22. 1458a18-19

Persuasion, Rhetorical

Enthymemes are the very body of persuasion.

RH—1. 1. 1354a14-15

Persuasion

We ought to be able to persuade on opposite sides of a question.

RH—Bk. 1. 1. 1355a29-30

The true and better side of the question is always naturally of a more easy inference and has, generally speaking, a greater tendency to persuade.

RH—Bk. 1. 1. 1355a36-38

Of means of persuading by speaking there are three species: some consist in the character of the speaker; others in the disposing the hearer a certain way; others in the thing itself which is said, by reason of its proving, or appearing to prove the point.

RH—Bk. 1. 2. 1356a1-4

Persuasion by Example

The common means of persuasion are example and enthymeme; example is of the nature of induction, which is a principle of reasoning. Of examples there are two species: for one is the quoting of real matters of fact which have actually taken place; another is the fabricating of them yourself; and of this method one species is illustration, the other fable, like those of Aesop and the African legends (Libyan).

RH—2. 20. 1393a23-30

Persuasiveness

Men of no education have more persuasive influence over the mob than men of high acquirements.

RH—Bk. 2. 22. 1395b26-27

Petitio Principii

Men appear to beg what was in the beginning in five ways, most evidently, indeed, and primarily, if any one begs the very thing which ought to be demonstrated; this, however, does not easily escape notice, as to the thing itself, but rather in synonyms, and wherein the name and the definition signify the same thing. Secondly, when what ought to be demonstrated particularly, any one asks for, universally, as when endeavoring to show there is one science of contraries, he demands it to be altogether granted, that there is one of opposites, for he seems to beg together with many things, that which he ought to demonstrate per se. Thirdly, if any one proposing to demonstrate the universal, begs the particular; as if when it is proposed, that there is one science of all contraries, some one should require it to be granted, that there is one of certain contraries; for he also seems to beg per se separately, that which he ought to show, together with many things. Again, if a person dividing the problem begs the thing proposed for discussion; as if when it is necessary to show that medicine belongs to the healthy, and the diseased, he should claim each of these, to be granted separately. Or if some one should beg one of these, which are necessarily consequent to each other, as that the side of a square is incommensurate with the diameter, when he ought to show that the diameter is incommensurate with the side.

T—8. 13. 162b34-163a13

Vide BEGGING THE QUESTION.

Petitio Principii, Fallacy of

Those fallacies which are from petitio principii arise in as many ways as it is possible to beg the original question; they seem, however, to confute from inability to perceive what is the same and what is different.

S E—5. 167a36-39

Phantasm

The phantasm arising from the motion of sensible perceptions, when it presents itself to him who is asleep, so far as he is asleep, is a dream.

DE SOM—3. 462a29-31

Phantasms occur in dreams similar to images in water.

DE DIV—2. 464b8-9

It is not unreasonable to suppose that some of the phantasms which present themselves in sleep are the causes of the actions which we perform when awake.

DE DIV—1. 463a21-23

Those that are asleep have a greater perception of small inward motions than those that are awake. But these motions produce phantasms, from which future events about things of this kind are foreseen.

DE DIV—2. 464a16-19

Philosopheme

Now a philosopheme is a demonstrative syllogism.

T—8. 11. 162a15-16

Philosopher

He that labors under perplexity and wonder thinks that

387

he is involved in ignorance. Therefore, also, the philosopher —that is, the lover of wisdom—is somehow a lover of fables, for the fable is made up of the things that are marvelous.

ME—1. 2. 982b17-19

Philosophizing, Value of

To philosophize is better than to acquire money, yet it is not more desirable to one in want of necessaries.

T—3. 2. 118a10-11

Philosophy

It is correct, also, that philosophy should be styled a science, speculative of the truth.

ME—1a. 1. 993b19-20

With regard to philosophy we must discuss these problems according to their truth; as regard dialectic, opinion suffices.

T—1. 14. 105b30-31

The value of philosophical teaching cannot be measured in money.

N E—9. 1. 1164b3-4

Philosophy, Speculative

Wherefore, according to this view of things, there would be three speculative philosophies; namely, the mathematical, the physical, the theological.

ME—5. 1. 1026a18-19

Philosophy (Metaphysics)

Philosophy . . . contemplates everything so far forth as it is entity.

ME—10. 4. 1061b25-27

Physicist (Natural Philosopher)

The entire attention of the physicist (natural philosopher) is engaged about those things that contain in themselves the principle of motion and rest.   ME–10. 1. 1059b16-18

Physics (Natural Philosophy)

To physics or natural science one ascribes the speculation of things as far forth as they partake of motion.

ME–10. 3. 1061b6-7

The investigation regarding sensible substance is the work of the physical and second philosophy; for not only is it necessary for the natural philosopher to afford information respecting matter, but also respecting that substance which is according to the definition, even still more.

ME–6. 11. 1037a14-17

Physics

Since physics happens to be conversant about a certain kind of entity (for about such a sort of substance is it concerned in which is contained in itself the principle of motion and rest) it is evident that it is neither practical nor productive.

ME–5. 1. 1025b19-21

Physical science is conversant about things that are inseparable, to be sure, but not immovable.

ME–5. 1. 1026a13-14

Pity

A sort of pain occasioned by an evil capable of hurting or destroying, appearing to befall one who does not deserve it, which one may himself expect to endure, or that some one connected with him will; and this when it appears near.

RH–2. 8. 1385b13-16

389

Placability

Placability is a subsiding and appeasement of anger.

RH–Bk. 2. 3. 1380a7-8

Place

The first immovable boundary of that which contains is place.

PHY–4. 4. 212a20-21

That there is such a thing, therefore, as place, appears to be evident from alternate mutation.

PHY–4. 1. 208b1-2

Place in a certain respect subsists together with the thing which it contains.

PHY–4. 4. 211a29-30

Place is not destroyed when the things which it contains are corrupted.

PHY–4. 1. 209a1-2

Place (a Continuous Quantity)

Place is of the number of continuous things, for the parts of a body occupy a certain place, which parts join at a certain common boundary, wherefore also the parts of place, which each part of the body occupies, join at the same boundary as the parts of the body, so that place will also be continuous, since its parts join at one common boundary.

CAT–6. 5a18-21

Plane

Every plane figure is either right-lined, or contained by a circumference.

DE C–2. 4. 286b13-14

Planets

Each of the planets is moved with many motions.

DE C–2. 12. 293a1-2

Plant

Plants live without having locomotion or sensibility, and many animals have not the use of intelligence.

DE A–1. 5. 410b25-26

Of plants, some only live for the space of a year, but others for a long time.

DE L ET B–1. 464b24-26

Plants are always renovated; and, therefore, they live for a long time.

DE L ET B–6. 467a12

The upward and downward parts are not only in animals, but also in plants.

DE IN–4. 705a29-31

In plants the male is not separated from the female.

DE G A–2. 4. 741a3-4

Platonic Forms

It would seem impossible for the substance to be separate from that of which it is the substance, therefore in what way can the ideas, when they are substances of things, exist separately from them.

ME–1. 9. 991b1-3

The assertion that these forms are exemplars and that the rest of entities participate in them is to speak vain words and to utter poetic metaphors.

ME–1. 9. 991a20-22

391

Pleasure

Pleasure is a psychical fact, and whatever a man is said to be fond of is pleasant to him.

N E—1. 9. 1099a8-9

Pleasure is a certain motion of the soul, and a settlement of it, at once rapid and perceptible, into its own proper nature.

RH—Bk. 1. 11. 1369b33-35

It is better to define it as an activity of the natural state of one's being.

N E—7. 13. 1153a14

Pleasures are an impediment to thoughtfulness.

N E—7. 12. 1152b16

Pleasure leaves the will free.

N E—3. 15. 1119a24

Pleasure is something which is whole and perfect.

N E—10. 3. 1174b7

It seems to be pleasure which most frequently deceives people, for pleasure appears to be good, and although it is not, the result is that they choose what is pleasant as if it were good, and avoid pain as if it were evil.

N E—3. 6. 1113a33-1113b2

Through pleasure, indeed, we act basely.

M M—1. 6. 1185b34-35

Pleasures are desirable, but not if they are immoral in their origin.

N E—10. 2. 1173b25-26

To make a good use of pleasures and pains is to be a good man, and to make a bad use of them is to be a bad man.

N E–2. 2. 1105a12-13

Pleasure is fostered in us all from early childhood, so that it is difficult to get rid of the emotion of pleasure, as it is deeply ingrained in our life.

N E–2. 2. 1105a1-3

Bodily pleasures too, as being violent, are pursued by people who are incapable of finding gratification in other pleasures.

N E–7. 15. 1154b2-3

The same thing is never constantly pleasant to us.

N E–7. 15. 1154b20-21

Pleasure perfects life.

N E–10. 4. 1175a15-16

Pleasure is felt not by Man only but by the lower animals.

N E–2. 2. 1104b34-35

Plot

The plot is the principal part and as it were the soul of tragedy.

P–6. 1450a38

A fable (plot) has an appropriate magnitude when the time of its duration is such as to render it probable that there can be a transition from prosperous to adverse, or from adverse to prosperous fortune, according to the necessary or probable order of things as they take place.

P–7. 1451a10-15

The plot, since it is an imitation of action, should be the imitation of one action, and of the whole of this, and the parts of the transactions should be so arranged, that any one of them being transposed, or taken away, the whole would become different and changed.

P—8. 1451a30-34

It is necessary that a plot which is well-constructed should be rather single than twofold, and that the change should not be into prosperity from adversity, but on the contrary into adversity from prosperity, not through depravity but through some great error.

P—13. 1453a12-16

I call the action simple from which taking place, as it has been defined, with continuity and unity, there is a transition without either reversal or discovery.

P—10. 1452a14-16

A plot is complex, from which there is a transition, together with discovery, or reversal, or both.

P—10. 1452a16-18

Solutions of fables ought to happen from the fable itself, and not from the machinery.

P—15. 1454a37-1454b2

In every tragedy there is a complication and unravelling.

P—18. 1455b24

Poet

It is evident that a poet ought rather to be the author of plots than of metres, inasmuch as he is a poet from imitation, and he imitates actions. Hence, though it should happen that he relates things which have happened, he is no less a poet.

P—9. 1451b27-30

It is requisite that the poet should speak in his own person as little as possible: for so far as he does so he is not an imitator.

P—24. 1460a7-8

It is not the province of a poet to relate things which have happened, but such as might have happened, and such things as are possible according to probability, or which would necessarily have happened.

P—9. 1451a36-38

Poetry
The style of poetry and that of prose is distinct.

RH—Bk. 3. 1. 1404a28

Two causes appear to have produced poetry in general. For to imitate is congenial to men from childhood. . . . Imitation, harmony, and rhythm being natural to us, the earliest among mankind, making a gradual progress in these things from the beginning, produced poetry from extemporaneous efforts.

P—4. 1448b4-24

Poetry is more philosophic, and more deserving of attention, than history. For poetry speaks more of universals, but history of particulars.

P—9. 1451b5-6

Point
That which is indivisible in every direction is a point, if it involves a position.

ME—4. 6. 1016b25-26

Not every thing is either infinite or finite: as, for instance, passive quality or a point.

PHY—3. 4. 202b31-32

Pole

It is evident therefore that the unapparent pole is the upward part of the heaven.

DE C—2. 2. 285b22-23

Police

As many persons stir up seditions that they may enjoy their own manner of living, there ought to be a particular officer to inspect the manners of all those whose lives are contrary to the interests of their own state.

POL—Bk. 5. 8. 1308b20-22

Polis

When many villages join themselves perfectly together into one society, that society is a state (polis), and contains in itself, if I may so speak, the perfection of independence; and it is first founded that men may live, but continued that they may live happily. For which reason every state is the work of nature, since the first social ties are such; for to this they all tend as to an end, and the nature of a thing is judged by its tendency. For what every being is in its perfect state, that certainly is the nature of that being, whether it be a man, a horse, or a house; besides, its own final cause and its end must be the perfection of any thing; but a government complete in itself constitutes a final cause and what is best.

POL—Bk. I. 2. 1252b27-1253a1

Political Justice

Political justice subsists by law and not by nature.

M M—1. 34. 1195a7-8

Political justice is partly natural and partly conventional.

N E—5. 10. 1134b18-19

Political Science

It is the political science or faculty which determines what sciences are necessary in states, and what kind of sciences should be learnt, and how far they should be learnt by particular people.

N E—1. 1. 1094a27-1094b2

The end of political science is the greatest good: justice.

POL—Bk. 3. 12. 1282b16-17

Politician

The lawgiver and the politician should know well what preserves and what destroys the democracy of the people or the oligarchy of the few.

POL—Bk. 5. 9. 1309b35-37

The political character wishes to be conversant with beautiful actions.

EE—1. 4. 1215b3

Politics

In politics, there is the government of the many, and the government of the few.

POL—Bk. 4. 3. 1290a15-16

Polity

When the citizens at large direct their policy to the public good, it is called simply a polity.

POL—Bk. 3. 7. 1279a37-39

A polity is the ordering and regulating of the state, and all of its offices, particularly of that wherein the supreme power is lodged; and this power is always possessed by the administration.

POL—Bk. 3. 6. 1278b8-11

There are three kinds of polity. The polities are kingship, aristocracy, and a third depending on a property qualification, which it seems proper to describe as timocratic. . . . Of these, kingship is the best and timocracy the worst.

N E—8. 12. 1160a31-36

Poor

In an oligarchy it is necessary to take great care of the poor, and to allot them public employments which are profitable.

POL—Bk. 5. 8. 1309a20-22

Position (as One of the Categories)

To be situated, like 'lying down' or 'seated.'

CAT—4. 2a2

Possession (as One of the Categories)

To possess, as 'to be shod,' 'armed.'

CAT—4. 2a3

Possession (to Have)

Possession has many meanings: the action of a thing according to the nature of that thing or according to the impulse of it; as that in whatever anything is inherent as being receptive; as a thing that embraces the things that are comprised; that which hinders in accordance with its own force anything from motion or action is said to possess this very thing.

ME—4. 23. 1023a8-23

Possession

It is impossible to have wealth or anything else without taking the trouble to have it.

N E—4. 2. 1120b18-19

Possibilities

By possibilities I mean such things as may be effected by our own actions.

N E—3. 5. 1112b26-27

Possible

To be possible and the possible I define to be that which, not being necessary, but being assumed to exist, nothing impossible will on this account arise, for we say that the necessary is possible equivocally.

P A—1. 13. 32a18-21

To be possible is predicated in two ways, one, that which happens for the most part and yet falls short of the necessary—for instance, for a man to become hoary, or to grow, or to waste, or in short whatever may naturally be, for this has not a continued necessity, for the man may not always exist, but while he does exist it is either of necessity or for the most part—the other way (the possible) is indefinite, and is that which may be possibly thus and not thus; or in short what occurs casually. . . .

P A—1. 13. 32b4-13

Posterior and Prior

Things which are posterior in generation are prior according to nature, and that which is last in generation is first by nature.

DE P A—2. 1. 646a25-27

Potentiality

That thing the existence of which is potential admits of both being and not being.

ME—8. 8. 1050b11-12

It must be assumed that what is in potentiality is different from what is in act.

DE S ET S—6. 445b30-31

399

Vide: POWER.

Potentiality (Power)

Potentiality is called the first principle of motion or change in another thing, or so far forth as it is another thing.

ME—4. 12. 1019a15-16

Power

The precise definition of the first potentiality would be a principle capable of bringing about a change in another thing, or so far forth as it is another.

ME—4. 12. 1020a4-6

Furthermore, power is the capacity of accomplishing this particular thing well, or doing so according to free-will.

ME—4. 12. 1019a23-24

Wherefore, is a thing powerful in respect of having a certain habit and first principle, and in respect of involving the privation of this, if it is admissible that it should involve privation.

ME—4. 12. 1019b8-10

No power pertains to that which has been, but to that which is, or will be.

DE C—1. 12. 283b13-14

If we take the various natural powers which belong to us, we first acquire the proper faculties and afterwards display the activities.

N E—2. 1. 1103a26-28

Let the regulation be made by the law, that no one shall have too much power by means either of his fortune or his friends.

POL—Bk. 5. 8. 1308b16-18

Power is not in the man who is member of the assembly or council, but in the assembly itself, and in the council and people, of which each individual of the whole community forms a part, as senator, adviser, or judge.

POL—Bk. 3. 11. 1282a34-37

Power, Supreme

As to the fact that the supreme power ought to be lodged with the many, rather than with those of the better sort, who are few, there would seem to be some doubt, though also some truth as well.

POL—Bk. 3. 11. 1281a40-42

Practicable Good

Practicable good likewise may be divided into that which is essentially good, and into that which is good with reference to something else which is essentially good.

E E—1. 7. 1217a35-37

Practical Science

Of practical science the end is a work.

M E—1a. 1. 993b21

Praise

Praise invariably implies a reference to a higher standard.

N E—1. 12. 1101b12-14

Predicated

Some things are predicated of a certain subject yet are in no subject as 'man' is predicated of a subject, i.e. of some certain man, yet is in no subject.

CAT—2. 1a20-21

Predicated of All

We say it is predicated of all when no instance of the subject can be found of which the term cannot be asserted.

P A—1. 1. 24b28-30

Predicated of None

We say 'to be predicated of none' when no instance can be found of which it can be said.

P A–1. 1. 24b30

Predicates

When one thing is predicated of another it will be predicated either in respect of what a thing is (the quiddity) or how it is, or how much, or a relative or an agent or a patient or where or when. Moreover, those which signify substance signify that the thing of which they are predicated is that which it is, or something belonging to it; but whatever do not signify substance, but are predicated of another subject, which is neither the thing itself nor something belonging to it, are accidents, as white is predicated of man.

PO A–1. 22. 83a21-28

Predication

When one thing is predicated of another, as of a subject, whatever things are said of the predicate, may be also said of the subject.

CAT–3. 1b10

Pregnancy

Pregnant women, also, are subject to all-various desires, and to a rapid change of their desires; which some call longing.

H A–7. 4. 584a17-19

Premise

The premises out of which enthymemes are deduced will be some of them necessary, but the greatest part contingent.

RH–Bk. 1. 2. 1357a30-32

Premiss

Vide: PROPOSITION.

Present

The present now is the boundary of the past and future time.

PHY—4. 13. 222a33-222b2

Present in a Subject

I mean by a thing being in a subject, that which is in anything not as a part but which cannot subsist without that in which it is.

CAT—2. 1a22-24

A certain grammatical art is in a soul as in a subject but it is not predicated of a subject.

CAT—1. 1a25

A certain whiteness is in a subject, the body, for every color is in a body, but it is predicated of no subject.

CAT—2. 1a27

Primary

What is primary and what is absolute, or simple, are strictly necessary.

ME—4. 5. 1015b11-12

Principle

That is a principle from whence the first of a thing not inherent is produced, and whence motion and change have first been naturally fitted to commence, as for example the child from the father and the mother.

ME—4. 1. 1013a7-9

Principle is either the principle of a certain thing, or of a certain number of things.

PHY—1. 2. 185a4

Common to all first principles is the being the original from whence a thing either is, or is produced, or is known.

ME—4. 1. 1013a17-19

It is necessary that all principles should neither be produced from each other, nor from other things.

PHY—1. 5. 188a27-28

That is called a principle from whence each thing would proceed in the best manner.

ME—4. 1. 1013a1-2

Whence a thing is known first, this is called a principle of that thing.

ME—4. 1. 1013a14-15

That is a principle from whence is produced the first of a thing that is inherent.

ME—4. 1. 1013a4

Of principles, however, there is no other cause, since they are eternal.

PHY—8. 1. 252b4-5

I call those principles in each genus, the existence of which it is impossible to demonstrate.

PO A—1. 10. 76a31-32

It is impossible to demonstrate the proper principles of each thing, for they will be the principles of all things, and the science of them the mistress of all (sciences).

PO A—1. 9. 76a16-18

Some principles are from necessity, but others contingent.

PO A—1. 32. 88b7-8

That is called a principle from whence anything has had motion imparted to it in the first instance.

M E—4. 1. 1012b34-35

A principle is greater in power than in magnitude.

DE C–1. 5. 271b12

That is a principle according to the free impulse of which things in motion are moved, and things undergoing a change are changed.

ME–4. 1. 1013a10-11

Just as a geometer by no means disputes with one who denies the principles of his science . . . so one who seeks physical principles does not dispute with one who denies physical principles.

PHY–1. 2. 185a1-3

Principles, Derived From Experience
Vide: EXPERIENCE.

Principles, First
First principles are known through themselves, but what are subordinate to them are known through them.

P A–2. 16. 64b35-36

The first principle of that which may be known constitutes, in regard to each genus, the one.

ME–4. 6. 1016b20

A first principle must not be predicated of a subject; for then there would be a first principle of a first principle; for the subject is a principle and prior to its predicate.

PHY–1. 6. 189a30-32

But so far forth as we obtain a knowledge of each thing by means of the definitions, and so far as first principles are

405

the genera of definitions, it is necessary also that first principles be the genera of things capable of definition.

ME—2. 3. 998b4-6

The most firm first principle of all is that concerning which there can be no possibility of deception, for such must needs be that which is most known . . . and it must needs be independent of hypothesis . . . this principle is: for the same thing to be present and not be present at the same time in the same subject and according to the same is impossible. This is the most firm of all first principles.

ME—3. 3. 1005b11-23

Principles of Evil Actions

The principles by whose motion men deliberately choose to hurt and do evil in contravention of law are depravity and moral weakness.

RH—1. 10. 1268b12-14

Prior

A thing is said to be prior to another in four respects: first and most properly, in respect of time . . . next, when it does not reciprocate according to the consequence of existence. . . . Thirdly, the prior is that predicated according to a certain order, as in the instance of science and discourses. . . . Moreover, the better and more excellent appear to be prior by nature.

CAT—12. 14a-b

That which in any respect is the cause of the existence of another may be said to be prior in this manner.

CAT—12. 14b12

Prior Analytics

It is first requisite to say what is the subject concerning which and why the present treatise is undertaken, namely

406

that it is concerning demonstration and for the sake of demonstrative science.

P A–1. 1. 24a10-11

Prior and Better Known

The prior and better known are such in two ways: for what is prior in nature, is not the same as that which is prior in regard to us, nor what is more known (simply) the same as what is more known to us. Now I call things prior and better known to us those which are nearer to sense and things prior and more known simply, those which are more remote from sense; and those things are most remote which are especially universal, and those nearest which are singular, and these are mutually opposed.

PO A–1. 2. 71b33-72a5

Prior and Posterior

Prior is that which is nearer a certain first principle defined either simply and by nature, or relatively, or according to place, or by certain things . . . other things prior and posterior are so in accordance with time. . . . Some things are prior and posterior according to motion, for that which is more immediate to the first moving power is prior . . . some things are prior according to potentiality, for that which is more potential is prior . . . also things are prior according to some order, as in a dance; in another way a thing is prior in knowledge as if it were absolutely prior; according to reason things that are universal are prior, but according to sense the singular are prior.

ME–4. 11. 1018b9-34

Privation

Privation is considered in one way if something does not have those things which by nature can be possessed, even if it itself is not fit by nature to have them; as for example a plant is said to be deprived of eyes. Another way, that is termed privation if a thing be by nature fit to have a thing

407

and yet does not have it, as a blind man deprived of sight; further is that privation, if a thing be by nature adapted to possess a quality, and when it is so adapted by nature to have it, it does not have it; further the violent removal of a thing is called a privation . . . moreover privation is found in the non-possession of a thing in every way.

ME—4. 22. 1022b22-1023a4

Privation is non-being per se.

PHY—1. 9. 192a5

Probability

Probability is what usually happens. It belongs to the contingent and variable.

RH—1. 2. 1357a34-36

Probabilities are those which appear to all, or to most men, or to the wise, and to those either to all or to the greater number, or to such as are especially renowned and illustrious.

T—1. 1. 100b21-23

Probability and sign are not the same, but the probable is what men know to have generally happened or not, or to be or not to be; this is a probability, for instance: that the envious, hate or that lovers show affection.

P A—2. 27. 70a3-7

Problems

Of problems, some are universal but others particular.

T—2. 1. 108b37-38

The things with which syllogisms are conversant are problems.

T—1. 4. 101b16

Procreation

The most natural act for living beings which are complete and not abortive or produced by spontaneous generation is to produce another being like themselves.

DE A–2. 4. 415a26-28

The seed is prolific which resembles hail, and males are generated from it more than females; and thin seed, and which is without globules, is prolific of females.

H A–7. 1. 582a29-32

Produced

That which has been produced must needs exist when first it has been produced.

ME–2. 4. 999b11-12

Production

All things that are produced arc produced by means of something, and from something, and become something.

ME–6. 7. 1032a13-14

Prologue

The prologue is the whole part of the tragedy, prior to the entrance of the chorus.

P–12. 1452b19-20

Proof

Proof should be demonstrative.

RH–Bk. 3. 17. 1417b21

Property

Property is that which does not show what a thing is, but is present to it alone, and is predicated convertibly with it. As it is the property of a man to be capable of grammar, for if he is a man he is capable of grammar, and

409

if he is capable of grammar he is a man; since no one calls property that which may possibly be present with something else.

T–1. 5. 102a18-23

By property we understand all such things as have their value measured by money.

N E–4. 1. 1119b26-27

Property is assigned either per se and always, or with relation to something else and sometimes.

T–5. 1. 128b16-17

The use of property consists in spending and giving.

N E–4. 1. 1120a8-9

Property is necessary for states, but property is no part of the state.

POL–Bk. 7. 8. 1328a33-35

Property, Private

It is very pleasant to oblige and assist our friends and companions, and strangers, which cannot be unless property be private; but this cannot result where they make the state too entirely one. And further, they destroy the offices of two principal virtues, modesty and liberality—modesty with respect to the female sex, for it is right to abstain from her who is another's; and liberality, as it relates to private property, without which no one can appear liberal, or do any generous action; for the office of liberality consists in imparting to others what is our own. This system of polity does indeed recommend itself by its good appearance, and specious pretences to humanity; and the man who hears it proposed will receive it gladly, concluding that there will be a wonderful bond of friendship between all its members, particularly when anyone censures the evils which are now

410

to be found in society, as arising from property not being common; as for example, the disputes which happen between man and man, upon their contracts with each other; the judgments passed to punish perjury, and the flattering of the rich; none of which arise from properties being private, but from the corruption of mankind. For we see those who live in one community and have all things in common, disputing with each other oftener than those who have their property separate; but we observe fewer instances of strife, because of the very small number of those who have property in common, compared with those where it is appropriated. It is also but right to mention not only the evils from which they who share property in common will be preserved, but also the advantages which they will lose; for viewed as a whole, this manner of life will be found impracticable. We must suppose then that the error of Socrates arose from the fact that his first principle was false; for we admit that both a family and a state ought to be one in some particulars, but not entirely so; for there is a point beyond which if a state proceeds towards oneness, it will be no longer a state. POL—Bk. 2. 5. 1263b5-34

Proportion

Justice then is a sort of proportion; for proportion is not peculiar to abstract quantity, but belongs to quantity generally, proportion being equality of ratios and implying four terms at least. N E–5. 6. 1131a29-32

Proportionate

That which is just then is that which is proportionate, and that which is unjust is that which is disproportionate. It follows that this disproportion may take the form either of excess or defect. N E–5. 7. 1131b16-18

Proposition

A proposition is a sentence which affirms or denies some-

411

thing of something, and this is universal, or particular, or indefinite.

P A—1. 1. 24a16-17

I denominate universal, the being present with all or none; particular, the being present with something or not with something or not with every thing; but the indefinite, the being present or not being present, without the universal or particular (sign).

P A—1. 1. 24a18-20

It is necessary that every proposition contain a verb or the tense of a verb, for the definition of man, unless 'is' or 'was' or 'will be' or something of this kind, be added is not yet a proposition.

DE I—5. 17a9-12

Not every sentence is a proposition, but only that in which there is truth or falsehood . . . as a prayer is a sentence but it is neither true nor false.

DE I—4. 17a2-5

Every proposition is either of that which is present, or is present necessarily or contingently.

P A—1. 2. 25a1-2

Every proposition and every problem shows either genus, property, or accident.

T—1. 4. 101b17-18

Some propositions are ethical, others physical, but others logical.

T—1. 14. 105b20

Proposition, Composite

All other (propositions) are one by conjunction . . . those propositions are complex (composite) which indicate many

412

facts or are without conjunction . . . a composite proposition is compounded of simple propositions. DE I–5. 17a8-24

Propositions, Contradictory

To every affirmation there is an opposite negation, and to every negation an opposite affirmation. And this is a contradiction: the affirmative and negative proposition with the same subject and predicate. DE I–6. 17a31-35

Wherefore I say that affirmation is opposed to negation contradictorily when the affirmation signifies the universal and the negation what is not universal, as 'every man is white,' 'not every man is white.' DE I–7. 17b16-19

We ought to consider these as opposite affirmations and negations: It is possible—it is impossible; it is contingent—it is not contingent; it is impossible—it is not impossible; it is necessary—it is not necessary; it is true—it is not true.

DE I–12. 22a11-13

Propositions, Contradictory Opposition of

I say they are opposed contradictorily which refer 'to all' and 'not to all' and 'to some' and 'to none.' P A–2. 8. 59b8-10

Propositions, Contrary

Now if anyone universally enunciates of a universal that something is and is not inherent, these propositions will be contrary. DE I–7. 17b3-5

Contrarily opposed (propositions) are the universal affirmative and universal negative, as "every man is white," "no man is white," "every man is just," "no man is just."

DE I–7. 17b20-23

413

Propositions, Contrary Opposition of

They are contrarily opposed as 'to all' and 'to none'; 'to some' and 'not to some.'

P A–2. 8. 59b10-11

Propositions, Conversion of

It is necessary that the universal negative proposition of what is present should be converted in its terms; for instance, if 'no pleasure is good,' 'neither will any good be pleasure.' But an affirmative proposition we must of necessity convert not universally, but particularly, as if 'all pleasure is good' it is also necessary that 'a certain good should be pleasure'; but of particular propositions we must convert the affirmative proposition particularly, since if 'a certain pleasure is good,' so also 'will a certain good be pleasure'; a negative proposition need not be thus converted, since it does not follow if 'man is not present with a certain animal' 'that animal also is not present with a certain man.'

P A–1. 2. 25a5-13

Proposition, Demonstrative

A demonstrative proposition differs from a dialectical in this, that the demonstrative is an assumption of one part of the contradiction, for a demonstrator does not interrogate, but assumes; but the dialectical is an interrogation of contradiction. As regards forming a syllogism from either proposition, there will be no difference between the one and the other, since he who demonstrates and he who interrogates syllogizes by positing that something is or is not present with something.

P A–1. 1. 24a22-27

A proposition is demonstrative if it is true and obtained through principles derived from the beginning.

P A–1. 1. 24a30-24b10

Proposition, Dialectical

The dialectical proposition is an interrogation of contradiction to him who inquires; but to the one who syllogizes, it is an assumption of what seems and is probable.

P A–1. 1. 24b10-12

Proposition, Dialectical

Differs from a demonstrative proposition.

Vide: PROPOSITION, DEMONSTRATIVE.

Proposition, Necessary

By necessary propositions I mean those out of which a syllogism is adduced.

RH–Bk. 1. 2. 1357b4-5

Proposition, Negative

It is necessary that the universal negative proposition of what is present should be convertible in its terms.

P A–1. 2. 25a5-6

A negative proposition need not be converted.

P A–1. 2. 25a12

A negative contingent proposition is not convertible.

P A–1. 17. 36b35-36

For the other propositions are converted, but the negative is not converted.

P A–2. 53a7-8

Proposition, Particular Affirmative

The particular affirmative proposition is proved through

415

the first figure and the third, in one mood in the first but in three moods in the third.   P A–1. 26. 42b35-38

Proposition, Particular Negative

The particular negative is proved in all the figures, but in the first in one mood, in the second in two moods, in the third in three moods.   P A–1. 26. 42b38-40

Propositions, Rules for Conversion of

A universal negative is universally convertible; but either affirmative proposition, particularly . . . but the particular negative never converts.   P A–1. 3. 25a28-36

Proposition, Simple

Simple propositions are either a simple affirmation or a simple denial . . . a simple proposition enunciates a simple fact or the parts of which form a simple whole. . . . A simple proposition asserts or denies something of something. A simple proposition is a significant expression regarding the presence or absence of something in a subject, according to the divisions of time.   DE I–5. 17a8-24

The affirmation and negation are simple which signify one thing of one, either of a universal taken universally, or otherwise as, "Every man is white," "not every man is white," "man is white," "man is not white," "no man is white," "some man is white," if 'white' signifies the same.

DE I–8. 18a13-17

Proposition, Syllogistic

Wherefore a syllogistic proposition will be simply an affirmation or negation of something concerning something.

P A–1. 1. 24a28-30

416

Proposition, Universal Affirmative

An universal affirmative is proved through the first figure alone and in one mood, only.

P A–1. 26. 42b32-33

Proposition, Universal Negative

The universal negative (is proved) both through the first (figure) and the second; through the first in one mood; through the second in two moods.

P A–1. 26. 42b34-35

Prosperity

Man, as being human, will require external prosperity.

N E–10. 9. 1178b33

Prosperous

Watch should be kept in turn over those who are most prosperous in the city.

POL–Bk. 5. 8. 1308b24-25

Prudence

Prudence is an intellectual virtue, by conforming to which men have the faculty of actually determining on the subjects of the good and evil, which pertain to happiness.

RH–Bk. 1. 9. 1366b20-22

Prudence is the antithesis of intuitive reason.

N E–6. 9. 1142a25

Prudence is a practical virtue.

N E–6. 8. 1141b16

The sphere of prudence as of opinion is that which is variable.

N E–6. 5. 1140b27-28

417

Prudence consists not merely in knowledge but in capacity for moral action.

N E–7. 11. 1152a8-9

While virtue ensures the correctness of the end which is in view, prudence ensures the correctness of the means to it.

N E–6. 13. 1145a5-6

It is impossible for a man to be prudent unless he is good.

N E–6. 13. 1144a36-1144b1

Prudence when alone is not perfect.   M M–1. 2. 1184a34-35

Prudence not only produces prosperity and virtue, but we also say that the prosperous do well, in consequence of prosperous fortune producing successful conduct.

E E–7. 14. 1246b37-1247a1

Prudence, in the strict sense, is generally taken to relate to one's own individual interests.   N E–6. 8. 1141b29-30

Public

It is necessary that the freemen and the bulk of the people should have absolute power in some things; but these are such as are not men of property, nor have they any reputation for virtue. And so it is not safe to trust them with the first offices in the state, both on account of their injustice and their ignorance; from the one of which they are likely to do what is wrong, from the other to make mistakes. And yet it is dangerous to allow them no power or share in the government; for when there are many poor people who are excluded from office, the state must necessarily have very many enemies in it. It remains, then, that they should have a place in the public assemblies, and in determining causes.

POL–Bk. 3. 11. 1281b24-31

Public Office

Men of family, independence, and fortune, with great propriety contend with each other for office; for those who hold office ought to be persons of independence and property: for a state can no more consist of all poor men, than it can of all slaves. POL–Bk. 3. 12. 1283a16-19

A pretension to offices of state should be founded on those qualifications which are part of itself.

POL–Bk. 3. 12. 1283a14-16

If once you are obliged to look among the wealthy for men who have leisure to serve, the evil follows, that the greatest offices, of king and general, will soon become venal. For this principle makes riches of more account than virtue, and causes the state to grow more avaricious: for whatever those who have the chief power regard as honorable, the opinion of the citizens necessarily follows in their wake; and where the first honors are not paid to virtue, there the aristocratic form of government cannot flourish firmly.

POL–Bk. 2. 11. 1273a35-1373b1

Public Opinion

The opinion of the multitude is to be neglected, though they nearly direct their attention to, and speak about every thing. E E–1. 3. 1214b34-1215a2

Punishment

Punishments are in a sense remedial measures.

N E–2. 2. 1104b16-17

Purpose

We only purpose what may, as we think, be possibly effected by our own action. N E–3. 4. 1111b25-26

Putrefaction

All other things putrefy except fire. DE M–4. 1. 379a14-15

Q

Quality

By quality, I mean that according to which certain things are said to be what they are, i.e. such and such.

CAT–8. 8b25

One species of quality is called habit and disposition. Habit differs from disposition in that it is more lasting and stable. Knowledge and virtue are habits, for knowledge seems to be of those things which are more stable and removed with difficulty. . . . But those are termed dispositions which are easily moved and quickly changed, as heat, cold, disease, health and such things.　CAT–8. 8b26-36

Another kind of quality is that according to which we say that men are prone to pugilism or to the course, or to health, or to disease, in short, whatever things are spoken of according to natural powers, or weakness.　CAT–8. 9a13

The third kind of quality consists of passive qualities and passions such as sweetness, bitterness, sourness and all their affinities, besides, warmth and cold and whiteness and blackness. Now that these are qualities is evident from the fact that their possessors are called such and such from them. (They are called passive qualities and passions) not from the fact that the possessors themselves suffer anything but from the fact that each of the above-mentioned qualities produces passion in the senses.　CAT–8. 9a28-9b10

The fourth kind of quality is figure and form which belong to a thing, besides straightness and curvedness and the like. . . . Thus a triangle or a square is said to be a thing of a certain quality.

CAT–8. 10a12

Quality is styled in one way the difference of substance.

ME–4. 14. 1020a33

Whatever besides quantity that inheres in substance.

ME–4. 14. 1020b6-7

Such things as supervene immediately upon birth from certain passions difficult of removal are called qualities.

CAT–8. 9b35

Quality admits of contraries, as justice is contrary to injustice, and whiteness is contrary to blackness and the like. . . . This does not happen in all cases for to the yellow or the pale or such like colors, though they are qualities, there is no contrary.

CAT–8. 10b12-15

What is white may be more or less white than another and the beautiful is said to be more or less beautiful than another. And one and the same is said to be more or less, as a body which is white is said to be whiter now than what it was before; and what is hot may be more or less hot.

CAT–5. 3b38-42

vide also CAT–8. 10b25

Whatever is changed in quality is so changed by sensibles.

PHY–7. 3. 245b2

421

Quality (as One of the Categories)

Examples of quality are like 'white,' 'grammatical.'

CAT—4. 1b25-26

Quality and Quantity

Every city is made up of quality and quantity: by quality I mean liberty, riches, education, and nobility, and by quantity the excess of its population.

POL—Bk. 4. 12. 1296b17-19

Quantity

Quantity is said to be that which is divisible into things that are inherent, of which either or each is adapted by nature to be a certain thing and a certain particular thing of this sort.

ME—4. 13. 1020a7-8

Quantity is not substance but rather that wherein qualities are inherent primarily, that is substance.

ME—6. 3. 1029a15-16

Of quantity, one kind is discrete, and another continuous; the one consists of parts, holding position with respect to each other, but the other of parts which have not that position.

CAT—6. 4b20

It is the special peculiarity of quantity to be called 'equal' and 'unequal.'

CAT—6. 6a26

Quantity does not appear capable of the greater and the less.

CAT—6. 6a19

Nothing is contrary to quantity.

CAT—6. 5b12

Quantity (as One of the Categories)

To speak generally . . . examples of quantity are like 'two cubits,' 'three cubits.'

CAT–4. 1b25

Quantity, Continuous

Quantity is either discrete or continuous; the one (continuous) consists of parts holding position with respect to each other . . . continuous as line, surface, body, time and place . . . a line is continuous for you may take a common term at which its parts meet, namely, a point, and of a surface, a line. Of the same sort are time and place, for the present time is joined both to the past and to the future. Again place is of the number of continuous things for the parts of a body occupy a certain place, which parts join at a certain common boundary, wherefore also the parts of place, which each part of the body occupies, join at the same boundary as the parts of the body, so that place will also be continuous, since its parts join at one common boundary.

CAT–6. 4b20-5a1-15

Quantity, Discrete

Parts have within them no relative position to each other. Discrete quantity is as number and speech . . . of the parts of number there is no common term by which its parts conjoin, as if 5 be a part of 10, 5 and 5 conjoin at no common boundary. . . .

CAT–6. 4b25

Quantity of Quality

So denominated by accident. If a man were to explain the quantity of whiteness, he will define it by the surface for as the quantity of the surface so is the quantity of the whiteness.

CAT–6. 5b1

423

Quarrel

Men quarrel concerning something of moment.

POL—Bk. 5. 4. 1303b18

Questions

There are four kinds of questions we ask: whether a thing is so, why it is so, if it exists, what it is.

PO A—2. 1. 89b23-25

R

Rabies

Of the diseases of dogs, rabies makes them mad; and those who are bitten (by mad dogs) are infected with rabies except man.

DE H A—8. 22. 604a5-7

Rain

Rain and dew are the same.

DE M—1. 11. 347b17

Water, therefore, when generated, causes the winds to cease, and when they cease rain is from these causes produced.

DE M—2. 4. 361a3-4

Rainbow

The rainbow indeed is formed in the day . . . and it is produced in the night, but seldom. The reason is, that in darkness colors are concealed.

DE M—3. 2. 327a21-25

Rare

A thing is said to be rare from the fact that its parts are distant from each other.

CAT—8. 10a22

Ratio

Always that which is higher is to that which is under it as form to matter.

DE C—4. 3. 310b14-15

425

There is no ratio of the infinite to the finite.

DE C—1. 6. 274a5-6

Ratiocination

Deliberation and ratiocination are identical.

N E—6. 1. 1139a12-13

Reason

Reason is the principle, as well in the productions of art, as in things which have a natural subsistence.

DE P A—1. 1. 639b14-16

All correction, rebuke and exhortation is a witness that the irrational part of the soul is in a sense subject to the influence of reason.

N E—1. 13. 1102b33-1103a1

Reasoning

Reasoning is an argument in which certain things being laid down, something different from the posita happens from necessity through the things laid down.

T—1. 1. 100a25-27

I call those forms of reasoning properly logical or rhetorical, in reference to which I use the expression *places*; such are those which apply with equal advantage to questions of justice, and natural philosophy, and of the philosophy of social life, and to numerous other subjects which differ in species.

RH—Bk. 1. 2. 1358a10-14

Reasoning, Method of

The method of proceeding in all (problems) both in philosophy and in every art and discipline, is the same, for we must collect about each of them those things which are with, and the subjects which they are with, and be provided with as many as possible of these, considering them also through three terms in one way subverting, but in another constructing according to truth (we reason) from those which are truly described to be inherent, but as regards dialectic syllogisms (we must reason) from probable propositions.

P A—1. 30. 46a3-10

Reasonings, Peculiar

I call peculiar reasonings all those reasonings which arise out of propositions conversant with each species and genus of subjects.

RH—Bk. 1. 2. 1358a16-17

Recessives

Children resemble their ancestors from whom nothing has come but the resemblances occur after many births as in the case of the woman of Elis who slept with an Ethiopian; she did not bear an Ethiopian daughter but the son born of her daughter was an Ethiopian.

DE G A—1. 18. 722a8-11

Recognition

Recognition of something may involve the previously known and also knowledge acquired at the same time, as of things falling under the universal of which he already has knowledge; for someone knew before that every triangle has angles equal to two right angles, but that this which is in a semi-circle is a triangle, he knew at the same time by induction.

PO A—1. 1. 71a17-21

Recollection

Recollection comes from the soul, and extends to the movements or remains of movements in the sense organs.

DE A—1. 4. 408b17-19

The recollection of time is twofold. For sometimes we do not remember it with measure, as that we did a certain thing on the third day, and sometimes we remember it with measure.

DE M ET R–2. 452b29-453a2

Recreation

A person who is fond of amusing himself is one who carries his recreation to excess.

N E–7. 8. 1150b18-19

Rectilinear

A rectilinear body when revolving in a circle will never occupy the same place.

DE C–2. 4. 287a15-16

Reflection

Among all animals, man alone has the prerogative of reflection.

H A–1. 1. 488b24-25

Reflex

The reflex is that which consists of periods.

RH–Bk. 3. 9. 1409a34-35

Refrigeration

Refrigeration is necessary to the preservation of the animal life; to guard against extinction by excess of heat.

DE R–8. 474b23-24

Refutation

A refutation (elenchus) is a syllogism of contradiction.

P A–2. 20. 66b11

A refutation is a syllogism with a contradiction of the given conclusion.

S E–1. 165a2-3

Rejection

There are three things which influence us to eschew them, viz. the shameful, the injurious, and the painful.

N E–2. 2. 1104b31-32

Relation (as one of the Categories)

Like 'double,' 'half,' 'greater than' are relations.

CAT–4. 1b26-27

Relatives

They are denominated, some of them, as a twofold to a half, and a threefold to a third, and in general, a multiple to a submultiple, and excess to that which is exceeded.

ME–4. 15. 1020b26-28

Relatives may have contraries as virtue is contrary to vice, each of them being relatives, and knowledge is contrary to ignorance. But contrariety is not inherent in all relatives, since there is nothing contrary to double, triple and things of this sort.

CAT–7. 6b15-18

All relatives, if properly designated, have a correlative.

CAT–7. 7a23

Habit, disposition, perception, knowledge and position are relatives . . . habit is said to be the habit of some one, knowledge the knowledge of something, and position the position of something, and so of the rest. CAT–7. 6b3-5

429

He who knows any one relative definitely, will also know what it is referred to, definitely.　　　　CAT–7. 8a35-36

Some things are termed relatives, which are said to be what they are, from belonging to other things, or in whatever other way they may be referred to something else.

CAT–7. 6a23-25

Relatives (Admit of Variation of Degree)

Relatives appear to admit of more and less, for the like and unlike are said to be so more and less and the equal and unequal are so called more or less, each of them being a relative, for the similar is said to be similar to something and the unequal, unequal to something. Yet, not all relatives admit of more and less, for double is not called more or less double, but all relatives are styled so by reciprocity as the servant is said to be servant of the master, and the master, master of the servant; and the double, double of the half, also the half, half of the double.　　　　CAT–7. 6b20-30

Relative to Absolute, Fallacy of

Other fallacies arise from some particular thing being said to be simply when it is so in a certain respect.

S E–5. 166b37-167a1

Relaxation

Relaxation is not an end.　　　　N E–10. 6. 1176b35-1177a1

Religion

The fortunate are lovers of the gods, and are disposed toward the deity with a sort of confidence, in consequence of the goods which have accrued to them from fortune.

RH–Bk. 2. 17. 1391b2-4

430

Remembering

Man alone has the gift of reminiscence. H A–1. 1. 488b26

Remembrance

From repeated remembrance of the same thing we get experience, for many remembrances in number constitute one experience.

PO A–2. 19. 100a3-5

We rapidly remember those things which frequently employ our thoughts.

DE M ET R–2. 452a28-29

Reminiscence

When, therefore, we exercise reminiscence, we are moved according to some one of prior motions, as long as we are moved, after which the recollection of what we investigate occurs.

DE M ET R–2. 451b16-18

Reminiscence differs from learning again, because he who exercises the former may in a certain respect be moved by himself to that which is posterior to the principle; but when he cannot accomplish this by himself, but through another, he no longer remembers. DE M ET R–2. 452a4-7

Renown

We call, however, those arts burdensome, which are alone exercised for the sake of obtaining renown.

E E–1. 4. 1215a29-30

Resemblance

For the most part, indeed, females more resemble their mother, but males their father. DE H A–7. 6. 586a4-6

431

Resistance

Resisting substances suffer something; but those which do not resist suffer nothing.

DE M–3. 1. 371a24-25

Respect

No one person can be entitled to unlimited respect.

N E–9. 2. 1164b30-31

Respiration

Nature caused animals to employ the power of respiration for the purpose of perceiving the odors of food.

DE S ET S–5. 444a25-27

Respiration is not common to all animals.

DE P A–3. 1. 662a16-18

Rest

Rest is contrary to motion.

CAT–14. 15b1

Rest in its nature partakes of unity.

ME–3. 2. 1004b28-29

There is an activity not only of motion but of immobility, and pleasure consists rather in rest than in motion.

N E–7. 15. 1154b26-28

Restitution

The restitution of a depraved nature is depraved; but of a good nature is good.

M M–2. 7. 1205b12-13

Retaliation

Retaliation also is just.

M M–1. 34. 1194a28

Retaliation brings a feeling of relief.

N E–4. 11. 1126a21-22

Revolt

Commotions arise in aristocracies partly because there are so few persons in power. . . . They will happen also when some great men are disgraced by those who have received higher honors than themselves, but to whom they are in no ways inferior in abilities; or when an ambitious man cannot get into power. . . . And also when some are too poor, and others too rich, which will most frequently happen in time of war. . . . They arise also when some person of very high rank might still be higher if he could rule alone.

POL—Bk. 5. 7. 1306b22-1307a3

Revolution

Revolutions are brought about in two ways, either by violence or fraud.

POL—Bk. 5. 4. 1304b8

The people do not easily change, but love their own ancient customs; and it is by small degrees only that one thing gains place from another; so that the ancient laws remain in force, while the power is with those who bring about a revolution in the state.

POL—Bk. 4. 5. 1292b17-21

Democracies will be most subject to revolutions from the dishonesty of their demagogues.

POL—Bk. 5. 5. 1304b20-21

An oligarchy is also subject to revolutions when the nobility spend their fortunes in luxury.

POL—Bk. 5. 6. 1305b39-40

Rhetoric

Rhetoric is a faculty of considering all the possible means of persuasion on every subject.

RH—Bk. 1. 2. 1355b26-27

The means of persuasion alone come properly within the sphere of the art, other things are merely additions.

RH—1. 1. 1354a13-14

433

It is plain that it is concerned with the means of persuasion, and as this is a sort of proof (because we are then most persuaded when we conceive that the point has been proved) but the proof of rhetoric is enthymeme . . . and the enthymeme is a sort of syllogism.

RH–1. 1. 1355a3-8

There are three types of rhetoric: deliberative (political), judicial (forensic) and demonstrative (ceremonial).

RH–1. 3. 1358b6-8

Its business is not absolute persuasion, but to consider on every subject what means of persuasion are inherent in it.

RH–Bk. 1. 1. 1355b9-10

Rhetoric is the counterpart of logic (dialectic), since both are conversant with subjects of such a nature as it is the business of all to have a certain knowledge of, and which belong to no distinct science.

RH–1. 1. 1354a1-3

Rhetoric is made up of the science of logic and of that branch of the science of social life which recognizes the subject of morals.

RH–Bk. 1. 4. 1359b9-11

Rhetoric is made up of the science of logic and of that branch of the science of social life which recognizes the subject of morals; and it partly resembles logic, partly the declamations of the sophists: and in exact proportion as one shall attempt to get up logic or rhetoric, not as they are general faculties but as distinct sciences, he will unwittingly do away their nature by his encroaching, in the act of so tricking them out, upon sciences of certain definite subject-matter, and not of words and forms of reasoning.

RH–1. 4. 1359b9-16

Rhetoric supplies itself from subjects which are usual matters of deliberation.

RH—Bk. 1. 2. 1356b36-1357a1

Rhetoric is useful, because truth and justice are in their nature stronger than their opposites.

RH—Bk. 1. 1. 1355a20-22

Deliberative is more difficult than judicial rhetoric.

RH—Bk. 3. 17. 1418a21-22

Of demonstrative the business is partly praise, partly blame.

RH—Bk. 1. 3. 1358b10-11

All reasonings of the orator are derived from four sources, and these four are probability, example, proof positive, and signs.

RH—Bk. 2. 25. 1402b12-14

Rhetoric, Propositions of

Positive proofs, probabilities and signs are the types of proof available to the rhetorician generally.

RH—1. 3. 1359a7-8

Rhythm

The diction ought to be measured, yet without metre; for what is destitute of measure is displeasing and indistinct. But by number all things are measured; and in modeling the diction, the number is rhythm, of which the metres are certain divisions. Hence the sentence should possess rhythm, though not metre; for then it will become verse; and its very rhythm should be without preciseness.

R H—3. 8. 1408b27-31

Rich

In an oligarchy it is necessary, if any of the rich insult

435

the poor, to let their punishment be severer than if they insulted one of their own rank.

POL–Bk. 5. 8. 1309a22-24

In democracies it is necessary that the rich should be protected, not only by not permitting their lands to be divided, but not even the produce of them.

POL–Bk. 5. 8. 1309a14-16

Riches

It should seem that some boundary should be set to riches, though in practice we see the contrary taking place; for all those who get riches add to their money without end.

POL–Bk. I. 9. 1257b32-34

Nature is stable and firm, but not riches.

E E–7. 2. 1238a12-13

Rights

Private individuals have the right of indicting any officers of state they like for violating the laws, while such as are so indicted have also an appeal to the court of justice, if the Council finds them guilty.

C–45

Rivalry

Where there is rivalry, there is also victory.

RH–Bk. 1. 11. 1371a6

River

All rivers, however, which do not flow into others, are seen to end in the sea; but no one is seen to end in the earth; for though they disappear, yet they again emerge.

DE M–2. 2. 356a22-24

Rough

(A thing is said to be rough) because of the fact that one part rises above another.

CAT–8. 10a24

S

Sagacity (Ready Wit)

Sagacity is a certain happy extempore conjecture of the middle term, as if a man perceiving that the moon always has that part lustrous which is toward the sun, should straightway understand why this occurs, viz. that it is illuminated by the sun.

PO A—1. 34. 89b10-13

Same

"The same," to speak in general terms, may appear to be divided in three ways, since we are accustomed to call something 'the same' either in number, in species or in genus: in number, when the names are many but the thing one, as a garment and a vestment; in species, when the things being many are without specific difference, as man with man, and horse with horse . . . they are the same in genus which are under the same genus as man and horse.

T—1. 7. 103a6-14

Those (things) which being derived from the same genus are by division mutually opposed, are said to be mutually simultaneous.

CAT—13. 14b33

Sameness

It is evident that sameness is a certain unity of the being of either many things, or when one employs anything as many.

ME—4. 9. 1018a7-9

437

Science

In every kind of theoretical investigation and every way of teaching, whether the more noble or the more ignoble, there appears to be two notions of proficiency: the one is called science while the other is a sort of skill, or education.

DE P A—1. 1. 639a1-4

Science, therefore, is conversant with that which may be scientifically known, and this is evolved in conjunction with demonstration and reason.
M M—1. 34. 1196b37-1197a1

We consider that we have scientific knowledge as opposed to a sophistical way of knowing through accidentals when we consider that we know the cause on account of which a thing is, that it is the cause of that thing, and that the latter cannot be otherwise.
PO A—1. 2. 71b9-12

Science is universal, and subsists through things necessary, and what is necessary cannot subsist otherwise than it does.
PO A—1. 33. 88b31-32

Science and intellect are always true, and no other kind of knowledge, except intellect, is more accurate than science.

PO A—2. 19. 100b7-9

All sciences communicate with each other according to common principles, and I mean by common those which men use as demonstrating from these, but not those alone which they demonstrate, nor that which they demonstrate, and dialectic is common to all sciences.
PO A—1. 11. 77a26-29

The scientific knowledge of each thing is had when we know the essence of each thing.
ME—6. 6. 1031b6-7

Sciences are distinguished into the speculative, the practical and the productive.

T—8. 1. 157a10-11

It is evident that there is no science of those things that are in a state of flux.

ME—12. 4. 1078b16-17

The most accurate of the sciences are those respecting things that are primary.

ME—1. 2. 982a25-26

It may be said that all science is capable of being taught, and that that which is an object of science is capable of being learnt.

N E—6. 3.1139b25-26

Is in the soul as in a subject, but it is predicated of a subject, viz. 'grammar.'

CAT—2. 1b1

But some things are both predicated of and are in a subject, as 'science' (knowledge) is in the soul but is predicated of a subject, grammar.

CAT—2. 1a34

Sciences are conversant about all things that are universal.

ME—2. 6. 1003a14-15

Science is a mode of conceiving universal and necessary truths.

N E—6. 6. 1140b31-32

The corruption of science is oblivion and deception.

DE L ET B—2. 465a23

Science is impossible without reasoning.

N E–6. 6. 1140b35

Science and demonstrative syllogism are not concerned with indefinites (or possibles) because the middle (term) is irregular, but to those things which may naturally exist.

P A–1. 13. 32b18-20

Science then may be defined as a demonstrative state of mind, i.e. a state in which the mind exercises its faculty of demonstration.

N E–6. 3. 1139b31-33

Science therefore is productive of pleasure.

M M–2. 7. 1206a7-8

Science and Its Object

The more valuable and honorable the object of a science, the more valuable and honorable the science.

RH–1. 7. 1364b7-8

Science, Demonstrative

For all demonstrative science is concerned with three things; those which it lays down as existing, the subject genus whose essential properties the science considers; and common things called axioms, from which as primaries they demonstrate; and thirdly, the attributes the signification of which the science assumes.

PO A–1. 10. 76b11-16

If then to know is what we have laid down, it is necessary that demonstrative science should be from things true, first, immediate, more known than, prior to and the causes of the conclusion, for thus there will be the appropriate first principles of whatever is demonstrated.

PO A–1. 2. 71b19-23

Science (Knowledge), Process of Acquiring

From sense, memory is produced, but from repeated remembrance of the same thing, we get experience, for many remembrances in number constitute one experience. From experience, however, the universal now established in the soul, the one beside the many, which is a single unit within them all, the principle of art and science arises: if it is conversant with coming-to-be, art; if with being, it is science. We conclude that these states of knowledge are neither innate in a determinate form nor are they produced from other habits more known, but from sensible experience, as when a flight occurs in battle, if one soldier makes a stand, another stands, and then another, until the fight is restored . . . when one of the individuals has made a stand, the first universal is formed in the soul, for the singular is indeed perceived by sense, but the content is of the universal, of man, not the man Callias. Again, the intellect stops in the individuals until they constitute the universal as from such an animal to animal, etc. It is clear, therefore, that primary things become necessarily known to us by induction, for thus sensible perception produces the universal. . . .

PO A–2. 19. 100a3-100b5

Scientific Knowledge

It is manifest that they (the philosophers) went in pursuit of scientific knowledge for the sake of understanding it, and not on account of any utility that it might possess.

ME–1. 2. 982b20-21

Neither is it possible to have scientific knowledge through sensation.

PO A–1. 31. 87b28

Science, Man of

Neither is everyone who possesses science to be questioned about everything, nor is every question to be

441

answered, but only those which concern the science in question.

PO A–1. 12. 77b6-9

Scientist

We are said to be scientists because we possess a particular branch of knowledge.

CAT–8. 11a35

Sea

The sea will never become dry. For that which before ascended, will again descend into the sea.

DE M–2. 3. 356b25-26

Security

The definition of security is the having possession there and in such manner that the enjoyment of the property is one's own.

RH–1. 5. 1361a19-21

Sedition

On account of profit and honor men rouse themselves against each other. . . . The other causes are haughtiness, fear, eminence, contempt, envy of those whose fortunes are beyond their rank. There are also other things which in a different manner occasion revolutions, as contention, neglect, want of numbers, and too great disparity of circumstances.

POL–Bk. 5. 2. 1302a38-1302b3

Inequality is always the occasion of sedition.

POL–Bk. 5. 1. 1301b28-30

Some raise seditions through desire of equality. Others do the same by not being content with equality, but aiming at superiority.

POL–Bk. 5. 2. 1302a26-28

They pursue their aim justly, when those who are inferior raise sedition for the sake of equality; unjustly, when those who are equal do so for superiority.

POL—Bk. 5. 2. 1302a29-31

Those who have been guilty of crimes will be the cause of sedition through fear of punishment.

POL—Bk. 5. 3. 1302b21-22

Seed

Seed is surplus.

DE L ET B—5. 466b8

Seed is the principal and the efficient of that which proceeds from it.

DE P A—1. 1. 641b29

Seed is twofold, *from which*, and *of which*.

DE P A—1. 1. 641b33

Self-Knowledge

When we wish to know ourselves, we shall obtain this knowledge by beholding our friends.

M M—2. 15. 1213a22-23

Self-Love

A good man ought to be a lover of self, as by his noble deeds he will benefit himself and serve others.

N E—9. 8. 1169a11-13

Self-Sufficient

We define the self-sufficient as that which, taken by itself, makes life desirable, and wholly free from want and this is our conception of happiness.

N E—1. 5. 1097b14-16

The man who is sufficient to himself, will also be in want of friendship.

M M–2. 15. 1213b1-2

Semen

Semen is a superfluity of useful and ultimate nutriment.

DE G A–1. 18. 726a26-27

Semivowel

That which has an audible sound with percussion.

P–20. 1456b27-28

Sensation

Sensation consists in being moved and in experiencing something; and it appears to be a sort of alteration that the being undergoes.

DE A–2. 5. 416b33-35

Sensation appears to be a kind of qualitative change.

DE A–2. 4. 415b24

Sensation arises from externals.

DE A–1. 4. 408b16-17

The object of sensation is prior to the sense. If the sensible is removed, sensation ceases; but if sensation ceases that does not destroy the sensible object.

CAT–7. 7b35-40

Nothing suffers without sensation.

DE C–2. 9. 290b33

Sensation of particular things is always true, even in animals.

DE A–3. 3. 427b12-13

Sensation is effected through the sanguineous parts.

DE P A–2. 10. 656b-19-20

Where there is sensation, there is pleasure and pain.

DE A–2. 2. 413b23

Sense

The sense is that which receives the sensible forms without matter.

DE A–2. 12. 424a17-19

Each sense is in the organ in so far as the organ is special.

DE A–3. 2. 426b8-9

Each sense is related to its own particular class of sensible qualities.

DE A–3. 2. 426b7-9

Sense is a ratio.

DE A–3. 2. 426b3

Sense is produced by the medium which is between sense and the sensible object being moved, that is to say it is produced by contact and not effluvia.

DE S ET S–3. 440a18-20

There are only five ordinary senses, I mean sight, hearing, smell, taste, and touch.

DE A–3. 1. 424b22-23

All the possible senses are possessed without exception by animals that are neither incomplete nor mutilated.

DE A–3. 1. 425a9-10

In order to live, it is not only necessary that the animal feels when it touches objects, it is necessary that it feels them from a distance; and that is what happens, if it can feel

445

through an intermediary because then this intermediary is affected and set in motion by the object that feels and the being is then set in motion by the intermediary.

DE A—3. 12. 434b26-29

Sense is not deceitful in what falls within its own peculiar province, but imagination is not the same with sense.

M E—3. 5. 1010b2-3

Sense is a certain knowledge.

DE G A—1. 23. 731a33-34

It is impossible for an animal to exist without sense.

DE P A—2. 1. 647a21

The first sense that belongs to all animals is touch.

DE A—2. 2. 413b4

The most developed sense in man is touch; in the second place, taste. In respect of the other senses, he is inferior to many animals.

H A—1. 15. 494b16-18

Without sense neither sleep nor wakefulness is present.

DE S—1. 454b28-29

We are easily deceived about the senses, when we are disturbed by any passions.

DE SOM—2. 460b3-4

By nature, then, indeed, are animals formed endowed with sense; but in some of them memory is not innate from sense, and in others it is.

ME—1. 1. 980a27-980b22

446

Sense Object

Sense itself is not of itself, but there is something else different from and independent of sense which must needs be prior to sense, for the moving cause is prior in nature to that which is being moved.

ME–3. 5. 1010b35-1011a1

Senses and Their Relationship to Induction and Demonstration

Vide   INDUCTION - DEMONSTRATION - UNIVERSALS.

Sensible

Sensibles can be taken in a three-fold manner: and within these three, two are indeed directly (per se) sensible and the other is indirectly sensible (per accidens); of the directly sensible one is proper to each sense and the other common to all. I say that the proper sensible is what cannot be sensed by another sense and about which error is impossible, as color as regards vision; common sensibles are motion, rest, number, figure, and magnitude (size). The indirectly sensible is considered, as for instance a certain white thing is the son of Diares; this is accidentally or indirectly sensed.

DE A–2. 6. 418a8-22

The act of the sensible object and the act of sensation are one and the same act.

DE A–3. 2.–425b25-26

Every thing sensible subsists in matter.

DE C–1. 9. 278a11

If animal is destroyed, sense is destroyed. But the sensible will remain, such as, body, warm, sweet, bitter and all the rest which are sensibles.

CAT–7. 8a4-5

447

All things sensible are in a process of corruption, and are in motion.

ME—2. 4. 999b4-5

All sensibles have contrariety, as in color, white is contrary to black; and in sapors, the sweet to the bitter.

DE S ET S—4. 442b17-19

That every thing sensible is magnitude, and that what is indivisible is not sensible, is evident.

DE S ET S—7. 449a20-21

Sensibility

Sensibility cannot be exercised without the body.

DE A—3. 4. 429b5

When there is sensibility, there is appetite.

DE A—2. 3. 414b1-2

Sensible Perception

They (animals) have an innate power, of judging, which they call sensible perception.

PO A—2. 19. 99b35

Sensoria

The sensoria of the touch and the taste are near the heart.

DE S ET S—2. 439a1-2

Sensorium

The sensorium is the recipient of sensibles.

DE P A—2. 1. 647a28

The sensorium of the odorable is in the head.

DE S ET S—5. 445a25-26

The sensorium of smelling is very reasonably situated between the eyes.

DE P A–2. 10. 656b31-32

Sensual Pleasures

Those who set themselves to live well often confine their view to the enjoyment of sensual pleasures; so that as this also seems to depend upon what a man has, all their care is to get money, and hence arises the second species of money-getting; for as their enjoyment is in excess, they seek means proportionate to supply this excess of enjoyment; and if they cannot do this merely by the art of dealing in money, they will endeavor to do it by other ways, and apply all their powers to a purpose which is not according to nature.

POL–Bk. I. 9. 1258a2-10

Sentence

A sentence is voice significant by compact, of which any part separately possesses signification, as indeed a word, yet not as affirmation or negation.

DE I–4. 16b26-28

A composite significant sound of which certain parts of themselves signify something . . . it is one in a two-fold way: it is either that which signifies one thing or that which becomes one by conjunction.

P–20. 1457a23-28

Sentiments

The parts of these are to demonstrate, to refute, and to excite the passions; such as pity, or fear, or anger, and such like; and besides these, to amplify and extenuate.

P–19. 1456a37-1456b2

449

Separation

Form and matter are not separated from the thing, but place may be separated from it.

PHY—4. 2. 209b22-24

Servility

In many instances human nature is servile.

ME—1. 2. 982b29-30

Sesquialter

The sesquialter in relation to the subsesquialter is according to number in relation to a definite number.

ME—4. 15. 1021a1-2

Sex

In the woman, every thing is by nature similar to what appears in man; the only difference consists in the womb.

H A—1. 14. 493a24-25

Nature has made one sex stronger and the other weaker.

ECO—Bk. 1. 3. 1343b30

Sex Determinant

Men and women vary in the production of males and females . . . the cause for which may be in the proportion or lack of proportion of what comes from the woman and the man or some other like cause.

DE G A—1. 18. 723a27-31

Shame

A kind of pain and agitation about evils present, past, or to come, which appear to tend to loss of character.

RH—Bk. 2. 6. 1383b13-15

450

Shame is occasioned by voluntary actions alone.

N E—4. 15. 1128b28

Shame is occasioned by misconduct.   N E—4. 15. 1128b22

Sheep

Sheep are the most stupid of all animals.

DE H A—9. 3. 610b23-24

Shoulders

Man does not walk unless he moves his shoulders.

DE IN—10. 709b25-26

Sight

What pertains to sight is the visible and the visible is color and colored objects.

DE A—2. 7. 418a26-27

The sight is of an aqueous nature; since this is the most easily preserved of all diaphanous substances.

DE P A—2. 10. 656a37-656b2

The eyes of a man have a sort of rampart and sheath, I mean the eyelids; and unless he moves his eyelids and opens them, he sees nothing.

DE A—2. 9. 421b28-30

We see according to a straight direction.

DE P A—2. 10. 656b30

The sight when it extends itself to a great distance is convolved through imbecility. And this perhaps is the cause of the twinkling of the fixed stars, and that the planets do not twinkle.

DE C—2. 8. 290a17-19

Sign

A sign seems to be a demonstrative proposition, necessary or probable, for that which when it exists a thing is, or which when it has happened, before or after, a thing has happened, this is a sign of a thing happening or being.

P A–2. 27. 70a7-10

Vide SYMBOLS.

Similar

Similar are those things styled both which everywhere undergo the same affection and undergo more of the same affections than of the diverse, and of which the quality is one, and in as many of the contraries as a change is possible, that which possesses more of these, or the more important amongst these, is similar to that thing.

ME–4. 9. 1018a15-18

Similar and Dissimilar

Things are said to be similar and dissimilar in respect of qualities alone.

CAT–8. 11a15

Simile

The simile is useful in prose, though seldom, since it carries with it the air of poetry.

RH–Bk. 3. 4. 1406b24-25

Simple (Undivided)

The undivided has two meanings: potentially and actually.

DE A–3. 6. 430b6-7

Simple or Composite

It is necessary then that every body should be either simple or composite.

DE C–1. 5. 271b17-18

452

Simple Bodies

That it is necessary that some motion should belong to all simple bodies is evident.

DE C—3. 3. 302b7-8

Simple (Incomplex Manner of Speaking)

Vide SPEECH.

CAT—2. 1a17-19

Simultaneous

Things are called simultaneous simply and most properly, whose generation occurs at the same time.

CAT—13. 14b23

Simultaneous, by Nature

But by nature those are simultaneous, which reciprocate according to the consequence of existence, although one is by no means the cause of the existence of the other, as in the double and the half.

CAT—13. 14b26

Singular

We speak of the singular as one in number.

ME—2. 4. 999b34-1000a1

Skull

The entire skull is a completely dry bone, round, and covered with a skin that has no flesh. In women, there is one joint only, that is circular. In men, there are three joints.

H A—1. 8. 491b1-4

Slave

He is by nature formed a slave, who is fitted to become the chattel of another person, and on that account is so, and

453

who has just reason enough to perceive that there is such a faculty as reason without being indued with the use of it.

POL—Bk. I. 5. 1254b20-23

A slave is an instrument in many arts: and as an estate is a multitude of instruments, so a slave is a living instrument.

POL—Bk. I. 4. 1253b29-32

As other men become worse when they get nothing for being better, and when no rewards are given for virtuous or vicious actions, so it is with slaves.

ECO—Bk. 1. 5. 1344b4-6

It is impossible to be friends with a slave qua slave, but not with a slave qua man.

N E—8. 13. 1161b5-6

Slavery

It is clear that some are free by nature, and others are slaves, and that in the case of the latter the lot of slavery is both advantageous and just.

POL—Bk. I. 5. 1255a1-2

Sleep

Sleep is a certain passion of the sensitive part, being, as it were, a certain bond and immobility.

DE S—1. 454b8-10

Sleep is the restriction of the first sensorium, so that it is not able to actualize its function.

DE S—3. 458a28-29

Sleep is not, as we have said, any impotency whatever of the sensitive part.

DE S—3. 456b9-10

454

Sleep is especially produced from food.   DE S–3. 457b7-8

In sleep we neither see, nor hear, nor, in short, have any sensible perception.

DE SOM–1. 458b33-459a1

It is evident that those who are awake, are awake, and those who are asleep, are asleep, by that power by which they are sentient.

DE S–1. 454a4-7

It is necessary that all sleep should be capable of awakening.

DE S–1. 454b14

Sense is possessed by animals even when asleep.

DE G A–5. 1. 779a13

Nor is every thing which is seen in sleep a dream. For, in the first place, it happens to some persons that they sensibly perceive after a certain manner sounds and light, sapor and the touch, yet feebly, and, as it were, at a distance. Thus, when asleep, we frequently seem to ourselves to see a certain light; but, when awake, we immediately know that it was the light of a lamp which caused this appearance.

DE SOM–3. 462a17-25

Sleeptalking
Some, also, answer in their sleep, when they are interrogated. For it is possible, simply, both to be awake and asleep.

DE SOM–3. 462a25-26

Slight
There are three species of slight: contempt, spite and contumely.

RH–Bk. 2. 2. 1378b13-15

Smooth

(A thing is said to be smooth) from the fact that its parts lie along a straight line (i.e. evenly).

CAT—8. 10a24

Snow

It is a constitutive property of snow to be white.

CAT—10. 12b36

Society

He who first established civil society was the cause of the greatest benefit; for as man, thus perfected, is the most excellent of all living beings, so without law and justice he would be the worst of all; for nothing is so savage as injustice in arms; but man is born with a faculty of gaining himself arms by prudence and virtue; arms which yet he may apply to the most opposite purposes.

POL—Bk. I. 2. 1253a30-35

If human society cannot subsist without actions at law, it certainly cannot exist without the infliction of penalties.

POL—Bk. 6. 8. 1322a5-7

Animals that form societies are those that have to perform an identical and common task; but all the animals living in groups do not form societies for this purpose. On the contrary, man, bees, wasps, ants, cranes form societies of this kind; and of these societies, some have a chief, while others have not.

H A—1. 1. 488a8-13

Society, Civil

If civil society was founded for the sake of preserving and increasing property, every one's right in the state would be in proportion to his fortune; and then the reasoning of

456

those who insist upon an oligarchy would be valid; for it would not be right that he who contributed one mina should have an equal share in the hundred, along with him who brought in all the rest, either of the original money or of what was afterwards acquired. Nor was civil society founded merely in order that its members might live, but that they might live well (for otherwise a state might be composed of slaves, or of the animal creation; which is far from the case, because these have no share in happiness, nor do they live after their own choice); nor is it an alliance mutually to defend each other from injuries, or for a commercial intercourse; for then the Tyrrhenians, and Carthaginians, and all other nations between whom treaties of commerce subsist, would be citizens of one state. For they have articles to regulate their imports, and engagements for mutual protection, and alliance for mutual defence; yet still they have not all the same magistrates established among them, but they are different among different people; nor does the one take any care that the morals of the other should be as they ought, or that none of those who have entered into the common agreements should be unjust, or in any degree vicious, but only that they shall not injure another confederate. But whosoever endeavors to establish wholesome laws in a state, attends to the virtues and the vices of each individual who composes it; and hence it is evident that the first care of a man who would found a state truly deserving that name, and not nominally so, must be to have his citizens virtuous; for otherwise it is merely an alliance for self-defence, differing only in place from those which are made between different people.

POL—Bk. 3. 9. 1280a25-1280b10

Socrates

There are two improvements in science which one might justly ascribe to Socrates: I allude to his employment of inductive arguments and his definition of the universal, both belonging to the principle of science.

ME—12. 4. 1078b27-30

457

Solecism

In a certain respect, a solecism is similar to those so called elenchi.

S E–1. 14. 174a5-6

Solution

A right solution is the detection of a false syllogism.

S E–18. 176b29-30

Sophism

A contentious syllogism.

T–8. 11. 162a16-17

Sophist

The art of the sophist is to appear to be wise without really being so; and the sophist makes money from a feigned wisdom.

S E–1. 1. 165a19-23

The character of sophist does not consist in the faculty (for the logician possesses this as well as he) but in his fixed design of abusing it.

RH–1. 1. 1355b17-18

Sophistical Refutation, Its Objects

We must assume how many are the objects which they aim at who contend and strive in disputations, and these are five in number: an elenchus (refutation), fallacy, paradox, solecism, needless repetition.

S E–1. 3. 165b12-22

Sophistry

For the sophistical art is a certain apparent, but not real wisdom.

S E–11. 171b33-34

458

The sophistical art is a certain art of making money from apparent wisdom.

S E—11. 171b27-29

Soul

It may be asked whether all passions of the soul are without exception common to the body that has the soul, or is any one peculiar to the soul itself.

DE A—1. 1. 403a3-5

In most cases, the soul does not appear to experience or do anything whatever without the body.

DE A—1. 1. 403a5-6

All the modifications of the soul appear to take place only in conjunction with the body.

DE A—1. 1. 403a15-16

The modifications of the soul are inseparable from the physical matter of living things.

DE A—1. 1. 403b17

Thus we may say that all the philosophers define the soul in three respects: movement, sensibility, and immateriality.

DE A—1. 2. 405b10-12

The soul appears to move the living thing by a sort of will and thought.

DE A—1. 3. 406b25-27

It is not correct to say that the soul is angry . . . it is better to say that man pities, or thinks or learns with or by the soul.

DE A—1. 4. 408b11-15

It is impossible for anything to be superior to the soul and dominate it; and that is still more impossible in the case of the mind.

DE A—1. 5. 410b12-14

459

Is it through the soul entirely that we think, act or suffer in each of these cases? Or is each different phenomenon related to different parts? DE A–1. 5. 411b1-3

It would appear rather that it is the soul that supports the body. As soon as it leaves the body, the latter ceases to breathe, and is soon corrupt. DE A–1. 5. 411b7-9

We see plants, and even certain insects, living very well after division; as if they had a soul identical in species, if not identical in number. Each of the parts has, in this case, sensation and movement for some time. . . . In each of the parts there exist all the parts of the soul identical with each other in their species, as in the entire soul, identical in so far as inseparable, identical with the entire soul, as if it were divisible. DE A–1. 5. 411b19-27

Necessarily, the soul cannot be substance, except as form of a natural body that has life potentially. DE A–2. 1. 412a19-21

In the life of the soul there are sleep and awakening. DE A–2. 1. 412a24

It is evident that the soul is not separate from the body. DE A–2. 1. 413a4

The soul is the principle of the following faculties and is defined by them: nourishment, sensibility, thought and movement. DE A–2. 2. 413b11-13

The soul must therefore be reason and form, and not matter or object. DE A–2. 2. 414a13-14

460

It is not a body, it partakes of the body. That is why it is in the body, and in the body made in such a way.

DE A–2. 2. 414a20-21

It is clear that the soul is an act and formula of what has the capacity of being a certain kind of thing.

DE A–2. 2. 414a27-28

The soul is the cause and the principle of the living body.

DE A–2. 4. 415b7-8

The soul is the plan and actuality of what is in potentiality.

DE A–2. 4. 415b14-15

The soul is a cause in as much as it is a final cause.

DE A–2. 4. 415b16-17

All bodies formed by Nature are the instruments of the soul.

DE A–2. 4. 415b18-19

The soul is the cause in so far as it is the principle from which arises movement.

DE A–2. 4. 415b21-22

It is the force capable of conserving what possesses it, whatever it is.

DE A–2. 4. 416b17-19

Soul is the substance and act of a certain body.

ME–7. 3. 1043a35-36

The soul is as it were all the things that are.

DE A–3. 8. 431b21

The soul in animals is distinguished by two faculties: judgement, which is the work of thought and sensation, and the locomotion with which the soul is endowed.

DE A—3. 9. 432a15-17

The soul has two parts, one irrational and the other possessing reason.

N E—1. 13. 1102a27-28

The qualities of the soul are three, viz. emotions, faculties, and moral states.

N E—2. 4. 1105b19-20

There are two parts of the soul, the rational and the irrational.

N E—6. 1. 1139a3-5

Prudence, virtue and pleasure are in the soul.

E E—2. 1. 1218b34-35

The soul of man may be divided into two parts; that which has reason itself, and that which has not but is capable of obeying its dictates.

POL—Bk. 7. 14. 1333a16-18

It is absurd to assert that soul is composed from the elements.

DE G ET C—2. 7. 334a9-10

The soul will at the same time perceive by one and the same thing, but not by the same reason.

DE S ET S—7. 449a16-19

Every living thing has a soul.

DE V—6. 470a19

It is impossible that the nutritive soul should exist without heat.

DE R–8. 474a25-26

The liberation of the soul is entirely without sensation.

DE R–17. 479a22-23

Soul, Traditional Definitions of

First, it is the greatest cause of movement, because it is self-moving: next, it is a body composed of the most minute particles: lastly, it is corporeal but less than any other body.

DE A–1. 5. 409b18-21

Soul, in Physics

It is the part of the physicist (natural philosopher) to institute an inquiry concerning a certain soul, such as is not unconnected with matter.

ME–5. 1. 1026a5-6

Soul and Body

Every living thing is composed of soul and body, and of these one is by nature the governor, the other the governed.

POL–Bk. I. 5. 1254a34-36

Sound

A thing moved in that which is not moved produces a sound.

DE C–2. 9. 291a16-17

Sound is double; one is an act and the other only a potential.

DE A–2. 8. 419b5

Sound appears to be the motion of something which is borne along.

DE S ET S–6. 446b30-447a1

463

Sound is the movement of what can be moved by smooth bodies when they are struck.

DE A–2. 8. 419b19-20

Transcendent sounds are injurious to the bulks of inanimate bodies. Thus the sound of thunder divides stones and the strongest bodies.

DE C–2. 9. 290b34-291a1

Sound and Silence

Sound and silence are known from a comparison with each other.

DE C–2. 9. 290b27-28

Species

Neither do gravity and levity, which tend to the same thing, differ in species.

PHY–5. 4. 228b29-31

Species and Genus

Of secondary substances, species is more substance than genus.

CAT–5. 2b8

Speculation

Happiness is coextensive with speculation.

N E–10. 8. 1178b32

Speculative

There are pleasures which are independent of pain or desire, as e.g. the activities of the speculative life.

N E–7. 13. 1152b36-1153a1

Speculative Sciences

It is evident that there are three kinds of speculative

464

sciences: the physical (physics), mathematical, (mathematics) and the theological (theology). . . . The most excellent is the genus of speculative sciences, and of these the one mentioned last possesses the greatest amount of excellence, for it is conversant about that one among entities which is more entitled to respect than the rest.

ME—10. 7. 1064b1-6

Of speculative science the end is truth.
ME—1a. 1. 993b20-21

Speculative Science, Excellence of

Each science is termed more excellent and more inferior according to its appropriate object of scientific knowledge.

ME—10. 7. 1064b5-6

Speech

Is more a property of a man than the exercise of the body.
RH—1. 1. 1355b1

Letters are formed partly by the tongue, and partly by the compression of the lips.
DE P A—2. 16. 660a5-7

Forms of speech are either simple or complex. Examples of the latter are such as 'the man runs,' 'the man wins'; of the former, 'man,' 'ox,' 'runs,' 'wins.'
CAT—2. 1a17-19

There are three points respecting a speech: one, the sources of the means of persuasion; second, the style, third, the proper arrangement of the parts of the speech.

RH—3. 1. 1403b6-8

Speech (a Discrete Quantity)

That speech is a quantity is evident, since it is measured

by a short and a long syllable; I mean a speech produced by the voice, since its parts concur at no common limit, for there is no common limit at which the syllables concur, but each is distinct by itself.

CAT–6. 4b32

Speed

Speed is both that which involves any motion whatever and an excess of motion, for there is a certain speed even of that which is slow.

ME–9. 1. 1052b29-30

Sperm

Not just anything rises from a certain sperm but like from like and not according to chance.

DE P A–1. 1. 641b27-28

Sphere

A sphere is of all figures the most useful for that motion which is produced in the same place.

DE C–2. 8. 290b1-3

Spontaneity

One can think spontaneously, when one wishes: but one cannot feel spontaneity, for of necessity there must be a thing to feel.

DE A–2. 5. 417b24-25

Spontaneous Generation

There are animals that are born spontaneously, and not from beings of the same genus as themselves.

H A–5. 1. 539a21-23

Stammering

In those persons whose tongue is not very much detached ... they stammer and stutter.

DE P A–2. 17. 660a25-27

Standard of Action

We make pleasure and pain in a greater or lesser degree the standard of our actions.

N E—2. 2. 1105a3-5

Stars

The motion of the stars is indeed swift, but remote.

DE M—1. 3. 341a21-22

No one of the stars is moved either with an animated or a violent motion.

DE C—2. 9. 291a22-24

Stasimon

The stasimon is the melody of the chorus.

P— 12. 1452b23

State

Although the good of an individual is identical with the good of a state, yet the good of the state, whether in attainment or in preservation, is evidently greater and more perfect.

N E— 1. 1. 1094b7-9

Every state is a society, and every society is established for the sake of some good end (for an apparent good is the spring of all human actions); it is evident that all societies aim at some good or other: and this is more especially true of that which aims at the highest possible end, and is itself the most excellent, and embraces all the rest. Now this is that which is called a state, and forms a political society.

POL—Bk. I. I. 1252a1-7

In the order of nature, the state is prior to the family or the individual; for the whole must necessarily be prior to the parts; for if you take away the whole body, you cannot say a foot or a hand remains, unless by equivocation, as if any one should call a hand, made of stone, a hand; for such only can it have when mutilated.   POL—Bk. I. 2. 1253a18-22

Now I am willing to admit that the state ought to be one as much as possible (for this is the principle which Socrates adopts), and yet it is evident that if it goes on till it becomes too much one, it will be no longer a state, for the state naturally supposes a multitude; so that if we proceed in this manner, from a state it will become a family, and from a family it will become an individual: for we should say that a family is one to a greater degree than a state, and a single person than a family; so that even if this end could be obtained, it should never be put in practice, as it would annihilate the state. For not only does a state consist of a large number of inhabitants, but they must also be of different sorts: for were they all alike there could be no state; for a confederacy and a state are two different things; a confederacy is valuable for its members, though all those who compose it are men of the same calling; for this is entered into for the sake of mutual defence, just as the addition of another weight makes the scale go down. The same distinction will prevail between a state and a tribe, when the people are not collected into separate villages, but live as the Arcadians. Now these things by which a state should become one are of different sorts; and it is the preserving a just and equal balance of power, which is the safety of states, as has already been mentioned in our treatise on Ethics. Now among freemen and equals this is absolutely necessary; for all cannot govern at the same time, but either by the year, or according to some other regulation or time. By this means, it follows that every one in his turn will be in office; as if the shoemakers and carpenters should exchange occupations, and not always be employed in the self-same calling. But as it is better that these should continue in their respective trades, so also in civil society, where

468

it is possible, it would be better that the government should continue in the same hands; but where it is not, there it is best to observe a rotation, and let those who are their equals by turns submit to those who are magistrates at the time, since they in turn will alternately be governors and governed, as if they were different men; by the same method different persons will execute different offices. Hence it is evident that a state cannot naturally be one in the manner that some persons propose; and that what has been said to be the greatest good of states, is really their destruction; though the good of anything tends to preserve it. For another reason also it is clear that it is not for the best to endeavor to make a state too much one, because a family is more sufficient in itself than a single person, and a state than a family; and indeed it can lay claim to the name of a state only when this sufficiency results to the members of the community. If then this sufficiency is preferable, a state which is less one, is better than that which is more nearly so.

POL—Bk. 2. 2. 1261a14-1261b15

Since a state is a collective body, and, like other wholes, composed of many parts, it is evident that our first point must be to inquire what a citizen is. For a state or city is a certain number of citizens.

POL—Bk. 3. 1. 1274b38-41

It is evident that when we speak of a state as being the same, we refer specially to the government there established; and it is possible to call it by the same name or any other, whether it be inhabited by the same men or by different ones. But whether or no it is right or not right to dissolve the community, when the state passes into an altered form of constitution, is another question.

POL—Bk. 3. 3. 1276b10-15

It is impossible that a state should consist entirely of excellent citizens.

POL—Bk. 3. 4. 1276b37-38

469

It is evident, then, that a state is not a mere community of place, nor established for the sake of mutual safety or traffic; but that these things are the necessary consequences of a state, although they may all exist where there is no state; but a state is a society of joining together with their families, and their children, to live well, for the sake of a perfect and independent life; and for this purpose it is necessary that they should live in one place, and intermarry with each other. Hence in all cities there are family meetings, clubs, sacrifices, and public entertainments, to promote friendship; for a love of sociability is friendship itself; so that the end for which a state is established is that the inhabitants of it may live happily; and these things are conducive to that end. For it is a community of families and villages, formed for the sake of a perfect independent life; that is, as we have already said, for the sake of living well and happily. The political state therefore is founded not for the purpose of men's merely living together, but for their living as men ought; for which reason those who contribute most to this end deserve to have greater power in the state than either those who are their equals in family and freedom, but their inferiors in civil virtue, or those who excel them in wealth, but are below them in worth.

POL—Bk. 3. 9. 1280b29-1281a8

The best is that in which a man is enabled to choose both to govern and to be governed with regard to virtue during his whole life.

POL—Bk. 3. 13. 1284a1-3

A state is not made up of one, but of many parts; one of which is those who supply provisions, called husbandmen; another called mechanics, whose employment is in the manual arts; the third sort are hucksters, I mean by these buyers, sellers, petty traffickers, and retail dealers; the fourth are hired laborers, or workmen; the fifth are the men-at-arms; to which may be added those who are members of the council.

The seventh sort are those who serve the public in expensive employments at their own charge; and these are called the opulent. The eighth are those who in like manner execute the different offices of the state. The offices of a senator, and of him who administers justice to litigants, alone now remain.

POL—Bk. 4. 4. 1290b38-1291a36

The union of the rich and the poor makes up a free state.

POL—Bk. 4. 8. 1294a16-17

State and Individual

It is evident that that very same life which is happy for each individual is happy also for the state and for every member of it.

POL—Bk. 7. 3. 1325b14-16

Statesman

There are three qualifications necessary for those who intend to fill the first departments in government. First of all, an affection for the established constitution; in the second place, abilities wholly equal to the business of their office; in the third, virtue and justice correspondent to the nature of that particular state in which they are placed.

POL—Bk. 5. 9. 1309a33-37

Statesmanship

Wisdom and statesmanship cannot be identical.

N E—6. 7. 1141a28-29

Statement (True or False)

A statement is said to be true or false inasmuch as it asserts that what is, is or what is not, is not.

CAT—5. 4b10

Strength

Strength is the capability of moving another at will.

RH—Bk. 1. 5. 1361b15

Style

The subject of style is clearly reducible to an art.

RH—Bk. 3. 1. 1404a16

The written style ought to be easily read and understood.

RH—Bk. 3. 5. 1407b11-12

But purity in speaking your language is the foundation of all style; and this depends of five particulars: first, on the connective particles; in using terms distinct and not vague; in terms not ambiguous; in using proper genders of nouns; in the proper numbers of nouns.

RH—3. 5. 1407a19-1407b11

Style will possess the quality of being in good taste, if it be expressive at once of feeling and character, and in proportion to the subject matter.

RH—Bk. 3. 7. 1408a10-11

The style needs be either continuous, and united by means of connectives . . . or reflex, and like the antistrophic odes of the old poets. Now the continuous style is the old style . . . the reflex is that which consists of periods. I call a period a form of words which has independently in itself a beginning and ending, and a length easily taken in at a glance.

RH—3. 9. 1409a24-1409b1

Style, Excellence of

Let excellence of style be defined to consist in its being

clear . . . and neither low, nor above the dignity of the subject, but in good taste.

RH–3. 2. 1404b1-5

Style, Frigidity of

Frigidity, as dependent on the style, consists in four points: in the use of compound words . . . the employment of foreign idioms . . . the employment of epithets either too long, out of place or too frequent . . . improper metaphors.

RH–3. 3. 1405b34-1406b20

Subalternate Genera

Vide GENUS.

Sublimity

The following expedients contribute to sublimity of style: using the definition in place of the noun; avoiding either if out of taste; illustration by metaphor and epithets; by using the plural for the singular; assigning to each word a distinct particle; using connectives; by negative qualities.

RH–3. 6. 1407b26-1408a10

Subsistence

There is therefore a subsistence for the sake of something in things which are produced by and exist from nature.

PHY–2. 8. 198b10-12

A being subsists just as long as it is nourished.

DE A–2. 4. 416b14-15

Whatever has a separate has also an essential subsistence.

ME–4. 18. 1022a35-36

473

Substance

Substance, in its strictest, first, and chief sense, is that which is neither predicated of any subject, nor is in any, as an individual man or horse.

CAT–5. 2a11

Substance, being one and the same in number, can receive contraries. It is by changing that substance admits of contraries . . . the modification takes place through a change in substance.

CAT–5. 4a10; 5. 4b17-19

It belongs also to substance that there is no contrary to them. . . . This is not the peculiarity of substance, but of many other things, as for instance of quantity.

CAT–5. 3b24

Substance appears not to admit of more or less. I mean . . . that substance is not said to be more or less that very thing that it is; as if the same substance be man, he will not be more or less man neither as regards himself at different times nor as regards other men.

CAT–5. 3b33-35

Substance is spoken of in four ways: for both the essence or the formal cause, and the universal and the genus seem to be substance in each thing and the fourth of these is the subject. But the subject is that of which other things are predicated, while it itself is no longer predicated of any other thing . . . substance appears especially to be the primary subject.

ME–6. 3. 1028b33-1029a2

Substance assumes, as we have said, three things: form, matter, and the composition, the result of these two elements.

DE A–2. 2. 414a14-16

474

Substances are three in number, and one of these is matter . . . another of these susbstances is Nature . . . Further, the third substance is that which subsists from these, and is ranked as a singular.

ME–11. 3. 1070a9-12

We assert first of all that substance is a particular genus of beings and that in substance we must distinguish, in the first place, matter, that is, what is not by itself such and such a special thing: next, form and species; and it is after them that the thing is specially named; and, in the third place, the composition that results from these first two elements.

DE A–2. 1. 412a6-9

Substances are three in number; one is cognizant by sense . . . and one part of this is eternal, and the other subject to decay. But another substance is immovable.

ME–11. 1. 1069a30-33

In some manner is matter denominated substance, but in another way form, and in a third, that which results from both or is a compound of both.

ME–6. 3. 1029a2-3

As regards substance, both simple bodies, as for instance, earth and fire and water and such like are called substances; and, in general, bodies are styled so; and animals consisting of these, and those things that are of the nature of demons, and the parts of these. Now, all these are called substances because they are not predicated of a subject, whereas other things are predicated of these.

ME–4. 8. 1017b10-14

Now substance seems to subsist in bodies most evidently; wherefore we say that both animals and plants and the parts of them are substances; and we say the same of natural or physical bodies, as fire and water and earth and everything of this sort; and as many as are either parts of these or are composed of these, either partly or entirely, as both the heaven and its parts, stars and moon and sun.

ME—6. 2. 1028b8-13

Every natural body endowed with life is substance.

DE A—2. 1. 412a15

That wherein qualities are inherent primarily.

ME—6. 3. 1029a15-16

It is not that which is predicated of the subject, but is that of which other things are predicated.

ME—6. 3. 1029a7-8

Nothing else is separable except substance since all others are said to be predicated of substance as of a subject.

PHY—1. 2. 185a31-32

Now substance happens to be called substance in two ways: both as the ultimate subject which is not predicated of anything else; and as that which may be this particular thing; but such is the form and species of each thing.

ME—4. 8. 1017b23-26

In another way is that styled substance whatever may be the cause of being, and may be inherent in such as are not predicated of a subject.

ME—4. 8. 1017b14-16

To speak generally, examples of substance are like man or horse.

CAT—4. 1b24-25

It is true of substances and differences that they are predicated univocally. For all these are predicated either of individuals or of species. There is no predication of first substance for it cannot be referred to any subject. Of second substances the species is predicated of the individual; the genus is predicated of the species and individuals.

CAT–5. 3a33-37

A universal substance does not subsist.

ME–6. 10. 1035b28-29

That, indeed, there exists a certain Eternal Substance, and a Substance that is Immovable, and possesses actually a subsistence separable from sensibles, is evident.

ME–11. 7. 1073a3-5

Substance, According to Plato

Plato considered both forms and mathematical entities as two substances, and, as a third, the substance of sensible bodies.

ME–6. 2. 1028b19-21

Substance and Form

Substance and form are each of them a certain energy (act).

ME–8. 8. 1050b2-3

Substance as Subject of Change

In all cases other than substance it is necessary that there be a subject of becoming; for when quantity or quality or relation, or time or place is said to change a subject is necessary, since substance alone is not predicated of another subject, but everything else of substance.

PHY–1. 7. 190a33-190b1

477

Substance, Primary

Primary substances are more especially termed substances because they underlie all others and all others are either predicated of them or are in them.

CAT—5. 2b15-17

In primary substances, no one is more substance than another; indeed, a certain man is no more a substance than a certain bull.

CAT—5. 2b26

As regards then the primary substances, it is unquestionably true that they signify a particular thing.

CAT—5. 3b10

Neither is the primal substance in a subject, nor is it predicated of any.

CAT—5. 3a8-9

Substance, Secondary

But secondary substances are they in which as species those primary substances (i.e. individuals) are inherent.

CAT—5. 2a12

Secondary substances are those in which as species those primarily-named substances are inherent, that is to say, both these and the genera of these species.

CAT—5. 2a14

Species and genera alone are termed secondary substances, since they alone declare the primary substances of the predicates.

CAT—5. 2b30

Substances, Sensible

Sensible substances— I mean such as are singulars; of

these there is neither definition nor demonstration, because they involve matter, the nature of which is such as to admit of the possibility both of being and not being; wherefore all the singulars of such are things subject to decay and corruption.

ME—6. 15. 1039b27-31

Substantial Nature

The substantial nature can be known by an analogy. Just as bronze is to the statue, or wood to a bed, or the matter and what lacks form before receiving form to the thing which has form, so is the substantial nature to what is the individual substance and being.

PHY—1. 7. 191a7-12

Suffering

That which acts and that which suffers are contraries.

DE G ET C—1. 7. 342a11-12

Suicide

Nor is any one of those who kill themselves in order to avoid pain, as many do, to be called brave.

E E—3. 1. 1229b39-40

Sun

That body which revolves around the earth, or which is hid by night.

ME—6. 15. 1040a30-31

The sun is circularly moved.

DE M—2. 4. 359b34

The sun always tends to the west and east.

DE M—2. 4. 361a8-9

The sun which especially seems to be hot, is seen to be white, and not of a fiery color.

DE M—1. 3. 341a35-36

The sun not only draws upward that moisture of the earth which emerges above the rest, but by the heat which it causes dries the earth itself.

DE M—2. 4. 360a6-8

The sun both causes blasts of wind to cease and co-excites them.

DE M—2. 5. 361b14

Superfluity

Nature does nothing superfluous.

DE P A—4. 11. 691b4

Superpartiens

Superpartient (superpartiens) in relation to superpartient is according to the indefinite in the same manner as the multiple is in relation to one.

ME—4. 15. 1021a2-3

Supreme Good

Happiness is the supreme good.

N E—1. 6. 1097b22

Surface

That which is divisible in a twofold respect is a surface.

ME—4. 6. 1016b26-27

Syllable

A syllable is a sound without signification.

P—20. 1456b34-35

480

Syllogism

A syllogism, indeed, is a discourse in which certain things being laid down, something else, different from what are laid down, follows from the fact that they are. I say "from the fact that they are" since it follows from them and it follows from them without the need of any extrinsic term to make the consequence necessary.

PA–1. 1. 24b18-22

A syllogism is a demonstration from necessary propositions.

PO A–1. 4. 73a24

A syllogism then is a discourse in which, certain things being laid down, something different from the posita happens from necessity through the things laid down.

T–1. 1. 100a25-27

It is evident, from what we have stated, that if the terms subsist towards each other there is necessarily a syllogism, and if there be a syllogism, the terms must thus subsist.

P A–1. 5. 28a1-2

A syllogism demonstrates something of something through a medium (middle term).

PO A–2. 4. 91a14-15

If both propositions are assumed contingent there is no syllogism.

P A–1. 17. 36b26-27

When both premises are assumed indefinite, or particular, there will not be a syllogism.

P A–1. 21. 40a1-2

When the negative is single, there will be a syllogism by conversion.

P A–I. 18. 38a3-4

481

Every syllogism consists of three terms.

PO A–1. 19. 81b10

Syllogism, Ad Impossibile

In the syllogism which leads to the impossible, one premise is laid down falsely.

P A–1. 29. 45b8-11

Syllogisms and Inductions, Means of Acquiring

The instruments by which we shall be well supplied with syllogisms and inductions are four: the securing of propositions, second, to be able to distinguish in how many ways each thing is predicated, third, to discover differences of things, and fourth, the consideration of the similar (likeness).

T–1. 13. 105a21-25

Syllogism, Contentious

A contentious syllogism is one which is constructed from apparent but not real probabilities, and which appears to consist of probabilities, or of apparent probabilities.

T–1. 1. 100b23-25

Syllogism, Demonstrative

Science and demonstrative syllogism are not concerned with indefinites (or possibles) because the middle (term) is irregular, but to those things which may naturally exist.

P A–1. 13. 32b18-20

Syllogism, (Dialectic)

Dialectic syllogism is that which is collected from probabilities.

T–1. 1. 100a30

Syllogism, Imperfect

An imperfect syllogism is one which requires either one

482

or more additions implied by the subject terms but not expressed through propositions.

P A—1. 1. 24b24-26

Syllogism not Produced

When a syllogism is not produced, both terms being affirmative or negative (and particular), nothing, in short, results of a necessary character.

P A—1. 7. 29a19-21

Syllogism, Ostensive

In the ostensive syllogism both premises are laid down according to the truth.

P A—1. 29. 45a8-11

Syllogism, Perfect

Wherefore I call a perfect syllogism that which requires nothing else besides the assumed premises for the necessary consequence to appear.

P A—1. 1. 24b22-24

When three terms so subsist, with reference to each other, that the last is in the whole of the middle, and the middle either is, or is not, in the whole of the first, then it is necessary that there should be a perfect syllogism of the extremes.

P A—1. 4. 25b32-35

Syllogism, Premises of

It is clear that a syllogism consists of two premises and no more.

P A—1. 25. 42a32-33

Syllogism, First Figure of

Of the figures, the first is especially adapted to science, for both the mathematical sciences carry out their demon-

483

strations by this, as arithmetic, geometry, optics and practically all the sciences that investigate causes since either entirely or for the most part the syllogism of the why is through this figure. Wherefore also, it will be especially adapted to science, for it is the highest property of knowledge to contemplate the 'why'; in the next place, it is possible through this figure alone to investigate the science of what a thing is.

PO A—1. 14. 79a17-24

Syllogism, Rules of First Figure of

Major premise universal.
Minor premise affirmative.

P A—1. 4. passim

Syllogism, Second Figure of

When the same is present with every one on the one hand and with none, on the other; or to all or none of each, a figure of this kind I call the second.

P A—1. 5. 26b34-36

Syllogism, Second Figure

Lastly, it appears that an affirmative syllogism is not found in this (second) figure, but all are negative, both the universal and the particular.

P A—1. 5. 28a7-9

Syllogism, Rules of Second Figure of

Major universal; one premise negative.

P A—1. 5. passim

Syllogism, Terms of

It appears that every demonstration will be by three terms and no more.

P A—1. 25. 41b36-37

It is evident that every demonstration and every syllogism will be through three terms only.

P A–1. 25. 42a30-31

Syllogism, Third Figure of

When with the same thing one is present with every, but the other with no individual, or both with every, or with none, such I call the third figure; and the middle in it, I call that of which we predicate both.

P A–1. 6. 28a10-14

Syllogism, Rules of Third Figure

Minor premise affirmative; conclusion particular.

P A–1. 6. passim

Syllogize

He who exercises reminiscence syllogizes.

DE M ET R–2. 453a9-10

Symbols

Spoken words are symbols of passions of the soul; written words are symbols of spoken words.

DE I–1. 16a3-4

Symphony

A particular sort of mixture of the sharp and the flat.

ME–7. 2. 1043a10-11

Synonyms

Those are called synonyms of which both the name is common, and the definition is the same.

CAT–1. 1a6

T

Tabula Rasa

The intellect is potential such as what it thinks is in it as in a tablet on which nothing is written.

DE A 3. 4. 429b30-430a2

Tall Men

Very tall men walk bent, and with the right shoulder inclining to the anterior, but the left hip more inclining to the posterior part, and with the middle of the body hollow and incurvated.

DE IN—7. 707b18-21

Taste

The taste is a certain touch.

DE S ET S—4. 441a3

Taste is a kind of touch; it is the sense of nutrition; and food is something that can be touched.

DE A—3. 12. 434b18-19

Teaching

All teaching and all learning grasped by reason proceeds from previous knowledge.

PO A—1. 1. 71a1-2

Teeth

Man has such and so many teeth principally for the sake of speech.

DE P A—3. 1. 661b14-15

Temperance

Temperance is a virtue by which men carry themselves so, in respect to the pleasures of the body, as the law directs.

RH–1. 9. 1366b13-15

Temperate

A temperate man becomes temperate by doing what is temperate.

N E–2. 3. 1105a18-19

Temperance and courage are destroyed by excess and deficiency but preserved by the mean state.

N E–2. 2. 1104a25-27

The temperate man is one who has no depraved desires.

M M–2. 6. 1203b17

It is by abstinence from pleasures that we become temperate, and when we have become temperate, we are best able to abstain from them.

N E–2. 2. 1104a33-35

Tendency

It is impossible for a thing to tend to that place at which nothing that is moved can arrive.

DE C–1. 8. 274b17-18

Term

I call that a term into which a proposition is resolved, as for instance, the predicate and that of which it is predicated, whether to be or not to be is added or separated.

P A–1. 1. 24b16-18

Term 'Included in' or 'Predicated of'

For one term to be 'included in another' as a whole is the

487

same as for the other to be 'predicated of' the whole of the other.

P A—1. 1. 24b26-28

Term, Extreme

The extreme is that which is itself in another and in which another also is.

P A—1. 4. 25b36-37

Term, Middle

I call that the middle which is itself in another whilst another is in it and which also becomes the middle (term) by position.

P A—1. 4. 25a35-36

Term, Middle (in Second Figure)

The middle term (in the second figure) I call that which is predicated of both extremes.

P A—1. 5. 26b36-37

Terminus

It is necessary that the terminus *from which* and the terminus *to which* a thing is naturally adapted to be moved should be specifically different.

DE C—1. 8. 277a13-15

Thesis

Of an immediate syllogistic principle, I call that the thesis, which it is not possible to demonstrate, nor is it necessary that he should possess it who intends to learn anything.

PO A—1. 2. 72a14-16

A thesis is also a problem, yet not every problem is a thesis.

T—1. 11. 104b29-30

488

A thesis is a paradoxical opinion of some one celebrated in philosophy, as that contradiction is impossible, as Antisthenes said, or that all things are in motion, according to Heraclitus, or that being is one, as Melissus asserted.

T—1. 11. 104b19-22

Thinking

Thinking and reflecting are not identical.

DE A—3. 3. 427b25-26

Thinking with Image

The soul never thinks without an image (phantasm).

DE A—3. 7. 431a16-17

Thirst

Thirst is desire for cold and liquid.

DE A—2. 3. 414b11-12

Thought

Thought, it may be said, resembles a rest and a cessation rather than a movement.

DE A—1. 3. 407a32-33

Thought deteriorates because some other thing deteriorates internally.

DE A—1. 4. 408b24-25

Accuracy of thought may be more clearly seen in smaller than in larger animals.

H A—9. 7. 612b19-21

Thunder

Why does it thunder? Because sound is produced in the clouds.

ME—6. 17. 1041a24-25

The sound of fire extinguished in the clouds.

PO A—2. 1. 94a4-5

The extinction of fire in a cloud.   PO A— 2. 8. 93b7-8

In the clouds a separation of the pneumatic substance taking place, and falling against the density of the clouds, produces thunder.

DE M—2. 9. 369a35-369b1

Thunder falls downward.   DE M—1. 4. 342a12-13

Thunder and Lightning

Thunder and lightning are divided, not by sound, but because the pneumatic substance is at the same time secreted, which produces the blow and the sound.

DE M—3. 1. 371b11-13

Time

A continuous quantity, none of the parts of time has an abiding existence, and what does not abide does not have position. It would be more appropriate to say that the parts have a relative order, in so far as one is prior to another.

CAT—6. 5a25

A continuous quantity. Its parts have a common boundary.   CAT—6. 4b24; 6. 5a7-8

All time is divisible.   DE S ET S—6. 446a30-446b1

No part is, in consequence of time being divisible.

PHY—4. 10. 218a5-6

490

Time does not appear to be composed from instants.

PHY—4. 10. 218a8

It is evident that time is not motion.

PHY—4. 10. 218b18

Time is not without mutation.

PHY—4. 11. 218b21

It is impossible for time to exist without motion.

DE G ET C—2. 10. 337a23-24

It is also evident why time is not said to be swift and slow; but much, a few, and long and short; for as far as it is continued, it is long and short; but so far as it is number, it is much and few.

PHY—4. 12. 220a32-220b3

No time is insensible.

DE S ET S—7. 448b16

That time, therefore, is the number of motion according to prior and posterior, and that it is continued, for it is of the continuous, is evident.

PHY—4. 11. 220a24-26

Time is a certain number. . . . Time is that which is numbered, and not that by which we number.

PHY—4. 11. 219b5-7

All time is one, simular, and at once.

PHY—4. 14. 223b10-12

The same time also is every where at once.

PHY—4. 18. 220b5-6

A verb . . . signifies time.

DE I–3. 16b6

Time and Motion

We not only, however, measure motion by time, but time by motion, because they are bounded by each other.

PHY–4. 12. 220b15-16

To Be

Neither 'to be' or 'not to be' is a sign of a thing; nor is 'being' taken all by itself; for it itself is nothing, however it cosignifies a certain composition which cannot be understood without the composing members.

DE I–3. 16b22-25

Topics, Use of the Treatise on

It will be consequent upon what we have stated to describe to what an extent and for what subjects this treatise is useful. It is so for three: mental exercise, discussion and philosophical science. That it is useful for mental exercise appears evident from these, that possessing method, we shall be able more easily to argue upon every proposed subject. But for discussion, because having enumerated the opinions of many, we shall converse with them, not from foreign, but from appropriate dogmas, confuting whatever they appear to us to have erroneously stated. Again, for philosophical science, because being able to dispute on both sides we shall more easily perceive in each the true and the false.

T–1. 2. 101a25-36

Torture

Torture is a kind of evidence, and appears to carry with it absolute credibility, because a kind of constraint is applied.

RH–Bk. 1. 15. 1376b31-32

Touch

Touch is the sense of alimentation.

DE A—2. 3. 414b7

In respect of the sense of touch, it is placed in a like part, for instance, in the flesh, or in some thing that replaces it.

H A—1. 3. 489a17-19

All animals without distinction have equally the fifth sense, that which is called touch.

H A—4. 8. 533a17-18

It is the only sense that all living things without exception possess.

DE A—2. 3. 414b3

Without touch it is impossible for a living thing to exist.

DE A—3. 13. 435b4-5

Tragedy

Tragedy aims at representing men as better than in actual life.

P—2. 1448a17-18

The Dorians lay claim to the invention of tragedy and comedy.

P—3. 1448a29-30

Tragedy is an imitation of a worthy or illustrious and perfect action, possessing magnitude, in pleasing language, using separately the several species of imitation in its parts, by men acting, and not through narration, through pity and fear effecting a purification from such like passions.

P—6. 1449b24-28

It is necessary that the parts of every tragedy should be six, from which the tragedy derives its quality. These are fable (plot) and character, diction and thought, spectacle and harmony.

P—6. 1450a7-10

The greatest is the combination of the incidents.

P—6. 1450a15

Tragedy is an imitation, not of men, but of actions.

P—6. 1450a16-17

The action and the fable (plot) are the end of tragedy. Without action, tragedy cannot exist.

P—6. 1450a22-24

Tragedy originated from those who led the dithyramb.

P—4. 1449a10-11

Tragedy is the imitation of a perfect and whole action, and of one which possesses a certain magnitude.

P—7. 1450b23-25

Tragedy is not only an imitation of a perfect action, but also of actions which are terrible and piteous.

P—9. 1452a1-3

The parts of tragedy are as follows: prologue, episode, exode, and chorus, of the parts of which one is the parados, but the other is the stasimon.

P—12. 1452b15-17

Tragedy is an imitation of better things.

P—15. 1454b8-9

Things in tragedy ought to be rendered apparent without teaching.

P—19. 1456b5

Tragedy has every thing which the epic possesses. To which may be added that it possesses perspicuity, both when it is read, and when it is acted.

P—26. 1462a14-17

Tragic Hero

Is one who neither excels in virtue and justice, nor is changed through vice and depravity into misfortune, from a state of great renown and prosperity, but has experienced this change through some error.

P—13. 1453a7-10

Transition

There is not a transition into another genus, as from length into superficies, and from superficies into body.

DE—1. 1. 268a30-268b2

Transposition

It is evident that when a noun and verb are transposed the same affirmation and negation result.

DE I—10. 20b10-12

Tree

That one part of a tree contains in capacity the whole tree, is evident from experience.

DE L ET B—6. 467a29-30

True

That which is true involves an affirmation in the case of composition, and a negation in the case of division; but that which is false involves the contradiction of this division.

ME—5. 4. 1027b20-24

That which subsists as true is entity.

ME–5. 4. 1027b18

True in Every Instance

I call that 'of every' which is not in a certain thing and in another thing is not, nor which is at one time and at another not; as if animal is predicated of every man, if it is truly said that this is a man, it is true also that he is an animal, and if now the one is true, so also is the other.

PO A–1. 4. 73a28-31

True and False

A statement is said to be true or false inasmuch as it asserts that what is, is or what is not, is not.

CAT–5. 4b10

In those things which are and have been the affirmation and negation must of necessity be true or false; and in universals taken universally, one is always true and the other false, and also in singulars . . . but in the case of universals not universally taken there is no such necessity.

DE I–9. 18a28-32

Of things enunciated without any connexion, none is either true or false; as "man," "white," "runs," "conquers." For every affirmation or negation seems to be either true or false.

CAT–4. 2a8

Nouns and verbs of themselves resemble conceptions without composition and division, as 'man' or 'white' . . . which are neither true nor false.

DE I–1. 16a13-16

For not in things themselves are the false and the true— as that which is good is true, but that which is bad is false

496

—but in the understanding; and the truth and falsehood concerning simples and essence are not in understanding either.

Neither is it possible that all assertions be false, nor all true, as well on account of many other difficulties which would be uttered in consequence of this position, supposing that they are false, neither will one who makes this very assertion speak what is true; but if all assertions are true, the person who says that all are false will not speak falsely.

ME—10. 6. 1063b30-35

True or False

The person that says that all things are true renders the statement contrary to this true also; wherefore he makes his own affirmation not true; for the contrary says that it is not true; but he that says that all things are false, even himself falsifies his own position.

ME—3. 8. 1012b15-18

True and Primary

Things true and primary are those which have certitude not through others but through themselves, as there is no necessity to investigate the 'why' in scientific principles, but each principle itself ought to be certain by itself.

T—1. 1. 100a30-100b21

Truth

The apprehension of truth is the function of both the intellectual parts of the soul.

N E—6. 2. 1139b12

It belongs to the same faculty of mind to recognize both truth and the semblance of truth.

RH—Bk. 1. 1. 1355a14-15

497

Mankind has a tolerable natural tendency toward that which is true.

RH—Bk. 1. 1. 1355a15-16

Truth is noble and laudable.

N E—4. 13. 1127a29-30

Truth and Falsehood

Truth and falsehood are involved in composition and division.

DE I—1. 16a13

Tyranny

A tyranny is a monarchy where the good of one man only is the object of government.

POL—Bk. 3. 7. 1279b6-7

A tyranny then is a monarchy where one person has a despotic power over the whole community.

POL—Bk. 3. 8. 1279b16-17

A tyranny is not according to nature, nor is the perversion of any other government whatsoever; for they are all contrary to it.

POL—Bk. 3. 17. 1287b39-41

Tyranny is the worst excess imaginable, as being a government the most contrary to a free state.

POL—Bk. 4. 2. 1289b2-3

Where one rules over his equals and superiors, without being accountable for his conduct, and whose object is his own advantage, and not the advantage of those whom he governs.

POL—Bk. 4. 10. 1295a19-22

498

The extreme of a democracy is a tyranny.

POL—Bk. 5. 10. 1312b5-6

Tyranny, Its End

The end of a tyranny is the protection of the tyrant's person.

RH—1. 8. 1366a6

Tyrant

His only object is pleasure.

POL—Bk. 5. 10. 1311a4

A tyrant is ambitious of engrossing wealth.

POL—Bk. 5. 10. 1311a5-6

A tyrant should endeavor to engage his subjects in a war, that they may have employment and may be for ever dependent upon their general.

POL—Bk. 5. 11. 1313b28-29

It is the part of a tyrant to place no confidence in friends, as every one desires to dethrone him.

POL—Bk. 5. 11. 1313b30-31

Neither slaves nor women conspire against tyrants; but when they are treated with kindness both of them are of necessity favorers of tyrants.

POL—Bk. 5. 11. 1313b35-37

Tyrants always love bad men.

POL—Bk. 5. 1. 1314a1-2

A tyrant should rather admit strangers than citizens to his table and familiarity, for the latter are his enemies.

POL—Bk. 5. 11. 1314a9-11

U

Ultimate

The end, together with the final cause, is a thing that is ultimate.

ME—4. 16. 1021b29-30

Understanding, Object of

Inasmuch as the object of the understanding is not a different thing from the understanding itself, in the case of as many things as do not involve a connexion with matter they will be the same thing; and the act of perception will be identical with the object of perception.

ME—11. 9. 1075a3-5

Unity and Being

Unity is predicated in as many ways as entity; and entity signifies partly this particular thing and partly quantity, and partly quality.

ME—6. 4. 1030b10-12

Universal

Of things, some are universal but others singular and by universal I mean whatever may naturally be predicated of many things, but by singular that which may not.

DE I—7. 17a38-40

By universal I mean whatever can be predicated of many.

DE I—7. 17a39-40

500

I call that universal which is both predicated 'of every' and 'per se' and so far as the thing is.

PO A–1. 4. 73b26-27

We speak of the universal as that which is common to these (i.e. singulars).

ME–2. 4. 1000a1

That which is universal is common, for that is said to be universal which by nature is fitted to be inherent in many things.

ME–6. 13. 1038b11-12

It is evident that nothing of those things that are universals can possess an existence apart from singulars.

ME–6. 16. 1040b26-27

Without universals it is not possible to attain to scientific knowledge; but the abstraction of them from singulars is a cause of the difficulties that ensue in regard to ideas.

ME–12. 9. 1086b5-7

Things universal are common. For we call those things universals, which are inherent in many things.

DE P A–1. 4. 644a27-28

That which is universal is a certain whole, since it comprehends many things as parts.

PHY–1. 1. 184a25

After a certain manner each body is many; but the all, or universe of which these are parts, is necessarily perfect.

DE C–1. 1. 268b9-10

The universal follows the particular. DE I–13. 23a18

Universal-Particular

The universal is more known in the order of reason; the individual in the order of sense.

PHY—1. 5. 189a5-7

Universal, Process of Acquiring Knowledge of

Vide SCIENCE, (KNOWLEDGE), PROCESS OF ACQUIRING.

Universal Statement

Wherefore in all syllogisms we must have a universal; a universal statement is established only when all the premises are universal; a particular in this way also, and from one particular.

PA—1. 24. 41b22-24

Universally

I mean universally enunciates of a universal as 'every man is white,' 'no man is white.'

DE I—7. 17b5-6

Universe

That the body of the universe therefore is not infinite, is manifest.

DE C—1. 7. 276a16-17

Univocally

Things are said to be named univocally which have in common both the name and the definition corresponding with the name.

CAT—1. 1a6

Unjust

The unjust is the unequal.

M M—1. 34. 1193b20

Unjust Man

Firstly, he who breaks the laws is considered unjust, and, secondly, he who takes more than his share, or the unfair man.

N E—5. 1. 1129b32-34

Upper Class

That which marks the upper classes is their fortune, their birth, their abilities, or their education, or any such like excellence which is attributed to them.

POL—Bk. 4. 4. 1291b28-30

Upward

Motion away from the center.

DE C—1. 2. 268b21-22

That which is upward in bipeds is towards the upward part of the universe.

DE IN—5. 706b3-4

That part whence nutriment and increase are imparted to animals and plants is the upward part.

DE IN—4. 705a32-33

Usury

Usury is most reasonably detested, as the increase of our fortune arises from the money itself, and not by employing it to the purpose for which it was intended. For it was devised for the sake of exchange, but usury multiplies it. And hence usury has received the name of 'produce'; for whatever is produced is itself like its parents; and usury is merely money born of money; so that of all means of money-making, this is the most contrary to nature.

POL—Bk. I. 10. 1258b2-8

V

Venality

In every state, it is necessary, both by the laws and every other method, that matters be so ordered as to shut out venality from state offices. POL—Bk. 5. 8. 1308b31-33

Vengeance

It is more natural to man to take vengeance than to forgive. N E—4. 11. 1126a30

Venial

They are venial, if they are mistakes committed not only in ignorance but from ignorance; but if they are not committed from ignorance but in ignorance, and from an emotion which is neither natural nor human, they are not venial.

N E—5. 10. 1136a5-9

Verb

A verb is that which, besides something else, signifies time; of which no part is separately significant, and it is always indicative of those things which are asserted of something else. DE I—3. 16b6-8

A composite sound significant with time, of which no part is of itself significant. P—20. 1457a14-16

Verbs taken by themselves are names and signify something but do not assert whether something is or is not.

DE I–3. 16b19-22

Vice

Pleasures and pains are the causes of vicious moral states, if we pursue and avoid such pleasures and pains as are wrong, or pursue and avoid them at the wrong time or in the wrong manner, or in any other of the various ways in which it is logically possible to do wrong.

N E–2. 2. 1104b21-24

Both vice and virtue are necessarily voluntary things.

E E–2. 11. 1228a7-8

It follows that our vices must be voluntary.

N E–3. 7. 1114b24

Vulgarity and meanness are vices.   N E–4. 4. 1122a30-31

Vicious

Every vicious person is ignorant of what he ought to do, and what he ought to abstain from doing.

N E–3. 2. 1110b28-29

Village

The society of many families, which was instituted for lasting and mutual advantage, is called a village, and a village is most naturally composed of the emigrant members of one family, whom some persons call 'clansmen,' the children and the children's children.

POL–Bk. I. 2. 1252b15-18

Virility

Most (men) are capable of generating till they are sixty

505

years old, and if they are capable after this period they possess a generative power till they are seventy years old.

DE H A–7. 6. 585b5-7

Virtue

It is a mean state as lying between two vices, a vice of excess on the one hand and a vice of deficiency on the other, and as aiming at the mean in the emotions and actions.

N E–2. 9. 1109a20-23

Virtue is a kind of good.

T–6. 4. 142b14

To speak summarily then, virtue is the best habit.

M M–1. 4. 1185a38

The virtues are not faculties. For we are not called either good or bad, nor are we praised or blamed, as having an abstract capacity for emotion.

N E–2. 4. 1106a6-9

Every virtue or excellence has the effect of producing a good condition of that of which it is a virtue or excellence, and of enabling it to perform its function well.

N E–2. 5. 1106a15-17

There are three dispositions, two being vices, viz. one the vice of excess and the other that of deficiency, and one virtue, which is the mean state between them.

N E–2. 8. 1108b11-13

Virtue and vice are both alike in our own power.

N E–3. 7. 1113b6-7

Virtue, if regarded in its essence or theoretical conception, is a mean state, but, if regarded from the point of view of the highest good, or of excellence, it is an extreme.

N E–2. 6. 1107a6-8

The virtues we acquire by first exercising them, as is the case with all the arts, for it is by doing what we ought to do when we have learnt the arts that we learn the arts themselves.

N E–2. 1. 1103a31-34

The virtues are in some sense deliberate purposes, or do not exist in the absence of deliberate purpose.

N E–2. 4. 1106a3-4

Virtue cannot be exercised, without the pleasure arising from virtuous conduct.

M M–2. 7. 1206a24-25

Virtue does not follow pleasure, but pleasure follows virtue.

M M–2. 11. 1209b37

All virtue is pre-elective, or the object of deliberate choice.

E E–3. 1. 1228a23-24

Actions in accordance with virtue are pleasant in themselves.

N E–1. 9. 1099a14-15

Virtue is the instrument of intellect.   E E–7. 14. 1248a29

By human virtue or excellence we mean not that of the body, but that of the soul.

N E–1. 13. 1102a16-17

But of virtue, there are two species, the one, indeed, being ethical, but the other dianoetical (or pertaining to the discursive energy of reason).

E E–2. 1. 1220a4-5

Virtue or excellence being twofold, partly intellectual and partly moral, intellectual virtue is both originated and fostered mainly by teaching.

N E–2. 1. 1103a14-16

It is necessary that ethical virtue should be conversant with certain media, and should be a certain medium.

E E–2. 3. 1220b34-35

It is clear that no moral virtue is implanted in us by nature.

N E–2. 1. 1103a19

Moral virtue tends to produce the best action in respect of pleasures and pains, and vice is its opposite.

N E–2. 2. 1105a10-13

Virtue will aim at the mean; I speak of moral virtue, as it is moral virtue which is concerned with emotions and actions and it is these which admit of excess and deficiency and the mean.

N E–2. 5. 1106b15-18

Virtuous actions are noble and have a noble motive.

N E–4. 2. 1120a23-24

It is easy to prove that it is not through external goods that men acquire virtue, but through virtue that they acquire them.

POL–Bk. 7. 1. 1323a40-41

Without virtue it is not easy to bear the gifts of fortune in good taste.

N E—4. 8. 1124a30-31

Virtue is greater than what is not positive virtue.

RH—1. 7. 1364a31-32

Those who use general terms deceive themselves, when they say that virtue consists in a good disposition of mind, or in doing what is right, or something of this sort. They do much better who enumerate the different virtues as Georgias did, than those who thus define them.

POL—Bk. I. 13. 1260a25-28

Virtue is a power (faculty) tending to provide us with goods and preserve them to us; a power moreover, capable of benefiting in many and important cases; of benefiting every object in every respect.

RH—1. 9. 1366a36-1366b1

The constituent parts of virtue are justice, courage, temperance, magnificence, magnanimity, liberality, placability, prudence, wisdom.

RH—Bk. 1. 9. 1366b1-3

Valor, justice, and wisdom have in a state the same force and form as in individuals; and it is only as he shares in these virtues that each man is said to be just, wise, and prudent.

POL—Bk. 7. 1. 1323b33-36

Virtue, Moral

Moral virtue is the outcome of habit.   N E—2. 1. 1103a17

Moral virtue is concerned with pleasures and pains.

N E—2. 2. 1104b8-9

Vision

Vision is produced only when the sensible organ experiences some affection.

DE A–2. 7. 419a17-18

It is the most deep-set eyes that, in every animal, have the most penetrating vision.

H A–1. 10. 492a9-10

Those whose nature is, as it were, loquacious and melancholy, see all-various visions.

DE DIV–2. 463b16-18

Voice

The voice is a sound expressing something. It is not a simple sound of the breathed-in air, like a cough.

DE A–2. 8. 420b29-31

Voice and sound are very different things.

H A–4. 9. 535a27-28

The voice is a sound produced by a living being.

DE A–2. 8. 420b5

The voice of girls is more acute than that of boys.

DE H A–7. 1. 581b10-11

Void

It must be admitted that there is neither a void body, nor that two magnitudes are in the same place, nor that any thing is increased by that which is incorporeal.

DE G ET C–1. 5. 321b15-16

Voluntary

It would seem to follow that it is voluntary if the agent

510

originates it with a knowledge of the particular circumstances of the action.

N E–3. 3. 1111a22-24

Men are voluntary agents in whatever they do wittingly and without compulsion.

RH–Bk. 1. 10. 1368b9-10

Voluntary actions we perform either with or without deliberate purpose—with it, if we perform them after previous deliberation, and without it, if without such deliberation.

N E–5. 10. 1135b8-11

The voluntary is that which possesses the principal authority in virtue.

M M–1. 12. 1187b33-34

It appears, therefore, that the voluntary subsists in virtue and vice.

M M–1. 9. 1187a28-29

Vote

When the people are masters of the vote, they become masters of the government.

C–9

Vowel

That which has an audible sound without percussion.

P–20. 1456b25-26

W

Waking

Because the blood is especially without separation after the introduction of nutriment, sleep is produced till the purest part of the blood is separated to the upper, and the most turbid to the lower parts. And when this happens the animal awakes, being liberated from the weight of the nutriment.

DE S—3. 458a22-25

Walking

In quadrupeds it is with the right part that walking begins.

H A—2. 1. 498b6-7

War

Since Nature makes nothing either imperfect or in vain, it necessarily follows that she has made all these things for the sake of man. For this reason the art of war is, in some sense, a part of the art of acquisition; for hunting is a part of it, which it is necessary for us to employ against wild beasts, and against those of mankind who, being intended by nature for slavery, are unwilling to submit to it. On this occasion, such a war is by nature just.

POL—Bk. I. 8. 1256b20-26

Water

Water is more generated in the winter and by night than by day.

DE M—2. 4. 360a2-3

All flowing waters are fontal waters.

DE M–2. 1. 353b19-20

Such things, therefore, as consist of water alone, these are fixed or congealed by cold.

DE P A–2. 2. 649a30

Hard and cold water is either the cause of sterility, or of the procreation of females.

DE G A–4. 2. 767a35

Wealth

The constituents of wealth are: plenty of money, being master of lands and seats, with the possession of personal property of live stock and slaves, such as are remarkable for number, stature, and comeliness; and all these should be secure and respectable and useful.

RH–1. 5. 1361a12-17

Weight

It is evident that not every body has either levity or gravity.

DE C–1. 3. 269b19-20

When

When, as 'yesterday,' 'the day before.'

CAT–4. 2a1-2

Where

Where, like 'in the market place,' 'in the Lyceum.'

CAT–4. 2a1

Whole

A whole is styled, first, that from which is absent no part of those things whereof the whole by nature is said to con-

513

sist; and secondly, that which contains the things contained, so that they form one certain thing.
ME—4. 26. 1023b26-28

The whole and the part tend naturally to the same thing, as for instance, all the earth and a small clod.
DE C—1. 3. 270a3-5

Wicked

It appears then that the wicked man has not a friendly disposition even to himself, as there is nothing lovable in him.
N E—9. 4. 1166b25-26

The wicked man may be compared to a State which carries out its laws, but whose laws are bad.
N E—7. 11. 1152a24

Wife

The well-ordered wife will justly consider the behavior of her husband as a model of her own life.
ECO—Bk. 1. 7. (Loeb p. 401 Bk. 3)

Neither splendor of vestments, nor pre-eminence of beauty, nor the amount of gold, contributes so much to the commendation of a woman, as good management in domestic affairs, and a noble and comely manner of life.
ECO—Bk. [1. 7]. Bk. 3. (Loeb ed. p. 401)

Will

The will is an appetite.
DE A—3. 10. 433a23

The will is a voluntary thing.
M M—1. 13. 1188a35

Every thing which a man wills is voluntary.
E E—2. 8. 1224a1

Neither are will and deliberate choice the same.

E E–2. 10. 1225b32

Will and opinion especially pertain to the end.

E E–2. 10. 1226a16

Wind

Wind is a certain quantity of dry exhalation, from the earth, moved about the earth.

DE M–2. 4. 361a30-31

Wind is rather the motion of air, since the same air remains both when it is moved and when it is stationary, so that, in short, wind is not air, for else there would be wind when the air is not moved, since the same air remains stationary which was wind.

T–4. 5. 127a4-8

Wind for the most part is produced after showers of rain, in those places in which it happens to rain, and the blasts of wind cease when it rains.

DE M–2. 4. 360b26-29

It is requisite to think that wind always accompanies and precedes thunder; but it is not visible, because it is without color. Hence it is moved before it strikes.

DE M–3. 1. 371b7-9

Tranquil winds are produced from two causes. For they either arise from cold, extinguishing the exhalation, as when thick ice is produced; or from the exhalation wasting away through suffocation.

DE M–2. 5. 361b24-27

Winds, however, do not seem to be hot, because they move the air which is full of a cold and abundant vapor, just as the breath which is blown through the mouth.

DE M–2. 8. 367a33-367b1

515

Wine

Wine is not beneficial either to children or nurses.

DE S—3. 457a14-15

Wine is pneumatic.

DE S—3. 457a16-17

Wing

They would be of no use to birds if they were erect.

DE IN—11. 710b32-711a1

Wisdom

Wisdom, therefore, is a science conversant about certain causes and first principles.

ME—1. 1. 981b27-29

Of the sciences that which is desirable for its own account, and for the sake of knowledge, we consider to be wisdom in preference to that which is eligible on account of its probable results, and that which is more qualified for preeminence we regard as wisdom, rather than that which is subordinate.

ME—1. 2. 982a14-17

But as far as wisdom has been defined a science of first causes, and of that which is especially capable of being scientifically known, so far such would be a science of substance.

ME—2. 2. 996b13-14

All other sciences may be more requisite than this one (wisdom) but none is more excellent.

ME—1. 2. 983a10-11

It may be defined as the capital science of the most honorable matters.

N E—6. 7. 1141a16-17

516

Wisdom will be the union of intuitive reason and science.

N E—6. 7. 1141b2-3

It is evident that wisdom is a virtue.

M M—1. 34. 1197b10-11

This (wisdom) alone of the sciences is free, for this alone subsists for its own sake.

ME—1. 2. 982b26-27

Wisdom in Physics

I admit there is a certain wisdom that is physics, but it is not the first.

ME—3. 3. 1005b1-2

Wisdom, Practical

Practical wisdom does not concern the governed, but only true opinion; the latter indeed are like flute makers, while he who governs is the musician who plays on the flutes.

POL—Bk. 3. 4. 1277b28-30

Wise Man

In the first place we go on the supposition that the wise man is acquainted with all things scientifically, as far as that is possible, not, however, having a scientific knowledge of them singly. In the next place, a person who is capable of knowing things that are difficult and not easy for a man to understand, such a one we deem wise (for perception of the senses is common to all, wherefore it is a thing that is easy and by no means wise). Further one who is more accurate, and more competent to give instruction in the causes of things, we regard more wise about every science.

ME—1. 2. 982a8-14

517

Wish

It will perhaps be best to say that in an absolute or true sense it is the good which is the object of wish, but that in reference to the individual it is that which appears to be good.

N E—3. 6. 1113a22-24

Nobody wishes what he does not think to be good.

N E—5. 11. 1136b7-8

Wit, Quick

Vide SAGACITY.

Woman

Vide FEMALE.

Wonder

For from wonder men, both now and at the first, began to philosophize, having felt astonishment originally at the things which were most obvious, indeed amongst those that were doubtful. . . .

ME—1. 2. 982b12-14

Wonderful

It is necessary in tragedies to produce the wonderful.

P—24. 1460a11-12

Words

Spoken words are symbols of passions of the soul; written words are symbols of spoken words.

DE I—1. 16a3-4

Words

We must employ but sparingly, and in very few places, exotic and compound words and those newly coined.

HR—Bk. 3. 2. 1404b28-29

World

The world is sensible. DE C–1. 9. 278a10

The whole world is composed from all its proper matter.

DE C–1. 9. 279a7-8

It is impossible that there should be more worlds than one.

DE C–1. 8. 276b21

There neither now are many worlds, nor were, nor can be produced; but this world is one, alone, and perfect.

DE C–1. 9. 279a9-11

Worm

It is a worm when, from a complete animal, another animal equally complete issues. H A–1. 5. 489b8-9

Worship

Whatever, either from defect or excess, prevents us from worshipping and contemplating God, is bad.

E E–7. 15. 1249b19-21

Worth

Men are worthy and good in three ways; and these are, by nature, by custom, by reason. POL–Bk. 7. 13. 1332a39-40

He is a man of worth who considers what is good because it is virtuous, as what is simply good. POL–Bk. 7. 13. 1332a22-23

A man, when he is perfectly worthy, is said to be beautiful and good; since the epithets the beautiful and the good are given to virtue. M M–2. 9. 1207b24-25

Writing

The demonstrative style is most adapted to writing. For its purpose is perusal.

RH—Bk. 3. 12. 1414a17-18

Wrong, to

To injure deliberately.

T—2. 2. 109b34-35

Y

Youth

The young are not proper students of political science, as they have no experience of the actions of life which form the premises and subjects of the reasonings.   N E–1. 1. 1095a2-4

It would seem that the friendship of the young is based upon pleasure; for they live by emotion and are most inclined to pursue what is pleasant to them at the moment.

N E–8. 3. 1156a31-33

Youth, Excellencies of

Accomplished in respect to personal excellence as stature, comeliness, strength, ability in the games; and as to that of the mind, temperance and courage; these all are the excellencies of youth.   RH–1. 5. 1361a1-5

Young

The young are in the highest degree apt to pursue the pleasures of love above all desires about which the body is concerned and in these they are incontinent.

RH–Bk. 2. 12. 1389a2-6

Young, Passions of

Ardent, inconstant, irritable, ambitious, sanguine, credulous, hopeful, rash, bashful, high-spirited, with a sense of honor, social, excessive, mischievous, facetious.

RH–2. 12. 1388b31-1389b12

Z

Zodiac

All the planets are moved in the zodiac, and not the sun alone.

DE M–1. 8. 345a21-22

BIBLIOGRAPHY

De Anima. Trans. into French by J. B-Saint-Hilaire. Paris: Librairie de Ladrange, 1846. Trans. by H. E. W.

De Partibus Animalium. Translated by T. Taylor. 9 volumes. Printed for the translator by R. Wilks, 1806-1812. Also by H. E. W.

Metaphysics. Trans. by J. H. M'Mahon. London: Bell, 1874.

Physics. Translated by T. Taylor.

Historia Animalium. Trans. by T. Taylor. Also H. E. W.

Politics. Trans. by E. Ealford. London: Bell, 1885

Constitution of Athens. Trans. by T. J. Dymes. London: Seeley and Co., 1891.

Poetics. Trans. by T. Buckley. London: Bell, 1872.

Magna Moralia. Trans. by T. Taylor.

Nicomachean Ethics. Trans. by R. W. Browne. London: Bohn, 1850.

Eudemian Ethics. Trans. by T. Taylor.

Rhetoric. Trans. by T. Buckley. London: Bell, 1872.

Organon, comprising:
> Categories.
> De Interpretatione.
> Prior Analytics.
> Posterior Analytics.
> Topics.
> Sophistici Elenchi.
> > Trans. by O. F. Owen. 2 vols. London: Bell, 1893, 1895.

De Caelo. Trans. by T. Taylor.

De Generatione et Corruptione. Trans. by T. Taylor.

Meteorologica. Trans. by T. Taylor.

Parva Naturalia, comprising:
> De Sensu et sensibili.
> De Memoria et reminiscentia.
> De Somno.
> De Somniis.

De Divinatione per somnum.
De longitudine et brevitate vitae.
De vita et morte.
De respiratione.
    Trans. by T. Taylor.
De Incessu Animalium. Trans. by T. Taylor.
De Motu Animalium. Trans. by T. Taylor.
De Generatione Animalium. Trans. by T. Taylor.